Municipal Reform in Canada

Reconfiguration, Re-Empowerment, and Rebalancing

edited by

Joseph Garcea and Edward C. LeSage Jr

OXFORD
UNIVERSITY PRESS

OXFORD
UNIVERSITY PRESS

70 Wynford Drive, Don Mills, Ontario M3C 1J9
www.oup.com/ca

Oxford University Press is a department of the University of Oxford.
It furthers the University's objective of excellence in research, scholarship,
and education by publishing worldwide in

Oxford   New York

Auckland   Cape Town   Dar es Salaam   Hong Kong   Karachi   Kuala Lumpur   Madrid
Melbourne   Mexico City   Nairobi   New Delhi   Shanghai   Taipei   Toronto

With offices in

Argentina   Austria   Brazil   Chile   Czech Republic   France   Greece   Guatemala
Hungary   Italy   Japan   Poland   Portugal   Singapore   South Korea   Switzerland
Thailand   Turkey   Ukraine   Vietnam

Oxford is a trade mark of Oxford University Press
in the UK and in certain other countries

Published in Canada
by Oxford University Press

Copyright © Oxford University Press Canada 2005

The moral rights of the author have been asserted

Database right Oxford University Press (maker)

First published 2005

Library and Archives Canada Cataloguing in Publication

Municipal reform in Canada : reconfiguration, re-empowerment and

rebalancing / edited by Joseph Garcea and Edward C. LeSage Jr.

Includes bibliographical references and index.

ISBN-13: 978-0-19-541810-1.—ISBN-10: 0-19-541810-7

1. Municipal reform—Canada—Provinces.

2. Municipal government—Canada—Provinces.

I. Garcea, Joseph   II. LeSage, Edward C.,1948-

JS1708.M87 2005   320.8'5'0971   C2004-906732-X

Cover design: Brett Miller
Cover image: CP/Toronto Star (Tony Bock)

1 2 3 4 – 08 07 06 05

This book is printed on permanent (acid-free) paper ∞.
Printed in Canada

Contents

Preface

This book is the product of a collaborative effort among 13 academics who share a strong interest in municipal governance and a belief that a detailed analysis of municipal reform in each province and territory in Canada during the turn-of-the-millennium period is both timely and valuable. The shared goal of the editors and contributors has been to produce a book that will be of interest and importance to a wide array of individuals within the academic, governmental, business, and voluntary sectors who want to understand both the recent municipal reforms and the evolution of municipal governance in Canada.

Within the academic sector this book should prove valuable for scholars of municipal government in Canada and other countries. Scholars teaching municipal governance to undergraduate and graduate students will find it useful as a core or reference text. For such academics and students this book is useful in three important ways. First, it provides a detailed account of reform initiatives, some of which were implemented and others which were not, during an especially active period of Canadian municipal reform that began in approximately 1990. Second, it provides insights into important thematic issues related to the purposes, nature and scope, politics, and effects of contemporary municipal reform. Third, it provides a general analytical framework consisting of conceptual and theoretical elements that either in its current form or in some modified form may prove useful for scholars in their research on reform agendas and initiatives either in the municipal sector or in any other governmental sector.

Within the governmental, business, and voluntary sectors the book is intended to serve as a reference resource for those who either are, or must become, well versed on contemporary municipal reforms in Canada. This includes not only elected and appointed officials in the municipal, provincial, federal, Aboriginal, health, and education sectors, but also the managers and staff of large and small business corporations and voluntary organizations.

It is fair to say that a book, rather than merely a chapter for each, could have been written on the reform agendas and initiatives of each province and territory. The hope of the editors and contributors is that this book stimulates further research into the many unexplored or under-explored aspects of those reform agendas and initiatives.

Acknowledgements

As editors we wish to express our sincere appreciation to numerous people who contributed to the production and publication of this book. First and foremost, we thank the contributors who committed themselves to writing chapters within an outline structure prescribed by us so that the reform story of each Canadian province and territory would be addressed in relatively uniform fashion. Although each of the contributors is an acknowledged academic expert in municipal government, production of these original essays involved considerable fact-finding and reflection. We are grateful for these efforts as they are the grist of the publication. And, since the contributors consulted widely within their jurisdictions to ensure the factual accuracy of what they wrote, we thank the many unnamed municipal and local government experts who aided their work. Second, we thank the staff at Oxford University Press, particularly Laura Macleod and Phyllis Wilson, and the copy editor, Richard Tallman, for providing valuable guidance and support at all stages of this project. The anonymous referees engaged by Oxford also deserve special thanks. Their contributions have been most valuable in assisting the contributors and us to focus and strengthen the chapters. Third, we thank our close colleagues and staff who provided valuable support either directly or indirectly in producing this book. This includes the academic personnel and staff of Government Studies, Faculty of Extension, at the University of Alberta, who supported the project by making extra efforts to shoulder Edward LeSage's work during the time of the book's development and writing. Special thanks also go to Deans of Extension Dr Gerry Glassford and Dr Cheryl McWatters for their support of his work. At the University of Saskatchewan special thanks are extended to the faculty and staff of the Department of Political Studies, who provided logistical and moral support for Joseph Garcea prior to and while working on this project. Fourth, we thank those who served as our research assistants for various parts of this project and whose contributions may not be visible but were very important. This includes Brenda Belokrinicev and Bernadette Logozar at the University of Alberta and Shane Garritty at the University of Saskatchewan. Last, but not least, we would like to thank our family members, as well as those of our contributors, whose support made this project possible.

Contributors

PETER G. BOSWELL is an Associate Professor in the Department of Political Science at Memorial University and served as Head of the department for nine years. Prior to attending university, he spent a number of years as a municipal administrator in Ontario. He served on Newfoundland's Constitutional Committee and the provincial Task Force on Municipal Regionalization. He has published several articles and chapters on Newfoundland municipal government and politics, and his *Municipal Councillor's Handbook*, 2nd edition, was recently published.

DANIEL BOURGEOIS is Lecturer in Municipal Governance at l'Université de Moncton. His municipal experience includes stints as Policy Analyst at the City of Moncton and Chair of the Commission of Three Communities. He conducts research on administrative nationalism and minority rule through sub-state institutions. His book on the Canadian bilingual districts will be published in 2005.

JOHN CROSSLEY taught political science and served as an academic administrator at the University of Prince Edward Island from 1987 to 2002. Since 2002 he has been Principal and Vice-Chancellor of Renison College at the University of Waterloo. His research on PEI government and public policy includes Aboriginal economic development, relations between the provincial government and First Nations, representation in the legislative assembly, and government reform.

JOSEPH GARCEA is an Associate Professor in the Department of Political Studies at the University of Saskatchewan where he teaches Canadian politics, local governance, public policy, public management, and intergovernmental relations. He is co-editor of *Indian Urban Reserves in Saskatchewan*, which devoted substantial attention to municipal-Aboriginal relations in the creation and operation of such reserves, and has served as Chair and Director of Research and Analysis for the Saskatchewan Task Force on Municipal Legislative Renewal.

KATHERINE A.H. GRAHAM is Dean of Public Affairs and Management at Carleton University. Her research interests focus on local government, Aboriginal policy, and Canada's North. She is one of Canada's leading researchers on governance and urban Aboriginal issues and has published extensively on these topics. Her many publications include her co-authorship of *Urban Governance in Canada: Representation, Resources, and Restructuring*, as well as several articles on municipal governance and reforms in Ontario.

PIERRE HAMEL is Professor of Sociology at the Université de Montréal. He has written extensively on social movements, urban politics, and local democracy. He is the author of *Action collective et démocratie locale* and has also co-edited several books, including two on social movements, *Urban Movements in a Globalising World* (2000) and *Globalization and Social Movements* (2001). He is currently completing a research project on Montreal's metropolitan governance.

CHRISTOPHER LEO is Professor of Political Science at the University of Winnipeg and Adjunct Professor of City Planning at the University of Manitoba. He is the author of numerous articles on local planning, development, and governance.

EDWARD C. LESAGE JR is a Professor of Extension at the University of Alberta, where he serves as Director of Government Studies. He is the author of articles and book chapters on provincial public administration, local and regional governance, and university continuing education. He has recently co-authored an in-depth study of inter-municipal collaboration in the Alberta capital region and collaborated with Jack K. Masson in the publication of *Alberta's Local Governments: Politics and Democracy*.

MARK PIEL holds a Master of Arts degree in political science from the University of Toronto. He is currently studying law at Osgoode Hall Law School, Toronto.

DALE H. POEL was a Professor in the School of Public Administration, Dalhousie University, at the beginning of this exercise in authorship. He produced several publications and reports on municipal reform in Halifax. He also co-edited a special issue of the *Canadian Journal of Regional Science* devoted to an assessment of the expectations and outcomes of provincial and municipal restructuring in Canada. He currently works as a consultant in the public sector, specializing in program evaluation and policy analysis.

DAVID SIEGEL is Dean of the Faculty of Social Sciences and Professor of Political Science at Brock University. He is the co-author of *Evolution, Revolution, Amalgamation: Restructuring in Three Ontario Municipalities* and co-editor of *Urban Policy Issues: Canadian Perspectives*. He has also published articles on various aspects of local governance, finance, and politics in numerous political science, public administration, and urban research journals.

PATRICK J. SMITH is a Professor, Department of Political Science, and Director of the Institute of Governance Studies at Simon Fraser University. His publications include works on Canadian local, regional, and metropolitan governance, provincial-municipal relations, global cities, and community planning and economic development. He is co-editor of the forthcoming book, *Metropolitan Governing: Canadian Cases, Comparative Lessons.*

KENNEDY STEWART is an Assistant Professor in the Public Policy Program at Simon Fraser University. He writes and teaches about democracy, democratic theory, research methods, and urban government. He has authored and co-authored several reports and articles on reforms to local governance in British Columbia, Metropolitan Toronto, and Greater London in England.

PART I

INTRODUCTION

CHAPTER 1

Municipal Reform Agendas and Initiatives: Analytical Framework and Overview

JOSEPH GARCEA AND EDWARD C. LESAGE JR

FOCUS OF THE BOOK

The turn of the new millennium has been marked by a plethora of interesting and important governance reform agendas and initiatives at the national, provincial, territorial, and local levels in Canada (Seidle, 1993; Aucoin, 1995; Shields and Evans, 1998; Kernaghan et al., 2000; Dunn, 2002; Lindquist, 2000). At the local level this has included an array of reform agendas and initiatives within the municipal sectors of all provinces and territories. These agendas and initiatives are the focus of analysis in this book.[1] Such reform within the municipal sectors has included three basic sets of activities: reviews on the need for reforms, proposals for reforms, and the implementation of reforms to the geographic boundaries, functions, finances, and jurisdictional powers of municipal governments. Notwithstanding the fact some reform initiatives have been undertaken in all provinces and territories, considerable differences exist between them in their precise focus and scope. In some provinces and territories the focus has been primarily on one or two of those four components of the municipal system—structures, functions, finances, powers—while other jurisdictions have dealt with all four. Moreover, whereas in some provinces and territories the municipal reform initiatives have been limited in scope, seeking to achieve minor adjustments to minor components of the municipal system, in others they have been wide-ranging with the intent to achieve major adjustments to major components of the municipal system.

Regardless of their precise focus and scope, such reform initiatives have produced debates of varying intensity among governmental and non-governmental stakeholders in each province and territory regarding an array of issues. Some of the debates surrounding those issues were short and muted and received little public or media attention; others were protracted and loud and received extensive public and media attention. Generally, such debates have tended to revolve primarily around issues of the adequacy or appropriateness of the following 10 aspects of the municipal systems and reforms to the same, which collectively constitute the broad parameters of the municipal reform agenda in Canada at the turn of the millennium (Graham et al., 1998: 12–14; Tindal and Tindal, 2004: 299–388):

- the boundaries of municipalities;
- the functions of municipal governments;
- the finances of municipal governments;
- the jurisdictional powers and constitutional status of municipal governments;
- the internal organizational and management frameworks of municipal governments;
- the relationships among municipal governments;
- the relationships between municipal governments and other levels of government, both inside and outside the Canadian polity;
- the relationships between municipal governments and their respective residents and ratepayers;
- the processes to be used for reviewing and reforming municipal systems;
- the effects of municipal reform initiatives that were proposed or implemented.

In addition to specific debates, there has also been an important overarching debate regarding the scope or magnitude of municipal reform. The debate has revolved around the question of whether at this juncture in history municipal governance is in need of a minor reconfiguration, a major reconfiguration, or a complete reinvention. The staunchest proponents of the reinvention of municipal governance have been many municipal officials, and particularly those from larger municipalities. For such officials the vision of the reinvention of municipal governance has not been limited to the conventional prescriptions found in the new public management literature regarding the realignment of the functions of municipal governments vis-à-vis both the for-profit and the not-for-profit sectors (Bennett, 1990; Siegel, 1993; Savoie, 1995; Borins, 1995; Barnett and Leach, 1996; Stein, 2001). Their vision has also included prescriptions for a fundamental realignment of the functions, finances, and powers of municipal governments, primarily through their respective provincial and territorial governments and to some extent also via the federal government (Cooper, 1996). The notable example of the latter has been the long-standing demands embodied within the reform agendas and initiatives of various municipal associations for the formal statutory and constitutional recognition of municipal government as a full-fledged order of government with what would be tantamount to a highly autonomous form of 'home rule' that would afford them greater authority and autonomy in relation to the provincial and territorial governments (Kitchen and McMillan, 1985; Canadian Federation of Municipalities, 1998).

In recent years such demands have been articulated most cogently and force-fully by some of the largest metropolitan municipalities, which have been demanding special functions, special financial arrangements with the provincial and federal governments, and special status and powers within the constitutional order (Edmonton, 2003). This is particularly true of the City of Toronto, which has expressed dissatisfaction with the modernized statutory framework recently adopted by Ontario. Toronto officials have been lobbying the provincial govern-ment for a special charter that would grant it unique jurisdictional authority and autonomy to transform it from a conventional city to a veritable 'city-state' (Toronto, 2000a, 2000b, 2000c, 2000d, 2000e). Their argument for such status is based largely on the logic of the importance for economic development of power-ful city-states in a time of ever-increasing globalization (Peirce, 1993; Martin, 1996).

OBJECTIVE OF BOOK

The central objective of this book is to chronicle and analyze various aspects of the extant, emerging, and prospective municipal reform agendas and initiatives in each province and territory in Canada during the 20 years that span the millennial divide from approximately 1990 to 2010, which in this volume is referred to as 'the turn-of-the-millennium municipal reform period'.

In exploring the municipal reform agendas and initiatives in each province and territory during this period, the present book focuses on five key topics that collectively can be referred to as the 5Ps of reform: the purposes, the pillars, the products, the processes, and the politics. The specific focus on each of these topics is explained, in turn, below.

Analysis of *purposes* focuses on the overarching goals and objectives of reform agendas and initiatives. These include both the stated and unstated major goals and objectives of the various governmental stakeholders—the provincial, territo-rial, and municipal governments, and various associations of municipalities and municipal officials. Some limited attention is also devoted to some of the goals and objectives of the federal government in light of its highly publicized 'new deal for municipalities' (Canada, 2002; Seidle, 2002; Berdahl, 2002; Martin, 2003; Canada, 2004; Plunkett, 2004).

The analysis of the *pillars* of municipal reform agendas and initiatives examines several components of the municipal system that are the objects of reform. This includes the structural, functional, financial, and jurisdictional components of the municipal systems in various provinces. The structural component of each municipal system comprises the overall configuration of the municipal system in terms of the number, types, and size of municipalities, quasi-municipalities, and municipal special-purpose bodies. The functional component consists of the formal and informal roles and responsibilities performed by various types of municipal governments and municipal authorities (Hobson and St-Hilaire, 1997). The financial component of the municipal system is made up of both the revenue and expenditure sides of the ledger; accordingly, the focus is on both the revenue sources and the expenditure responsibilities of municipal governments and their agencies. In the case of revenue sources, attention is devoted to the property tax assessment system and the level of reliance on the property tax base by municipalities and other governing entities. The jurisdictional component involves the authority and autonomy of municipal governments and municipal special-purpose bodies related to any facet of the municipal system. This includes their authority and autonomy to make decisions regarding, among other things, the structures, functions, and finances of municipal governments and municipal special-purpose bodies, as well as various types of intergovernmental relations. The principal issue related to jurisdictional authority for such matters is its distribution not only between the municipal and provincial or territorial governments, but also among various types or levels of municipal governments. Another important pillar of municipal reform that could be examined, but which is formally beyond the scope of this book, is the internal organizational, administrative, and managerial apparatus (Kernaghan et al., 2000; Richmond and Siegel, 1994). This includes the structures and functions of their councils and council-committee systems, the configuration of their administrative units, and the management of their respective human and financial resources, as well as various other types of assets and the delivery of their municipal services.

The analysis of the *products* of reform agendas and initiatives focuses on 'outputs' and 'outcomes'. Examination of outputs involves both reform proposals and actual reforms. These can be embodied in any one or more of the following:

- various types of reports commissioned by provincial, territorial, or municipal governments;
- provincial draft legislation;
- provincial statutes, regulations, policies;
- programs that impinge on various components of the municipal system.

With outcomes, attention is devoted to the effects of reforms for, among other things, the stated and unstated overarching goals and objectives of the reform agendas and initiatives in each province and territory (Vojnovic and Poel, 2000).

The analysis of the *processes* of municipal reform agendas and initiatives deals with decision-making with attention devoted to the modes and mechanisms of decision-making (Higgins, 1986b). In examining the modes of decision-making, the objects of analysis are the general approaches or, if you will, styles of decision-making. Pertinent areas of investigation include:

- whether decision-making processes entail either intra-governmental or intergovernmental negotiations;
- whether decision-making processes include public consultations;
- whether reforms are initiated, developed, or implemented by the provincial and territorial governments, their respective municipal governments, or jointly;
- whether reform initiatives are mandated for municipal governments by provincial or territorial governments, or whether municipal governments are

granted either complete or limited discretion and choice in matters related to reforms.

When we consider the mechanisms of decision-making the focus is on various types of organizational instruments used for addressing issues of reform. Examples of such analysis include whether they involve legislative committees or task forces and commissions created by the provincial, territorial, or municipal governments, either on a separate or joint basis; and the membership of such task forces and commissions, which might include elected or appointed officials of the various orders of government, academics and members of various professions who deal with municipal governance, and representatives of various communities or segments of the population.

In regard to the *politics* of municipal agendas and initiatives the focus is both on the configuration of key governmental and non-governmental political actors involved in the deliberations on reform, and on the patterns of collaboration and confrontation among these actors and the determinants of these patterns.

In summary, the principal emphases here are the purposes, pillars, products, processes, and politics of municipal reforms in the Canadian provinces and territories during the turn-of-the-millennium period. The book also devotes some attention to the prospects for municipal reform agendas and initiatives in the near future. Thus, the six research questions addressed in the various chapters of this book are:

- What were the purposes (i.e., goals and objectives) of the municipal reform agendas and initiatives in the provinces and territories?
- What were the similarities and differences in the nature and scope of the reform agendas and initiatives across the provinces and territories?
- What effect did the reform initiatives in each province and territory have on the purposes for which they were framed and implemented?
- What types of processes were used in framing and implementing municipal reform agendas and initiatives?
- What types of politics did those reform agendas and initiatives generate, and what were the determinants of the same?
- What types of municipal reform agendas and initiatives are likely to emerge in each province and territory in the near future?

CONTRIBUTION OF THE BOOK

The decision to chronicle and analyze the municipal reform agendas and initiatives of this period is based on two major interrelated considerations. The first is that this is an interesting and arguably important period for Canadian municipalities:

- All levels of government and a substantial portion of the general public recognized that the quality of municipal governance matters very much in the grand scheme of governance and political, economic, and social development in light of phenomena such as 'multi-level governance' (Bradford, 2004; Gibbins, 2001) and 'glocalization'(Courchene, 1995).

- A large number of reform agendas and initiatives emerged in all provinces and territories at approximately the same time.
- A high level of attention has been devoted to municipal reform in every province and territory.
- Governmental and non-governmental stakeholders and analysts have been engaged in an array of debates regarding the purpose, nature, and effects of the various reform agendas and initiatives.
- Various types of political machinations have surrounded the move towards reform in each province and territory.

The debate that is likely to persist for some time focuses on the effects that various reform initiatives have had on the configuration of several components of the municipal system, and also on some aspects of governance at the municipal, provincial, territorial, and national levels. The key issue in that particular debate is the extent to which reforms to date have had either a transformational effect or a marginal effect on the fundamental nature of municipal systems and municipal governance.

There is no question that the turn-of-the-millennium period of municipal reform is interesting and distinctive, and that it deserves serious academic attention. This much is true regardless of whether the recent period is ultimately judged as transformationally significant—comparable to 'the turn-of-the-century municipal reform era' of 100 years earlier (Tindal and Tindal, 2004: 1, 44–60)—or as a mere adjustment to municipal governance. However, the suggestion that this is a distinct period should not be interpreted to mean that it is necessarily a unique time. Comparable types of reform agendas and reform initiatives that emerged in previous distinct municipal reform periods in Canada have been analyzed in various monographs (Plunkett, 1973), chapters in edited volumes (Plunkett and Graham, 1982; Feldman and Graham, 1981; Magnusson and Sancton, 1983), and leading textbooks on municipal governance (Crawford, 1954; Dickerson et al., 1980; Higgins, 1986a; Tindal and Tindal, 2004). The common thrust of reforms among the various reform periods is the effort to modernize municipal governance by eliminating or at least modifying what are deemed problematic, anachronistic elements of the systems. In some respects, therefore, each reform period constitutes an attempt to modernize parts of the municipal systems that were institutionalized through so-called modernization efforts in previous reform periods. Thus, the turn-of-the-millennium period constitutes another important modernization initiative designed to help municipal governments, and to some extent their respective provincial and territorial governments, deal with challenges posed not only by demographic, economic, and social factors in the domestic and international environments, but also their own past policy decisions and those of other governments within the Canadian and international political systems (Frisken, 1994; Coffey, 1994a; Sancton, 1994; Blais, 1994; Andrew,

1995; Boswell, 1995; Magnusson, 1996; Andrew, 1997; Graham et al., 1998; Tindal and Tindal, 2004: 1–21, 61–84; Sancton, 2000a).

The second major consideration for chronicling and analyzing the present period is that until now it has not received a comprehensive and integrated academic treatment. Although several books and journal articles on municipal governance in Canada devote some attention to recent and ongoing municipal reform agendas and initiatives, none provides a comprehensive and up-to-date analysis of reform in each province and territory. Canadian literature that devotes some attention to municipal reform agendas and initiatives during this period consists of the following: books that focus on the evolving nature of various elements of municipal systems as a whole (Tindal and Tindal, 2004; McAllister, 2004); books that focus on municipal governance in metropolitan areas (Graham et al., 1998; Sancton, 1992; Lightbody, 1995; Thomas, 1997; Sancton, 2002b); journal articles devoted to city-regions (Coffey, 1994b; Sancton, 1994; Blais, 1994; Hutton, 1996; Smith, 1996; Gertler, 1996; O'Brien, 1996; Sancton, 1996b; Tomlinson, 1996; Quesnel, 2000); books that focus on urban policy issues (Fowler and Siegel, 2002); books that focus primarily on structural reforms (Sancton, 1991; Sancton, 2000b); books that focus on functional reforms (Hobson and St-Hilaire, 1997); books, monographs, and chapters in edited volumes that focus on financial reforms (Treff and Perry, 1998; Siegel, 2002; Kitchen, 2003; Boothe, 2004); journal articles devoted to structural and functional reforms in some provinces (Sancton, 1996a; Downey and Williams, 1998; Graham and Phillips, 1998; Graham and Phillips, 1999; Williams and Downey, 1999; Sancton, 2000c; Garcea, 2002a; Fischler et al., 2004); and journal articles and monographs devoted to jurisdictional reforms in various provinces (Canaran, 1996; Lidstone, 1998; Gagnon and Lidstone, 1998; Garcea, 2002b).

The bibliographic references in this chapter, together with those in subsequent chapters, reveal a growing body of literature that addresses various aspects of the municipal reforms in each province and territory during the last 15 years. The collective efforts of all analysts involved in chronicling and analyzing the plethora of reforms in this period are valuable because they shed much needed light on the extant reform agendas and initiatives and those that are likely to emerge in the near future. The analysis of municipal reform in Canada is also important from an international comparative context in that it contributes to a growing body of literature on municipal reform throughout the world. The comparative literature on municipal reform reveals that similar types of agendas and initiatives, and the political machinations that drive reform, have been evident in other countries during the same period (King and Pierre, 1990; Bennett, 1990; Vajpeyi, 1990; Stewart and Stoker, 1995; McCarney, 1996; Pierre, 1998; John, 2001; Amnå and Montin, 2000; Bukowski and Rajagopalan, 2000). The major difference across various countries has been in the precise configuration of reform agendas and initiatives based on differences in what are deemed to be the most salient problems and the best means by which to address them. This is equally true of industrialized countries (Dente and Kjellberg, 1988; Keating, 1991; John, 2001; Kersting

and Vetter, 2003; Bäck et al., 2003; Dollery and Marshall, 2003), developing countries (Vajpeyi, 1990), and post-communist countries (Coulson, 1995; McCarney,
1996: Baldersheim et al., 2003).

OVERVIEW

In Part II, 'Municipal Reforms in the Provinces and Territories: Case Studies',
analyses are presented on the state of municipal reform in each of Canada's
provinces and territories.

Chapter 2 examines municipal reform in British Columbia. Patrick Smith and
Kennedy Stewart's analysis commences with the 1991 election of Michael
Harcourt's New Democrat government and concludes with the recent passage of
the Gordon Campbell Liberal government's Community Charter legislation. The
chapter reveals that this has been an active time of legislating reform but that,
despite the activity, very little has changed in the fundamental features of the
municipal system and its operations. Smith and Stewart observe that the principal
focus has been jurisdictional reform, with structural, functional, and financial
reform receiving little attention. This imbalance in the reform agenda is captured
in their phrase 'one oar in the water' pulling for efficiency, rather than two pulling
for democratic accountability as well as efficiency. Another significant observation
is that under four successive premiers, efficiency improvements have been stressed
over reforms in democratic accountability; that is, to use the conceptual language
of this book, capacity development has been emphasized over reform to municipal-community relations. The authors devote attention to stalled or abandoned
accountability reforms, including the ones in which they were significantly
involved in an advisory capacity. While commending efficiency reforms, they
decry the lack of balance in the provincial reform agenda. In particular, they worry
that British Columbia's Community Charter legislation will result in providing
municipalities with greater powers while not providing the citizenry with the
requisite means to hold them in check.

Chapter 3 looks at Alberta. Edward LeSage catalogues the antecedents to
Alberta's groundbreaking Municipal Government Act (1994) and reviews the
novel particulars of that legislation, which has provided a template for jurisdictional reforms in other provinces and territories. Legislatively defined purposes of
municipalities, 'natural person' powers, spheres of jurisdiction, and general bylaw-
making powers are considered with special interest. LeSage observes that Alberta's
efforts have been heavily oriented towards jurisdictional and financial reforms and
less focused on functional and structural matters. Functional and financial debates
are currently at the top of the provincial-municipal agenda, with Alberta's urban
municipalities energetically arguing for a comprehensive new deal. A key observation is that despite the now widespread adoption of selected jurisdictional reforms
across the country, there is little evidence of the efficacy of the 1994 Act. While
some Alberta municipalities have taken advantage of the enabling features of the
new legislation, many municipalities are wary of the putatively liberating provisions and have not embraced them. A court challenge (only recently resolved in
favour of municipalities at the Supreme Court of Canada) is cited as one reason

for slow adoption of the legislated innovations. However, there is also an apparent paradox of freedom in play.

In Chapter 4, Joseph Garcea examines municipal reform initiatives in Saskatchewan. Despite extensive efforts at producing substantial structural, functional, financial, and jurisdictional reforms, ultimately the only notable reforms were a modernization of the property assessment system, a modest statutory framework to facilitate voluntary amalgamations, and a new statutory and jurisdictional framework for cities. Garcea argues that those reforms did not produce a substantial change to the capacity of municipalities, to provincial-municipal relations, to inter-municipal relations, or to municipal-community relations. He concludes that it is unlikely that more substantial structural, functional, financial, or jurisdictional reforms will be implemented in the near future. Such reforms, according to Garcea, will only occur if either the provincial and municipal representatives are prepared to make major concessions to accommodate each other on their preferred reform options, or the provincial government decides to reform the municipal system despite the preferences of municipal representatives. These developments are highly unlikely given the history of recent Saskatchewan politics. The one possible exception, following the recommendations of a provincially appointed task force, might be a change in the extent to which education authorities rely on or have access to property tax revenues. Even such a change, however, is highly contingent on the provincial government's fiscal capacity to implement those recommendations, which at the time of writing is not improving.

Chapter 5 surveys municipal reform initiatives in Manitoba. Authors Christopher Leo and Mark Piel devote the bulk of the chapter to describing reforms to the two distinct components of the municipal system in Manitoba: Winnipeg and the rest of the province's municipalities. Commentary on the municipal system outside Winnipeg focuses on the new Municipal Act of 1996, while the discussion of Winnipeg provides the historical context for understanding the fundamental nature and scope of the City of Winnipeg Charter Act (2003). Leo and Piel's central theme is that Manitoba's statutory reforms represent a shift in three directions—greater uniformity in the treatment of municipalities by the province, increased authority for municipal government, and a market model for service delivery. The authors conclude that although the reforms have left Manitoba's municipalities with noticeable increases in authority, the jury is still out on the effect that this will have on municipal governance. The same can be said in regard to the relative merits of the use of corporate powers in the general municipal legislation and of 'natural person' powers in Winnipeg's charter. The authors note that the increased powers and responsibilities have resulted in the institutionalization of market mechanisms and market philosophies into the municipal legislative architecture in Manitoba, the intent being to help municipalities deal with the forces of globalization.

In Chapter 6, David Siegel examines Ontario's extensive reform initiatives. Siegel explains and assesses the broad system-wide structural changes that reconstituted most of the province's municipal structure, including the venerable Ontario county system, regional governments, and city-region governmental reform. Details of the nature and effects of Ontario's bold, but only partially successful, efforts to achieve a clearer functional division between municipal and provincial governments are also catalogued. So, too, are Ontario's financial reforms, which included a provincial-municipal swap wherein municipalities inherited the whole of the property tax in exchange for dramatic reductions in provincial grants for a wide range of functionally realigned services. Siegel's assessment of the relative gains and losses for municipalities as a result of those reforms should be of special interest to all municipal reformers across Canada. On balance, Siegel sees the emergence of a more self-reliant and somewhat more empowered municipal sector that continues to wrestle with the challenges of balancing functions with financial resources. Siegel observes that the reform tide has clearly run its course in Ontario, if for no other reason than that Premier Mike Harris's Conservative government expended a great deal of political capital on that initiative, and Premier Dalton McGuinty's Liberal government is clearly not prepared to do the same. He points to survey data that reveal a general subsidence of hard feelings that were intensely held among certain elements of the public and municipal officials, and infers that the Liberals, elected to office in 2003, are not anxious to do anything that will reverse that trend.

Chapter 7 explores municipal reform initiatives in Quebec. Pierre Hamel reveals that structural reforms were by far the most publicized and significant. It was largely in conjunction with structural reforms that some minor functional, financial, and jurisdictional reforms were implemented. The initial structural reforms implemented by the Parti Québécois government using a combination of a voluntary approach with positive and negative incentives and a mandatory approach touched much of the Quebec municipal system and involved both the amalgamation of several hundred municipalities and the reconfiguration of the regional municipal authorities in metropolitan, urban, and rural areas throughout the province. Subsequent structural reforms initiated by Premier Jean Charest's Liberal government involved the historic de-amalgamation process that provided the communities within municipalities that had been amalgamated since 2000 the opportunity to hold referendums on whether they wanted their former municipality to be reconstituted. As a result of those referendums 32 municipalities are scheduled to be re-established on 1 January 2005. Functional reforms entailed a minor realignment of the roles and responsibilities both between the provincial and municipal governments and among the reconfigured regional authorities and municipal governments. Financial reforms amounted to an exchange of financial resources between the province and municipalities. Jurisdictional reforms were also relatively minor and focused largely on increasing municipal authority and autonomy in raising and managing financial resources. Hamel questions whether the corpus of reforms produced substantial change or results. He concludes that while additional tinkering with the system is likely, it is unlikely that more substantial reforms comparable to the structural reforms of the past decade will be implemented in the near future. The reason for this is the reform fatigue felt by provincial and municipal officials and the political imperatives facing the provincial government to avoid doing anything that could alienate any of its political support among municipal governments and their ratepayers. The prospects for substantial reforms in the near future are highest in the financial sphere. Financial reforms could be triggered by any major agreements that may be reached between the federal government and the Quebec provincial government, with Ottawa transferring funds designated for municipalities to Quebec as part of Prime Minister Paul Martin's promise of a new deal for municipalities.

Chapter 8 addresses New Brunswick's reforms. Daniel Bourgeois's survey focuses on the initiatives of two provincial governments—Frank McKenna's Liberals and Bernard Lord's Tories. This is done with an allusion to the lasting and increasingly problematic effects of the Byrne Commission reforms instituted in the 1960s. Bourgeois observes that although McKenna's government considered a wide range of reforms and announced ambitious legislative plans, most of the actual reforms were structural. Especially notable were the amalgamations in select urban areas and the creation of various regional commissions. Functional reform was not given much attention and plans for financial reform were comparatively modest. McKenna's government proposed legislation that would liberate municipalities from the confines of the 'express authority' doctrine, but this never passed. Lord's Conservative government, elected in 1999, halted prospective McKenna financial and jurisdictional reforms and set out to construct its own comprehensive reform agenda. While certain initiatives have gone forward, such as regionalizing economic development through the creation of new authorities, the Lord administration's reform agenda has yet to be made concrete in legislation. Bourgeois highlights four key reform 'lessons' derived from two cases presented in the chapter, one of which examines the regionalization of police services and the other the creation of a 911 central dispatch service in the Moncton region. Although the cases are drawn from the New Brunswick experience, the lessons appear to be broadly applicable.

In Chapter 9, Dale Poel provides an overview of municipal reform initiatives in Nova Scotia since the early 1990s. Poel commences with a brief survey that underscores the lasting legacy of the renowned Graham Commission and notes that while the province's regionalization initiatives have received the most attention in academic and public comment, other reform initiatives have been on the agenda. He suggests that the general thrust of those reform initiatives has been to improve both the capacity and performance of municipal governments and the alignment of roles and responsibilities between the provincial and municipal governments. Legislation establishing regional municipal governments in Cape Breton and Halifax, realignment of functions between the provincial and municipal governments, and the transfer of financial responsibility for property assessment from the province to municipalities have been among the most significant reforms. Despite the implementation of significant reforms, much remains on that province's reform agenda. Unresolved issues include the appropriate alignment of functions and finances between the provincial and municipal governments. Poel appears confident that the issues will be tackled but concludes that the effectiveness of reforms resides in the political will and the quality of leadership exercised at the municipal and provincial levels.

Chapter 10 examines Newfoundland's municipal reform agenda since 1990. Peter Boswell's analysis suggests that although the municipal reform agenda for structural, functional, financial, and jurisdictional reforms in that province was relatively ambitious, the nature and scope of the actual reforms have turned out to be relatively limited. He points out that structural reforms—amalgamation and regionalization—were abandoned in the face of strong opposition, and observes that functional reforms did not entail any major transfers between the province and municipalities. Financial reforms were minor, involving grant cutbacks and minor adjustments to municipal legislative powers on taxation, budgeting, and debt restructuring. Jurisdictional reforms entailed the elimination of some statutory provisions that were generally unworkable and the clarification of some unclear or ambiguous provisions. In looking to the future, Boswell concludes that it is unlikely that any major reforms are on the horizon. By his account, there will be some minor amalgamations on a voluntary basis if rural communities continue to lose population and as urban communities expand, and some minor tinkering with financial arrangements between the provincial and municipal governments. A consolidated Cities Act also may be in the offing. The only prospect for a changed scenario would be a dramatic change for the better in Newfoundland's economic prospects.

In Chapter 11, John Crossley paints the historical context in which municipal reform in Prince Edward Island was contemplated during the turn-of-the-millennium period. Structural reforms were the most pronounced. Provincially mandated amalgamations were concluded within PEI's most heavily populated urban areas. Badly needed rural structural reform was considered but never seriously pursued. Functional, financial, and jurisdictional reforms were much less ambitious although perhaps not less needed. In contrast to the prevailing pattern across the country, Crossley notes that functional reforms involved the transfer of roles and responsibilities to the province. There is little evidence of provincial downloading or offloading, largely owing to the feeble capacity of most PEI municipal authorities. In fact, the proliferation of special-purpose bodies can be traced to provincial confidence in their capacity over that of existing municipal administration. Major municipal financial reforms were introduced in the early 1980s and remain in place despite persistent issues that Crossley attributes to structural and functional problems. Nonetheless, the financial administration appears to suit current circumstances. Crossley observes that in recent years there have been few calls for jurisdictional reform and no legislative amendments to change the powers and autonomy of PEI municipal government. Crossley discounts prospects for major new reform initiatives in the near future, citing the relatively weak leverage of municipal government on the public policy agenda.

In Chapter 12, Katherine Graham analyzes the municipal reform agenda in Yukon, the Northwest Territories, and Nunavut. She observes that reform initiatives were similar in nature and scope to those undertaken in the smaller provinces. Her analysis contains several key themes. One is that, despite some similarities, the three territorial governments have had different priorities for, and approaches to, municipal reform. Contrary to what some might assume, one size does not fit all in the territorial North. Another theme is that local governance is central to community development and sustainability in the territories. Unfortunately, northern municipal government is very fragile due to economic and administrative challenges. Among the most important challenges are inadequate financial resources, staff retention, and developing permanent indigenous municipal employees. In Nunavut, determining the roles and resources of local government is a work in progress, as this new territory evolves. In considering potential reform initiatives, Graham believes that territorial governments will strive to further modernize the basic municipal legislation and to advance the larger project of 'territory-building'. She adds that in light of the history and current challenges faced by each of the territorial governments, territory-building may be the most important source of change to the nature and roles of municipal governance in the three territories. The transitional issues related to the emergence and evolution of more autonomous Aboriginal governments in Yukon and the Northwest Territories may represent another source of change to municipal governance in those two territories.

The concluding chapter, by Garcea and LeSage, consists of three major sections based largely on the information and analyses in the previous 11 chapters and to some extent also on the extant literature on municipal reform. The first section summarizes and analyzes the purposes, pillars, products, processes, and politics of the municipal reform agendas and initiatives. The second section offers some prognostications regarding municipal reform in the near future. The third section suggests some directions for further research.

The principal observation regarding the purposes of reform is that the various reform initiatives were largely designed to advance three overarching goals or objectives:

- improved governance capacity both at the municipal level and at the provincial and territorial levels;
- improved intergovernmental relations between municipal governments and their respective provincial or territorial governments and also among the municipal governments;
- improved relations between municipal governments and members of their respective communities related to issues of accessibility, responsiveness, and accountability.

Notably, the goals and objectives of reform have not always been shared equally by all provincial and municipal governments. Indeed, in some instances they have articulated quite different purposes.

In regard to the pillars of municipal reform, all jurisdictions devoted some attention to structural, functional, financial, and jurisdictional reforms, and the degree of attention devoted to each of those four categories of reforms varied not only across the various provinces and territories but also within each of them.

Structural reforms were contemplated and in some instances undertaken largely through amalgamation and the creation of one-tier rather than two-tier systems of municipal governance. Restructuring was initiated or at least studied in most jurisdictions and substantial structural reforms were implemented in Ontario, Quebec, Nova Scotia, New Brunswick, PEI, and in some respects also in the northern territories as a result of the creation of Nunavut, which effectively hived off a substantial portion of the local authorities from the Northwest Territories.

Functional reform sought to realign the responsibilities of municipal governments and their respective provincial and territorial governments. Such realignment was contemplated in several provinces and territories, but ultimately significant reforms were implemented only in Ontario and Nova Scotia. This said, some form of functional realignment, however modest, occurred in just about every jurisdiction. Such realignments often involved some measure of downloading, uploading, or off-loading of provincial functional responsibilities and varying degrees of disentanglement and entanglement among the various levels of government.

Financial reforms were designed to achieve one or more of the following: a realignment of the financial responsibilities between the municipal and provincial governments; increased access for municipal governments to various revenue resources; increased flexibility of municipal governments in generating revenues through various revenue sources; and changes to various aspects of the property tax assessment systems. Some financial reform was evident in most every jurisdiction, but in no case were radical reforms implemented. Indeed, most financial reforms were essentially relatively minor adjustments to the status quo.

Jurisdictional reform initiatives were designed to adjust the level of authority and autonomy that municipal governments had vis-à-vis their respective provincial and territorial governments. Such reforms were contemplated in every jurisdiction and implemented in all provinces and territories. Notwithstanding much fanfare regarding the generation of putatively 'new-style' municipal statutes—exemplified by Alberta's 1994 Municipal Government Act—which contained provisions to enhance the scope of municipal authority and autonomy, jurisdictional authority and autonomy for many municipal governments were not altered dramatically. In fact, perhaps the most radical changes occurred in the Northwest Territories, where new forms of First Nation local governance arrangements were forged.

The two major observations regarding the products in terms of outputs of structural, functional, financial, and jurisdictional reform initiatives are: first, overall the scope of the actual reforms that were ultimately adopted or implemented was significantly more limited than what was considered or proposed; and second, there was considerable variation among the provinces and territories in the nature and scope of the reforms that were implemented.

The jury is still out in regard to the effects of implemented reforms. It is difficult to conclude whether municipal governance is improved today over what it had been 10–15 years ago. Depending on one's perspective and focus, credible arguments can be made for positive, negative, or neutral consequences. Although the effects of specific reforms are highly debatable, the overall effect of reform is less debatable. The fundamental transformation or reinvention that some sought in municipal governance did not happen. After all, regardless of what conclusions one reaches regarding the precise effect of each of the reforms implemented, neither the fundamental purpose of municipal governance nor the fundamental nature of the constitutional status, functions, or finances of municipal governments has been radically transformed by recent municipal reforms.

In regard to the processes of reforms: they entailed a combination of intergovernmental negotiations and public consultations; and reviews and public consultations tended to rely extensively on special task forces appointed by the appropriate provincial minister or by cabinet as a whole and much less on legislative committees. These task forces were largely comprised of members with either academic or practical expertise on municipal governance. Municipal associations and other formal stakeholder organizations did, on occasion, establish separate venues and processes in seeking to achieve their preferred reforms, but usually they did so in reaction to processes initiated by the provincial and territorial governments.

The politics of reform varied in nature and intensity not only across the provinces and territories but, in many instances, also across the different reform initiatives undertaken within each province and territory. Reform politics was largely intergovernmental in nature, involving extensive and intense negotiations between municipal governments—either individually or collectively—and their respective provincial or territorial governments. Insofar as non-governmental stakeholders were engaged in the political machinations of municipal reform, it was generally in reaction to initiatives of the governmental stakeholders. Political controversy accompanying negotiations differed noticeably around the various foci of reform. Negotiations were often highly publicized and controversial on matters related to structural reforms and certain types of functional and financial reforms, such as the realignment of roles and responsibilities between orders of government for major programs like welfare and changes in property assessments. They were less publicized and controversial in regard to other types of functional and financial reforms that did not entail major changes in the financial burden, either for governments or for ratepayers. Similarly, most jurisdictional reforms that involved, for example, changes in roles and responsibilities for public health and ambulatory services from municipal to health authorities also created little public debate.

In proffering some prognostications regarding the nature and scope of the reform agenda and the adoption or implementation of potential reforms, the concluding chapter postulates that what will happen in the future, as in the past, is highly contingent on the interests and imperatives of provincial, territorial, local, federal, and Aboriginal governmental leaders as well as various non-governmental community leaders with a stake in municipal government affairs. All indications are, however, that we can expect continuity rather than discontinuity not only in the nature and scope of proposed reforms, but also in the reforms that are actually adopted or implemented in the near future. Indeed, in some cases the reforms considered and adopted or implemented are likely to entail either minor adjustments to what has already been implemented in the recent past, or the implementation of reforms that were considered but to date have still not been implemented. In short, in the near future it is unlikely that there will be any radical departures from the reform agenda and reforms of recent vintage.

NOTE

It is useful to define two key concepts—'reform agendas' and 'reform initiatives'. Whereas 'reform agendas' are sets of municipal reform issues that are under active consideration by various governmental and non-governmental stakeholders, 'reform initiatives' are the actions of governmental actors directed either at examining or implementing reforms. This includes activities such as reviews on the need for reforms, proposals for reforms, and reforms that are actually implemented. The foregoing definition of 'reform agendas' is influenced by John Kingdon's notion of policy agenda: 'a list of subjects or problems to which governmental officials, and people outside government closely associated with those officials, are paying some serious attention at any given time' (Kingdon, 1984: 3). Also influential in our conceptualization of reform agendas are Cobb and Elder, who distinguished between 'institutional' or governmental agendas, which consist of issues and options that governments perceive as in need of attention, and 'systemic' or public agendas, which consist of issues and options that the broader community perceives as in need of attention (Cobb and Elder, 1972: 85). Given that in cases of multi-level governance, such as that found in the municipal sector, each order of government is likely to have its own reform agenda, which may be the same as or different from that of other order(s) of government. Unless there is a specific reference to a particular institutional or governmental agenda, in this book the concept reform agenda(s) is used in the same way as Kingdon's concept of policy agenda, to refer to the list of subjects or problems under active consideration by governmental and non-governmental officials.

REFERENCES

Amnå, Erik, and Stig Montin. 2000. *Towards a New Concept of Local Self-Government? Recent Local Government Legislation in Comparative Perspective.* Bergen: Fagbokforlaget.

Andrew, Caroline. 1995. 'Provincial-Municipal Relations; or Hyper-Fractional Quasi-Subordination Revisited', in James Lightbody, ed., *Canadian Metropolitics: Governing Our Cities.* Mississauga, Ont.: Copp Clark, 137–60.

———. 1997. 'Globalization and Local Action', in Timothy L. Thomas, ed., *The Politics of the City: A Canadian Perspective.* Scarborough, Ont.: Nelson Canada, 139–49.

Aucoin, Peter. 1995. *The New Public Management: Canada in Comparative Perspective.* Montreal: Institute for Research on Public Policy.

Barnett, Neil, and Robert Leach. 1996. 'The New Public Management and Local Governance', in Ian Hampsher-Monk and Jeffrey Stanyer, eds, *Contemporary Political Studies, 1996.* London: Political Studies Association of the United Kingdom, 1508–38.

Bennett, Robert J., ed. 1990. *Decentralization, Local Governments, and Markets: Towards a Post-Welfare Agenda.* Oxford: Clarendon Press.

Berdahl, Loleen. 2002. *Structuring Federal Urban Engagement: A Principled Approach.* Calgary: Canada West Foundation.

Blais, Pamela. 1994. 'The Competitive Advantage of City-Regions', *Policy Options* 15, 4: 15–19.

Borins, Sandford. 1995. 'The New Public Management is Here to Stay', *Canadian Public Administration* 38, 1: 122–32.

Boswell, Peter G. 1996. 'Provincial-Municipal Relations', in Christopher Dunn, ed., *Provinces: Canadian Provincial Politics*. Peterborough, Ont.: Broadview Press, 253–74

Boothe, Paul, ed. 2003. *Paying for Cities: The Search for Sustainable Municipal Revenues*. Western Studies in Economic Policy No. 9. Edmonton: Institute for Public Economics.

Bradford, Neil. 2004. 'Place Matters in Multi-Level Governance: Perspectives on a New Urban Policy Paradigm', *Policy Options* 30, 1: 39–44.

Bukowski, Jeanie J., and Swarna Rajagopalan, eds. 2000. *Redistribution of Authority: A Cross-Regional Perspective*. London: Praeger.

Canada. 2002. *Canada's Urban Strategy—A Blueprint for Action*. Final Report of Prime Minister's Task Force on Urban Issues. At: www.judysgro.com

———. 2004. Speech from the Throne. Mimeo.

Canadian Federation of Municipalities. 1998. 'Future Role of Municipal Government'. Mimeo.

Canaran, Hemant R. 1996. 'Local Government Legislation and Structures Are Outdated Says Vancouver Lawyer Lidstone', *Municipal World* (Aug.): 6–7.

Cobb, Roger, and Charles D. Elder. 1972. *Participation in American Politics: The Dynamics of Agenda-Building*. Boston: Allyn and Bacon.

Coffey, William J. 1994a. *The Evolution of Canada's Metropolitan Economies*. Montreal: Institute for Research on Public Policy.

———. 1994b. 'City-Regions in the New Economy: The Economic Role of Metropolitan Areas', *Policy Options* 15, 4: 5–11.

Cooper, Reid. 1996. 'Municipal Law, Delegated Legislation and Democracy', *Canadian Public Administration* 39, 3: 290–313.

Coulson, Andrew. 1995. *Local Government in Eastern Europe: Establishing Democracy at the Grassroots*. London: Edward Elgar.

Courchene, T.J. 1995. 'Glocalization: The Regional/International Interface', *Canadian Journal of Regional Science* 18, 1: 1–20.

Crawford, K. Grant. 1954. *Canadian Municipal Government*. Toronto: University of Toronto Press.

Dente, Bruno, and Francesco Kjellberg, eds. 1988. *The Dynamics of Institutional Change: Local Government Reorganization in Western Democracies*. London: Sage.

Dickerson, M.O., S. Drabek, and J.T. Woods. 1980. *Problems of Change in Urban Government*. Waterloo, Ont.: Wilfred Laurier University Press.

Dollery, Brian, and Neil Marshall, eds. 2003. *Reshaping Australian Local Government*. Sydney: University of New South Wales Press.

Downey, Terence, and Robert Williams. 1998. 'Provincial Agendas, Local Responses: The "Common Sense" Restructuring of Ontario's Municipal Governments', *Canadian Public Administration* 41: 234–5.

Edmonton. 2003. *Identifying and Addressing Inequities in the City of Edmonton's Relationship with the Provincial Government*. Edmonton: Corporate Services Department, Dec.

Feldman, Lionel D., and Katherine A. Graham. 1981. 'Local Governmental Reform in Canada', in Arthur B. Gunlicks, ed., *Local Government Reform and Reorganization: An International Perspective*. Port Washington, NY: Kennikat Press, 151–68.

Fischler, Raphael, John Meligrana, and Jeanne M. Wolfe. 2004. 'Canadian Experiences of Local Government Boundary Reform: A Comparison of Quebec and Ontario', in Meligrana, ed., *Redrawing Local Government Boundaries: An International Study of Politics, Procedures, and Decisions*. Vancouver: University of British Columbia Press, 75–105.

Fowler, Edmund P., and David Siegel. 2002. *Urban Policy Issues: Canadian Perspectives*, 2nd edn. Toronto: Oxford University Press.

Frisken, Frances. 1994. 'Metropolitan Change and the Challenge to Public Policy', in Frisken, ed., *The Changing Canadian Metropolis*. Berkeley, Calif.: Institute of Governmental Studies Press, 1–35.

Gagnon, Kristin, and Donald Lidstone. 1998. 'A Comparison of New and Proposed Municipal Acts of the Provinces', paper prepared for the 1998 annual conference of the Federation of Canadian Municipalities, Regina.

Garcea, Joseph. 2002a. 'Municipal Reform in Western Canada: plus ça change plus c'est la même chose', *Organizations & Territoires* 11, 3: 101–10.

———. 2002b. 'Modern Municipal Statutory Frameworks in Canada', *Journal of Governance: International Review* 3, 2: 1–14.

Gertler, Meric. 1996. 'City-Regions and the Global Economy: Choices Facing Toronto: Principles to Guide Toronto Policy Makers', *Policy Options* 17, 7: 12–15.

Gibbins, Roger. 2001. 'Local Governance and Federal Political Systems', *International Social Science Journal* 53, 1: 163–70.

Graham, Katherine A., and Susan D. Phillips. 1998. '"Who Does What' in Ontario: The Process of Provincial-Municipal Disentanglement', *Canadian Public Administration* 41, 2: 175–209.

——— and ———. 1999. 'Emerging Solitudes: The New Era in Provincial-Municipal Relations', in Martin W. Westmacott and Hugh P. Mellon, eds, *Public Administration and Public Policy: Governing in Challenging Times*. Scarborough, Ont.: Prentice-Hall, 73–88.

———, ———, and Allan A. Maslove. 1998. *Urban Governance in Canada: Representation, Resources, and Restructuring*. Toronto: Harcourt Brace Canada.

Gross Stein, Janice. 2001. *The Cult of Efficiency*. Don Mills, Ont.: Anansi.

Higgins, Donald J.H. 1986a. *Local and Urban Politics in Canada*. Toronto: Gage Educational Publishing.

———. 1986b. 'The Process of Reorganizing Local Government in Canada', *Canadian Journal of Political Science* 19, 2: 219–42.

Hobson, Paul A.R., and Frances St-Hilaire, eds. 1997. *Urban Governance and Finance: A Question of Who Does What*. Montreal: Institute for Research on Public Policy.

Hutton, Thomas. 1996. 'Structural Change and the Urban Policy Challenge: Policy Responses to Transformational Change', *Policy Options* 17, 7: 3–6.

John, Peter. 2001. *Local Governance in Western Europe*. London: Sage.

Keating, Michael. 1991. *Comparative Urban Politics: Power and the City in the United States, Canada, Britain and France*. Brookfield, Vermont: Edward Elgar.

Kernaghan, Kenneth, Brian Marson, and Sandford Borins. 2000. *The New Public Organization*. Toronto: Institute of Public Administration of Canada.

King, Desmond S., and Jon Pierre, eds. 1990. *Challenges to Local Government*. London: Sage.

Kingdon, John W. 1984. *Agendas, Alternatives, and Public Policies*. Boston: Little, Brown and Company.

Kitchen, Harry M. 2003. *Municipal Revenue and Expenditure Issues in Canada*. Toronto: Canadian Tax Foundation, Tax Paper No. 107.

——— and Melville L. McMillan. 1985. 'Local Government and Canadian Federalism', in Richard Simeon (research coordinator), *Intergovernmental Relations*, vol. 63 of the studies of the Royal Commission on the Economic Union and Development Prospects for Canada. Toronto: University of Toronto Press, 215–61.

Lidstone, Donald. 1998. 'Lidstone Compares New and Proposed Legislation', *Municipal World* (Aug.): 9–12.

Lightbody, James, ed. 1995. *Canadian Metropolitics: Governing Our Cities*. Toronto: Copp Clark.

Lindquist, Evert, ed. 2000. *Government Restructuring and Career Public Service*. Toronto: Institute of Public Administration of Canada.

McAllister, Mary Louise. 2004. *Governing Ourselves? The Politics of Canadian Communities.* Vancouver: University of British Columbia Press.

McCarney, Patricia L., ed. 1996. *The Changing Nature of Local Government in Developing Countries.* Toronto: Centre for Urban and Community Studies, University of Toronto, and Federation of Canadian Municipalities, International Office.

Magnusson, Warren. 1996. *The Search for Political Space.* Toronto: University of Toronto Press.

———— and Andrew Sancton, eds. 1983. *City Politics in Canada.* Toronto: University of Toronto Press.

Martin, Fernand. 1996. 'Montréal devant la mondialisation: Le modèle optimal reste à construire', *Policy Options* 17, 7: 16–19.

Martin, Paul. 2003. 'Towards a New Deal for Cities', presented at the Creative Cities Conference, Winnipeg, 29 May. At: www.paulmartintimes.ca

O'Brien, Allan. 1996. 'Municipal Reform in Halifax: Assessing the Amalgamation in Halifax', *Policy Options* 17, 7: 20–2.

Peirce, Neal, with Curtis Johnson and John Stuart Hall. 1993. *Citistates: How Urban America Can Prosper in a Competitive World.* Washington, DC: Seven Locks Press.

Pierre, Jon, ed. 1998. *Partnership in Urban Governance: European and American Experience.* London: Macmillan.

Plunkett, Thomas J. 1973. 'Structural Reform of Local Government in Canada', *Public Administration Review* 33, 1: 40–51.

————. 2004. 'A Nation of Cities Awaits Paul Martin's "New Deal"—Federal Funds for "Creatures of the Provinces"', *Policy Options* 30, 1: 19–25.

———— and Katherine Graham. 1982. 'Whither Municipal Government?', *Canadian Public Administration* 25, 4: 603–18.

Quesnel, Louise. 2000. 'Municipal Reorganization in Quebec', *Canadian Journal of Regional Science* 23, 1: 115–34.

Richmond, Dale, and David Siegel, eds. 1994. *Agencies, Boards, and Commissions in Canadian Local Government.* Toronto: Institute of Public Administration of Canada.

Sancton, Andrew 1991. *Local Government Restructuring Since 1975.* Toronto: ICURR.

————. 1992. 'Canada as a Highly Urbanized Nation: New Implications for Government', *Canadian Public Administration* 35, 2: 281–98.

————. 1994. 'Governing Canada's City Regions: The Search for a New Framework', *Policy Options* 15, 4: 12–15.

————. 1996a. 'Reducing Costs by Amalgamating Municipalities: New Brunswick, Nova Scotia and Ontario', *Canadian Public Administration* 39, 3: 267–89.

————. 1996b. 'Assessing the GTA Task Force's Proposal: A Politically More Acceptable Alternative', *Policy Options* 17, 7: 38–40.

————. 2000a. 'The Municipal Role in the Governance of Canadian Cities', in Trudi Bunting and Pierre Filion, eds, *Canadian Cities in Transition: The Twenty-First Century*, 2nd edn. Toronto: Oxford University Press, 425–42.

————. 2000b. *Merger Mania: The Assault on Local Government.* Westmount, Que.: Price-Patterson.

————. 2000c. 'Amalgamations, Service Realignment, and Property Taxes: Did the Harris Government Have a Plan for Ontario Municipalities?', *Canadian Journal of Regional Studies* 23, 1: 135–56.

————. 2002a. 'Municipalities, Cities, and Globalization: Implications for Canadian Federalism', in Herman Bakvis and Grace Skogstad, eds, *Canadian Federalism: Performance, Effectiveness, and Legitimacy.* Toronto: Oxford University Press, 261–77.

————. 2002b. 'Metropolitan and Regional Governance', in Fowler and Siegel (2002: 54–68).

Savoie, Donald. 1995. 'What Is Wrong with the New Public Management?', *Canadian Public Administration* 38, 1: 112–21.

Seidle, Leslie, ed. 1993. *Rethinking Government: Reform or Reinvention?* Montreal: Institute for Research on Public Policy.

———. 2002. *The Federal Role in Canada's Cities: Overview of Issues and Proposed Actions*. Ottawa: Canadian Policy Research Networks, Discussion Paper F/27, (Nov.).

Shields, John, and Mitchell Evans. 1998. *Shrinking the State: Globalization and Public Administration 'Reform'*. Halifax: Fernwood.

Siegel, David. 1993. 'Reinventing Local Government: The Promise and the Problems', in Seidle (1993: 175–202).

———. 2002. 'Urban Finance at the Turn of the Century: Be Careful What You Wish For', in Fowler and Siegel (2002: 36–53).

Smith, Patrick J. 1996. 'Metropolitan Governance: Vancouver and B.C. Regions: Workable Alternatives to Regional Government', *Policy Options* 17, 7: 7–11.

Stewart, John, and Gerry Stoker, eds. 1995. *Local Government in the 1990s*. London: Macmillan.

Thomas, Timothy, ed. 1997. *The Politics of the City: A Canadian Perspective*. Scarborough, Ont.: ITP Nelson.

Tindal, C. Richard, and Susan Nobes Tindal. 2004. *Local Government in Canada*, 6th edn. Scarborough, Ont.: Nelson Canada.

Toronto. 2000a. 'Towards a New Relationship with Ontario and Canada', press release.

———. 2000b. 'Towards a New Relationship with Ontario and Canada', Staff Report.

———. 2000c. 'The Time Is Right for New Relationships with Ontario and Canada', Background Report.

———. 2000d. 'Power of Canadian Cities—The Legal Framework', Background Report.

———. 2000e. 'Comparison of Powers and Revenue Sources of Selected Cities', Background Report.

Treff, Karen, and David B. Perry. 1998. *Finances of the Nation: A Review of Expenditures and Revenues of the Federal, Provincial, and Local Governments of Canada*. Toronto: Canadian Tax Foundation.

Vajpeyi, Dhirendra, ed. 1990. *Local Government and Politics in the Third World: Issues and Trends*. New Delhi: Heritage Publishers.

Vojnovic, Igor, and Dale Poel. 2000. 'Provincial and Municipal Restructuring in Canada: Assessing Expectations and Outcomes', *Canadian Journal of Regional Science* 13, 1: 1–6.

Williams, Robert J., and Terrence J. Downey. 1999. 'Reforming Rural Ontario', *Canadian Public Administration* 42, 2: 160–92.

PART II

MUNICIPAL REFORM IN THE PROVINCES AND TERRITORIES

CHAPTER 2

Local Government Reform in British Columbia, 1991–2005: One Oar in the Water

PATRICK J. SMITH AND KENNEDY STEWART

INTRODUCTION AND OVERVIEW

On 16 May 2001, the British Columbia Liberal Party captured 58 per cent of the votes in the British Columbia general election and 77 of 79 legislative seats. One of the first promises of incoming Premier Gordon Campbell was a major reform of BC's municipal government legislation. Proclaimed as the Community Charter in May 2003 and in effect since 1 January 2004, this legislation marked yet another attempt by a British Columbia provincial government in recent years to reform municipal government.[1] This chapter reflects on the past decade and a half of municipal legislative reform in British Columbia including: (1) a brief background of the prelude to municipal legislative review in BC and early reform success under the NDP regime of Mike Harcourt; (2) an evaluation of decentralization initiatives under Premier Glen Clark and his NDP successors Dan Miller and Ujjal Dosanjh; and (3) an assessment of what recent reform measures under BC Liberal Premier Gordon Campbell mean to current and future municipal governance in British Columbia.

In following the general framework of this book, we describe legislation affecting local government according to how each Act affected the structural, functional, financial, and jurisdictional features of BC local governments. We have added two additional themes—efficiency and accountability—'efficiency' gains reflect improved service delivery with reduced costs and 'accountability' increases indicate a closer linking of governmental policy with public will. As described by Peter Self (1977) and others (e.g., Smith, 1979), these two themes are inextricably linked and efficiency will often only rise when decision-makers are held responsible for their actions. Decentralization is a common method for raising local government efficiency as it removes the bureaucratic barriers to local innovation.

Table 2.1   Acts Pertaining to Municipal Government, 1991–2005

Years	Administration	Total Acts	Primary Topic Municipal Reform	%	Municipal Reform of Some Relevance	%
1991–5	Harcourt	281	21	8	36	13
1996–01	Clark/Miller/Dosanjh	243	11	6	33	14
2001–5	Campbell	267	8	3	48	18
1991–2005 Total		**791**	**40**	**5**	**117**	**15**

However, as has been recognized in Britain and elsewhere, an increase in local control should be accompanied by an increase in local accountability to avoid corruption or capture by local interest groups or by the professional bureaucracy (Smith and Stewart, 2005). Conflict of interest guidelines, freedom of information legislation, and open meetings can enhance public control of officials, but the electoral system is the base upon which local democracy rests and thus must be the primary concern of any upper-tier government with an eye to offloading decision-making power to lower-tier governments (Stewart, 2003).

As shown in Table 2.1, municipal reform has been high on the agendas of all three British Columbia governmental regimes since 1991. Of the 791 legislative acts passed in these years, local government has been the primary topic of 5 per cent of all acts passed while 15 per cent of BC legislative activity has had at least some relevance to municipalities. Considering the finite amount of legislative time available and the large number of provincial responsibilities, it would appear that this issue ranks high with most provincial governments—although it would appear to have ranked higher with some than others (see Appendix III for a detailed listing of relevant legislation). But upon reviewing what clearly has been an active period of local government reform, readers may be surprised that almost nothing has changed with regard to the local government structure or the functions for which they are responsible. While attempts have been made to enhance efficiency, almost no attempts have been made to increase accountability of local officials; and where there has been change it has seldom been accompanied by increased local fiscal capacity.

The creation of the Greater Vancouver Transit Authority (GVTA) marks the only structural change, and a relatively minor one at that, as the enabling legislation merely moved responsibility for transit in the Lower Mainland from a provincially appointed body to one that is indirectly elected/appointed regionally.[2] A minor functional change accompanied this structural change as the GVTA; its membership is primarily drawn from the indirectly elected Greater Vancouver Regional District, which has been given responsibility for overseeing transit and transportation development and operation in the metropolitan region. In terms of how local governments conduct their business, recent legislation has brought a few financial and jurisdictional changes—most of which have been aimed at increasing efficiency by freeing the hands of local governments. Under Premier Glen Clark's

Municipal Affairs Minister, Mike Farnsworth, local governments were given new authority to initiate Public-Private Partnerships (P3s) and slightly broadened corporate powers—moves that the incoming Liberal government sought to enhance in its Community Charter. Overall, the last decade and a half has brought much legislative action but little real reform to local government institutions in British Columbia.

Successive British Columbia governments have attempted to increase local government efficiency through decentralization but with either no or only a token effort to improving accountability. With the exception of the measures brought in under Mike Harcourt's Electoral Reform Act in the early 1990s, local councillors and officials are no more accountable to their local electors now than before decentralization began. While Clark and his various Municipal/Local Government ministers demonstrated on a number of occasions that they understood the crucial link between efficiency and accountability, they failed to deliver on the accountability side. Clark's successors, Dan Miller and Ujjal Dosanjh, almost completely ignored municipal government reform and did nothing to correct the local government accountability deficit. Elected in 2001, the Liberals promised a new package of legislation to increase accountability—including a much needed review of local electoral law. To avoid accusations of having only 'one oar in the water', like his predecessors, Gordon Campbell and his ministers would have had to have followed through on these accountability promises in a timely fashion or risk creating local governments that are even less accountable to their electors. With the BC election set for 17 May 2005,[3] Campbell's Liberals have left British Columbia's local government's rowing in the water with only one oar. As this chapter demonstrates, more accountable local government remains little more than a notion in British Columbia at the start of the twenty-first century.

BALANCED OBJECTIVES: HARCOURT'S ELECTORAL REFORM AND REGIONAL GROWTH STRATEGIES, 1991–6

There are several antecedents to municipal legislative review in British Columbia. These include initiatives involving the Federation of Canadian Municipalities (FCM) and provincial counterparts such as the Union of British Columbia Municipalities (UBCM) regarding provincial reform of planning and growth management legislation in the early to mid-1990s and more recent efforts to apply subsidiarity principles to the issues of who does what in the provincial-local universe. Whether in discussions about federal and provincial support for urban infrastructure renewal programs or constitutionalizing the local 'first order' of government in the late 1970s to mid-1980s, local governmental lobbying for recognition, responsibility, rights, and revenue all were to the fore (Bergamini, 1991; Smith, 1993a). From the late 1980s to the mid-1990s, there were increasing calls for a local 'Bill of Rights' as municipal jurisdictions confronted downloading and offloading without concomitant revenue-raising capacity. Local governance reform efforts were also affected by subsidiarity inquiries (invariably instituted by senior provincial authorities with answers often predetermined) of 'who does what?' All this came about around continuing arguments to decentralize decision-making and free up local governments' potential for innovation and efficiency (BC Ministry of Municipal Affairs, 1993). Some of the latter had already been demonstrated in an increasing range of international municipal exchanges, some of which dated back to World War II (Fry et al., 1989; Hobbes, 1995; Smith, 1992).

In 1991 the New Democratic Party finally ended Social Credit's stranglehold on provincial power in British Columbia. Whereas the right-of-centre Bennett, Vander Zalm, and Johnston Social Credit administrations (1975–91)— the latter two premiers with local governmental office experience—often talked the local autonomy talk but preferred a more centralized walk, expectations among local government watchers were high that much needed reforms would take place when former Vancouver mayor Harcourt was first elected in 1991. Harcourt's team did not disappoint and promptly modified the local electoral process with the Local Elections Reform Act, 1993. After appointing former Vancouver councillor Darlene Marzari as Minister of Municipal Affairs, the government then legislated important changes on regional planning and growth management through the Growth Strategies Statutes Amendment Act, 1995. Consistent with Harcourt's deliberative style, these reforms occurred after an extensive provincial-municipal consultation process that formed a firm basis for the success that followed (Smith, 1998b).

Changes brought in under the Local Elections Reform Act, 1993 were largely administrative, but Harcourt's decision to allow candidates to include the names of elector/party organizations on local ballots sparked a growth in political parties in some of the larger municipalities across the province (Smith and Stewart, 1998). In addition, requiring candidates to report campaign contributions and expenses rendered the electoral process more transparent and for the first time local electors could see who paid for the campaigns of mayors and councillors. In initiating these reforms, Harcourt demonstrated that he understood the importance of making municipal governments more accountable to local citizens and that major advancement could be achieved without changing the structural, functional, financial, or jurisdictional features of local government.

The other component of the Harcourt local government reform agenda was to further entrench a co-operative approach to regional growth management. Rather than using the more traditional carrot-and-stick method where compliance is achieved through reward and punishment, Marzari preferred the notion of carrot and big carrot—the carrot being respect for local-local/local-regional decision-making and the big carrot being funding for local improvements in growth strategy infrastructure such as mass transit improvements. Preparatory work began in 1992 and involved extensive comparative examination of other jurisdictional responses to growth management, particularly in the United States and Canada (Smith, 1993b). Central to this discussion, the Union of British Columbia Municipalities mostly defended the status quo while recognizing the need for some legislative adjustments. The result of this research agenda and consultation was agreement on nine basic principles (see Appendix I) from which was crafted the Growth Strategies Statutes Amendment Act, 1995. This initial promise of a local-regional-provincial co-operative approach resulted in later agreements such as the Greater Vancouver Regional District's Livable Region Strategic Plan (LRSP) and the subsequent Master Implementation Agreement (MIA) signed by the province and the GVRD in 1997. This Agreement identified four key elements of such provincial-regional co-operation:

1. *Shared goals*, including a 'partnership approach' to ensure 'coordinated and mutually reinforcing actions' and to maintain 'ongoing consultation and cooperation between the province and the GVRD. Through a variety of *Implementation Agreements*, both the Province and the Region agree to be bound by the process and agreements achieved.'

2. *Partnership principles*, including a 'recognition that responsibility for development of the Greater Vancouver region is shared and requires a coordinated response by the Province and local governments', 'mutual respect', 'harmonization of policies', and public involvement.

3. *Administrative procedures*, including sharing information, a five-year commitment to review the master agreement, and structures to resolve outstanding issues on an ongoing basis.

4. *Co-ordination of policy and action*, including agreement to co-ordinate and harmonize regional and provincial activities. Both the province and the GVRD undertake particular individual and joint policy/action to ensure this harmonization, including:

   a. *For the province*, appointment of provincial representatives to the region's Intergovernmental Advisory Committee, provincial direction to these representatives, co-operation in working to implement the Livable Region Strategic Plan (LRSP), including early/timely consideration of GVRD suggestions for legislative, financial, and regulatory actions to assist in this, early notification to the GVRD of substantial provincial matters affecting the LRSP, and a commitment to seek environmental sustainability in the Georgia Basin/Puget Sound;

   b. *For the GVRD*, implementing the LRSP in accordance with the provincial Growth Strategies Act, providing regional services in accordance with the LRSP, working with member municipalities to achieve agreement on the regional context statements, regional information-gathering, and consideration of additional important watercourses through the region's Green Zone.

   c. *Jointly*, the GVRD and province will prepare implementation agreements— on the Green Zone and major roads/highways, to achieve a compact metropolitan region better served by public transit and 'complete communities' (Ministry of Municipal Affairs Growth Strategies Office, 1998).

Regarding this book's focus on four facets of reform—structural, functional, financial, and jurisdictional—the 1995 Growth Strategies Act of the Harcourt government built upon previous success by formalizing an informal structure that had existed since the mid-1960s when the regional district system was established. With the Local Elections Reform Act, 1993, Harcourt brought forth a useful reform without any major changes to the institutional character of municipal government

(Oberlander and Smith, 1993). Such reform action was clear indication of a co-operative provincial-municipal approach, subsequently reinforced by regional and senior provincial authorities planning for the Greater Vancouver region and in the other regions of the province under the Growth Strategies Act (Smith and Oberlander, 1998). The goal of the latter legislative reform was to improve on what was seen to be an already efficient method of land-use planning by ensuring that the process stayed decentralized. Importantly, this entrenchment, when coupled with changes that increased local electoral accountability through increasing the vitality of local party systems and forcing local politicians to reveal funding sources, demonstrated that the Harcourt regime recognized—and implemented legislation appropriate to reinforce—the critical efficiency/accountability balance.

HALF THE AGENDA: THE CLARK REGIME AND THE MILLER/DOSANJH POSTSCRIPT, 1996–2001

In 1996, British Columbians returned the New Democratic Party to power under Glen Clark with just 39 per cent of the votes, compared with 42 per cent for the opposition Liberals. When the Clark government was first elected, Municipal Affairs received little attention and was one of a bundle of portfolio responsibilities assigned to Deputy Premier Dan Miller. But when new Premier Glen Clark received a rough reception by mayors and councillors at his first Union of British Columbia Municipalities convention in September 1996, former Port Coquitlam city councillor Mike Farnworth was appointed to head the Ministry of Municipal Affairs. Recreating positive provincial-municipal relations was placed high on his agenda by the Premier. After enjoying a productive ministerial term, in 1998 Farnworth was rewarded with a cabinet promotion to Employment and Investment (including responsibility for gambling licensing, the issue that eventually brought down the Clark administration). Former Vancouver city councillor Jenny Kwan took over as Minister of Municipal Affairs. Three important pieces of local legislation were passed between 1996, when Clark came to power, and 1999, when he was replaced by Dan Miller: the Local Government Statutes Amendment Act, 1998 (Bill 31), the Greater Vancouver Transportation Authority Act (Bill 36), and the Local Government Statutes Amendment Act, 1999 (Bill 88). Though these Acts sought to improve municipal government efficiency through decentralization they did not strengthen local communities' capacity to control their politicians.

Farnworth's Strong Start

With considerable work already done to deal with the pressures of fast growth in BC's major urban regions, Premier Clark brought in Mike Farnworth to pick up where Harcourt left off. The new plan was to increase local government efficiency through further decentralization, balanced with an increase in local accountability to the public by improving electoral and non-electoral mechanisms of control and oversight. To repair relations with local government officials Farnworth conducted a Harcourtesque provincial-municipal consultation process in which he elicited major local input from a Provincial/Local Government Joint Council that he created with the Union of British Columbia Municipalities in 1996. In 1997, the

UBCM agreed with the minister on the principles and protocols to guide this phase of local government legislative reform, and Farnworth began to construct Bill 31— a peace offering that further decentralized power by overhauling BC's Municipal Act. As a set of principles, it was a logical step, consistent with the minister's provincial party platform, governmental policy, and his own commitment to democratic reform. The bill was premised on subsidiarity, devolving responsibilities to the most appropriate—generally local—level, and when enacted it substantially reformed the BC Municipal Act by:

1. Recognizing local government as an independent, responsible, and accountable order of government.
2. Empowering local governments with broad corporate powers in the areas of:
   a. agreements respecting activities, works, or services (e.g., with a private partner; with a local government in another province);
   b. acquiring, managing, and disposing of land and any other type of property (e.g., disposal of land directly to a person in exchange for other land);
   c. granting assistance to benefit the community (e.g., exempt a community group from a user fee; guarantee repayment of borrowing for a non-profit housing society);
   d. delegating its powers to members, officers, employees, committees of other local government bodies (e.g., various permits issued by staff; hearings held by a panel of council members).
3. Consolidating these broad corporate powers in one part of the Act, along with the general requirements for and limitations on their use.
4. Adding special provisions to facilitate local government public-private partnerships.
5. Providing general authority to incur a future liability under an agreement subject to a counter petition requirement if the liability extends beyond five years, and by making a parallel change to require a counter petition opportunity for loan authorization bylaws.
6. Ensuring that the public has information on the intended use of corporate powers and an opportunity for input on significant matters (e.g., notice of assistance under a partnering agreement; counter petition opportunity for disposal of utilities; elector assent for disposal of water or sewer works).
7. Providing more flexible local government authority to establish officer positions; eliminating required titles of municipal clerk, regional district secretary, and treasurer; and recognizing the chief administrative officer position.

Farnworth's Bill 31 did not produce any structural or functional change but did affect financial and jurisdictional arrangements. Financially, the possibility of public-private partnerships and future local funding options reflected the trend towards a less-controlling provincial government. In jurisdictional terms, these reforms set the stage for improvements in both efficiency and accountability: (i) further decentralization based on subsidiarity principles, and (ii) necessary concomitant accountability amendments to bring clearer democratic control to these increasingly empowered local governments. Farnworth left the task of guiding Bill 31 through the legislature and initiating a new bill that would increase local government accountability through electoral and non-electoral reforms to his cabinet successor, Jenny Kwan. This was a job that she clearly understood and, at least initially, seemed inclined to undertake.

Dropping the Accountability Baton

At the September 1998 annual meeting of the UBCM, Kwan reiterated the key principles contained in Bill 31 and her commitment to carry these forward in additional reforms to the Municipal (now Local Government) Act. She called the changes promised and undertaken as 'landmark':

> . . . of all the provincial governments in Canada, only British Columbia has provided local government with this degree of recognition. . . . With Bill 31, you have an unprecedented degree of control over your own affairs. In addition there are new tools to help you govern your communities effectively, including broad corporate powers in such areas as: making agreements respecting activities, works or services acquiring, managing and disposing of land and granting financial assistance.

Echoing the themes of Harcourt's early reforms and following the agenda set by Farnworth, Kwan made an early commitment to balance decentralized power with more accountable municipal government. Kwan branded these reforms her 'number one priority':

> Local government accountability will also be a key part of our 1999 legislative agenda . . . because there can be no authority without corresponding accountability. It is important that we have an accountability model that recognizes the diversity of local government types and sizes. . . . The traditional ways of doing business are changing. The ground rules that governed our relationship for decades are being rewritten.

A report written for the Ministry of Municipal Affairs by the Institute of Governance Studies (IGS) at Simon Fraser University outlined the road ahead for Kwan to meet her pledge. Commissioned by Farnworth's department in 1997, the two-volume report, entitled *Making Local Accountability Work in British Columbia*, was submitted to Kwan in early 1998. In a press release announcing the report's findings, co-authors Patrick Smith and Kennedy Stewart claimed that municipal governance in BC was nearing an accountability crisis, requiring both electoral and non-electoral reform (Smith and Stewart, 1998). The IGS study provided the ministry with evidence of the extent of the problem in local democracy in the province, as well as recommendations on how accountability shortfalls could be addressed (see Appendix II for overview).

On the non-electoral side, Smith and Stewart made recommendations regarding changes to existing conflict of interest, freedom of information and privacy, and ombudsman legislation. Noting that there were currently no conflict of interest

Figure 2.1 Voter Turnout in British Columbia Municipal Elections, 1986–96

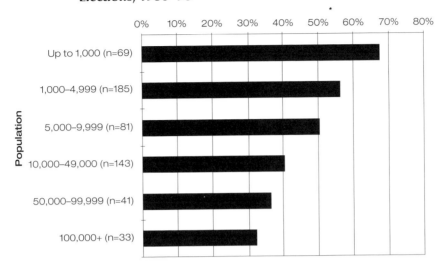

provisions covering municipal politicians in the province, the report recommended that the province's conflict of interest legislation be extended to cover all municipal politicians and that a position of Deputy Conflict Commissioner—with specific responsibility for municipal officials—be established. In terms of freedom of information, the report recommended that existing freedom of information provisions be extended to include many 'in-camera' meetings to allow for maximum public access to deliberations and decision-making. While the non-electoral recommendations and changes could make the day-to-day running of municipal business more transparent and accessible to the public, as argued by Smith and Stewart, the province's local electoral systems were sorely in need of reform.

Since the 1930s local elections in all BC municipalities have been contested under at-large systems in which council members are elected by plurality vote in a single constituency spanning an entire municipality. As shown in Figure 2.1, a survey of voter participation in more than 500 BC municipal elections over 10 years found that while turnout in small and medium-sized municipalities routinely ranged from 50 to 70 per cent, participation rates in British Columbia's largest municipalities—such as Vancouver, Surrey, Burnaby, Richmond, Abbotsford, Coquitlam, and Saanich (all above 100,000 in population)—hovered just over the 30 per cent mark. Moreover, as decreases in voter turnout do not occur evenly across the voting population of larger municipalities, some community groups living in metropolitan areas—particularly ethnic communities—will be permanently or almost permanently absent from the electoral process (Stewart, 1997, 2003: 19–27). From these results, and because the at-large system unacceptably distorts vote-to-seat proportionality (Stewart, 2003: 19–21), the authors concluded that the electoral system should be radically overhauled in all large communities. Other major recommendations by Smith and Stewart included extending the existing provincial election expense limit and tax credit legislation to cover municipal parties and local elections as well as partially reimbursing candidates for election expenses—in other words, bringing the system up to the levels or standards of electoral regulations that apply for federal and provincial elections in Canada.

Despite the evidence and recommendations of this report and her bold talk at the UBCM annual meeting, within months new Municipal Affairs Minister Kwan and the Clark cabinet misstepped badly before beginning the tough task of tightening local government accountability. In February 1999, Kwan unilaterally (and unpredictably) announced a $40 million cut in municipal grants after most local authorities had already completed their budgetary projections. All $40 million in cuts came from the budgets of BC's largest municipalities. In her defence, the minister noted that 'the province has already started to implement a three-year plan to reform the Municipal Act, which will provide new revenue-generating powers to local governments' (Ministry of Municipal Affairs, 1999). The UBCM's response was to withdraw from the still-new Joint Council partnership. The minister's reply was a call for a return to joint decision-making either through the Joint Council or an alternative process.

With this single action, the Clark government undid much of the goodwill that had been generated under Harcourt and through Farnworth's faith-building efforts. Then UBCM president Steve Wallace had called the Farnworth/early Kwan reforms 'the beginning of a new era in relations with the province . . . a renewed partnership that recognizes local government as a separate order of government.' But with Kwan's $40 million cut he noted a return to 'the old top-down model' so familiar in the provincial-municipal universe (Wallace, 1999). At this stage Kwan was left with a real efficiency-accountability dilemma: although the municipal sector had been granted new powers, no serious steps had been taken to enact accountability reforms. At the same time, due to provincial actions, her new municipal partners were also showing signs of rebelling.

Subsequent in-depth consultations with UBCM took place in February 1999—just as the unilateral provincial grant cuts were pending—at the second annual Symposium for New Legislation for Local Government, with over 230 mayors, regional district chairs, and senior local government staff in attendance. However, much of the early policy promise had given way to policy stalemate, followed by inertia. Caving in to the demands of UBCM members, Kwan was not inclined to proceed with the accountability reforms needed to complete her government's policy package. The reform package that Kwan introduced focused only on minor, non-electoral changes such as more open meetings and small additions to conflict of interest legislation—not without value, but far from enough to bring about real local accountability.

In sum, Kwan's Bill 88 (Local Government Statutes Amendment Act, 1999) changes amounted to little more than tinkering. Farnworth had already initiated most of the Phase I efficiency changes before Kwan started her term. Under the

Kwan/Clark regime, no new structures were created and no real functional reforms occurred. After calling the local/provincial agreement (between the ministry and the UBCM) 'historic', Kwan and her cabinet colleagues started by cutting municipal grants in the traditional way—without consultation and with little regard for local needs. Despite a career premised on seeking accountability changes, Kwan defended her inaction by stating that 'no one is crying out for change. . . . It would be presumptuous for me to impose it' (Armstrong, 1999). In the end, it simply may have been that the Local Government Minister did not have sufficient clout with her cabinet colleagues.

The Greater Vancouver Transportation Authority (GVTA)

Ironically, the only local government structural reform to occur during Clark's premiership did not originate from the Ministry of Municipal Affairs but rather from the Ministry of Finance, when Joy MacPhail (then Minister responsible for BC Transit) introduced the bill that was to become the Greater Vancouver Transportation Authority Act. Whereas the Harcourt/Marzari and Clark/Farnworth reforms applied to all municipal bodies in the province, the Greater Vancouver Transportation Authority Act transferred select powers for transportation and related services in metropolitan Vancouver from the provincially appointed British Columbia Transit to a new Greater Vancouver Transportation Authority (now known as 'Translink') (Ginnell and Smith, 2001). The Act mandated that Translink and the GVRD must 'work together to establish a mutually agreeable strategic transportation plan and growth management strategy' (Rock, 2001). But while the provincial legislation legally established Translink as a separate entity from the GVRD, the two organizations are joined in many formal and, most importantly, informal ways. For example, members of the GVRD hold 15 of the 18 Translink board positions (Rock, 2001).The other three are provincial appointments, now not filled by the senior government.[4]

The functional mandate of Translink is to 'plan and finance a regional transportation system that moves people and goods efficiently and supports the regional growth strategy, air quality objectives and economic development of the Greater Vancouver Regional District' (Translink, 2001). Provincial funding for Translink's operations was approximately $545 million in 2000 and as of 2004 the province had approved a $3.9 billion 10-year transportation improvement plan.[5] Translink was also given the ability to increase revenues through several other 'taxation' instruments, such as the possibility of tolls, parking taxes, vehicle levies, etc., though in some instances these need provincial assistance for collection. The Translink board's institutional image is as almost an arm's-length provider of management for the several subsidiary companies and programs it established under its jurisdiction. It describes its role or management style as 'steering not rowing' (Rock, 2001).

In creating the GVTA/Translink, the province undertook *one* minor structural change in one regional district—albeit the largest one, representing close to one-half of the provincial population. Whereas BC Transit was a purely provincial entity under the supervision of the appropriate minister, Translink can be said to be a new addition to the family of local/regional administrative bodies because its board is controlled by indirectly elected GVRD members. With a change in structure comes a corresponding change in function in that the Greater Vancouver Transportation Authority Act moves responsibility for Greater Vancouver transportation into the hands of locally elected officials. Financially, the capacity to toll and tax—even if provincial assistance in collection is still needed in many instances—marks a change in the de facto financial power of those holding seats on the GVRD/GVTA.

In terms of efficiency and accountability, moving control over transit to a regional body continues the trend of decentralization that an optimist might describe as an attempt to unleash the innovational power of local officials and make transit more efficient. But Translink has created a new problem—it has more fully empowered indirectly elected officials who are now two steps removed from their constituents. While the GVRD has primarily been a forum where locally elected mayors and councillors could discuss and come to agreement on issues such as regional growth, there was little need for them to be directly elected. But now that these same officials are vested with the power to make decisions over service provision and taxation with little provincial supervision, a strong argument can be made for direct regional elections. For example, late in 2000 Translink attempted to use one of its new revenue-generating instruments to levy a direct vehicle tax. The proposed levy generated widespread public opposition from many different sectors and was ultimately abandoned when the province refused to collect the new tax.   This underscored the fact that while GVRD/Translink now has the jurisdictional capacity to impose such charges, it often lacks the administrative capacity to collect such taxes. More importantly, the public outcry against the vehicle levy highlighted the ongoing regional accountability gap. This gap became a ravine during the summer 2002 Vancouver bus strike; lasting over several hot summer months, no one could find any accountable politician at Translink, which had turned management of its buses over to a subsidiary, Coast Mountain Bus Company Ltd (Fershau, 2003). In this instance, the lack of an accountability oar to match the one intended for efficiency was clear and apparent.

The lack of accountability of Translink—and the continuing interest in more traditional provincial meddling in local-regional affairs—came to a head again in 2004. Due to 2010 Olympic excitement and the possibility of federal infrastructure dollars, the province 'offered' $300–$400 million, matched with federal dollars, *if* Translink would approve (and share in costs) of a P3 to build a Richmond Airport–Vancouver (RAV) rapid transit line. On two occasions in 2004 the regional board voted against the deal as 'too rich' for local taxpayers—and as inconsistent with LRSP-defined priorities of service first to the fast-growing northeast municipalities in Greater Vancouver. With threats of lost revenues from the province, an unprecedented third vote was held on 30 June 2004. The RAV project was approved subject to upper limits being placed on public dollar contributions and an extra $170 million in provincial support to complete the higher-priority northeast section of the region's still-new millennium line (Translink, 2004).

The Miller/Dosanjh Postscript, 1999–2001
The last days of the NDP reign were unspectacular in terms of municipal reform. Neither Premiers Dan Miller or Ujjal Dosanjh nor their Ministers of Municipal Affairs attempted to deal with the increasing electoral/accountability deficit. Dosanjh's Minister of Municipal Affairs, Cathy McGregor, did introduce the Local Government Statute Amendment Act, 2000, but it was of limited consequence. Possible accountability reforms were again ignored. However, during the final BC legislative session under the NDP, some last efforts were made by several governmental insiders to bring the missing accountability reforms to the attention of the outgoing administration. For example, representatives from labour unions, the Coalition of Progressive Electors (COPE)—the leftist municipal political party in Vancouver—and academe raised the issue of local electoral/accountability reforms on several occasions with senior ministers, including then Minister of Municipal Affairs Jim Doyle. These reform proposals were included in a draft BC Local Elections Transparency Act that included proposals for:

- election spending limits for individuals, parties, and electoral associations running for municipal office;
- disclosure of all election spending (including third-party expenses);
- moving municipal elections reporting/record-keeping to the purview of the provincial Chief Electoral Office;
- tax credits for municipal party donations;
- election expense limits for third parties; and,
- a commitment to create a process by which the municipal electoral system could be reformed (Local Electoral Reform Coalition, 2000).

With their own re-election squarely on the minds of outgoing ministers, however, these reform efforts were quickly replaced by a focus on avoiding an NDP electoral deluge. In the end, 'la deluge' was what arrived, with just two New Democrats returned to the BC legislature—one of them, former Deputy Premier Joy McPhail, the other, former Municipal Affairs Minister Jenny Kwan. The neglect of the NDP to enact any of the necessary local accountability reforms during the latter part of its mandates in 1999–2001 under Clark, Miller, or Dosanjh represents a failure to understand even the interests of the party itself in strengthening local democracy. Given the earlier success of BC municipal legislative reform—on growth strategies and on local governmental empowerment—the weak, almost non-existent accountability measures represented a significant omission in the NDP reform agenda. Moreover, where Harcourt had handed Clark a strong model on which to base future municipal government reforms and a smoothly working provincial/local relationship based on mutual respect, by the time Dan Miller replaced Clark as premier, Clark and his later ministers had not only managed to diminish any goodwill that may have existed but had also lost a grip on ensuring a balance between efficiency and accountability reforms. In short, from 1996 to 2001 the NDP had let the local governmental sheep run away with the carrots. The only structural and functional changes during the period came with the enacting of the Greater Vancouver Transit Authority Act, and these changes only affected a single authority within a single region. Financially and jurisdictionally, however, actions had been taken, and the hands of local officials were somewhat freed, particularly by the Bill 31 'efficiency' reforms. Yet, it was still not clear whose bidding was to be done by those hands.

GORDON CAMPBELL'S COMMUNITY CHARTER AND OTHER LEGISLATIVE REFORMS, 2001–5

In the BC Liberal Party's 'new era' election platform of 2001, one of the commitments for the 'first 90 days' was action on the creation of new municipal legislation—a Community Charter. However, at the end of 90 days, instead of new legislation, British Columbians got process. Campbell appointed an 11-member Community Charter Council made up of current and past municipal/regional officials and provincial appointees. Four members were selected by the UBCM, four members-at-large were selected by the provincial cabinet on the recommendation of the UBCM, and the provincial government appointed three members to represent provincial interests; it reported to the Minister of State for the Community Charter. Given the task of consulting and developing draft legislation, in October 2001 the Charter Council published *The Community Charter: A Discussion Paper*. Much preliminary work had already been done while the Liberals waited their turn to govern in BC. Initially, public input was limited to a small number of municipal officials and representatives from the Union of BC Municipalities, but after considerable criticism the process was broadened to include input from elected officials from various parts of the province (Vance, 2002). In May 2002, the Ministry of Community, Aboriginal and Women's Services (MCAWS—which had 'replaced' Municipal Affairs) released *The Community Charter: A New Legislative Framework for Local Government*. According to Ted Nebbling, the Minister of State for the Community Charter, the new legislation would:

> replace a provincial tradition of rigid rules and paternalism with flexibility and co-operation, . . . will encourage municipalities to be more self-reliant . . . [and] presents simple, concise legislation that balances broad municipal abilities with public accountability and protection of province-wide interests in key areas like the economy, environment and public health. (Ministry of Community, Aboriginal and Women's Services, 2002: 3)

Structurally and functionally, little has changed under the Community Charter, but the legislation did bring about a number of financial and jurisdictional reforms—all aimed at freeing up the hands of local government:

- *'Natural person' powers.* Under legislation prior to the Community Charter, BC municipalities were corporate entities, meaning that their powers were subject to some limitations on the making of agreements and providing assistance. 'Natural person' powers do away with itemized corporate powers and increase the corporate capacity of the municipality in relation to already delegated powers.

- *Service powers.* Municipal councils may now provide any service they consider necessary and bylaws are no longer required to establish or abolish services.
- *Agreements.* In terms of public-private partnerships, municipalities gain a simplified authority to grant an exclusive or limited franchise for transportation, water, or energy systems, and the requirement of provincial approval for agreements between a municipality and a public authority in another province is eliminated.
- *Additional revenue sources.* The Community Charter 'puts forward for discussion', but does not yet commit the province to, a number of potential municipal revenue sources outside of property taxes, including: fuel tax, resort tax, local entertainment tax, parking stall tax, hotel room revenue tax, and road tolls. In the case of Greater Vancouver's transportation authority, some of these tax powers were already transferred.

In addition, the Community Charter went to some lengths to clarify local-provincial relations by recognizing municipalities as 'an order to government' and promising:

- *Consultation.* The provincial government agrees to consult with the UBCM before changing local government enactments or reducing revenue transfers.
- *No forced amalgamations.* Amalgamations between two or more municipalities will not occur unless electors within the affected communities approve the merger.
- *Reduction of provincial approvals.* Under the Community Charter the number of routine provincial government approvals will be reduced. As well, the Community Charter allows the province to reduce approvals further over time through regulations.

These commitments indicated that the Liberals wished to increase administrative flexibility and, as much as possible, free local authorities from time-consuming provincial interference—a move underscored by the shift from corporate to 'natural person' powers, reduced provincial oversight, and promises of consultation and increased revenue-generating capacity. Thus, this initial Liberal round of municipal legislative reform in British Columbia could be seen as an attempt to increase efficiency through decentralization based on limited financial and jurisdictional tinkering and no major structural or functional reforms. However, BC local governments appear wise to be wary of such promises. After all, since the 2001 provincial general election, local BC school boards have been dealt with in ways entirely opposite to the sentiments expressed in the Community Charter. Not long after being elected, the Liberals imposed a three-year teachers' pay settlement, then announced that school boards would be responsible for the pay increases for years two and three without any additional compensation despite their earlier promise not to cut education funding. As a result of this de facto cut most school boards had to lay off teachers and close schools. Even when some of the funding was restored, local school boards were left significantly disadvantaged and having to deal with the political fallout from local cuts. Similarly, restructured health boards (now just six for BC) found that many decisions on costs and closures were left to them, after health budgets were limited, despite the provincial government's promise that there would be 'no cuts to health-care funding'. Again, the 'dirty work' of cutbacks fell on the 'local' authorities.

In terms of accountability, the Liberals argued that they were shifting responsibility for monitoring local councils from provincial ministries to local communities: 'The Charter is founded on a principle that municipalities are accountable to the public, not the province. Therefore, the . . . Charter does not call for reporting to the province but rather to citizens' (Minister of Community, Aboriginal and Women's Services, 2002: 14). The Liberals appeared to recognize that municipal policy decisions would more likely reflect the will of the local community only if local accountability were improved. However, by adding only an 'annual reporting' requirement and minor changes to the conflict of interest legislation, the Liberals ran the risk of further freeing the hands of under-accountable local governmental bodies. When asked about the possibility of including substantive accountability (i.e., electoral) reforms in what was initially termed the Phase I version of the Community Charter, officials at MCAWS, the Ministry of State for the Community Charter, and the Community Charter Council conceded that such reforms were problematic and 'would have to wait until 2004–2005—*a timetable sufficient to prevent discussion of electoral reforms through the next plus one municipal electoral cycle*' (Ministry of State for the Community Charter, 2002; emphasis added). As current BC government thinking attests, no such reforms on accountability are now planned until after the May 2005 election.[6] Even then, they remain in doubt.

After much delay to its Community Charter legislative reform package, the intention of the BC Liberal government had been to meet once more with the UBCM at its annual conference in Whistler, BC, in September 2002. The government then planned to introduce its Community Charter bill to the BC legislature for autumn 2002 approval. However, the more UBCM members considered the draft charter, the more concerns they expressed. For example, they found that although the Community Charter promised no provincial 'downloading' to municipalities without consultation and equivalent fiscal compensation, no such consideration was to be made when the province simply 'off-loaded' a responsibility or service. The Union of British Columbia Municipalities understood the meaning of the more traditional 'downloading', where responsibility is simply given to local authorities—often without concomitant funding from the province to support the new responsibilities. 'Off-loading', they discovered, was when the provincial government simply abandoned a service, leaving local citizens to urge the municipality to restore the service, but again—and with no exception—without the municipality receiving any financial support from the senior level of government. This has meant that municipalities have had to buy their community hospitals (as Kimberley, BC, did after provincial cuts forced its closure) or hold referendums (as Delta did in the November 2002 municipal election to get voter approval for a local tax increase to fund its hospital emergency ward on a 24-hour basis as opposed to the ward operating only during the day and early evening as a result of cuts imposed by the provincially appointed regional health board).

The concerns raised by local governments meant another delay until spring 2003 as the new timetable for legislative reform. That decision, and the time and energy devoted to the Community Charter Transitional Provisions, Consequential Amendments and Other Amendments Act, 2003 (Bill 76), pushed back any planned Phase II Community Charter regional district reforms until after the legislatively established 17 May 2005 BC general election (Paget, 2004). It also meant that no serious local accountability reforms (Phase III) should be anticipated in any possible second mandate (2005–9) for the BC Liberals (Walisser, 2004). The key reform test for the Campbell Liberals was whether accountability was a sufficient priority to be on the government's 2001–5 agenda. With Phase II and Phase III of the Community Charter falling off the provincial government's to-do list, it is likely to be a long incubation before real regional district and local governmental accountability reforms return to active policy consideration in British Columbia. That may fit with Premier Campbell's commitment to undertake a review of provincial electoral matters (Campbell, 2001)[7]—a process that, if successful, would not bring more general provincial electoral reform prior to a 2009 general election.

As with previous NDP governments throughout the 1990s, the Liberals are clearly aware that if they are to bring efficiency through decentralization they must also empower local citizens with the appropriate tools to help them hold local officials responsible for their actions. Although Community Charter provisions for annual reports and revised conflict of interest legislation are a start, these efficiency measures will be effective only if barriers to electoral participation are lowered, local elector organizations are helped to mature, and council seats are distributed more fairly. These latter considerations were only evident in the City of Vancouver—its (Berger) Electoral Reform Commission recommended democratic reforms—including an October 2004 referendum—in time for the November 2005 city elections (see www.city.vancouver.bc.ca/erc; also City of Vancouver, 2004, and personal correspondence with Thomas Berger, Commissioner, Vancouver Electoral Reform Commission). Such reforms failed to materialize.

Thus the picture at the end of the first Campbell mandate is not promising. The Community Charter (Bill 14), in place since 1 January 2004, set out its purpose in language recognizable to at least some advocates of modest home rule. For Canadian urbanists, BC's Community Charter legislation also includes language that constitutional scholars recognize as maintaining the potential for provincial jurisdictional oversight (section 92[8] of the Constitution Act, 1867). This is clearest in the purposes of the new Community Charter:

3. The purposes of this Act are to provide municipalities and their councils with
   (a) a legal framework for the powers, duties and functions that are necessary to fulfill their purposes,

(b) the authority and discretion to address existing and future community needs, and

(c) the flexibility to determine the public interest of their communities and to respond to the different needs and changing circumstances of their communities.[8]

The principles of the Act sound closer to the views of those who advocate local autonomy. They reflect a stated desire to clarify both municipal and provincial components of the provincial-municipal relationship in British Columbia and, potentially, to add to local autonomy:

Principles, Purposes and Interpretation Principles of municipal governance

1 (1) Municipalities and their councils are recognized as an order of government within their jurisdiction that

(a) is democratically elected, autonomous, responsible and accountable,

(b) is established and continued by the will of the residents of their communities, and

(c) provides for the municipal purposes of their communities.

(2) In relation to subsection (1), the Provincial government recognizes that municipalities require

(a) adequate powers and discretion to address existing and future community needs,

(b) authority to determine the public interest of their communities, within a legislative framework that supports balance and certainty in relation to the differing interests of their communities,

(c) the ability to draw on financial and other resources that are adequate to support community needs,

(d) authority to determine the levels of municipal expenditures and taxation that are appropriate for their purposes, and

(e) authority to provide effective management and delivery of services in a manner that is responsive to community needs.

Principles of municipal-provincial relations

2 (1) The citizens of British Columbia are best served when, in their relationship, municipalities and the Provincial government

(a) acknowledge and respect the jurisdiction of each,

(b) work towards harmonization of Provincial and municipal enactments, policies and programs, and

(c) foster cooperative approaches to matters of mutual interest.

(2) The relationship between municipalities and the Provincial government is based on the following principles:

(a) the Provincial government respects municipal authority and municipalities respect Provincial authority;

(b) the Provincial government must not assign responsibilities to municipalities unless there is provision for resources required to fulfill the responsibilities;

   (c) consultation is needed on matters of mutual interest, including
       consultation by the Provincial government on
       (i)   proposed changes to local government legislation,
       (ii) proposed changes to revenue transfers to municipalities, and
       (iii) proposed changes to Provincial programs that will have a signif-
             icant impact in relation to matters that are within municipal
             authority;
   (d) the Provincial government respects the varying needs and conditions
       of different municipalities in different areas of British Columbia;
   (e) consideration of municipal interests is needed when the Provincial
       government participates in interprovincial, national or international
       discussions on matters that affect municipalities;
   (f) the authority of municipalities is balanced by the responsibility of
       the Provincial government to consider the interests of the citizens of
       British Columbia generally;
   (g) the Provincial government and municipalities should attempt to
       resolve conflicts between them by consultation, negotiation, facilita-
       tion and other forms of dispute resolution.

This legislative language hides as much as it illuminates, however. For example, despite talk of limiting interference by the senior provincial authority, should local governments under BC's Community Charter decide to raise local taxes—such as to businesses—rather than opt for the newly preferred user fees and the like, the province reserves the right to impose limits on property tax rates, in direct contradiction of the Community Charter's expressed intent to empower local autonomy. And under a redefined provincial-municipal relationship, the Community Charter reminds local governments that apart from acknowledging and respecting each other's jurisdiction, the legislative intent is to 'work towards harmonization of provincial and municipal enactments, policies and programs.'[9] This may work in many instances, but not where a local government wishes to take a rather divergent policy tack. Here, the intergovernmental game becomes more perilous for local authorities.

The dismissal of school boards and the 'over a weekend' elimination by Order-in-Council of the GVRD's authority over the region's watershed, when it tried to block provincial implementation of a natural gas pipeline through that watershed to Vancouver Island, serve as historical reminders of such senior provincial powers.[10] The more recent provincial overturning of a local governmental (Delta) bylaw to limit negative air quality impacts of large greenhouses by requiring them to use natural gas or propane as opposed to wood waste,[11] the use of similar provincial powers (right-to-farm legislation) to prevent local coastal municipalities from using their bylaw powers to limit possible negative environmental impacts from fish farms, and the provincial 'return' of fines to fish-farm operators continue to serve as current reminders that constitutional authority does matter when significant policy differences arise between local and provincial players. So did the summer 2004 provincial decision to determine the route, cost, and P3 provider of the West Vancouver segment of the sea-to-sky highway upgrade for the Vancouver–Whistler 2010 Winter Olympics. In the process, the province listened to, and then ignored, the clearly negative views of the local municipal council. The municipality's response has been political protest and legal action against the province.[12]

One of the best indicators of the Liberals' failure to move the accountability markers is found in the BC Community Charter provisions for counter-petitions 'against a proposed bylaw, action or other matter of a local government'. These are a carry-over from the old Local Government Act. Members of the community can circulate a petition and if they get 10 per cent of the local electorate to sign (it used to 5 per cent under the Local Government Act), then the bylaw must be subject to referendum, which is only binding if the referendum fails. In other words, this provision is effectively toothless—if anything, the new Charter measure have made councils slightly less rather than more accountable. A pre-Charter MCAWS survey found that:

- Local governments are making good use of the counter-petition mechanisms and getting appropriate results.
- Of the 55 issues counter-petitioned, 87 per cent were insufficient (i.e., did not meet the 5 per cent threshold), confirming that the process appears to be working for non-controversial matters.
- Seven (13 per cent) of the counter-petitions were sufficient, with four proceeding to a vote, where two failed (with 68 per cent and 64 per cent against) and two passed (57 and 59 per cent in favour). In other words, out of 55 issues for which counter-petitions were attempted, only two of these petitions ultimately succeeded.

The issues that were successfully counter-petitioned and proceeded to a vote involved the borrowing of funds (a majority of counter petitions that were not successful involved approval for borrowing as well) or were politically significant, such as the disposal of parkland or the sale of property housing a community hall—the proceeds of which would be used for a special reserve fund to maintain heritage properties. On significant issues such as these it would seem appropriate that a community may indicate its desire for a vote.

While the survey indicated that, overall, the current assent mechanisms were working, it suggested that some minor changes may be necessary, particularly in the areas of notice provision, misinformation issues, and determining petition sufficiency. The survey results did not indicate that the 5 per cent threshold should be increased or that 5 per cent is an inappropriate threshold for smaller communities. Indeed, it would appear that where petitions were successful, it was because the matter or matters related to the petition were significant and that petition success was not related to community size (BC, 2000). The 10 per cent threshold in the new Community Charter simply made such citizen action more difficult.

Perhaps Robert Bish's recent comments on the Community Charter sum up the situation best:

One change in the Charter that increases corporate authority is the increase in requirement that a counter-petition have signatures from 10 per cent . . . of voters on the voters roll. . . . A requirement of 5 per cent of all voters is already a high requirement compared to referendum signature requirements in the US, where requirements are usually specified as a percentage of voters who voted in the last election. In effect, 5 per cent of all voters is likely to mean 10 to 15 per cent of actual voters, and a 10 per cent of voters requirement is likely to mean 20 to 30 per cent of all voters in the last election. What the increased requirement does is limit the like-lihood of a successful petition to only those decisions opposed by very well-organized interest groups, not just a club or group of citizens. . . . A requirement for referenda on major decisions, especially for capital projects that will have implications for many future councils, needs to be carefully evaluated from many perspectives. . . . I believe local governments would be more accountable if referenda were required on major capital projects and that a citizen-initiated referenda process [should] be available for any bylaw. This is the practice for local governments in all Western US states and it has not led to an excessive number of referenda. The referenda that do occur, however, help keep people interested in their local government. This is itself useful now that elections are only once every three years. In summary, upping the counter-petition requirements for decisions that should be considered in a referendum is a move away from, not toward, accountability to citizens. . . . (Bish, 2002)

Beyond provisions on counter-petitions, perhaps the most stunning erosion of the new Community Charter promise is BC's Bill 75—the Significant Projects Streamlining Act. Introduced and passed in just three weeks in November 2003, the Act allows the provincial government to override any local governmental opposition on any project deemed of significant provincial interest.[13] Minister of State for Deregulation and Transportation Kevin Falcon noted that the intent of the Act was to 'cut red tape', 'remove unnecessary and costly delays', and 'create new economic activities'. The Significant Projects initiative produced an official, highly critical UBCM response with over half of the UBCM member municipalities passing motions condemning Bill 75. According to a UBCM press release:

The UBCM Executive is shocked by the degree of intrusion of this legislation into local affairs. It allows any Minister . . . to replace *any* local government bylaw, plan, regulation, policy, etc. to facilitate the approval or development of a 'provincially significant project'. Cabinet can make that determination without *any prior* notice to the local government or the community. The Community Charter . . . promised us recognition as an independent, accountable and responsible order of government. . . . The Community Charter touted public accountability and openness but Bill 75 replaces local, publicly developed plans (including those developed through public hearing processes) with fiats from the provincial Minister. We recognize there is a need to balance local and provincial interests. . . . This is just not the way to achieve it. The Executive is calling on the provincial government to remove local government from Bill 75. (UBCM, 2003)

Similar school board experience in several of Ontario's largest cities in the late period of Harris/Eves Tory rule mirrored these lessons. If proof is in the pudding, it would appear necessary to go back to basic recipe ingredients on local empowerment and accountability and start again.

The year 2004 started as 2003 did, with the province again showing a disregard for local decision-making. In another example of provincial interference in local affairs, local police forces found out on 30 December 2003 that all bars and restaurants in BC would be allowed to stay open the next day, New Year's Eve, until 4 a.m. The provincial Liquor Control and Licensing Act was amended in late 2002 allowing for this change but it was not implemented. Local police forces first learned of the change less than 48 hours before its impact, resulting in expensive overtime/shift changes, with all costs borne by the municipalities. The provincial legislation overrides municipal bylaws, and even when the changed hours were decided by the provincial agency no one informed municipal/policing officials until they found out the day before; the reason given by the province for this oversight: the legislation 'did not require' notification to local governments.

The summer/fall 2004 provincial pressure on West Vancouver over the sea-to-sky highway route and on the GVRD and Translink over a provincially preferred public-private partnership to build the RAV rapid transit line were simply two more recent reminders that despite legislative language change, the provincial-municipal relationship in BC was still more top-down than locally based. The lead-up to the 2010 Winter Olympics suggests that this fact of life may be the most important determinant on the local intergovernmental file in 2005–10 in British Columbia, with provincial impatience at having to consider local interests carrying the day despite the policy promise in BC's Community Charter.

CONCLUSIONS: EVALUATING INSTITUTIONAL CHANGE, EFFICIENCY, AND ACCOUNTABILITY

It is astounding to think that although a massive amount of legislation has been formulated, consulted on, debated, passed, and implemented over the last 14 years, BC local governments of today closely resemble those of the early 1990s. Of the approximately 140 Acts affecting local governments passed since 1992, few have impacted the structure or function of local government in British Columbia. As was clear under the NDP and likewise the Liberals, successive BC governments have been satisfied with the basic components of the municipal system and are content to make financial and jurisdictional alterations rather than engage in more fundamental structural or functional reforms.

As shown in Table 2.2, the only major *structural* reform has come through the changes made to regional transit in Greater Vancouver in legislation that was of little general consequence to municipal authorities in the largest city-region and of no significance for those located in the rest of the province. The Greater Vancouver Transportation Authority Act, 1998 also represents the only major *functional* change over the last 15 years. Whereas Harcourt's reforms were administrative in nature, all significant changes since 1996 have affected the *financial* and

Table 2.2 Overview of Significant Local Legislative Reform Efforts, 1991–2004

Regime	Legislation	S	F	Fi	J	E	A
Harcourt	Local Elections Reform Act, 1993	N	N	N	N	N	Y
	Growth Strategies Statutes Amendment Act, 1995	N	N	N	N	Y	N
Clark	Local Government Statutes Amendment Act, 1998	N	N	Y	Y	Y	N
	Greater Vancouver Transportation Authority Act, 1998	Y	Y	Y	Y	Y	N
	Local Government Statutes Amendment Act, 1999	N	N	Y	Y	Y	N
Campbell	Community Charter	N	N	Y	Y	Y	N
	Significant Projects Streamlining Act, 2003	N	N	N	Y	N	N

Key: S = Structural, F = Functional, Fi = Financial, J = Jurisdictional, E = Efficiency, A = Accountability, Y = Yes, N = No

jurisdictional capacities of municipal governments in BC. These changes include NDP and Liberal efforts to reduce oversight by the provincial government and NDP/Liberal promises to allow more taxation powers and to transform municipalities from corporations into 'natural persons'. The last two columns in Table 2.2 illustrate how efficiency and accountability were affected by the listed acts. Looking at the three electoral terms, the Harcourt era (1991–6) can be seen as having introduced the most balanced municipal reforms, with the Clark/Miller/Dosanjh and current Campbell governments focusing on efficiency and virtually ignoring accountability. Under Municipal Affairs Minister Darlene Marzari, the Harcourt New Democrats showed insight in partially devolving power to create a more co-operative municipal/provincial relationship and in achieving widespread agreement on the Growth Strategies Act. On the accountability side, allowing local parties to be identified on local election ballots and forcing candidates to disclose their funding sources helped speed the development of municipal political parties and increased election transparency in BC's larger municipalities. As strong and active local political parties often represent one of the most significant challenges to long-entrenched urban regimes, Harcourt's 'minor' administrative changes encouraging municipal political party formation represent the single largest accountability reform of the past 15 years in British Columbia.

While Clark, Miller, Dosanjh, and their respective ministers were aware that an efficiency/accountability balance needed to be struck, not only did they fail to implement accountability reforms but they also threatened the atmosphere of co-operation cultivated by Harcourt. Mike Farnworth's reforms, embodied in Bill 31, the Local Government Act, began a process of empowering local governments. The task of strengthening the power of local citizens to control municipal officials was left to Jenny Kwan, Farnworth's successor in the Municipal Affairs portfolio. However, Kwan and her cabinet colleagues were not up to the challenge and her

Bill 88 changes were largely ineffective, as were those of her NDP successors. Community Charter reforms under Liberal Premier Gordon Campbell—a former Vancouver mayor and GVRD chair—suggest an overemphasis on efficiency versus accountability again. Despite strong language in the Community Charter about 'a new deal for BC's municipalities', unless substantive electoral and non-electoral accountability reforms are included in subsequent legislation, all that may occur is a further empowering of under-accountable local governments in BC. The one exception might have been the City of Vancouver, left to make some of its own democratic reform choices; here, the November 2005 civic election will tell the tale.

Among other things, this BC experience supports several conclusions:

1. Local governmental issues command significant attention of provincial governments in British Columbia.
2. Legislative reform increasingly allows municipal governments more decisional capacity—though more limited fiscal capability.
3. Each substantial reform plan has included the promise of concomitant democratic reforms (on the accountability side), but in almost every case such promise has remained unfulfilled.

The argument here is not against the empowerment of local governments—this notion has been part of the policy discourse since Lord Durham noted that the Rebellions of 1837–8 were partly caused by the fact that colonial powers had not taken advantage of local governmental development 'as a training ground for democracy' (Smith, 1998a; Craig, 1985). Decentralization has been on the agendas of the Canadian Federation of Mayors and Municipalities/Federation of Canadian Municipalities at least since the 1976 report, *Puppets on a Shoestring*, and it was not only in Paul Martin's last speech as federal Finance Minister to the FCM in May 2002 (Canadian Federation of Mayors and Municipalities, 1976; Martin, 2002) but also in Martin's first Throne Speech in January 2004 after he succeeded Jean Chrétien as Liberal Party leader and Prime Minister. It remains on the federal government agenda with the July 2004 post-election cabinet appointed by Prime Minister Martin and the creation of the Ministry of State for Infrastructure, Cities and Communities.

Rather, the point is that if substantive decision-making capacity is to shift from provincial to local hands, then the local citizenry must be given the tools to control their officials. Otherwise, they may have less say than if power had remained centralized.

As it stands, British Columbia's largest municipalities (and regions) have a serious accountability deficit. Although useful as part of an overall package, tinkering with conflict of interest laws, open meetings, and annual reports are simply not sufficient. Avoiding the central questions of electoral accountability and local democratic disengagement will not solve the problem. As Allan Lambert and fellow commissioners noted in the *Report* of the 1979 Royal Commission on

Financial Management and Accountability, 'you cannot have efficiency in democratic government without accountability.' Floating around with one oar in the water will not get the BC municipal boat to the accountability shore. Thus, adding accountability to local government reforms remains the primary task for the Campbell Liberal government—or any future government—in BC. Whether the Liberal legacy will be the establishment of a true 'Community' Charter or simply another 'Local Government' Charter remains to be seen. Early twenty-first-century evidence from British Columbia strongly suggests this lesson: 'Less is less!'

In terms of short-term prognostications, the Community Charter process and product to date suggest that the likelihood of an ongoing democratic deficit in British Columbia is high. Bill 75, on Significant Projects, and provincial decisions on right to farm versus local bylaws or with West Vancouver's objections on routing of provincial highways suggest a provincial government that wishes to continue to steer *and* row. In the 16 November 2002 BC municipal elections, the turnout in larger municipalities was approximately 30 per cent, which is substantially less than for either provincial or federal elections. There is perhaps no more telling conclusion than the continued municipal disengagement of British Columbians despite a decade and a half of continuous local legislative reform efforts. Only real democratic reforms will begin to alter this democratic deficit. To date, no British Columbia government has seemed prepared to grasp that political reform nettle. Until one does, real local democracy will remain nothing more than an ideal.

Appendix I:
Harcourt's Nine Basic Regional Planning Principles

1. *No new institutions*—partly a by-product of political and fiscal realities, and a recognition that BC already had a strong local planning system.
2. *Voluntary participation . . . most of the time*—premised on the notion of voluntary planning and the idea that 'planning works best when there is buy-in', but allowing for provincial requirements for regional growth strategies in instances of 'extreme' growth or where 'local governments are slow to react cooperatively'.
3. *Compatibility . . . a bias towards agreement*—to ensure compatibility and consistency among local and regional growth strategies. Subsidiarity principles included here with an 'interactive' system giving 'equal weight' to OCPs (Official Community Plans) and regional strategies.
4. *Dispute resolution . . . as a last resort*—recognition of the need for a 'closure' requirement; while preferring locally negotiated 'collaborative solutions', a provincial capacity—and mechanism—to ensure that 'differences' are, in the end, 'resolved'.
5. *Broad-based consultation . . . early and often*—a commitment that 'everyone who has to live with the outcomes should have a say in the development of plans': municipalities, community groups, and other interested publics.
6. *Regional diversity/regional flexibility*—a planning system flexible enough to accommodate regional diversity in economy, geography, objectives, and issues.

7. *Provincial direction and support*—a provincial commitment to stating all of its expectations clearly.

8. *Early provincial involvement*—recognition that a wide range of provincial decisions, for example, on capital expenditures for highways/transit, health/education facilities, or energy projects, can significantly affect settlement patterns; and a provincial commitment to 'come to the table early and stay involved continuously throughout the regionally led planning processes'.

9. *Provincial commitment*—an acceptance that the province should itself 'be guided by regional growth strategies' and ensure its actions/investments 'are consistent with local governments' initiatives' (Ministry of Municipal Affairs, 1998).

APPENDIX II:
SUMMARY OF MAKING LOCAL ACCOUNTABILITY WORK IN BC

- While local democracy has been reflected positively in British Columbia, especially in the vast majority of small to medium-size municipalities, in the province's larger municipalities there is evidence that democratic, representative, and accountability deficits exist. More importantly, in BC's largest municipalities, irrespective of political persuasion of local council, local democracy increasingly fails to reflect generally agreed international standards of democratic accountability.

- Certain democratic electoral fundamentals in BC's larger municipalities have decayed to the point where, in comparative terms, they are not considered adequate, failing generally agreed democratic tests of political equality, representation of viewpoints, overall importance of electoral contests, and, most importantly, accountability.

- Comparative research also indicates that political systems, such as are found in BC's largest municipalities, verge on democratic crisis when they exhibit unhealthy patterns of participation (e.g., very low voter turnout).

- There is a seamless web between electoral and non-electoral accountability. Reform recommendations to ensure accountability in local governance must include both. Non-electoral reforms, such as on conflict of interest, freedom of information, and administrative review are necessary, but alone they are not sufficient to the task. Electoral reforms, while paramount, will be aided by non-electoral changes.

- On structure, the conclusion of this report clearly is that one size does not fit all. The democratic deficit identified is not apparent in smaller municipalities in British Columbia and structural change is not necessary in these local settings. In BC's larger municipalities, democratic weaknesses are evident and only structural change can redress the balance.

- Most importantly, the public in BC's larger municipalities is dissatisfied with the status quo, wishes to remain engaged in their governance, and wants local accountability to work. Many of those involved in government—at both the provincial and local levels—recognize this public demand and are prepared to act.

Appendix III:
Legislation of Relevance to Municipal Government, 1991–2005

Harcourt (NDP)

Year	Bill	Legislation
1992	20	Ministry of Municipal Affairs, Recreation and Housing Statutes Amendment Act, 1992*
1992	25	Property Purchase Tax Amendment Act, 1992*
1992	28	Municipal Finance Authority Amendment Act, 1992*
1992	45	Statute Revision Miscellaneous Amendment Act, 1992
1992	48	Municipal Affairs, Recreation and Housing Statutes Amendment Act (No. 2), 1992*
1992	66	Assessment and Property Tax Reform Act, 1992*
1992	77	Municipal Amendment Act (No. 2), 1992*
1992	81	Miscellaneous Statutes Amendment Act, 1992
1992	84	Labour Relations Code
1993	12	Municipalities Enabling and Validating (No. 2) Amendment Act, 1993*
1993	19	School Amendment Act, 1993*
1993	26	Waste Management Amendment Act, 1993*
1993	35	Local Elections Reform Act, 1993*
1993	38	Emergency Program Act
1993	42	Cabinet Appeals Abolition Act
1993	43	Municipalities Enabling and Validating (No. 2) Amendment Act (No.2), 1993*
1993	57	Municipal Affairs Recreation and Housing Statutes Amendment Act, 1993*
1993	58	Municipal Affairs Recreation and Housing Statutes Amendment Act (2), 1993*
1993	73	Land Title Amendment Act, 1993*
1994	12	Library Act*
1994	20	Local Government Grants Act*
1994	21	Heritage Conservation Statutes Amendment Act, 1994
1994	25	Municipal Affairs Statutes Amendment Act, 1994*
1994	30	Agricultural Land Commission Amendment Act, 1994
1994	31	Municipal Amendment Act, 1994*
1994	37	Skills Development and Fair Wage Act
1994	49	Attorney General Statutes Amendment Act, 1994
1994	56	Forest Land Reserve Act
1995	10	Mountain Resort Association Act
1995	11	Growth Strategies Statutes Amendment Act, 1995*
1995	22	Farm Practices (Right to Farm) Act
1995	24	Miscellaneous Statutes Amendment Act (No. 2), 1995
1995	29	Employment Standards Act
1995	31	Municipal Affairs Statutes Amendment Act, 1995*
1995	43	School Sites Acquisition Statutes Amendment Act, 1995*
1995	55	Miscellaneous Statutes Amendment Act (No.3), 1995

Clark/Miller/Dosanjh (NDP)

Year	Bill	Legislation
1996	2	Budget Measures Implementation Act, 1996
1996	8	Municipal Affairs and Housing Statutes Amendment Act, 1996*
1996	14	BC Benefits (Income Assistance) Act
1997	2	Budget Measures Implementation Act, 1997
1997	11	Agriculture, Fisheries and Food Statutes Amendment Act, 1997
1997	16	Police Amendment Act, 1997
1997	17	Capital Region Water Supply and Sooke Hills Protection Act
1997	22	Miscellaneous Statutes Amendment Act, 1997
1997	26	Local Government Statutes Amendment Act, 1997*
1997	30	Technical University of British Columbia Act
1997	35	Municipalities Enabling and Validating (No.2) Amendment Act, 1997*
1997	45	School Amendment Act, 1997
1997	46	Local Government Statutes Amendment Act (No. 2), 1997*
1998	10	Miscellaneous Statutes Amendment Act, 1998
1998	21	Assessment Amendment Act, 1998
1998	31	Local Government Statutes Amendment Act, 1998*
1998	35	Education Statutes Amendment Act, 1998*
1998	36	Greater Vancouver Transportation Authority Act*
1998	47	Strata Property Act*
1998	50	Miscellaneous Statutes Amendment Act (No. 3), 1998
1999	51	Nisga'a Final Agreement Act
1999	53	Pension Benefits Standards Amendment Act, 1999
1999	62	Miscellaneous Statutes Amendment Act, 1999
1999	65	Labour Statutes Amendment Act, 1999
1999	66	Attorney General Statutes Amendment Act, 1999
1999	74	Miscellaneous Statutes Amendment Act (No. 2), 1999
1999	79	Land Reserve Commission Act
1999	88	Local Government Statutes Amendment Act, 1999*
1999	91	Unclaimed Property Act*
2000	12	Regulatory Streamlining Miscellaneous Statutes Amendment Act, 2000
2000	14	Local Government Statutes Amendment Act, 2000*
2000	24	Miscellaneous Statutes Amendment Act (No.2), 2000
2001	20	Drinking Water Protection Act

Campbell (Liberal)

Year	Bill	Legislation
2001	25	Municipalities Enabling and Validating Act (No. 3)*
2002	8	Deregulation Statutes Amendment Act, 2002
2002	11	Miscellaneous Statutes Amendment Act, 2002
2002	21	Agricultural Land Commission Act
2002	30	Trustee Investment Statutes Amendment Act, 2002

2002	32	Waste Management Amendment Act, 2002*
2002	36	Energy and Mines Statutes Amendment Act, 2002
2002	37	Food Safety Act
2002	38	Environmental Assessment Act
2002	50	Advanced Education Statutes Amendment Act, 2002*
2002	54	Miscellaneous Statutes Amendment Act (No. 2), 2002
2002	62	Miscellaneous Statutes Amendment Act (No. 3), 2002
2002	70	Residential Tenancy Act
2002	73	Community Care and Assisted Living Act
2003	6	Budget Measures Implementation Act, 2003
2003	14**	Community Charter*
2003	15	Unclaimed Property Amendment Act, 2003
2003	18	Coastal Ferry Act
2003	22	Community, Aboriginal and Women's Services Statutes Amendment Act, 2003
2003	48	Employment Standards Amendment Act, 2002
2003	55	Water, Land and Air Protection Statutes Amendment Act, 2003
2003	56	Flood Hazard Statutes Amendment Act, 2003
2003	57	Environmental Management Act
2003	59	Financial Administration Amendment Act, 2003
2003	60	Business Corporations Amendment Act, 2003
2003	65	Local Government Bylaw Notice Enforcement Act*
2003	68	Administrative Tribunals Appointment and Administration Act
2003	73	Community Care and Assisted Living Act
2003	75	Significant Projects Streamlining Act*
2003	76	Community Charter Transitional Provisions, Consequential Amendments & Other Amendments Act, 2003*
2003	88	Private Managed Forest Land Act
2004	71	Safe Streets Act*
2004		(Fifteen additional Acts, for which municipal government is not primary topic)

*   Municipal government primary topic of legislation.
** Bill 14 came into effect in 2004.

NOTES

1. The BC Community Charter legislation was given royal assent on 29 May 2003. It came into effect on 1 January 2004.
2. The GVTA is made up of locally elected mayors and councillors; like the GVRD, they then are selected to serve on the GVTA board. On this GVRD model, see Smith and Oberlander (1998).
3. British Columbia now has legislatively established election dates. The following election will likely be in October 2009, although the provincial legislature will not set the date until after the 2005 election.
4. The other three board seats are held by provincial MLAs, appointed by the government; at the end of the NDP era these MLAs were not attending meetings and there remains an intention to eliminate this provincial membership component. That has continued under the 2001–5 Campbell Liberal administration.
5. See Greater Vancouver Transportation Authority, *2005–2007 Three Year Plan + Ten Year Outlook: Strategic Transportation Plan Amendment* (Burnaby, BC: Translink, Feb. 2004).
6. MCAWS officials and BC politicians have concluded that after several years of 'reforms',

no new initiatives are planned prior to the 2005 BC general election. (BC government interviews, Feb.–Mar. and Aug. 2004.)

7. A Citizens' Assembly has worked on the province-wide electoral reform issue, reporting in December 2004, for May 2005 BC general election consideration in a province-wide referendum (see www.citizensassembly.bc.ca).

8. Bill 14, Community Charter Act, Third Reading, 4th Session, 37th Parliament, proclaimed 29 May 2003. In effect from 1 January 2004. Victoria: Queen's Printer.

9. Bill 14, the Community Charter, 'Principles of the Provincial-Municipal Relationship', Part 1, Sec. 2.

10. On this example, see Smith and Oberlander (1998).

11. See Derrick Penner, 'Tomato King cheers right to burn wood: Court overturns bylaw that restricted growers fuel—Delta bylaw "set undue restrictions"', *Vancouver Sun*, 19 Apr. 2003, C1–2. In this case the Municipality of Delta had passed a bylaw to provide some local controls of large (e.g., in this case 18-acre) greenhouse operations, in particular their use of less-clean fuel sources for heating. The BC government intervened when a grower challenged the bylaw, citing right-to-farm legislation over the right of a municipality to legislate on local businesses. The province also argued that the local bylaw contradicted the provincial Waste Management Act, which exempts agricultural operations. Urban-rural issues of this sort are not new to Delta, a Vancouver suburb. In the late 1980s and 1990s, Delta held the longest land-use dispute hearing in Canadian history over efforts to develop farmland for urban use. The debates over the so-called Spetifore lands near the Tsawassen ferry terminal to Vancouver Island initially led to the Bill Bennett Social Credit government abolishing regional planning in 1983 when the GVRD initially prevented development plans by a Delta Social Credit supporter. The Minister of Agriculture/Fisheries has since precluded use of local bylaws to prevent/regulate coastal fish farms in BC as well.

12. On the fish-farm issues, see, for example, Charlie Anderson, 'Auditor-General to look into return of (fish-)farm fines after a complaint by the Sierra Legal Defence Fund', *The Province*, 15 Feb. 2004, A6. The pressure against fish farming has continued provincially and internationally throughout the summer and fall of 2004. On the West Vancouver dispute with the province on the sea-to-sky highway, see, e.g., 'Decision on overland route for sea to sky slammed', District of West Vancouver news release, 17 July 2004, in which the municipality stated that it was 'extremely disappointed with the province's decision'. In a statement to council on 20 July, West Vancouver Mayor Woods noted that the province had 'consistently misstated the issues and the District of West Vancouver's position'. A municipal legal challenge against the province on environmental assessment grounds is underway.

13. See, for example, 'Bill 75, the Significant Projects Streamlining Act, introduced November 3, 2003', at: <www.gov.bc.ca> and <www.dogwoodinitiative.org/SignificantProjectsStreamliningAct.htm>. The Act was given royal assent on 2 December 2003: <www.civicnet.bc.ca>.

References

Armstrong, J. 1999. 'The Forces That Cut Vancouver in Half', *Globe and Mail*, May, 1, 7.

Bergamini, M. 1991. *A Constitutional Role for Municipalities: Prospects and Options*. Ottawa: Federation of Canadian Municipalities, Sept.

Bish, Robert L. 2002. 'The Draft Community Charter: Comments', paper prepared for the Workshop on the Community Charter sponsored by the Local Government Institute and the School of Public Administration, University of Victoria, June 14.

British Columbia. 2000. 'Assent Proposals', in *Ministry of Municipal Affairs Issue Summaries and Recommendations for Symposium on New Local Government Legislation March 1–2.* Victoria: Ministry of Municipal Affairs.

Campbell, G. 2001. Premier Gordon Campbell Speech at Cabinet Swearing-In Ceremony, 5 June. At: www.gov.bc.ca/prem/popt/speech/June_5_Premier _speech.htm

Canadian Federation of Mayors and Municipalities. 1976. *Puppets on a Shoestring: The Effects on Municipal Government of Canada's System of Public Finance.* Ottawa: Canadian Federation of Mayors and Municipalities.

City of Vancouver. 1996. *Administrative Report: Amendment to Election Procedures Bylaws.* Vancouver, 9 July.

———. 2004. *A City of Neighbourhoods: Report of the 2004 Vancouver Electoral Reform Commission,* Thomas Berger, Commissioner. Vancouver, June.

Craig, G.M., ed. 1982. *Lord Durham's Report.* Ottawa: Carleton University Press.

Fershau, J. 2003. 'Muddling through Urban Regionalism: Rational Actors, Arenas without Rules and Transportation Governance in the Greater Vancouver Regional District', Master's thesis, Simon Fraser University.

Fry, E., L. Radebaugh, and P. Soldatos, eds. 1989. *The New International Cities Era: The Global Activities of North American Municipal Government.* Provo, Utah: Brigham Young University Press.

Ginnell, K., and P.J. Smith. 2001. 'Habitat@25: Lessons (Still) from Vancouver', in *Shelter and Governance—Report for the Special Session of the UN General Assembly for an Overall Review and Appraisal of the Implementation of the Habitat Agenda.* Vancouver: Institute of Governance Studies, Simon Fraser University, and Centre for Human Settlements, University of British Columbia, June.

Hobbes, H. 1994. *City Hall Going Abroad.* Thousand Oaks, Calif.: Sage.

Local Electoral Reform Coalition. 2000. *Draft Local Elections Transparency Act.* Vancouver: Local Electoral Reform Coalition.

Martin, P. 2002. 'Keynote Address to the Federation of Canadian Municipalities', Hamilton, Ont., 31 May. At: www.fin.gc.ca/news02/02-046e.html

Ministry for Community, Aboriginal and Women's Services. 2002. *The Community Charter: A New Legislative Framework for Local Government.* Victoria: Queen's Printer.

Ministry of Municipal Affairs. 1997a. *Getting Our Municipal Act Together: A Discussion Paper On Principles.* Victoria: Queen's Printer, Oct.

———. 1997b. *Master Implementation Agreement between the Province and the Greater Vancouver Regional District.* Victoria: Ministry of Municipal Affairs.

———. 1999. 'Statement from Jenny Kwan, Minister of Municipal Affairs', press release, 17 Feb. At: www.marh.gov.bc.ca/LGPOLICY/ MAR/

———, Growth Strategies Office. 1998. *An Explanatory Guide to BC's Growth Strategies Act.* Victoria: Queen's Printer.

Oberlander, H.P., and P.J. Smith. 1993. 'Governing Metropolitan Vancouver: Regional Intergovernmental Relations in British Columbia', in D. Rothblatt and A. Sancton, eds, *Metropolitan Governance: American/Canadian Intergovernmental Perspectives.* Berkeley: Institute of Governmental Studies, University of California, 329–73.

Paget, G. 2004. Executive Director, Governance and Structure Division, BC Ministry of Community, Aboriginal and Women's Services, interview, 13 Feb.

Rock, C. 2001. Translink Manager, interview, 27 Feb.

Razin, E., and P.J. Smith, eds. 2005. *Metropolitan Governing: Canadian Cases, Comparative Lessons.* Jerusalem: Magnes Press, Hebrew University of Jerusalem.

Royal Commission on Financial Management and Accountability (Lambert Commission). 1979. *Report.* Ottawa: Queen's Printer.

Saddlemyer, K. 2002. Community Charter Council member, interview, 27 July.

Self, P. 1977. *Administrative Theories and Politics.* London: Allen and Unwin.

Smith, P.J. 1992. 'The Making of a Global City: Fifty Years of Constituent Diplomacy—The Case of Vancouver', *Canadian Journal of Urban Research* 1, 1: 90–112.

———. 1993a. *Redrawing the Map: Is Bigger Better?* Edmonton: Federation of Canadian Municipalities.

———. 1993b. *Leadership, Accountability and Governability: The Ontario Regional Experience—Report for the BC Ministry of Municipal Affairs*. Vancouver.

———. 1998a. 'Local Government: An Introduction', in M. Howlett and D. Laycock, eds, *The Puzzles of Power: An Introduction to Political Science*, 2nd edn. Toronto: Oxford University Press, 393–403.

———. 1998b. 'Public Participation and Policy-Making in the Vancouver Region', in K. Graham and S. Phillips, eds, *Citizen Engagement: Lessons in Participation from Local Government*. Toronto: Institute of Public Administration of Canada, 49–77.

——— and T.H. Cohn. 1995. 'Developing Global Cities in the Pacific Northwest: The Cases of Vancouver and Seattle', in P.K. Kresl and G. Gappert, eds, *North American Cities and the Global Economy: Challengers and Opportunities*. Thousand Oaks, Calif.: Sage.

———, with P. Nicoll. 1979. 'Municipal Planning Administration in England and Canada', *London Review of Public Administration* 12 (Nov.): 29–64.

——— and H.P. Oberlander. 1998. 'Restructuring Metropolitan Governance: Greater Vancouver—British Columbia Reforms', in D. Rothblatt and A. Sancton, eds, *Metropolitan Governance Revisited: American/Canadian Intergovernmental Perspectives*. Berkeley: Institute of Governmental Studies, University of California, 371–406.

———, with H.P. Oberlander. 2005 (forthcoming). 'Governing Metropolitan Vancouver: Past Its "Best Before" Date', in E. Razin and P. Smith, eds, *Metropolitan Governing: Canadian Cases, Comparative Lessons*. Jerusalem: Magnes Press, Hebrew University of Jerusalem.

——— and K. Stewart. 1998. *Making Local Accountability Work in British Columbia*. Burnaby: Institute of Governance Studies, Simon Fraser University.

——— and ———. 2004. 'Eager Beavers, Lazy Cats and the Mushy Middle Thesis: Understanding Intergovernmental Policy-making Capacity of Local Governments', in Robert Young and Christian Leuprecht, eds, *Canada: The State of the Federation, 2004*. Kingston: Institute of Intergovernmental Relations, Queen's University.

——— and ———. 2005 (forthcoming). 'Unaided Politicians in Unaided City Councils: Explaining Policy Advice in Canadian Cities', in M. Howlett, D. Laycock, and L. Dobuzinskis, eds, *Policy Analysis in Canada: The State of the Art*. Toronto: University of Toronto Press.

Stewart, K. 1997. 'Measuring Local Democracy: The Case of Vancouver', *Canadian Journal of Urban Research* 6, 2: 160–82.

———. 2003. *Think Democracy: Options for Local Democratic Reform in Vancouver*. Vancouver: IGS Press, Simon Fraser University.

———. 2005 (forthcoming). 'Product Over Process: Elite and Public Support for Metropolitan Governance Reform in Greater London and Metropolitan Toronto', in E. Razin and P.J. Smith, eds, *Metropolitan Governing: Canadian Cases, Comparative Lessons*. Jerusalem: Magnes Press, Hebrew University of Jerusalem.

Translink. 2001. About Us. At: www.Translink.bc.ca/aboutus/gvrd.htm

———. 2004. 'Rapid Transit Expansion', news release. At: www.Translink.bc.ca/whatsnew/newsreleases/news06300401.asp

Union of British Columbia Municipalities. 2004. Press release, 7 Nov.

Vance, K. 2002. Union of British Columbia Municipalities Staff, interview, 25 July.

Walisser, B. 2002, 2004. Local Government Section, Ministry for Community, Aboriginal and Women's Services, interviews, 23 July 2002 and 13 Feb. 2004.

Wallace, S. 1999. Union of British Columbia Municipalities, interview, 12 Feb.

CHAPTER 3

Municipal Reform in Alberta: Breaking Ground at the New Millennium

EDWARD C. LESAGE JR

INTRODUCTION

This chapter[1] examines municipal reform in Alberta in the period beginning with Premier Don Getty's 1986 throne speech announcing a review of the province's municipal legislation and ending with a stalled provincial-municipal effort to negotiate broad new functional and financial arrangements. During this period Alberta introduced groundbreaking new municipal legislation, and tinkered to a greater or lesser extent with functional, financial, and structural features of its municipal system.

Analysis of Alberta municipal reform is of interest for a least four reasons. First, Alberta's Municipal Government Act (1994) introduced truly novel features to Canadian municipal legislation, freeing municipalities from close provincial oversight and providing them with greater administrative flexibility. Second, although other provinces were initially reticent to adopt Alberta-style municipal legislation, over the following decade several passed new municipal legislation built firmly on the new Alberta foundation. The trend seems certain to continue. Third, the consequential results of the Alberta approach are instructive insofar as the Alberta experience is the longest-running test of an effort to overturn Dillon's rule—the premise that a municipality cannot take action unless authorized to do so by provincial statute. Most interesting is that the results are notably less demonstrable than might have been expected given the trumpeting of those who brought forth the enabling legislation. Finally, the Alberta reform story is arguably an instructive parable of revolutionary reform. At the heart of this parable is the lesson that revolutions are born out of unusual circumstances and carry with them something of a natural history. Further, revolutionary reform is often a rough business that bends utopian designs, if not laying waste to them.

Alberta's most significant reforms were jurisdictional and resulted in introducing what was at the time pioneering legislation designed to reduce direct provincial control over municipalities and to strengthen municipal authority and autonomy within defined spheres of jurisdiction. Provincial officials asserted that with the proclamation of the Municipal Government Act (MGA) (1994) municipalities were no longer mere children of the province and that a new basis for municipal governance had been established. Over the years municipal governments have disparaged these claims—perhaps rightly insofar as municipal finances and a host of other functions remain under heavy provincial prescription—but something changed on the books with the new legislation. If nothing else, there is a theoretical elegance to the 'new' MGA reflected in an effort to shift the burden of democratic oversight and control from the provincial government to the local citizenry.

The most significant financial reform involved conversion of assessment valuation practices from a 'fair actual value' scheme to market value assessment. With this new regime came companion changes to assessment equation practice, which in part were necessitated by the province's direct move to manage the education property tax on a province-wide basis. The shift to market value assessment brought Alberta practices into line with those of other provinces and provided municipalities with a more equitable and easily administered assessment regime. Other financial reforms were designed to move the Alberta regime towards greater jurisdictional autonomy for municipalities (most particularly in relation to incurring debt) and financial flexibility. However, very little was provided by way of new revenue sources and at present many of the province's municipalities express deep criticism of the provincial government's closed purse.

Nothing radical was attempted by way of functional reforms during the turn-of-the-millennium reform period. In fact, the province's municipal associations and large municipalities engaged in what now appears to be a failed effort to rationalize functions between the provincial and municipal levels. Functional adjustments between the province and municipalities were pushed forward in the mid-1990s, but much of this was less reform than aggressive provincial downloading and off-loading. Likewise, not much reform was attempted through restructuring. Alberta sought to reduce the number of smaller municipalities through the ministerial bully pulpit and eliminated the whole dysfunctional category of 'improvement districts' and the moot Alberta county arrangement while also stripping away the province's regional planning architecture. There was also another failed attempt to reform governance in the capital region.

Several themes are woven into this chapter. One bares the rationalist architecture of the new legislation and of selected aspects of the provincial government's program reform. Draft legislation emanating from the extended Municipal Statutes Review Committee (MSRC) exercise was crafted in the light of citizen and interest group input and informed by considerable debate and reflection by committee members. A second theme traces the political ideation entwined with the reform effort. In this there is a revelation of a 'sea change' in public mood that affected the course of the MSRC initiative. Although it was little appreciated at the time, reformers tapped a rising populist sentiment that favoured greater auton-omy from what was perceived to be an overbuilt and increasingly out of touch provincial administration. This tide would bring in another type of Tory govern-ment that was putatively sympathetic to the populist sentiments of the new Act while paradoxically jealous of its prerogatives and public treasury. A third theme also explores another paradox: that of the fear of or disinterest in freedom. Even though many municipal leaders and active observers of the municipal scene pushed for greater autonomy, once this was granted many municipalities were either wary of it or continued to subscribe to the old ways of doing things, thereby largely ignoring their new-found autonomy. Finally, and as alluded to above, there is an overarching theme of what might be best described as the 'natural history' a revolutionary reform. Within the chapter this is revealed as a dialectic in which the contradictions of the old order increased to such a degree that new ideas were cast up, providing the basis for a dramatic departure with the past. As with any revolu-tion, there are the required zealots, reactionaries, and the mass of the affected whose existence is changed, though never quite as the revolutionaries would hope. What is especially interesting about Alberta's municipal reform proposals, which were brought forth through the Municipal Statues Review Committee, is that they were twice abandoned—once, prior to the so-called 'Klein Revolution' that rescued them in a spasm of far-reaching reform to the whole of the provincial government and its progeny sectors; and again, recently, when the reforms have been eclipsed (and effectively forgotten) by new reform demands relating to func-tion and finance.

Separate sections devoted to jurisdictional, financial, functional, and structural reforms follow. A final section reflects on reforms with attention to politics, processes, and results.

JURISDICTIONAL REFORM

Prior to the statutory reforms of the mid-1990s, the last major reforms to Alberta's Municipal Government Act were concluded in 1968 (Laux, 2002: 1–2). The 1968 MGA was essentially a merger of several former Acts that had been applied to different forms of municipalities (e.g., cities, towns, villages, and municipal districts). Veterans of the 1968 reform opine that no significant policy review accompanied that exercise since its objectives were consolidating and otherwise relatively narrow. Effectively, then, in its broad construction and jurisdictional premises the 1968 Municipal Government Act reflected a legislative scheme drawn from the 1940s and, arguably, from an even earlier period.[2]

By the 1980s Alberta municipal legislation had become voluminous and complex because the Municipal Government Act had been amended on many occasions. Even more problematic was the dispersed and sometimes contradictory character of legislation bearing on municipalities. Subsequent analysis revealed that nearly 100 pieces of provincial legislation affected municipal operations (Alberta, 1989a). The legislation and its many regulations did not reflect a coher-ent policy of provincial-municipal relations. Further, some aspects of the existing legislation shouted the need for reform since they were either antiquated or had become politically controversial. The general division of powers between province and municipal government and the freedoms accorded municipalities to conduct business dealings, annexation, planning, financial administration, assessment, and taxation were among the more noteworthy areas where friction or acknowledged deficiencies existed.

This tangle of municipal legislation and a general (if low-grade) malaise in provincial-municipal relations prompted the Progressive Conservative government of Premier Don Getty to announce its intention to review and update Alberta's municipal legislation.[3] The resulting Alberta Municipal Statutes Review Committee (MSRC) operated between 1987 and 1991. Its terms, defined by the Minister of Municipal Affairs, directed the members to examine emerging trends in Alberta and elsewhere and make recommendations on legislation appropriate to Alberta municipal government in the last decade of the twentieth century and into the twenty-first century.[4]

The MSRC concluded its work with an ambitious and novel draft bill in its final report (Alberta, 1991) that can be viewed as jurisdictional reform within two broad reform objectives. The first objective was to increase the jurisdictional autonomy and operating freedom of municipalities. MSRC members were convinced that the Alberta municipal system was sufficiently mature by the end of the twentieth century to be accorded considerably greater autonomy. This is certainly the message they received from many municipalities and others whom they consulted. Autonomy was desired within general areas of competence in which municipalities had long demonstrated their abilities to provide good government and services of reasonable quality. Operating freedom was an administrative corollary to this autonomy.

The second broad objective was to enhance good governance. To this end, the MSRC concluded that there was a need for greater citizen involvement and greater transparency in local policy-making. The Committee also concluded that the processes of local policy-making and administration could be improved, and said the same in regard to intergovernmental relations. Parenthetically, the MSRC sought to create municipal legislation that was accessible and 'user-friendly'. The welter of municipal legislation and the abstruseness of the statutes themselves promoted this ambition, but so did the ambition to promote good government through a more active citizenry. Comprehensible legislation would presumably aid an active citizenry.

Bill 51 was draft legislation based on principles introduced by the MSRC. The first and second broad reform objectives were very much in evidence in the bill, which died on the order paper.[5] In fact, Alberta's sweeping municipal reform would likely have died outright in 1992 were it not for larger events occurring in the body politic. Ralph Klein succeeded Don Getty as Tory leader and Alberta's Premier in December 1992. By all logic, Bill 51 should have been a crowning achievement of the Getty government. Municipal reform was a policy objective declared in Getty's first throne speech and the MSRC process lasted for most of the Getty premiership. However, by 1992 municipal reform had ceased to be a high priority of the beleaguered and increasingly inward-looking government.

Moreover, after six years and several ministers of municipal affairs, sweeping municipal reform had no natural champion in cabinet. Klein's Progressive Conservative forces won the June 1993 provincial election that followed; this was an election in which the PCs and the provincial Liberals each promised to be more fiscally conservative than the other. Shortly after the election the Klein government unveiled a comprehensive program of fiscal restraint and governmental reorganization that was so dramatic in its conception that it has been commonly referred to as the 'Klein Revolution'.

The Klein government resurrected the municipal legislative reform initiative, claiming that Bill 51, in fact, strongly reflected many aspects of the Premier's new governance agenda. These aspects, according to the then Deputy Minister of Municipal Affairs, included consultation, simplification of legislation and regulations, search for efficiency, and empowerment.[6] Municipal legislative reform was back in business. The Klein government's Bill 31 would be passed pretty much in whole as the first installment of Alberta's new Municipal Government Act. Much of what had been in Bill 51 was retained, although certain features of the antecedent bill were removed.[7] Bill 31 also included substantial new parts relating to property assessment, taxation, tax recovery, and selected other matters that were previously defined in separate legislation.[8]

An extraordinary amount of detailed legislation is contained in the new Municipal Government Act. However, for purposes of discussing reforms directed towards greater municipal autonomy and operating freedom, focus can be narrowed to a handful of sections in the initial two parts of the Act. First, within section 3, there is a description of the purposes of a municipality:

The purposes of a municipality are
(a) to provide good government,
(b) to provide services, facilities or other things that, in the opinion of council, are necessary or desirable for all or a part of the municipality, and
(c) to develop and maintain safe and viable communities.

This statement is a novel addition to municipal legislation since nothing of this sort existed in the former MGA or, it would seem, in Canadian legislation. While not granting any specific powers to a municipality, the legislature indicated, up front, that municipalities possess broad jurisdiction and powers over local affairs. The section, in effect, frames the whole of the Act and was offered for the benefit of the courts as well as municipal officials and citizens. Obviously it is not unqualified since the more specific prescriptions of the Act and other provincial legislation bear upon it. Nonetheless, it serves as a guide for those proposing municipal initiatives or scrutinizing them.

Section 6 provides the second advance towards greater autonomy and operating freedom. This section extends 'natural person' powers to municipalities. 'Natural person' powers are almost endless. An organization possessing them can enter into contracts, purchase or sell goods and services, borrow money, provide loans and guarantees, make investments, set up a company, hire employees, construct or lease buildings, set up non-profit organizations, purchase shares in a company, enter into partnerships or joint ventures, and much more. These powers had long existed in the corporate world but were never extended to municipalities. Instead, prior to the introduction of this innovation, municipalities conducted their non-legislative functions and provided services to citizens as specifically authorized by numerous sections of legislation.

When coupled with section 3, and viewed within the scope of authorities given to municipalities in subsequent sections, 'natural person' powers provide an elegant statutory device for municipalities to conduct a wide range of business affairs less encumbered by legislated prescription. For example, Alberta munici-palities can operate public utilities under the authority of section 6 even though the actual operations are governed by other parts of the Act and other legislation, and within these the minister holds approval powers. Municipalities can provide a wide range of health services authorized under the section, produce or arrange for fire protection, and arrange for a great range of cultural and recreation services. Moreover, the ways in which these services can be produced—direct provision, contracting out, joint-venturing—are matters both authorized and left to munic-ipal discretion under 'natural person' powers. The freedom to pursue corporate activity under these powers to further the purposes of the municipality is extraor-dinary, as seemingly is the potential for innovation.

'Natural person' powers are not unlimited in general law and in the case of the MGA specific restrictions apply. The province purposefully sought to restrict certain activities that municipalities might pursue under the 'natural person' powers. Among these restrictions are investments, borrowing, controlling corpo-rations, and providing loans and guarantees. In brief, 'natural person' powers extended to Alberta municipalities do not go as far as those applied to business corporations.

During the MSRC discourse, the concept of 'spheres of jurisdiction' was intro-duced. The concept, drawn from federated governance systems theory, would have municipalities given broad grants of authority in which they could make local law within their own boundaries. When first proposed, the concept stood in sharp contrast to the existing regime in which grants of municipal legislative authority were tightly defined within specific sections of municipal and other legislation. The spheres concept is realized in section 7 of the new MGA. The 'spheres' to which general bylaw-making authority is extended to municipalities by the Act include:

- safety, health, and welfare of people and the protection of people and property;
- people, activities, and things in, on, or near a public place or place that is open to the public;
- nuisances, including unsightly property;
- transport and transportation systems;
- business, business activities, and persons engaged in business;
- services provided by or on behalf of the municipality;
- public utilities;

- wild and domestic animals and activities in relation to them;
- enforcement of all bylaws.

Section 8 defines the scope of municipal power to pass bylaws under the broad provisions of section 7. Two things are important to note in the context of the present discussion. First, section 8 is written broadly and specifically declares that it does not seek to limit section 7. The declaration was inserted in anticipation that the courts and policy-makers would try to use the section to limit the broad spheres through appeal to the specific examples provided in section 8. Second, the Act provides municipalities with a new general power to 'prohibit', which complements the previous power to regulate. Thus, municipalities gained an important new tool to aid local governance.

Section 9 is a final complement to this suite of legislative provisions that boost municipal autonomy and flexibility. It reminds readers, and again perhaps especially the courts, that the Alberta legislature fully intended to provide municipalities with broad authority to make law in local affairs. Specifically, it provides that the power to pass bylaws under the spheres of jurisdiction domains:

> is stated in general terms . . . to give broad authority to councils and to respect their right to govern municipalities in whatever way the councils consider appropriate with the jurisdiction given to them under this or any other enactment.

Greater autonomy and flexibility were also promoted through a host of significant but for present purposes less central measures. For example, the number of officials that are necessarily appointed by councils was reduced to include only the chief administrative officer (s. 205). The only other requisite appointment is that of an auditor, who technically is not an administrative official of the municipality (s. 280). Other officials can be appointed at the discretion of council. Councils were provided scope to delegate 'powers, duties or functions under this or any other enactment or a bylaw to a council committee, the chief administrative officer or a designated officer, unless this or any other enactment or bylaw provides otherwise' (s. 203[1]). A municipal council's ability to borrow and conduct certain other financial administration activity was greatly simplified as the approval regime was lightened; this business will be discussed under 'Financial Reforms', below.

Promoting greater autonomy and flexibility was not concluded with the passage of the 1994 legislation. Indeed, this legislation represented only part of the municipal jurisdictional reform effort. Bill 32, the Municipal Government Amendment Act, 1995, was in itself a substantial piece of legislation containing 105 sections and bringing the whole of a reconstituted Planning Act and a reconstituted Regional Municipal Services Act into the compendium.

New sections of the Act dealing with planning (part 17) issued from yet another public consultation—the Planning Act review. The broad conclusions of this review were that Alberta's planning legislation should be delayered and deregulated. Thus, revisions through Bill 32 sought to increase local autonomy, reduce duplication and competition among authorities in the planning regime, and streamline approval processes. Much of the province's existing planning oversight and control machinery was eliminated through the new planning administration introduced in the 1995 addition to the Act. More will be said about selected particulars of the new planning administration regime in the following discussions on functional and structural revisions.

Strengthening democratic governance, the second broad objective of reformers, was aided through several innovations. Public participation is given a whole part in the Act (part 7). Citizens gained power to petition a public meeting, which councils are required to convene if the petition is validated (s. 229). Through petition, the citizenry also obtained the power to force public votes on new bylaws and resolutions and to force the amendment or repeal of existing bylaws and resolutions (s. 232). The actual rendering of these provisions is something less than straightforward insofar as different prescriptions apply to advertised bylaws (s. 231) and those not advertised, and to bylaws enacted through public votes(s. 234). Moreover, certain bylaws under the financial administration, assessment, taxation, and planning sections of the legislation are either subject to special provisions or excluded from the public vote provisions (s. 232). With all this noted, it remains that citizens gained important new opportunities to affect local public policy-making through the public vote machinery. Of special interest are provisions that allow for bylaws enacted through public votes to stand for some time against council adulteration. Although subject to specific exceptions, locally, during the first three years following the passage of a bylaw through a public vote, only a public vote can amend or revoke the local legislation. Between three and ten years' time a council must advertise that it intends to amend or revoke such local legislation (s. 240). Councils are provided the option of evoking a one-year moratorium on petitions dealing with the same or a similar subject if a bylaw on this has been passed by a public vote (s. 239). The wisdom of this provision is clearly to give the citizenry and council a little breathing room between petition-evoked plebiscites.

Open government provisions were also extended to the conduct of council business. Councils would enjoy less freedom in holding in camera meetings. The new Act contained access to information provisions under the public participation section but most of these sections were repealed in 1999 with the coming into force of section 1(1)(p)(vi) of the Freedom of Information and Protection of Privacy Act (s. 217). Another addition very much in keeping with the transparent government principles espoused by the Klein administration is a provision requiring disclosure of salary information for council members, the chief administrative officer, and designated officers (s. 217[3]). When new planning legislation was invested into the MGA with passage of Bill 32, citizens gained additional opportunities for input into local planning policy and administration through various public hearing and appeal mechanisms.

Provincial legislators also sought to strengthen local governance through improving the quality of local public policy. Within the 1994 legislation there is a deliberate attempt to separate policy-making and administrative domains. Councils were assigned duties for developing and evaluating the policies and programs of their municipalities, ensuring that the powers, duties, and functions of the municipality are carried out and that legislatively prescribed powers, duties, and functions are executed (s. 201). To help engineer a division between the council and administrative domains, the authors of the legislation created the position of chief administrative officer (CAO). They invested a significant number of duties and responsibilities into the CAO position and, importantly, declared 'a council must not exercise a power or function or perform a duty that is by this or another enactment or bylaw specifically assigned to the chief administrative officer or a designated officer' (s. 201[2]). Students of public administration may think these provisions somewhat naive, given the normal prescriptions of political science, but the problem addressed in the new MGA was especially aimed at council meddling in local administration and not bureaucratic usurpation of elected democratic authority.

To further discipline local policy-making the legislation prescribed that councillors would be held personally liable for funds expended outside a budget or otherwise not authorized by council (s. 249) and for amounts borrowed, loaned, or guaranteed where these actions cause the municipality to exceed its debt limits (s. 275). Fairly, however, the provisions would only apply to those who voted in favour of such measures, and the penalties would not apply where ministerial approvals were acquired. While broadly protected from liability or loss under legislation in the performance or intended performance of their functions, duties, and powers, councillors and municipal officers would forfeit such protection in matters involving defamation, dishonesty, 'wilful misconduct', and gross negligence (s. 535[2]). Once again, while the architects of the new legislation offered autonomy and greater operating freedom they also raised the responsibility ante to remind council members and officials that they would need to exercise their authority with care. However, it is worth noting that in 2002, under Bill 23, Municipal Government Amendment Act, 2002, s. 535(2) was amended to insert the words 'in good faith', as in:

> are not liable for loss or damage caused by anything said or done or omitted to be done *in good faith* in the performance or intended performance of their functions, duties or powers under this Act or any other enactment.

The change in legislation reflected concerns vigorously articulated by Alberta's two major municipal associations to the effect that recent court decisions (rendered in other provinces) potentially exposed them to significant risk as a consequence of the wording of the Alberta legislation.

Mediation processes to resolve various intergovernmental disputes were discussed during the Municipal Statutes Review exercise but were not introduced into the Act until the introduction of the revised planning legislation in 1995. In 1999, amendments were made to the Act to require mediation as a step to address annexation disputes (s. 211.1). In the case of planning legislation the Act instructs the Municipal Government Board to inquire as to why mediation was not attempted in disputes arising over statutory plan amendments and land-use bylaw amendments (s. 690) and in special cases concerning subdivision approvals, development permits, and other authorizations (s. 619).

Financial Reform

Through its 1994 legislation, Alberta introduced a significantly different regime relating to deficits, borrowing, debt limits, investments, tax recovery, and the provincial structures for overseeing these matters. In that the province was concomitantly passing legislation that would discipline its spending, it is little surprise that it would write new provisions concerning the regulation of municipal debt and the orderly administration of budgets. Under the legislation, budget deficits are permitted for a maximum of three consecutive years. Where deficits occur beyond the third year, the province requires the municipality to eliminate the accumulated deficiency and balance the budget (s. 244[1]). When this is not possible there are provisions for the minister to approve the elimination of the deficiency over a longer period. However, the minister also possesses the power to dictate the municipality's budget until such time as the deficiency is eliminated.

Under the old regime the Local Authorities Board approved municipal borrowing according to its internally established guidelines. Under the new Municipal Government Act the government adopted a radically different scheme that, generally speaking, was consistent with the general tenor of the Municipal Statute Review Committee findings and the Klein government's espoused philosophy. The Local Authorities Board—the province's central authority for managing municipal borrowing, annexation, and selected other municipal functions—was eliminated with the proclamation of the new Act. In the Board's stead, reformers established a system controlled by ministerial regulation of municipal debt limits (s. 252). These debt limits take the province out of the approval process by setting a benchmark that lenders can use to assess municipal creditworthiness. Prior to the new legislation, the Alberta Municipal Financing Corporation (AMFC) had a near monopoly on financing municipal borrowing, which certainly was advantageous to many of the province's smaller authorities. Under the new regime municipalities are likely to continue arrangements through the AMFC, but they can choose to seek better financing on the open market. Municipalities gained broader investment powers that permitted them to invest through a wider range of instruments, notwithstanding that the scope of these investments are still strictly prescribed (s. 250).

Assessment legislation was revised and consolidated into the new MGA. 'Revised', in fact, is hardly the proper term for the changes to the assessment and taxation regime. Under long-standing legislation Alberta municipalities conducted assessments for most residential properties using a 'fair actual value' system based on standards and methods prescribed by the Minister of Municipal Affairs. This was a depreciated replacement cost approach to assessment that had been developed to provide a reasonable and equitable standard of assessed value. It was introduced at a time when there was little administrative capacity to conduct equitable market-based assessments which themselves were not especially well suited to the boom-bust cycles of the earlier, largely undiversified Alberta economy. The trouble with the system was that it was difficult to administer and it produced assessment values that were not intuitive insofar as the general public was concerned.

Initial proposals for assessment reform envisioned market value assessment applied to all property other than farmland, linear property, and railways. The scheme was controversial, especially in rural areas, which led the Municipal Affairs department to abandon direct specification of the market value approach in the new MGA, although the provisions would be written into legislation through regulations and fully implemented by 1998. In any event, the result was to establish a market value system on all real property across the whole of the province except that which is regulated.

Tax exemption provisions were significantly altered under the new MGA. Exemptions remained for certain types of property, including farm residences and buildings, and school, environmental, municipal, and undeveloped utility property (s. 361). There were also broad exemptions written for government, churches, and other bodies such as universities (s. 382). Under the previous legislation non-profit organizations applied to the Local Authorities Board for exemptions from property taxation that were, in turn, ratified by the Lieutenant-Governor in Council. Under the new regime, exemptions established under existing legislation through Order-in-Council or private members' bills were to remain in force until removed by a municipality (s. 363[2]). All these particulars should not, however, cloud the significant change in the new approach to tax exemptions; municipalities were given broad powers to determine tax exemptions largely as they pleased, subject to the above-mentioned restrictions. In 1998 the power was strengthened so that exemptions could be made by resolution instead of bylaw.

Municipalities were given authority and responsibility for tax recovery. Provincial involvement in tax recovery matters would be limited to Alberta registries maintaining land title information on tax recovery property (part 10, division 8). The process itself would be streamlined and the time for completing the process reduced significantly. Further, municipalities were given protection from being forced to assume the title of properties that were not sold at a tax auction (s. 242). Prior to enactment of the new legislation the lack of such protection had been a major issue for municipalities as the previous rules forced some jurisdictions to assume ownership of contaminated sites with all their liabilities. In 1998 the province passed the Municipal Government Amendment Act, which contained additional relief by providing a stable and certain regime for tax recovery on vexingly peripatetic manufactured homes.

New taxation provisions under the 1994 legislation opened opportunities for municipalities to levy a special tax to raise revenue to pay for a long list of services. These services included waterworks, sewer, dust treatment, paving, the repair and maintenance of roads, ambulance services, fire protection, and recreation services. Special taxation could also be used to pay incentives for health professionals to reside and practise their professions in the municipality (s. 382[1]). Further, the

legislation permits council to impose the tax on any area of the municipality benefiting from the service for which the tax is levied. Under previous legislation
municipalities could effect a local improvement tax to facilitate capital project
developments. The special tax builds on this, addressing the issue of continuing
maintenance where expenditures are extraordinary and the beneficiaries can be
identified. Provisions for the local improvement tax remain (part 10, division 7).

A new arrangement was also implemented for inter-municipal tax-sharing (s.
55). Under the old municipal legislation, disputes involving inter-municipal tax-
sharing were resolved through adjudication by the Local Authorities Board. The
new Act eliminated this process and turned the settlement of these matters back to
municipalities, which must find resolution through negotiation and mediation.
The rationale behind this shift was similar to that supporting other autonomy-
producing innovations—municipalities were to be the architects of their own fate.
Alberta Municipal Affairs provides mediation services to municipalities to assist
them in instances where tax-sharing agreements are not easily negotiated. In the
toughest cases, such as a recent one in northern Alberta, the minister has raised
the question of the viability of the municipal structure in the region. This was
undoubtedly done to remind the municipalities of the full range of policy options
available to the minister if parties cannot reach a reasonable conclusion to their
negotiations.

One of the most dramatic changes wrought by the Klein government in its
sweeping reforms of the mid-1990s was the wholesale amalgamation of local
school authorities. The number of authorities was reduced from 141 operating in
January 1994 to 60 when the tide of reform was complete (Bruce and Schwartz,
1996). More significant for present purposes was the attendant change to educational financing, which directly affected municipalities. Alberta scrapped the
school finance regime that had existed since 1960 and replaced it with one that is
centrally administered and relies for approximately half its revenue on provincial
levies on local properties, which are collected by municipalities for the province
(University of Alberta, 2000: 7-26–7-29).

The change in the school requisition was introduced at the same time as the
market value assessment system was initiated. Although the province had an
assessment equalization administration in place, it was strained by the uneven
quality of the mass market value assessments produced by local assessors and by
the inadequacy of the equalization reporting system. The province established an
Alberta Equalized Assessment Panel late in 1998 to explore what might be done to
reduce the stresses caused by the confluence of these intertwined initiatives.
Through this a comprehensive strategy was developed to bolster uniform assessment standards, assessor professional education, and provincial monitoring of the
application of assessment standards (Alberta, 2000b). Amendments to the
Municipal Government Act passed in 2002—to be phased in over two years—
provide greater transparency of the equalized assessment system, full disclosure of
assessment information for the purpose of requisitions, and elimination of the
one-year time lag between the preparation of current and equalized assessments
(Alberta, 2002b). Assessor education was addressed earlier through regulation.

Sharing of provincially collected taxes has not been popular with the Alberta government and this remains a point of dispute between the province and municipalities in their discussions within the Minister's Provincial/Municipal Council (see below). The one notable exception—ultimately one that has hardened the municipal lobby—has been the province's granting its two largest cities a rebated share of the provincial fuel tax collected within their boundaries. A 1999 agreement between the province and the cities saw five of nine cents of taxes collected by the province on a litre of gasoline at the pump returned to the cities for transportation infrastructure development. However, with the reading of the 2002 budget the province unilaterally cancelled the five-cent-per-litre transfer. The mayors of Calgary and Edmonton were livid, threatened court action, and generally pilloried the provincial government for its poor financial planning. The province relented and reinstated the agreement but declared that although the cities could expect some per-litre amount from the gas tax, there was no ironclad guarantee that it would remain as high as five cents per litre. The amount has remained at this level through subsequent provincial budgets, however.

FUNCTIONAL REFORM

Functional reform was largely tomorrow's business for the Municipal Statutes Review Committee and for drafters of Alberta's new MGA. This said, there were two notable exceptions. The first concerns the regime for administering land-use planning. Prior to Bill 32, Alberta's municipal land-use planning was governed by a structure with the Alberta Planning Board at the apex and 10 regional planning commissions with authority over a large percentage of the province's population (Laux, 2002: 1–42 ff.). The Planning Board exercised significant powers over the province's municipal land-use planning, including the ratification of regional plans to ensure that they conformed to provincial policy. It frequently exercised its power to deny and return plans that did not meet its approval. The Board similarly approved amendments to regional plans and also functioned as a subdivision appeal authority. From the mid-1980s the Board's powers over municipalities were attenuated to some degree as the province granted municipalities increased discretion in approving subdivision plans and wider latitude in other areas (Masson, 1994: 417 ff.).

Regional planning commissions were responsible for developing regional plans that all member municipalities were statutorily required to honour. Commissions developed plans in which regional planning goals were defined and, pursuant to these, developed broad guidelines that applied to subdivision and other land-use planning activities of regional importance. Power was given to the commissions so that they could exercise their subdivision approval authority over all municipalities within their jurisdictions except those that were given subdivision approval authority by the province.[9] The commissions also acted as planning resource bodies to many municipalities in their regions. Additional assistance to many smaller and remote municipalities in planning matters came from the province's Municipal Affairs' Planning Services Division. The division assisted these authorities in developing general municipal plans and attendant land-use bylaws and, in certain instances, functioned as the subdivision approval authority. The division also aided the government in drafting municipal land-use policies that were enacted by the province through Orders-in-Council.

With Bill 32 the whole provincial and regional planning structure was largely wiped away. The new legislation eliminated the Alberta Planning Board, eradicated the regional planning commissions, and generally gave municipal land-use development over to municipalities (Elder, 1995; Laux, 2002). All municipalities are now required to adopt a land-use bylaw that divides municipalities into districts, defines various land uses within these districts, and provides for the issuance of development permits (s. 639). Municipalities with populations of 3,500 or more were henceforth required to adopt a municipal development plan while those of less population were given the option to do so (s. 632). Within these plans options were left open to establish area structure and area redevelopment plans. In the absence of the regional planning architecture, municipalities are given the choice to develop jointly an inter-municipal development plan or to address inter-municipal policies in their municipal development plans. If the latter route is chosen, consultation with adjacent municipalities is mandatory. Further, municipalities are required to establish development and subdivision authorities and a subdivision and development appeal board. The province retained the power to establish land-use policies under Order-in-Council. Every statutory plan, land-use bylaw, and action taken by municipalities, subdivision and development authorities, and appeal boards (including the Municipal Government Board) must be consistent with these policies (s. 622). However, in practice, these policies have been broadly conceived and are portrayed by Municipal Affairs officials as 'facilitative'. Municipal Affairs' Planning Services Division also fell under the axe so the provision of planning services is now a matter of local municipal concern.

The second functional change involved creation of the Municipal Government Board. The Board is a quasi-judicial tribunal charged with addressing a number of matters previously handled by either the Local Authorities Board or the Alberta Planning Board. Among the list of matters addressed by the Board are appeals on property assessment, equalized assessment, linear property assessment, and subdivisions involving a provincial interest. Inter-municipal disputes fall under the Board's purview, as do conflicts between municipalities and housing authorities, annexation matters, and any other matters referred by the Minister or Lieutenant Governor (s. 488[1]). With the creation of the Board and the definition of its responsibilities, the province gave a freer rein to municipalities in planning and financial matters.

After nearly a decade under Alberta's new MGA most parties agree that there is a need to sort out roles and responsibilities. On 16 November 2001, Guy Boutilier, the Minister of Municipal Affairs, announced the establishment of the Minister's Provincial/Municipal Council on Roles and Responsibilities in the 21st Century.[10] This ministerial initiative was launched in response to vigorous municipal association entreaties inviting the province to engage them in a 'disentanglement' dialogue. The province's municipalities were deeply disturbed by the heavy burdens that they were shouldering as a result of provincial off-loading and downloading of services and responsibilities for which they received little or no resource compensation.

Council membership is a high-level affair comprising the two municipal association presidents, the mayors of Edmonton and Calgary, a representative from the Alberta Economic Development Authority, three MLAs, and the minister, who chairs the body. Council duties include:

- Identifying and prioritizing issues to be addressed by the Council.
- Developing a process to resolve provincial/municipal issues.
- Clarifying the roles and responsibilities of the provincial and municipal governments.
- Recommending how to develop an improved partnership focused on providing the most efficient, effective, and co-ordinated level of service to Albertans from both orders of government.
- Developing a provincial position on urban and rural issues that incorporates the views of municipalities and is consistent with the values of Albertans.

In quick order the municipal representatives sought to add 'resource' issues to the discussion and the terms of reference were changed accordingly. The council was also officially renamed the Minister's Provincial/Municipal Council on Roles, Responsibilities and Resources in the 21st Century.

The Alberta Urban Municipalities Association has proposed a 'framework' within which the province and municipalities would relate. Core to the association's proposal is the requirement that the two 'orders' of government should work together as equals. Indeed, the association seeks 'power equally divided between the two orders of government' (AUMA, 2002b: 6). Among other tenets of the AUMA proposal are those that seek a clear division of responsibilities, flexibility in provincial policy and legislation, program flexibility, consistency and stability in intergovernmental relationships, and, lastly, an appeal to contemplate the citizenry's interests first. Some of the same global points are reportedly made in a joint submission presented early on in deliberations by the cities of Edmonton and Calgary, although these governments used the occasion to emphasize special considerations owed to them. Purportedly the large authorities made claim on special provincial policies and program elements to assist them with their unique burdens in areas such as transit, social services, and economic development.

Of special interest in the efforts to define roles and responsibilities is the AUMA's current 'three Rs' (roles, responsibilities, and resources) initiative and, particularly, some of the background research that has contributed to the discussion. It champions a rationalization of the roles, responsibilities, and allocation of resources between the municipal and provincial levels of government. An initial round of consultations with the AUMA membership identified prime program and service areas in which role and responsibility issues are especially acute (AUMA, 2002a). At the top of the list are public transit, police, ambulance, solid waste, social services, and social housing.

Provincial policy-makers are not unaware of these issues and in some instances they have made efforts to study and propose solutions. Recently, separate ad hoc Tory caucus committees investigated and reported on policing and ambulance issues. To underscore the distance between the province and municipalities on many of the key issues, the most eye-catching recommendation of the MLA Policing Review Committee's final report was to have all municipalities pay full freight for policing services (Alberta, 2002c). Under a long-established arrangement, municipalities under 2,500 population and rural municipalities do not pay for such services. The Committee proposed to create a 'Policing Support Grant Fund' that would be financed by diversion of 25 per cent of provincial revenue from traffic fines. Grants from this fund would be provided to municipalities based on a formula using a municipality's equalized assessment and crime rate.[11] Needless to say, these proposals were unpopular with small authorities that feared changes in the formula and increasingly heavy financial burdens for policing. Since 2002 the issue of police services grants has become politically more intense. The core of the issue transmogrified over the interval with the proposal for direct payment by all municipalities slipping off the table. Pressing issues on the policy agenda have included inadequate funding for the larger urban centres and the injustice of municipalities with populations of 5,000 and less not receiving the same subsidies as those of 2,500 and less. News of a new formula was introduced in the 2004 Speech from the Throne and details leaked slowly from the government in the following weeks. Under the new arrangement the province will extend the base funding for policing to all municipalities with populations of 5,000 or less. It will also provide additional funding through per capita grants. Communities with full subsidies will not receive revenue from traffic fines, while others will receive shares on some proportion.

Tory caucus committee proposals addressing the ambulance services were perhaps less controversial, but offered little towards municipal preferences around roles and responsibilities. The main proposal concerning municipalities is that Regional Health Authorities (RHAs) should be linked into the governance of ambulance services and that this should be accomplished through the formation of regional ambulance districts. Indeed, the caucus committee examining ambulance services called for the Minister of Health to provide leadership in restructuring the delivery of these services by creating formal partnerships between municipalities and RHAs (Alberta, 2001b). Following the 2004 Speech from the Throne and the 2004 budget address, a new arrangement was announced in which '[g]overnance and funding responsibility for ground ambulance services will be shifted from municipalities to health regions' (Alberta, 2004). To facilitate the transition the province committed an additional $13 million for ground ambulance services. This arrangement went decidedly further than the MLA committee proposal and transferred the land ambulance function to the RHAs. Municipalities are generally pleased with this development, not least because the new arrangement promises to create over $50 million in new tax room for the province's municipalities. Interestingly, even though the RHAs will assume governance and funding responsibility for land ambulance services, many municipalities will continue to deliver the services under contract to the health authorities.

Structural Reform

The most dramatic changes to the municipal structure during the halcyon days of Klein's reforms were the elimination of Alberta counties and the previously described overhaul of the land-use planning, changes to the property assessment administration, and creation of the Municipal Government Board. Structural reform involving Alberta's counties is a straightforward enough tale. The Alberta system of county administration was established in the early 1950s to provide a governmental structure with coterminous municipal and school boundaries (Masson, 1994: 108–17). This was done to facilitate co-ordination of rural road improvements and maintenance with school transportation. To a lesser degree, the innovation also sought to promote administrative efficiencies through integrated municipal and school governance and (to a lesser extent) administration. The structures could not survive Klein's restructuring of the school system that obviated the coterminous boundaries through the creation of much larger rural school authorities.[12]

Alberta has not been completely without 'reforming' amalgamations and other forms of consolidation. Beginning in the mid-1990s, Alberta Municipal Affairs committed itself to a program that encouraged municipalities to evaluate their viability as independent corporate entities. The province published assessments of the financial viability of all the province's municipalities and encouraged the local authorities to measure their viability on several other dimensions. This initiative was first aimed at some of the smallest municipalities, which were clearly suffering under provincial grant reductions, and other somewhat larger authorities that had leveraged themselves to such an extent that the reductions were also taking a bite. Department officials were available to conduct analyses and, if conditions permitted and the local populations were willing, to dissolve the authorities or amalgamate them with other municipalities. Despite these efforts there were relatively few takers. Between 2000 and 2002, for example, there were only three 'dissolutions', all of which were villages that reverted to hamlet status within municipal districts. Perhaps the most significant consolidation occurring in the 1990s was that involving the creation of the Town of Cold Lake, later to be renamed the City of Cold Lake. The town was formed by the amalgamation of the Town of Cold Lake and the Town of Grand Centre and by annexation of land from the Municipal District of Bonnyville No. 87. To put this initiative in perspective, the population of the city is a little under 12,000 and it appears to be losing people. Another 'significant' change of the late 1990s was amalgamation of the City of Drumheller and the Municipal District of Badlands No. 7 to form the Town of Drumheller. Precisely why the amalgamated town does not possess Specialized Municipality status (discussed below) is unclear.

If there is an Alberta approach to dealing with regional problems in recent times it most certainly involves creating the mechanisms and processes that permit voluntary collective municipal action within a geographic region. Changes made in 1994 to the Regional Municipal Services Act made it possible for regional

services commissions (RSCs) more readily to serve as general vehicles for municipal co-operation. Prior to 1994, RSCs only could be involved in hard utilities (e.g.,
water, sewer, and waste management). With the change of legislation the purview
has been expanded to include airports and emergency response facilities among
other services, including inter-municipal planning administration. It was anticipated that the commissions would quickly blossom and address a variety of services with the proclamation of the new MGA. However, only in recent times has this
promise begun to emerge. There has been a spurt of growth in the number of
these authorities. In early 2001 there were 32 RSCs; within a year the number had
jumped to 41, and in mid-2004 the total stood at 52. Municipal Affairs officials say
that this number is likely to continue to increase.

For a while it looked as if the Alberta pattern of voluntary municipal restructuring might be altered by a high-profile ministerial initiative. In December 1998 the
Minister of Alberta Municipal Affairs launched the Alberta Capital Regional
Governance Review (ACRGR). The chair of the ACRGR was given instructions to
'recommend approaches to the governance of the capital region which will
address the broad range of challenges and opportunities the region will face over
the next 30 years or more' (Alberta, 2000a: 7). To this was added the comment of
the minister of the day that the 'status quo would not do.'

The ACRGR final report, published in May 2001, proposed a two-track approach
to strengthening the region: a partnership track and a shared services track. Shared
services would build on the extensive bilateral and multilateral shared services
arrangements that the Review discovered within the region (Alberta, 2001a). At the
heart of the partnership track route would be a regional body with mandatory
municipal membership and voting rules devised to respect regional sensitivities.
This, effectively, was a regional governance body by another name. All of the
ACRGR recommendations were accepted by the province save that recommending
creation of a formal regional partnership agreement and another proposing that
regions' municipalities select 'the best approach' for long-term delivery of water,
waste water, and solid waste services. Since the publication of the report, progress
has been made on several recommendations relating to the shared services track.
The Alberta Capital Region Alliance (see below) has completed a regional transportation master plan, federal and provincial funds have aided the development of
a regional emergency response plan, and the provincial government has
contributed over $400,000 to help the region's municipalities create a regional GIS
system. The regions' economic development authorities also have moved to collaborate with one another in attracting new industries and businesses.

It is likely that the most significant consequence of the Governance Review
initiative is the creation of the Alberta Capital Region Alliance. The Alliance is a
non-profit body established by the Capital Region's 22 municipalities to effect
collaborative action and lobby government on behalf of the region. It is a harbinger of what appears to be a growing movement towards an American-style 'council
of governments' or Australian 'regional organizations and councils' in Alberta.
Recently, Calgary has pursued development of a regional partnership with its area
municipalities. While broadly modelled on the Capital Region initiative, the

Calgary region has sought to define voting decision rules to promote collective action. This stands in contrast to the Capital Region, which has purposefully adopted a consensus decision-making approach. The Red Deer region has also fashioned a regional partnership among area municipalities, but unlike the initiatives in the two major metropolitan centres this effort concentrates principally on economic development and industry attraction. Across the province other regional partnerships have been formed, in part owing to provincial grant incentives that reward inter-municipal collaboration.

Specialized Municipalities are a new classification of municipal government created through the new MGA (s. 83). The Act allows the minister to create a Specialized Municipality when no other classification of municipal government can meet the needs of residents of the proposed municipality. This form of government allows for unique combinations of responsibilities and special institutional arrangements to effect good government. The legislated classification also permits the province to create authorities of quite different forms without having to resort to special and unique legislation. At present there are four Specialized Municipalities in the province: Strathcona County, the Regional Municipality of Wood Buffalo, the Municipal District of Mackenzie No. 23, and the Municipality of Jasper. The reasons for creating the specific Specialized Municipalities are principally variations on a couple of themes. In the Wood Buffalo case, the logic was to bring the large industrial assessments associated with oil sands production and the scattered rural populations into the same municipal structure as the principal urban entity in the area (i.e., Fort McMurray). Strathcona County effectively had accomplished the same feat as Wood Buffalo under an ingenious arrangement in which the county's principal urban entity remained classified as a hamlet despite growing to a population in excess of 40,000. Specialized Municipality status permitted the county to organize a more rational representational system while ensuring that the urban centre would remain imbedded within the larger and significantly rural municipality. The Mackenzie municipality contains two separately incorporated towns within its boundaries but also a number of hamlets scattered across its expansive northern territory. The special status was granted to address concerns over municipal management and government among distinct hamlet communities. Specialized Municipality status for Jasper was granted in light of the municipality's location in a national park, but this also recognized that it would be best if the Jasper region operated as an urban-rural structure.

Improvement Districts once dotted the Alberta landscape. These unincorporated rural administrative units are the responsibility of the provincial government, which, through Municipal Affairs, levies and collects taxes and oversees service provision. Since the 1940s there have been occasional provincial initiatives to reduce the number of Improvement Districts. At the beginning of the 1990s there were 18 (Masson, 1994: 134) and today there are only seven. Of these seven, five exist with boundaries that are coterminous with national parks and two with boundaries coterminous with provincial parks. During the late 1980s residents of Improvement Districts and the province agreed that a transitional form of government was needed to promote conversion to full-fledged rural municipal governments (i.e., counties or municipal districts). Thus, the Rural District Act was passed in 1991. This legislation was short-lived since it was repealed with the creation of the new MGA.

REFLECTIONS ON THE MUNICIPAL REFORM EXPERIENCE IN ALBERTA

When municipal officials are asked to express the most significant features of Alberta's reforms they tend to cite councils' confidence to legislate and regulate without frequent need to consult with Alberta Municipal Affairs. This point is likely the most widely acknowledged salubrious outcome of the new MGA. 'Natural person' powers are part of this, as are the general bylaw-making powers that fall within the eight local legislative spheres of jurisdiction. Municipal officials cite a range of new opportunities for corporate action that have been effected by the new legislation. For example, a small city has established a business to provide high-speed communication services within the authority, and a county has gone into the business of selling used bridge timbers acquired from the provincial transportation department. A specialized municipality has been especially aggressive in exercising 'natural person' powers. It has established a commercial partnership with a major private bus corporation to produce public transit services and has joint-ventured with a major telecommunication corporation to produce a 911 answer-and-dispatch service for over 30 communities inside and outside its region. Two urban municipalities have partnered with a county to create a non-profit corporation that operates a large recreation centre that the three authorities co-operatively financed and built. A small town has entered into a partnership with a private restaurateur to operate a food facility on municipal property.

Other officials cite the loosened financial administration prescription and borrowing provisions as welcome innovations. Administrators celebrate the division between council and administrative functions, and they also view the CAO model and elimination of several statutory positions named in the previous Act as welcome reform. Chief administrative officers are now largely free to appoint whom they wish to administrative posts. This was often not the case under previous legislation. The lightened and notably more locally administered planning regime is cited by officials as a laudable improvement. Within this, the local administration of subdivision and development appeals appears to be something appreciated by authorities, who felt hard done by under the regional planning commission structure. Further, there is some relief in the removal of previous absurdities such as those associated with the former tax recovery regime and with the prohibitions against charging varying rates, even if those to be charged agreed to the variance, under the previous regional municipal services legislation. Rural municipalities appreciate the elimination of any effective distinction between them and urban municipalities in planning matters, as existed under previous legislation—this has resulted from Municipal Government Board rulings that have in effect said 'a municipality is a municipality.'

Although many municipalities have embraced the liberating features of the new MGA, many others have been cautious. Thus, one of the principal outcomes of the Alberta reform process has been widespread 'business as usual'. Provincial and municipal officials, and lawyers who specialize in municipal matters, give various explanations for this lack of engagement. The most common of these is that municipalities hesitate to innovate for fear of the legal and political risk associated with innovation. There is certainly some credibility to this observation. Since 1994, every municipal association general assembly meeting has featured a cavalcade of municipalities putting forward resolutions requesting that the province clarify or add some clause or section to the Act. In the 1990s, the loose draftsmanship of the parts of the MGA encouraged such resolutions, but beyond this, many municipalities were uncomfortable with the broad enabling features of the Act—and this remains the case. The concern turns significantly on both legal and political risks that are, of course, highly correlated. In effect, there is an apparent paradox of freedom: while the municipal community has agitated for greater authority and flexibility, many hesitate to exercise these freedoms.

Other explanations for this paradox exist. One is that municipalities simply did not need the autonomy provided by the new MGA. Startling evidence of this comes from a progressive CAO employed by a rural county who shared with the author the fact that between 1995 and 2002 his authority passed only five bylaws out of 32 proposed that specifically relied on section 7 of the Act. No bylaws passed by his council relied on section 3 and none relied specifically on the 'natural person' provisions of section 6. Indeed, most of the bylaws passed by the municipality were required by municipal government or other provincial legislation (e.g., a property tax bylaw as required by the MGA) or were elective under municipal or other provincial legislation. Other CAOs have mentioned similar experiences.

While municipalities have been broadly cautious about exercising the autonomy-enhancing sections of the new Act for fear of successful court challenges, until recently there has been little legal challenge to these provisions. Dire consequences predicted in the application of the 'natural person' powers have not occurred at all (Manderscheid, 1998). However, one important case recently resolved in favour of the City of Calgary at the Supreme Court of Canada threatened the foundations of the autonomy-enhancing sections of the Act—and, it would seem, the foundations of many other new municipal government Acts derived from the Alberta legislation. In 2002, the Court of Appeal of Alberta ruled that the City of Calgary had acted beyond its powers in its administration of taxi licences. The decision reversed a Court of Queen's Bench decision favouring the city in the *United Taxi Drivers of Southern Alberta v. Calgary* case. At issue was the lack of precisely specified powers in the Municipal Government Act supporting the city's actions. The court decision suggested that when common-law rights are interfered with, municipalities must act with a specific grant of power (Court of Appeal of Alberta, 2002). As a 'case comment' on the decision provides, '[t]he majority judgement in this case challenges the foundation of the MGA and the manner in which municipalities have governed since 1995. It is a decision that may have broad-reaching implications for all Alberta municipalities' (Bardsley, 2002: 7). Put another way, Dillon's rule appeared to be alive and well, notwithstanding the intentions of the Legislative Assembly of Alberta. What was so surprising about the Court of Appeal's judgement was that it countermanded a lower court decision that made immanent sense to those who had worked with the new legislation. It was therefore with considerable relief that the Supreme Court ruled in favour of the appeal mounted by the City of Calgary and the Attorney General of Alberta (Supreme Court of Canada, 2004). Whether additional court challenges will be mounted against the autonomy-enhancing provisions of the new legislation remains to be seen. At present, however, municipal concern over the legal fragility of the legislation appears to be calmed.

There is a politics to the past two decades of Alberta municipal reform that cannot be fully explored in a chapter relating mostly news from the front. Still, a few observations are necessary by way of conclusion. Officials involved in the creation of the MGA have commented that the MSRC was much ahead of its time within Alberta, not to mention the rest of Canada. Within Canada the vanguard character of the new MGA has been broadly recognized, but little acknowledgement is given within Alberta to the precociousness of the legislation in relation to what would later become known as the Klein Revolution. The Municipal Statutes Review Committee engaged in extensive consultations over its long duration. These tapped a growing political sentiment within Alberta that, when mobilized, was at the core of Preston Manning's and the federal Reform movement's rise, and it propelled the hard swing in Alberta towards provincial fiscal conservatism, downsizing, less regulated government, and the 'reinvention of government'. Municipal politicians and administrators clamoured for greater freedom and a loosening of the provincial grip on their activities. They claimed that they were better managers of their affairs than the provincial government of Don Getty, which many regarded as remote, profligate, and lacking good judgement in many other ways. These sentiments were by no means fully realized in the new MGA but they are certainly evident. More important, the elements of Bill 51 that evolved from the MSRC were adopted by the new Klein crew in 1993 as their own. And, after a fashion, they were.

Perhaps it was only happenstance, but the minister delivered to the Department of Municipal Affairs following Klein's taking the Premier's seat was assuredly the most energetic and ideologically committed advocate of the government's evolving neo-conservative agenda. Dr Steve West made rough work of the new Act by speeding up the consolidation of municipal legislation. He commanded what, in retrospect, may have been profoundly dysfunctional initiatives, including the elimination of the regional planning commissions, the wholesale conversion of the municipal assessment regime, and the abandonment of many provincial services that aided municipalities. The flotsam and jetsam of these decisions continue to float to the top. Nonetheless, something must be said in grudging admiration for the heroic creation of an omnibus Act that contains so many reforming sections. Revolutionaries are more into sculpting with chainsaws than fine chisels, so the indictment of Dr West must be considered in perspective.

Whether the current Minister's Council on Provincial/Municipal Roles, Responsibilities, and Resources will serve as an effective venue to provide a clearer logic for provincial-municipal relations is something to hope for, but a modest dose of pessimism should be swallowed to temper any great expectation. The

Council remains a creation of the Minister of Municipal Affairs and, therefore, it is subject to ministerial enthusiasms. One only need go back into the near-history of the Alberta Capital Region Governance Review to be reminded that a campaign that starts out with fanfare under one minister can end in near silence under another. Moreover, while the present minister, Guy Boutilier, is widely acknowledged to be both intelligent and energetic, history has not delivered to him the stuff of real opportunity.

Old realities following the Klein halcyon period have reasserted themselves on the Department of Municipal Affairs and its client municipalities. Creation of a new deal between municipalities and the province might be relatively simple if Municipal Affairs is the only provincial department to which municipalities relate. This is not the case, and while the minister may speak with authority within government on matters relating to municipal legislation, many of municipalities' most important relations are with other departments and other ministers. Moreover, the ministers of these other departments often find it to their advantage to deal directly with municipalities and their associations.

At the heart of it, then, significant new municipal reform of the sort now being called for by the Alberta Urban Municipalities Association and others looks like a political long shot. The venue of the reform conversation is a council conceived by a novice minister in a government that continues to be concerned most recently (and perhaps perpetually) with the retirement of debt and management to prevent deficits. The reform ante is higher now since provincial-municipal finances are the topic of discussion, as are new powers to municipalities. Beyond this, there is little urgency within the provincial government to push ahead with the types of reform demanded by the cities and the urban municipal association since these would invariably involve complications with more highly touted policy objectives.

Besides, it is likely that in any new arrangement of roles and responsibilities municipalities would have to take on new roles and heightened responsibilities. If nearly a decade of living under significant reform is anything to judge by, it is an even bet that, when pushed, many municipalities will not welcome new responsibilities, and more than an even bet that they will not readily embrace new reforms. If the Alberta experience is anything to go by, the authorship of truly significant reform appears to be something that occurs periodically and, perhaps, in abbreviated fashion. Moreover, even with the mandating of bold new designs for the future, it seems that the real change that follows is uneven and frequently unrealized in the near term. Historians often seek to identify the moment at which new epochs begin. For all the usefulness of this, their accounts usually relate rapid advance by the vanguards that is followed by a long, staggered advance by the rest. When considering municipal reform in Alberta at the turn of the new millennium, this would seem about right.

NOTES

1.   I am grateful to members of Alberta Municipal Affairs for the considerable assistance they provided me in preparing this chapter. The verity of the contents is solely my

responsibility and any errors or omissions do not reflect on the department or its helpful and knowledgeable staff.

2.   For a brief survey of municipal legislative reform, see Laux (2002: ch. 1).

3.   Premier Getty announced his intention to review the legislation in his government's first Throne Speech (1986) and repeated the pledge in the next Throne Speech that followed the 1986 provincial elections.

4.   See Ministerial Order MO 728/87, referenced in Municipal Statutes Review Committee (1991).

5.   The demise of Bill 51 was intentional insofar as the purpose of circulating the draft bill after first reading was to invite debate and public feedback.

6.   Jack Davis, Deputy Minister of Alberta Municipal Affairs, provided these observations in two speeches. The first was to the Canadian Association of Municipal Administrators on 26 May 1993. The second was delivered to the Federation of Canadian Municipalities conference 'Tools of Government Workshop' on 29 May 1993. Both presentations were in Calgary.

7.   For example, the purposes of a municipality section (now section 3 of the MGA) were altered, as was the list of general bylaw-making spheres, which was shortened from 11 to eight. The percentage of the population in municipalities under 10,000 required to effect a valid petition was lowered, provisions for in camera meetings were narrowed, and the proposal for a local governance commission was scrapped.

8.   When the new MGA came into force on 1 January 1995, it consolidated or repealed 21 Acts. The MGA was subsequently amended a number of times and consolidated or repealed another five Acts, bringing the total number of Acts consolidated or repealed to 26. A list of Acts either consolidated into the new MGA or repealed between the passage of Bill 31 and June 2004 include the following: Agricultural Relief Advances Act, Assessment Appeal Board Act, Border Areas Act, County Act, Crown Property Municipal Grants Act, Crowsnest Pass Municipal Unification Act, Electric Power and Pipe Line Assessment Act, Improvement Districts Act, Local Authorities Board Act, Local Tax Arrears Consolidation Act, Municipal and Provincial Properties Valuation Act, Municipal and School Administration Act, Municipal District of Badlands No. 7 Incorporation Act, Municipal District of Bighorn No. 8 Incorporation Act, Municipal District of Brazeau No. 77 Incorporation Act, Municipal District of Clearwater No. 99 Incorporation Act, Municipal District of Cypress No. 1 Incorporation Act, Municipal Government Act (RSA 1980 CM-26), Municipal Tax Exemption Act, Municipal Taxation Act, Municipalities Assessment and Equalization Act, New Towns Act, Planning Act, Regional Municipal Services Act, Rural Districts Act, Tax Recovery Act.

9.   The Planning Act, 1977 permitted municipalities to function as their own subdivision approval authority upon petition to and approval by the minister. The Department of Municipal Affairs was reticent to respond to such petitions since they would obviate the logic of the regional planning regime.

10. See 'Minister's council to ensure stronger and more effective provincial/municipal partnerships for the 21st century', Government of Alberta news release, Edmonton, 16 Nov. 2001. At: <www.gov.ab.ca/acn/200111/11577.html>.

11. For a listing of principal recommendations of the MLA Policing Review Committee and access to the complete report, see <www.gov.ab.ca/home/news/dsp_feature.cfm?lkFid=187>.

12. Acute observers will note that a number of Alberta municipalities continue to feature the word 'county' in their formal names. This is a municipal preference but the name has no status under the MGA. Municipalities with the word 'county' in their names are either municipal districts or, in one case, a specialized municipality.

References

Alberta. 1988a. Municipal Statues Review Committee. 'External Relations', Preliminary Draft Discussion Paper No. 5 (July).

———. 1988b. Municipal Statutes Review Committee. 'What are Municipal Services?', Preliminary Draft Discussion Paper No. 2 (Apr.).

———. 1988c. Municipal Statutes Review Committee. 'How should we be structured?', Preliminary Draft Discussion Paper No. 3 (May).

———. 1988d. Municipal Statutes Review Committee. 'How should municipalities be financed?', Preliminary Draft Discussion Paper No. 4 (June).

———. 1988e. Municipal Statutes Review Committee. 'The Discussion Papers' (Nov.).

———. 1989a. Municipal Statutes Review Committee. 'Municipal Government in Alberta: A review of yesterday and today—A proposal for tomorrow'.

———. 1989b. Municipal Statutes Review Committee. 'Establishment of Municipalities', Legislation Paper No. 1, Preliminary Discussion Draft.

———. 1990. Municipal Statutes Review Committee. 'The Municipal Government Act: Local Autonomy, You Want It, You Got It', Second Discussion Draft.

———. 1991. Municipal Statutes Review Committee. *Municipal Government in Alberta: A Municipal Government Act for the 21st Century* (Mar.).

———. 1992. Bill 51, The Municipal Government Act, 1992.

———. 1994. Bill 31, The Municipal Government Act, 1994.

———. 1995. Bill 32, The Municipal Government Amendment Act, 1995.

———. 1996a. Municipal Affairs. '1995 Viability Data'.

———. 1996b. Municipal Affairs. 'Land Use Policies' (6 Nov.).

———. 1998. Municipal Affairs. 'Proposed Amendments for 1998 to the Municipal Government Act'.

———. 1999a. Municipal Affairs. 'Proposed Amendments to the Municipal Government Act'.

———. 1999b. MLA Farm Property Assessment Review Committee. 'Farm Consultation Report: Assessing Issues and Taking the Next Steps' (May).

———. 2000a. Alberta Capital Region Governance Review. 'Preamble', First Report (Mar.).

———. 2000b. Alberta Equalized Assessment Panel. 'Report and Recommendations to the Minister of Municipal Affairs on Equalized Assessment in Alberta' (July).

———. 2001a. Alberta Capital Region Governance Review. 'An Agenda for Action' (May).

———. 2001b. MLA Review of Ambulance Service. 'Patient-Focussed Emergency Medical Services: MLA Review of Ambulance Service Delivery 2001 *Draft Report*' (May).

———. 2002a. Alberta Municipal Affairs. 'Proposed Amendments to the Control of Corporations Regulation (AR 373/94): Consultation document and questionnaire'.

———. 2002b. Bill 23, Municipal Government Amendment Act, 2002.

———. 2002c. MLA Policing Review Committee. 'Report of the MLA Policing Review Committee' (July).

———. 2004. 'Budget 2004 strengthens rural and urban communities', news release, 24 Mar.

Alberta Urban Municipalities Association (AUMA). 2002a. 'Final Report: Three R's Project—Phase 1' (Feb.).

———. 2002b. 'Creating Accountability—Roles, Responsibilities and Resources: A Working Paper', presented to the Minister's Council on Provincial/Municipal Roles, Responsibilities, and Resources, 11 June.

———. 2002c. 'Discussion Paper on the 3Rs: Results of the 3 Rs Survey—Phase II' (Summer).

————, Protective Services Task Force. 2002d. 'Report on the Royal Canadian Mounted Police Contract in Alberta', 28 June.

Bardsley, Tim W. 2002. 'Court ruling challenges interpretation of broad municipal powers', *Urban Perspective* 22, 4: 7.

Bruce, Christopher J., and Arthur M. Schwartz. 1996. 'Education: Meeting the Challenge', in Christopher J. Bruce, Ronald D. Kneebone, and Kenneth J. McKenzie, eds, *A Government Reinvented: A Study of Alberta's Deficit Elimination Program.* Toronto: Oxford University Press, 383–416.

Court of Appeal of Alberta. 2002. *United Taxi Drivers' Fellowship of Southern Alberta v. Calgary (City of)*, 2002 ABCA 131.

Elder, P.S. 1995. 'Alberta's 1995 Planning Legislation', *Journal of Environment Law and Practice* 6: 23–58.

KPMG. 1996. 'Inter-municipal Cooperation—Survey Results', prepared for Alberta Association of Municipal Districts & Counties and Alberta Urban Municipalities Association, 7 Nov.

Laux, Frederick A. 2002. *Planning Law and Practice in Alberta.* Edmonton: Juniber.

Manderscheid, Don. 1998. 'The Alberta Municipality: The New Person on the Block', *Alberta Law Review* 36, 3: 692–706.

Masson, Jack, with Edward C. LeSage Jr. 1994. *Alberta Local Governments: Politics and Democracy.* Edmonton: University of Alberta Press.

Supreme Court of Canada. 2004. Judgement in Appeal 29321: *City of Calgary v. United Taxi Drivers' Fellowship of Southern Alberta, Rashpal Singh Gosal, Haringer Singh Dhesi, Aero Cab Ltd and Air Linker Cab Ltd—and—Attorney General of Alberta.* (Alta.) 2004 SCC 19/2004 CSC 19.

University of Alberta, Faculty of Extension. 2000. *Property Assessment and Taxation,* Module 7 'Property Taxation' (Sept.).

CHAPTER 4

Saskatchewan's Municipal Reform Agenda: Plethora of Processes and Proposals but Paucity of Products

JOSEPH GARCEA

INTRODUCTION

Saskatchewan's municipal reform agenda during the past 15 years can be described as a plethora of substantial reform processes and proposals but a paucity of substantial reform products. The result has been a major gap between the nature and scope of the reform proposals that were developed and debated and the reforms that were implemented. The major cause of that gap has been the reticence and in some instances the resistance on the part of municipal and provincial officials to accept reform proposals put forth by the other level of government or by various committees and task forces that they established. Although Saskatchewan's provincial and municipal governments have agreed on the overarching goals of the municipal reform agenda, they have often disagreed on the means by which to achieve them. This chapter provides an overview of the broad goals of the municipal reform agenda in Saskatchewan; an overview of the major structural, functional, financial, and jurisdictional reform proposals and actual reforms; and an overview of the politics of reforms. The chapter concludes with an assessment of the municipal reform agenda and some prognostications on future reform.

THE GOALS OF THE REFORM AGENDA

Although Saskatchewan's provincial and municipal governments agreed on the principal goals of reform, they often disagreed on the means by which to achieve them. Four major goals for the municipal system were municipal capacity-building, inter-municipal co-ordination and co-operation, municipal-provincial co-ordination, and good municipal governance. These goals were echoed in the terms of reference and reports of various task forces as well as in ministerial statements made in conjunction with various municipal reform initiatives (e.g., Saskatchewan, 1986; SUMA, 1995b; Saskatchewan, 1997; Saskatchewan, 2000f).

The first programmatic goal of the reform agenda was what might be termed municipal capacity-building. This refers to the goal of increased fiscal, planning, development, and service delivery capacity of municipal governments. During the recent period of municipal reform there was a genuine desire on the part of provincial and municipal officials to consider whether municipalities had the requisite jurisdictional authority and financial resources to do what they must for their communities in light of an increasingly complex, challenging, and rapidly changing environment. They were particularly concerned about the continuing and compounding negative effects of the depopulation of some municipalities due to migration from smaller to larger communities, and the effects of financial constraints facing many municipalities due to declining revenues and increased operating costs. Given such challenges, both provincial and municipal officials were concerned that municipalities could become increasingly dependent on the provincial government not only for financial resources, but also for administrative and operational support in matters related to governance, management, and service delivery. There was a shared desire on the part of the municipal and provincial governments to improve the capacity of municipalities for dealing with problems or challenges that confronted their communities, but there were differences between them on the best means to achieve this goal. The prevailing view among municipal officials was that they simply needed more jurisdictional authority and power; on the other hand, provincial officials believed that municipalities needed greater organizational capacity through various means, including in many instances the consolidation of neighbouring municipalities. This position was stated in a provincial government publication on provincial assistance for local government reorganizations: 'With a limited and shrinking tax base and population, some small villages and rural municipalities are experiencing difficulty in maintaining local government structures. Moreover, municipal governments are finding it increasingly difficult to raise the necessary resources to function independently and provide services' (Saskatchewan, 1995d: 1).

A second major and closely related goal of municipal reforms was inter-municipal co-operation and co-ordination. There was a shared belief that increasing such co-operation and co-ordination is essential in maximizing the capacity of municipal governments to perform their core functions and also to minimize problematic inter-municipal spillovers. Despite the fact that they shared this goal, there were some significant disagreements as to how to achieve it. While the prevailing view among municipal officials was that the provincial government should merely provide financial incentives to achieve such co-operation and co-ordination, provincial officials felt that to get the requisite type and level of such co-operation and co-ordination, financial incentives alone would not suffice. Instead, they maintained that some mandating by the provincial government for inter-municipal co-operation and co-ordination would be required.

A third overarching goal of the municipal reform agenda was provincial-municipal co-ordination and co-operation in developing and implementing their respective policies and programs. An important focus of such co-ordination and co-operation was disentanglement in performing their respective functions. Such disentanglement had less to do with shifting responsibility for performing service delivery or regulatory functions from one order of government to the other than with altering the administrative supports and political oversight and control provided by the province for various governance and management functions performed by the municipal governments. Another dimension of disentanglement existed in the financial sphere, where the goal was to minimize the types and number of financial transfers between the provincial and municipal governments. There was a shared concern that the provincial and municipal governments were somewhat more entangled than they needed to be in the functional and financial spheres and that this caused planning and political problems for both orders of government. They differed, however, on the precise changes needed in the nature and scope of co-ordination, co-operation, and disentanglement.

The fourth principal goal of the municipal reform agenda was 'good governance', that is, sound governance and management practices based on fundamental political and administrative principles such as efficiency, effectiveness, equity, equality, accountability, transparency, and majority rule. Although provincial and municipal officials shared this goal, they differed in regard to the best means to achieve it. The most significant difference between them was on how much provincial oversight and control was required to ensure good governance.

The Nature and Scope of the Municipal Reform Agenda

Saskatchewan has had an interesting and important municipal reform agenda, which has focused on various types of reform—structural, functional, financial, and jurisdictional. The key elements of that reform agenda are explained, in turn, below.

The Structural Reform Agenda

Unlike some other jurisdictions where major restructuring has occurred, either through the creation of new regional governments or in the reconfiguration of existing ones, in Saskatchewan there was no major restructuring. The only structural reforms during the past 15 years were very minor and resulted from two types of reforms. The first entailed the periodic creation or dissolution of a few municipalities due to fluctuations in the population of various local communities. The second type entailed the conversion of either all or a substantial part of five northern municipalities and small parts of some urban and rural municipalities in southern Saskatchewan to Indian reserve status as part of the Treaty Land Entitlement Framework Agreement process (Barron and Garcea, 1999). These structural reforms did not produce a substantial change either to the number or types of municipalities in the province. Its traditional one-tier municipal system consisting of approximately 1,000 municipalities and quasi-municipalities has remained intact. Consequently, at the start of the twenty-first century Saskatchewan had the distinction of having the second highest number of municipalities with the smallest average population per municipality in the country (Saskatchewan, 2000c: 247).

Although there were no major structural reforms to Saskatchewan's municipal system, there were some notable amendments to the statutory framework that could potentially produce some structural reforms, but to date this has not happened. The amendments enacted in 2001 were designed to facilitate amalgamation on a voluntary basis (i.e., Bill No.23—Rural Municipality Amendment Act, 2001, and Bill No. 24—The Urban Municipality Amendment Act, 2001). The key provisions in those statutory amendments were designed to maximize municipal authority and autonomy of the amalgamating municipalities in making important decisions regarding the geographic, political, service, and fiscal frameworks of the resulting municipalities with minimal provincial involvement (Saskatchewan, Hansard, 15 June 2001, 1844–6).

The statutory framework for voluntary amalgamation enacted in 2000 was the product of a compromise reached between the provincial government and the two associations of municipalities, the Saskatchewan Urban Municipalities Association (SUMA) and the Saskatchewan Association of Rural Municipalities (SARM). The agreement was reached shortly after the public hearings on the highly controversial interim report of the Task Force on Municipal Legislative Renewal, which recommended an extensive amalgamation program to reduce the number of municipalities and municipal entities to fewer than 125 as a means of increasing the capacity of the municipal government sector to deal with its needs and preferences. The Task Force was not the first to recommend extensive amalgamation of municipalities. Such recommendations had been made by several provincially appointed bodies that investigated the need for municipal reform, including the Royal Commission on Agriculture and Rural Life in the 1950s (Saskatchewan, 1956), the Local Government Finance Commission in the 1980s (Saskatchewan, 1986), and the Consensus Saskatchewan Advisory Committee (Saskatchewan, 1990) and the Inter-Community Cooperation and Community Quality of Life Advisory Committee (Saskatchewan, 1993) in the 1990s. In recent decades various academics, including one of Canada's leading political scientists (Smiley, 1960: 313) and two Saskatchewan economists with expertise in regional economics (Stabler and Olfert, 2000), have also recommended amalgamation as a solution to problems in Saskatchewan's municipal sector.

In the spring of 2000 the Municipal-Provincial Roundtable, consisting of SARM, SUMA, and provincial government representatives, decided to examine the issue of voluntary amalgamation. It did so because it was constrained to wrestle with the highly volatile amalgamation genie released from the bottle by the Task Force on Municipal Legislative Renewal with its recommendation for what it termed a 'directed consultative approach' to amalgamation. Its recommendation of such an approach was based on the strong opposition within the municipal sector, and particularly the rural municipal sector, against the Services District Act (Bill 33) introduced by the Romanow government in 1996 (Garcea, 1997). In light of that opposition, the proposed legislation, which authorized municipalities to establish such service districts on an entirely voluntary basis for essentially any purposes that they deemed appropriate, was ultimately withdrawn by the provincial government.

After extensive negotiations, members of the Municipal-Provincial Roundtable agreed to enact a statutory framework for voluntary amalgamation—it was in the interest of both the provincial and municipal governments to demonstrate not only that they were committed to municipal reform, but also that they were willing to be flexible in achieving it (Saskatchewan, 2000b). Unfortunately, but not surprisingly, the new statute for voluntary amalgamation ended up serving a symbolic rather than a practical function. This was a case of history repeating itself. In 1962 the CCF government had enacted the Municipal Units and County Act amid extensive resistance from within the municipal sector. That Act included provisions for voluntary and mandatory amalgamations, but neither approach was used to achieve extensive amalgamations in the 22 years from the time it was enacted until it was eventually repealed in 1984 (SARM, 1995: 52–3).

The Functional Reform Agenda

Saskatchewan's functional reform agenda during this period was limited in scope and did not result in any major reform initiatives. For better or worse, there was no disentanglement, downloading, or uploading of any major functions related to either hard or soft services. Instead, there were only very small adjustments to the alignment of roles or responsibilities between the provincial and municipal governments for some relatively minor functions such as certification of municipal officials, training of firefighters for some communities, and providing building inspectors for small urban and rural communities. In all of those cases the province was attempting either to terminate or at least to reduce its role and responsibility in performing such functions. Ironically, despite those attempts, the provincial government found that in certain instances the lack of capacity in the municipal sector actually forced it and its various agencies either to perform or to pay for some additional functions. The notable example of this was the responsibility for monitoring and managing the safety of the water supply for some communities. The problems experienced in the highly publicized case of the contamination of North Battleford's water supply drew attention to the lack of capacity of many other municipalities to ensure a continued supply of safe water. The result was that the provincial government had to devote money to the improvement of local water and sewage treatment systems, and in some instances its water agency (SaskWater) had to become increasingly involved in providing safe water on a contractual basis to smaller communities (SARM, *Rural Councillor* 37, 4 [Aug./Sept. 2002]: 27).

The absence of substantial functional reforms was not for lack of effort on the part of the provincial government. After all, it initiated several reviews to examine options for a realignment of functions between itself and the municipal governments, and to examine options for the performance of some functions through inter-municipal co-operation. Invariably, the municipal associations were reticent and in some cases strongly opposed to the realignment of any functions between the provincial and municipal governments, largely because they feared that it could have placed added financial burdens on them. Moreover, they opposed having to perform some functions through inter-municipal co-operation because they feared it would result in inequities in financial contributions and constitute the thin edge of the wedge towards mandated amalgamation.

Such reticence and opposition on the part of the municipal associations to explore any functional reforms was clearly evident during the early to mid-1990s in the context of discussions of enhancing inter-municipal co-operation for the purpose of performing various functions more effectively and efficiently. This occurred in conjunction with both the provincially appointed advisory committee on Inter-Community Cooperation and Community Quality of Life (Saskatchewan, 1993) and the SUMA Task Force on Urban Governance Renewal (SUMA, 1996). It also happened when the provincial government introduced the Services District Act (Bill 33) in 1996 as a means to provide municipalities with the requisite framework to facilitate the creation of inter-municipal regional authorities on a voluntary basis to perform various municipal service and development functions. Ultimately, however, the provincial government had to withdraw Bill 33 due to the strong opposition to it because it was perceived as the proverbial 'slippery slope' towards forced amalgamation.

Similar reticence and resistance were also evident in the case of the provincial-municipal Memorandum of Understanding (MOU) developed after Bill 33 was withdrawn by the provincial government due to the intense pressure by one municipal association (i.e., SARM) and the decision of the other (i.e., SUMA) to support it in a grand, albeit reluctant, gesture of solidarity. One of the major components of the MOU was to examine the alignment of functions between the provincial and municipal governments as part of the broader effort to review and possibly reconfigure not only the functional, but also the financial and jurisdictional relationships between them. What looked like a promising trilateral review and reform process, involving the provincial government and those two municipal associations, was terminated largely due to a lack of strong commitment on the part of those associations to devote the requisite time and resources to it. Evidently, their lack of commitment stemmed from a lack of sufficient professional staff to perform the key tasks and a widespread disenchantment with the provincial government's decision at the time to cut the level of funding for the municipal revenue-sharing pools. The result was that although some basic background papers were produced, neither reform proposals nor reforms resulted from the MOU initiative.

The issue of functional reforms re-emerged two years later, in 1998, with the appointment of the Task Force on Municipal Legislative Renewal. As part of its broad mandate, the Task Force considered the alignment of functions and the need for co-ordination and co-operation in performing them between and among the provincial and municipal governments as well as various local authorities. In its interim and final reports, the Task Force recommended that the realignment of functions should be considered as part of a broader and substantial reform initiative that would also include structural, financial, and jurisdictional reforms (Saskatchewan, 2000a, 2000c, and 2000d). That recommendation was based on the belief that such a multi-dimensional approach to reform was likely to be more productive than an approach focused on only one dimension of the municipal system. Unfortunately, the antipathy towards the Task Force's recommendations on structural reform ultimately overshadowed all of its other recommendations, including those on functional reform. The result was an intense, limited, and relatively unproductive debate on the need for and nature of reforms.

Municipal reticence and resistance to functional reform re-emerged in the context of the Municipal-Provincial Roundtable process undertaken between May and October 2000 in the wake of the furor caused by the recommendations in the interim report of the Task Force on Municipal Legislative Renewal. On several occasions during the Roundtable process provincial representatives attempted to place on the agenda a review of potential changes to the alignment of functions between municipal governments and both the provincial government and various local authorities, but on each occasion the municipal associations refused. As part of their efforts to stimulate interest in initiating discussions on functional reform during the Roundtable process, provincial officials prepared a short issues and options paper, 'Updating Municipal-Provincial Roles and Responsibilities' (Saskatchewan, 2000e). The position of provincial officials as articulated in that paper was that 'the Municipal-Provincial Roundtable [should] undertake a process of reviewing and updating municipal government roles and responsibilities (functions) in relation to those of the provincial government and other authorities, using a similar process to that used by the Roundtable in the identification of impediments to voluntary restructuring' (ibid., 1). To that end a process was 'needed to agree on appropriate municipal functions, to provide the basis for future discussions regarding the clarification and redefinition of municipal powers, municipal finances, reduced provincial involvement, and other legislative or policy renewal' (ibid.). In that paper provincial officials also suggested that the process would provide a forum to discuss the following:

- changes in municipal roles and responsibilities as a result of public expectations, government priorities, social and demographic trends, and emerging issues and problems;
- the capacity of municipalities to perform their jobs, including the resources required (human and financial) and concern about the safety and quality of municipal services in relation to this capacity (e.g., water supply);
- innovations in public service delivery (ibid.).

Provincial officials also identified the following general functional areas, with specific issues that had to be addressed:

- regional parks and libraries—municipal government concerns about funding responsibilities and cost-sharing;
- building standards and fire inspections—municipal capacity to perform, requirements for bylaw approval (e.g., setting fees);
- water quality monitoring—municipal capacity to perform, safety issues;
- planning and development—the department's role both in approving bylaws and in assisting or even preparing plans and bylaws;

- municipal lands, reserves, and streets—overlapping jurisdiction, requirements to approve fees (e.g., plumbing); and
- traffic control—overlapping jurisdiction, requirements for approval (e.g., school bus and snowmobile operations) (ibid., 3).

That paper also outlined the following approaches for reviewing functions that provincial officials hoped would be acceptable to their municipal counterparts.

- a systematic review of both optional and mandatory municipal functions in current legislation in relation to the above noted objectives and issues;
- a selected review of key functional areas and functions in which issues and concerns have been raised by municipalities, municipal associations, and the department, as well as by others identified by the Roundtable;
- a thematic review of municipal-provincial roles and responsibilities in relation to: services to property vs services to people (or 'hard' vs 'soft services'); functions of a local nature vs functions of a provincial nature; and/or functions requiring shared responsibility vs those of sole responsibility (ibid., 2).

Despite their concerted efforts and a willingness to be flexible both on substantive and procedural matters, provincial officials were unable to convince their municipal counterparts involved in the Roundtable to undertake any consultations on the need for and nature of functional reforms.

The Financial Reform Agenda
The financial reform agenda yielded more substantial results than either the structural or functional reform agendas. In discussing the nature and scope of financial reform and its results, it is useful to distinguish between three major categories of reform initiatives. The first category entails substantial reform initiatives produced through major adjustments. This includes two major sets of reforms—those to the property tax assessment system and to the system of provincial grants in lieu of taxes. The second category entails minor reforms through adjustments. This includes both the provincial-municipal revenue-sharing system and the provincial-municipal cost-sharing system. The third category involves exploratory initiatives that to date have not produced reforms. This includes the sharing of the property tax base by municipal governments and education authorities and inter-municipal cost-sharing.

Reforms to the Property Assessment System
The property assessment system has undergone some important reforms in recent years. These focused largely on modernizing and updating the property tax system and on minimizing what were deemed to be inequities therein among properties caused either by outdated assessments or by property tax exemptions for too many different types of properties.

The reforms to the property assessment system occurred during two rounds of reforms. The first round, undertaken in the mid-1990s and largely based on the reform agenda of the Saskatchewan Assessment Management Agency (SAMA), produced the most important reforms to the municipal statutes and policies on the property assessment system. This entailed the movement towards a 'full market value' system from a 'fair market value' system, the computerized calculation of assessments so that they could be updated frequently and quickly, and the refinement of the statutory and policy frameworks (Hanselmann, 2000). Over the eight years since its founding in 1987, SAMA made several efforts to implement the new system. Its efforts, however, were met with some reticence and resistance from municipalities, ratepayers, and even successive provincial governments. Indeed, both Grant Devine's Conservative government prior to 1991 and Roy Romanow's NDP government thereafter wanted some consensus to be achieved at least within the municipal sector before proceeding with the proposed reforms. To that end, in 1993 and 1994 SAMA undertook some public consultations that included large public meetings that were usually packed with ratepayers who vented their concerns regarding the potential effects of reassessment on their tax bills. Opposition to the proposed reforms started to subside somewhat after some special consultations were undertaken in 1995 and 1996 with key stakeholders to provide them with the facts regarding the nature and effects of the proposed reforms. Shortly after those consultations were concluded, the provincial government decided to enact the requisite statutory and policy frameworks for the implementation of the new property assessment system in 1997 (Hanselmann, 2000).

The second round of reforms to the property assessment system was undertaken between 1999 and 2002. That round was based on an agenda that emerged from both the so-called 1997 Reassessment Review Committee, which was mandated to review and make recommendations on issues related to the 1997 reassessment (Saskatchewan, 1999b; Garcea, 1999), and the Tax Exemptions Review Committee, which reviewed and made recommendations on property tax exemptions (Saskatchewan, 1999c; Garcea, 1999). Those reviews produced numerous recommendations and ultimately several reforms. The reforms included statutory amendments that changed several elements of the assessment system:

- The timetable for reassessment was extended from three to four years.
- The property tax assessment appeals process was streamlined.
- The statutory provisions became more consistent regarding property tax exemptions for urban, rural, and northern municipalities.
- Municipal councillors were prohibited from sitting on local assessment appeals boards.
- Municipalities gained greater autonomy to use alternative assessment approaches for businesses, such as sales and income taxes, rather than just the replacement cost approach.

Although there was no major change to the taxing authority of municipal governments beyond the property tax system during the latter part of this period, the municipal governments were also given various tax tools that, directly or indirectly, were related either to the property tax system or to the provision of services for property. These tools included mill rate factors, minimum taxes, base taxes, tax phase-in, establishing subclasses, and allowing variable mill rates in rural municipalities for various types of service areas and communities. In effect these tax tools were intended to provide municipalities with more freedom in determining whether to base their tax regimes on the value of property or the value of specific bundles of public services provided to properties. Most of those reforms were produced with remarkably little fanfare and controversy. The major reason for this is likely that the committees recommending these reforms consisted of representatives from key stakeholders, including the provincial government as well as various associations in the municipal, educational, library, and business sectors. Moreover, both of those reviews generally focused on relatively technical matters that were not seen as problematic by the governmental stakeholders or ratepayers. The notable exception to this was the elimination of tax exemptions for two types of properties—the land value of residential acreages and the education portion of taxes on seasonal resort properties in provincial as well as regional parks. The elimination of those exemptions was strongly resisted by representatives of the ratepayers who lost those exemptions.

Reforms to the System of Payments in Lieu of Taxes
Another major financial reform during the contemporary era was the phasing in of a system of provincial payments in lieu of taxes for properties owned by the Saskatchewan Property Management Corporation. In the 1998–9 fiscal year the provincial government started the four-year phasing in of that system. At the end of the phasing-in period the provincial government was paying grants in lieu of taxes at the same level as if those properties were privately owned. This particular reform stemmed from the provincial government's realization that it could not behave as 'free rider' while constraining others not to behave in such a fashion by making them pay for a share of municipal operating and service costs. This realization emerged during the review of property tax exemptions. The provincial government could hardly approve legislation or encourage municipalities to enact bylaws that eliminated tax exemptions for various types of properties when it continued to exercise Crown privilege on its own properties. To some extent, however, the provincial government's decision was also part of an effort to appease municipalities in their continued demands for greater provincial transfers in the form of either revenue-sharing or cost-sharing programs.

Reforms to the Revenue-Sharing System
Although there were some minor adjustments to the revenue-sharing system, there were no major reforms. Indeed, the basic form of the revenue-sharing system continued to be essentially as it had been when it was first established in 1978 (SUMA, *Urban Voice* 7, 3 [Apr. 2002]: 1, 3). The only significant change in the intervening years was the level of funds transferred to municipalities annually through the revenue-sharing pools. The downward trend in the level of funds transferred through those pools occurred in two major stages. In the first stage, the Conservative government of Premier Grant Devine froze the escalator index

built in to the revenue-sharing system to ensure that revenues would be adjusted with changes in the level of provincial revenues. Interestingly, it did this after a few years of exceeding the transfers that were warranted pursuant to the escalator index. In the second stage, the New Democratic government of Premier Roy Romanow went a step further by completely disregarding the escalator index and reducing the amount of funds for revenue-sharing (SUMA, *Urban Voice 7*, 5 [July/Aug. 2002]: 5). Both of those governments were trying to reduce the amounts of funds that would be directed to revenue-sharing as part of their efforts to control provincial expenditures pursuant to their respective deficit and debt reduction initiatives.

In an effort to appease municipal officials for the reductions in revenue-sharing, the Romanow government eliminated one provincial levy on the municipalities and modified two other such levies. It eliminated the two-mill hospital levy and imposed a corresponding dollar-for-dollar reduction in provincial transfers to municipalities through the revenue-sharing program. At the same time it also reduced the level of the public health levy and the social assistance levy by a total of $5 million without imposing a corresponding dollar-for-dollar reduction in provincial transfers through the revenue-sharing program. The elimination of the hospital levy and the reduction in the public health and social assistance levies helped to appease municipal officials. However, given that the elimination and reduction of those levies constituted only a fraction of the cuts to revenue-sharing, municipal officials continued to press the provincial government for an increase in transfers through the revenue-sharing pools (ibid.). After those initial cutbacks, no additional money was directed to the revenue-sharing system for several years. Eventually, however, in 2001–2 approximately $10 million was added to the revenue-sharing system for all three major groups of municipalities (i.e., northern, rural, and urban). Despite that additional funding, during the first few years of this century the revenue-sharing fund stands at approximately 50 per cent of what it was when first established. Rather than putting additional money into this system, the provincial government opted to direct some of its financial contributions to municipalities into targeted cost-shared programs and projects. This trend is discussed in greater detail below.

In 2002, provincial and municipal officials were discussing a review of the distribution formula for the revenue-sharing system in light of the relatively low level of funds (ibid.). This occurred after the revenue-sharing system was reformed by splitting the urban revenue fund into two major pools, one for cities and one for towns and villages. This was done to address concerns expressed over the years by the city officials that the funding had been gradually shifted away from the cities and towards the towns and villages. Even with that change considerable disenchantment remained within the urban sector regarding revenue-sharing due to what municipal officials saw as insufficient financial transfers. The cities were so dissatisfied with their level of funding that they advocated scrapping the program altogether and replacing it with an unconditional grant program for infrastructure set at $100 per capita. The cities' proposal was not accepted, in part because there was no agreement on it among two other types of smaller urban municipalities (i.e., towns and villages), which felt that such a funding formula would not be advantageous for them.

In an effort to arrive at some agreement on the issue in the fall of 2002 the provincial government produced an issues and options paper for the stated purpose of entering into discussions with the Saskatchewan Urban Municipalities Association and its members. For comparative purposes, that paper focused on the unconditional grant distribution formulas of Manitoba, New Brunswick, and Nova Scotia, ostensibly because those provinces still provided a significant share of funding for municipalities on an unconditional basis (Saskatchewan, 2002c). Some of the key issues regarding distribution of unconditional grants examined in that paper included: 'potential principles for a distribution formula; whether or not there should be a separate funding pool for cities; whether there should be a minimum grant; and the concept of equalization' (ibid., iv). The paper added that potential principles to consider in developing a new formula include: 'predictability and stability in funding; a simple and transparent distribution formula; fiscal equity; basic or minimum grant; and unconditional versus conditional funding' (ibid.). The paper concluded with a discussion of next steps, which included consultations within the urban municipal sector and negotiations between the provincial government and SUMA to arrive at an agreement. In the event that an agreement could not be reached, there were two basic options—'to continue with the status quo . . . or for the province to unilaterally develop a new distribution formula' (ibid., 18). Negotiations are ongoing and it remains to be seen what, if any, changes will be made to the revenue-sharing system.

Reform to the Provincial-Municipal Cost-Sharing System
The paucity of major innovative reforms has also been evident in the provincial-municipal cost-sharing system. There were what might be described as minor adjustments to the number and nature of, as well as the criteria for, provincial-municipal cost-sharing programs. A major thrust of such adjustment was a reduction in the level of funding for and the number of conditional and unconditional cost-shared programs provided to municipalities. During this period the provincial government was moving deliberately and steadily towards targeted funding for programs, projects, and services that the provincial and federal governments deemed to be of a high priority. At the same time the provincial government also began moving away from universal per capita grants for all municipalities to targeted grants based on the needs of communities according to criteria established either exclusively by the provincial government or jointly by the provincial and federal governments. A notable example of this is the Canada-Saskatchewan Infrastructure program, which targeted approximately $70 million for improvements to water and sewer systems based on pressing needs.

At least two other issues were considered on the financial reform agenda. The proportion of funding for education drawn from the property tax base was one of the main issues examined as part of the municipal reform agenda, but this did not result in any reforms. The central objective was to determine the feasibility of reducing the level of reliance by the education sector on the property tax base (SUMA, SARM, and SSTA, 1991). More specifically, the objective was to reverse the trend of the past few decades that produced a decline in provincial support for education from approximately 60 per cent in previous decades to 40 per cent during the most recent decade. The desirability of reducing the degree of reliance of school boards on the local property tax base was underscored both by the 1997 Reassessment Review Committee (Saskatchewan, 1999b) and the Tax Exemptions Review Committee (Saskatchewan, 1999c), both of which included representatives from the municipal and educational governing authorities as well as from the provincial government. Despite the emerging consensus to reduce the level of reliance by school boards on the property tax system, no major initiatives were undertaken to achieve this. Two major obstacles prevented change in this area— the provincial government's fiscal constraints, and the inability of the municipal governments to provide the province with some assurances that they would not increase their property taxes to the point where they would be using all of the tax room created by the provincial funding for education. This was something that the provincial government deemed potentially problematic in its efforts to reduce the overall level of taxation in Saskatchewan to ensure that the province would not lose ground to other provinces in terms of tax competitiveness. To prevent this, the provincial government decided to provide some ratepayers with a rebate on the education portion of their tax bill rather than giving money directly to educational authorities. This had the additional benefit of providing the provincial government with political credit for the rebate. This is precisely what the provincial government did in a limited way for two years when it implemented the property tax rebate only for the education portion of the assessment on farmland. That rebate program was introduced by the government in its budget for the 2000–1 fiscal year and terminated in the 2002–3 budget (Saskatchewan, 2000g).

Although the rebate program was terminated, the education portion of the property tax moved to the top of the policy agenda when the provincial government announced in the 2003 budget speech the creation of the Commission on Financing K–12 Education to review and make recommendations on the issue by 31 December 2003. The Commission's precise mandate was to review how public education is funded in Saskatchewan and to identify options for change on several critical issues:

- the appropriate balance between provincial and school board contributions;
- the appropriate balance between the use of property taxes and other sources of taxation;
- fairness and equity in financing education among the existing classes of property taxpayers (agricultural, commercial, and residential);
- the wide variation in the fiscal capacity of school divisions to raise tax revenues and the variations in assessment and spending per student among school divisions, including the impact on access to quality education for students; and

- any other issues about financing K–12 education that the government and the Commission agree should be addressed as priority issues (Saskatchewan, 2003b).

The Commission's final report, submitted to the provincial government on 8 January 2004, recommended that there should be a reduction in the level of funding for education from the property tax base, and that $200 million per year in additional provincial funding for education should be derived from a 1 per cent increase in an expanded provincial sales tax that would include snack food and restaurant meals. The ultimate goal is that within five years 80 per cent of K–12 funding will be derived from the general revenue fund and 20 per cent from the property tax base (Saskatchewan, 2004a). The government's initial reaction was that it would take at least two months to study the report and the various issues and options raised therein before it could respond in a more definitive manner on its plans for reforming the funding framework for K–12 education (Saskatchewan, 2004b). This cautious reaction was based largely on two important considerations—raising the provincial sales tax was unacceptable to a substantial proportion of the population and to the official opposition (Saskatchewan Party, 2004), and a substantial portion of the population felt that reliance on the property tax for funding education was acceptable.

Another issue that was explored as part of the financial reform agenda is intermunicipal cost-sharing. A major initiative on the part of the provincial government was to try to increase the degree of equity in cost-sharing for programs, projects, and services among neighbouring municipalities. The most concerted effort for that purpose was the sharing of costs for policing among rural municipalities and villages with populations under 500. To that end a tripartite task force was established in 1999 with representatives from the major types of municipalities and the provincial government. This task force found it difficult to achieve substantial progress on the issue. The lack of progress after nearly three years of deliberations ultimately led SUMA to announce that it would withdraw from the task force (see SUMA, 2002: 1; *Urban Voice* 7, 5 [July/Aug.]: 1). The failure to move forward on this issue is indicative of the challenges that the municipal sector has faced in the past and is likely to continue to face in the future in achieving much progress in the laudable cause of inter-municipal co-operation and co-ordination.

The Jurisdictional Reform Agenda

For most of the recent reform period there had been no major jurisdictional reforms, but during the last five years at least two major sets of such reforms have been implemented. The first of these, enacted in 2001, consisted of a series of amendments to the existing municipal statutes and were designed to empower various types of municipalities in matters related to voluntary amalgamation, discussed earlier, and to increase the scope of the authority and autonomy of municipalities both in managing their own internal organizational affairs and in enacting local regulations. These reforms, introduced in the legislature on 4 May 2001, were embodied in statutory amendments to the existing municipal Acts

(Garcea, 2001). The amendments aimed to accomplish two major goals—the restructuring of the municipal system by removing barriers to voluntary restructuring, and the reconfiguration of the provincial-municipal relationship designed to reduce provincial government involvement in local decision-making. In introducing the changes to the municipal statutes the Minister of Municipal Affairs indicated that the amendments responded to the recommendations of the Municipal-Provincial Roundtable, which had identified statutory barriers to municipal amalgamation on a voluntary basis and helped to clarify 'the provincial-municipal relationship and remove unnecessary provincial intrusion in municipal affairs' (Saskatchewan, news release, 4 May 2001). The amendments to increase the jurisdictional authority of municipal governments for voluntary amalgamation have already been explained in conjunction with structural reforms. Here it remains to explain the amendments to increase the jurisdictional authority of the municipal governments for governance and management.

The package of amendments to the municipal statutory framework introduced on 4 May 2001 contained several key provisions designed to increase the authority and autonomy of municipal governments both for managing their own organizational affairs and for performing their local regulatory functions (Saskatchewan Hansard, 4 May 2001: 934). These included: (a) financial management, (b) taxation and licensing, (c) personnel management, (d) records management, (e) licensing and location of businesses, and (f) local traffic systems. Significant amendments related to financial management included increased authority and autonomy for municipalities in the accounting systems they use, borrowing, capital trust funds, investments, and disposal of municipal property at any price of their choice. Amendments on property assessment included increased authority and autonomy for municipalities in establishing subclasses of property assessments by cities, setting licence fees for direct sellers, and the level of discounts that rural municipalities give on the prompt payment of property taxes. Amendments related to regulatory matters included: (a) regulations related to businesses; (b) regulations pertaining to street closures and traffic control; (c) regulations pertaining to the certification of municipal administrators; and (d) regulations pertaining to conflict of interest rules for council members.

These amendments were particularly important for cities, which found the existing statutory framework much too paternalistic and cumbersome for their purposes. It would not be an exaggeration to say that were it not for the impetus provided by a brief prepared by the City Mayors Group and its representations both to the Task Force on Municipal Legislative Renewal and, more importantly, to the provincial government, this particular set of amendments would have not been introduced. The amendments were an important concession to the cities, which had been seeking separate cities legislation tailored to meet their particular statutory needs. Ultimately, cities saw these amendments as an important step in the right direction but still far short of what they sought in terms of jurisdictional authority and autonomy, and therefore they continued to pressure the provincial government for a separate and more empowering Act tailored specifically to serve their governance and management purposes.

A new Act, designed to increase the jurisdictional authority and autonomy of cities, was passed in 2002 (SUMA, *Urban Voice* 7, 5 [June 2002]: 1). Although the legislation was approved in July it did not come into force until January 2003. The Act constituted a return to the past practice when separate legislation existed for various types of urban municipalities, including cities. The enactment of a separate statute was the product of nearly three years of negotiations between the city mayors and the provincial government. As part of that initiative the city mayors produced both a position paper and the requisite draft legislation. Initially the provincial government wanted to deal with the demands of the city mayors as part of broader and more comprehensive statutory reform based on the work of the Task Force on Municipal Legislative Renewal. This would have entailed some important linkages among the jurisdictional authority, functions, finances, and structures of all municipalities. However, when it became clear that comprehensive reform to make such linkage possible would not occur in the near future, the city mayors, with the help of their provincial municipal association, pressed the provincial government to enact the legislation they had drafted and revised following consultations with provincial officials in 2001.

In response to that pressure, Premier Lorne Calvert initially stated that although he was prepared to introduce the proposed legislation in the spring legislative session of 2002 so that it could be reviewed and debated by the legislature and the public, his government was not prepared to enact it during that particular session. A major consideration for taking that position was that it was unclear whether all other types of municipalities, regardless of their capacity to operate within such a statutory framework, would demand a comparable statutory framework. Shortly thereafter, however, the Premier changed his position and acceded to the demands of the city mayors to enact the Cities Act (Saskatchewan, 2002b). What accounts for the change of position is not perfectly clear. However, undoubtedly the desire to be seen as receptive and responsive in a timely fashion to at least part of the municipal sector was an important consideration. The new Premier recognized that his government had some proverbial bridges to repair in its efforts to build confidence and support within the municipal sector following the rancour that had been generated regarding the restructuring agenda recommended by the Task Force on Municipal Legislative Renewal. Another potentially important consideration was that representatives for other types of municipalities were not eager to adopt comparable legislation until they had seen how it worked for cities (SUMA, *Urban Voice* 7, 5 [July/Aug. 2002]: 1, 3).

The stated purpose of the Act was to enhance the scope of the cities' jurisdictional authority and autonomy. For that purpose the Act was essentially the same as those that had been adopted in Alberta and Ontario in that it included the two innovative statutory conventions contained in the municipal legislation of those provinces—'natural person' powers and areas of jurisdiction. In the case of the former the Act states that 'a city has the capacity and subject to any limitations that may be contained in this or any other Act, the rights, powers and privileges of a natural person' [Part II, section 4(1)]. In the case of areas of jurisdiction the Act contains a relatively long list of what are referred to as areas of 'jurisdiction to enact bylaws'. The list ranges from general areas, such as 'the peace, order, and good government', to relatively specific matters, such as 'wild and domestic animals and matters related to them'. Despite the provision on 'natural person' powers and areas of jurisdiction, the Act makes it clear that although cities are autonomous, they are not sovereign because they remain subordinate to the provincial government and subject to provincial laws. The wording in section 5 of the Act states that cities '(a) are a responsible and accountable level of government within their jurisdiction, being created and empowered by the Province of Saskatchewan; and (b) are subject to provincial laws and to certain limits and restrictions in the provincial interest as set out in this and other Acts' (Saskatchewan, 2002a; Saskatchewan, 2002b). The Act also made it clear that it would not apply automatically to all cities. Each city would have to choose through the adoption of a formal resolution either to operate under the Cities Act or to continue operating under the Urban Municipalities Act. Within one year all Saskatchewan cities had opted for the Cities Act. Shortly after they adopted it the cities began to seek various amendments to it in an effort to add some provisions and refine others in order to maximize clarity and to block potentially problematic loopholes. As had been the case with Alberta's innovative municipal statutory framework, more details were required in the statute than had initially been envisioned. This suggests that a fine balance must be reached between relatively general provisions and detailed provisions in these new Acts. It also suggests that when new statutes are enacted there is likely to be an initial adjustment period and, based on past experience, subsequent readjustments thereafter.

Before the Cities Act was even passed, towns and villages started to consider whether to seek a comparable statutory framework. Shortly after its passage, SUMA established the Towns and Villages Legislative Review Committee to consider whether to amend the existing Urban Municipalities Act or to broaden the application of the new Cities Act to include all types of urban municipalities (SUMA, *Urban Voice* 7, 5 [July/Aug. 2002]: 1, 3). During its deliberations the Committee produced draft legislation that was essentially a hybrid of the extant Urban Municipalities Act and the Cities Act. At the time of writing that Committee continues to work on producing a new Act for towns and villages. If it manages to do so this will be the second statute produced largely by SUMA members to be submitted to the provincial government for formal enactment. However, the implementation of the draft legislation for towns and villages is by no means a foregone conclusion—provincial and municipal representatives have been debating whether there should be a single municipal statute that applies to all urban municipalities, and possibly also to all rural and northern municipalities, or whether entirely different legislation for each of the different orders of municipality should be adopted.

To date, the jurisdictional reforms were implemented in an effort to appease municipal associations. As in other jurisdictions, for most of this period the municipal associations lamented their subordinate constitutional and statutory status vis-à-vis the provincial governments and periodically made demands for improvements in their status. In addition to some form of recognition as an order of government at the constitutional or at least the statutory level, their demands also included an increase in the scope of their jurisdictional authority or autonomy vis-à-vis the provincial government. Again, as in other jurisdictions, the Saskatchewan government was quite reticent most of the time to bow to such demands. It felt that the problem was not that municipal governments did not have the requisite authority and autonomy within the existing statutory framework to perform their functions, but that many of them did not have the requisite organizational capacity in terms of human and financial resources to perform such functions. As well, the provincial government thought that municipal governments were asking for a level of authority and autonomy that in the case of a vast number of them was more than they could use effectively without creating problems for themselves and others. Although the provincial government was reticent to undertake major changes to the balance of jurisdictional authority and autonomy between itself and the municipal governments, particularly in the absence of reforms to other elements of the municipal system, eventually it agreed to some of the demands from various types of municipalities for such changes. It remains to be seen whether it will also accept some of the other outstanding demands for jurisdictional reforms, particularly the demands of the towns and villages for a new and more permissive statute.

THE POLITICS OF MUNICIPAL REFORM

Saskatchewan's municipal reform agenda produced a plethora of political machinations. The bulk of those political machinations were largely intergovernmental in nature, involving the provincial and municipal governments. Members of the general public were generally more likely to react to reforms proposed by provincial and municipal officials than to pressure them for reforms. This was particularly true in cases where the members of the general public felt that their financial interests were likely to be affected. Notable examples of this were the strong and spontaneous grassroots opposition to some business taxation regimes and to the reassessment initiatives during the early to mid-1990s (Hanselman, 2000). A similar type of grassroots resistance was also evident in response to the restructuring proposals of the Task Force on Municipal Legislative Renewal (Garcea, 2001). Although concerns regarding the financial and service implications for ratepayers were a major factor behind the massive mobilization against the Task Force's recommendations on restructuring, it is doubtful that much of that opposition would have materialized had it not been mobilized by elected and appointed municipal officials and their provincial associations, particularly those in the rural municipal sector, who expended vast organizational and personal resources in their efforts to mobilize ratepayers against the proposed structural reforms. Their ability to mobilize opposition to substantial reforms has rendered them a major obstacle to such reforms to date, and is likely to continue to render them so in the near future.

To some extent, however, the provincial government has also been an obstacle to reform because it has been either unwilling or unable to produce the right comprehensive package of reforms that would be attractive to associations of municipalities and municipal officials. Such unwillingness or inability is largely a function of three potential types of losses—fear of losing control over municipalities, fear of losing some of its governance powers, and fear of losing provincial elections.

Conclusions

The foregoing analysis reveals that whereas Saskatchewan's municipal reform agenda over the past 15 years was relatively broad in scope, the reforms actually implemented were relatively limited. This is particularly true of the structural and functional reform agendas, which did not yield any major reforms either to the structure of the municipal system or to the functions that municipal governments perform. By contrast, the financial and jurisdictional agendas yielded several reforms. The most notable of the financial reforms was the modernization of the property assessment system, and the most notable of the jurisdictional reforms were the enactment of the Cities Act and amendments to some of the other municipal statutes designed to empower municipal governments in regulating local affairs and in the management of internal affairs within their institutions.

What the foregoing analysis does not reveal but merits some attention is the effect of the municipal reform processes on the fundamental goals of the overall reform agenda identified in the first section of this chapter (i.e., municipal capacity-building, inter-municipal co-operation and co-ordination, provincial-municipal co-ordination and co-operation, and good municipal governance). Notwithstanding some good efforts and intentions of various provincial and municipal officials to produce and implement reforms that would contribute to those goals, there is little to suggest that they were very successful. This is not to imply that they have had no effect at all, but the reforms have not had either an extensive or a transformative effect. Indeed, even the most generous assessors of the effects of those reforms would be hard-pressed to suggest that they have been extensive or transformative.

This is certainly true in the case of governance capacity. Although the jurisdictional authority and autonomy of municipal governments has been increased somewhat by various reforms, their overall capacity has changed little, if at all. This is as true of the cities, which now operate under the new Cities Act, as it is of other municipalities, which have been operating under a slightly revamped statutory framework. Even in the case of cities now under the new Cities Act, their governance capacity has not increased substantially as was generally believed would be the case with their newly acquired 'natural person' powers and clearly defined areas of jurisdiction. Part of the reason for this is that governance capacity depends as much, if not more, on financial resources as on jurisdictional authority.

Similarly, the reforms have not had a significant effect on inter-municipal co-operation and co-ordination. There is nothing to indicate a substantial increase in inter-municipal initiatives such as joint approaches to programming, administration, and financing or the sharing facilities and equipment. The statutory amendments designed to foster and facilitate both inter-municipal co-operation and co-ordination and voluntary amalgamation have not produced any substantial results. This is also true of provincial-municipal co-operation and co-ordination. The state of such co-operation and co-ordination is not substantially different today from what it was 15 years ago. At most, some of the statutory reforms clarified a few minor jurisdictional issues that impinge on such co-operation and co-ordination. However, no major statutory or organizational framework for provincial-municipal co-operation and co-ordination emerged as a result of the reform initiatives.

Finally, the goal of good municipal governance was not advanced very much as a result of the various reform initiatives. Neither democratic processes and practices nor political accountability within the municipal sector has been improved substantially. By the end of this period, the electoral processes, decision-making processes, and the political accountability systems remained essentially as they had been at the start.

In summary, the municipal reforms during this period were limited both in their scope and in their effect on the overarching goals of reform. The reforms that were implemented amounted to tinkering with various elements of the municipal system, rather than the transformation or reinvention of municipal governance. The tinkering occurred largely because, for better or worse, the vision for the transformation or reinvention of municipal governance in Saskatchewan articulated in the interim and final reports of the Task Force on Municipal Legislative Renewal was rejected by an influential group of elected and appointed municipal officials. Their rejection of this restructuring agenda was rooted largely in what they perceived as the possibility of a significant amalgamation program, to which they were adamantly opposed.

Saskatchewan municipal officials were much more effective in protecting their preferred municipal structural arrangements than their counterparts in Ontario and Quebec largely because of the near-death experience suffered by the Romanow government in the 1999 election, which produced a coalition government between the New Democrats and the Liberals. That experience sapped the Premier and influential members of his cabinet and staff of the resolve to pursue the amalgamation agenda through either the 'directed consultative approach' recommended by the Task Force or by any other means. In short, 'the government blinked' in the face of strong opposition from municipal officials who were much more interested and adept at preserving the status quo than building a new municipal system for the future. Evidently, the government's decision not to press ahead with a restructuring agenda was rooted in part in the broken promise by representatives of the municipal associations to begin exploring options for increased inter-municipal co-operation and even amalgamation where necessary. That was not the first time that representatives of the municipal associations made and broke that promise. One cannot help but wonder how many more times it will be made and broken before any substantial structural change occurs to Saskatchewan's municipal sector.

The prospects for substantial municipal reforms in Saskatchewan in the future are highly contingent on at least three factors. The first is the recognition on the part of a critical mass of municipal officials and members of the general public of the magnitude of social and economics costs of not undertaking some major reforms to the municipal system. Unfortunately, too few people recognize the significant social and economic costs—in the form of lost opportunities—that stem from the nature of the current configuration of the municipal system.

The second factor that could foster substantial reforms in the future is the proper diagnosis of the obstacles to reform. Contrary to what many officials in the municipal sector may think and suggest, the major obstacles to reforming or reinventing Saskatchewan's system of municipal governance have never been the provisions in the statutory framework or the configuration of the financial framework. Instead, the key obstacle has been their strong attachment to the status quo, which has been valued much more than a fundamentally reformed, transformed, or reinvented system of municipal governance. This is particularly true of the basic structural features of the municipal system.

The third factor that could foster substantial reforms in the future is the willingness of the provincial and municipal governments to make substantial compromises in formulating and implementing a comprehensive package of reforms. If recent history is any indication, however, it is highly unlikely that either the municipal or provincial governments will be willing to make the requisite compromises for that purpose. Instead, each level of government is likely to expect the other to accede to their respective demands, while they themselves tend to be inflexible and uncompromising.

There is little to suggest that any of the aforementioned factors for fostering municipal reforms exist today or that they will exist in the near future. Consequently, the prospects for substantial municipal reforms in Saskatchewan are unlikely to be very different in the near future from what they have been in the recent past. This is an ironic and paradoxical situation for a province that for several decades in the post-World War II period prided itself, and deservedly so, for being a courageous and influential leader in designing and implementing innovative governance reforms, many of which were emulated by other provinces (Poel, 1976; Lutz, 1986). In the municipal sector, however, Saskatchewan has never been a courageous leader or even a courageous follower. The precise implications of this for the province in terms of social and economic costs are difficult to calculate but are nonetheless real. This is a view espoused by many practitioners and observers, some of whom have articulated their opinion publicly and others who have articulated it privately to avoid being criticized by influential power brokers within the municipal sector who disagree with them. It is absolutely imperative that provincial and municipal leaders recognize that the economic and social development of Saskatchewan depends in large part on substantial and appropriate municipal reforms as much as, if not more than, it does on some other types of major reforms that are often advocated. Finally, all future reformers would do well to remember a central theme in the report of the Task Force on Municipal Legislative Renewal that municipal restructuring alone is not enough; other major reforms—both to provincial and municipal governance, and possibly also to federal and Aboriginal governance—are needed to create a governance framework that contributes to the province's prosperity and progress.

REFERENCES

Barron, Laurie F., and Joseph Garcea. 1999. *Indian Urban Reserves in Saskatchewan.* Saskatoon: Purich Publishing.

Colligan-Yano, Fiona, and Mervyn Norton. 1996. *The Urban Age: Building a Place for Urban Government in Saskatchewan.* Saskatchewan Urban Municipalities Association. Regina: Century Archive Publishing.

Garcea Joseph. 1997. 'Saskatchewan's Aborted Municipal Service Districts Act (Bill 33): Pegagus or Trojan Horse?', paper presented at the Canadian Political Association annual meeting.

———. 1999. 'Municipal Legislative Renewal in Saskatchewan: Purposes, Politics, and Process', paper presented at the Canadian Political Association annual meeting.

———. 2001. 'Municipal Reform in Saskatchewan 1998–2001: Restructuring the Municipal System and Realigning the Provincial-Municipal Relationship', paper presented at the Canadian Political Association annual meeting.

Hanselmann, Calvin. 2000. 'Agenda Setting Saskatchewan Property Assessment System Reforms, 1987–1995', MA thesis, University of Saskatchewan.

Lutz, James M. 1989. 'Emulations and Policy Adoptions in the Canadian Provinces', *Canadian Journal of Political Science* 22, 1 (Mar. 1989): 147–54.

Morton, Jenni. 1995. *The Building of a Province: The Saskatchewan Association of Rural Municipalities.* Regina: PrintWest.

Poel, Dale. 1976. 'The Diffusion of Legislation among the Canadian Provinces', *Canadian Journal of Political Science* 9 (Mar. 1976): 605–26.

Saskatchewan. 1956. *Royal Commission on Agriculture and Rural Life: Rural Roads and Local Government, A Summary.* Regina: Queen's Printer.

———. 1961. *Continuing Local Government Committee.* Regina: Queen's Printer.

———. 1976. *Report of the Rural Development Advisory Group.* Regina: Queen's Printer.

———. 1980. *Minister's Committee to Review Urban Law.* Regina: Queen's Printer.

———. 1985. *Strategy for the Development of Rural Saskatchewan* (Special Task Force Report).

———. 1986. *Local Government Finance Commission, Final Report.*

———. 1990–2002. Hansard.

———. 1990. Consensus Saskatchewan Committee. *Leading the Way: A Blue Print for Saskatchewan.*

———. 1993a. *Report of the Advisory Committee on Inter-Community Cooperation and Community Quality of Life.*

———. 1993b. *Partnership for Municipal Service Delivery: A Review of Intermunicipal Arrangements in Saskatchewan.*

———. 1993c. *Partnerships for Municipal Service Delivery: Examples of Intermunicipal Approaches in Other Provinces.*

———. 1995a. *Intermunicipal Arrangements in Rural Municipalities.*

———. 1995b. *Review of Emergency and Protective Services.*

———. 1995c. *Provincial Assistance for Local Government Restructuring.*

———. 1995d. *Inter-Community Cooperation Program: Program Guidelines.*

———. 1996a. *Preparing for the New Century: Making Choices for Today and Tomorrow* (Final Report on Public Input), Jan.

———. 1996b. An Act Respecting Service Districts (Bill 33).

———. 1996c. *The Municipal Restructuring Assistance Program.*

———. 1999a. Task Force on Municipal Legislative Renewal. *Municipal Governance for Saskatchewan in the 21st Century: A Discussion Paper.*

———. 1999b. *Phase 1 Report of the 1997 Reassessment Review Committee: Executive Summary.*

————. 1999c. *Final Report of the Property Tax Exemptions Review Committee: Executive Summary for Discussion Purposes.*

————. 2000a. Task Force on Municipal Legislative Renewal. *Municipal Governance for Saskatchewan in the 21st Century: Interim Report.*

————. 2000b.Task Force on Municipal Legislative Renewal. Report of Public Hearings and Submissions on the Interim Report.

————. 2000c. Task Force on Municipal Legislative Renewal. *Municipal Governance for Saskatchewan in the 21st Century: Final Report on the Urban and Rural Municipal Sectors.*

————. 2000d. Task Force on Municipal Legislative Renewal. *Municipal Governance for Saskatchewan in the 21st Century: Final Report on the Northern Municipal Sector.*

————. 2000e. *Updating Municipal-Provincial Roles and Responsibilities: Review of Municipal Functions.*

————. 2000f. Saskatchewan Municipal-Provincial Roundtable. *Impediments to Voluntary Restructuring: A Review of the Legislative and Financial Impediments to Voluntary Restructuring in Saskatchewan.*

————. 2000g. 'A Plan for Growth and Opportunity', Budget Address, 2000.

————. 2002a. *Statutes of Saskatchewan*, 'Cities Act, 2002'.

————. 2002b. 'New Cities Act Introduced', news release, 12 June.

————. 2002c. *Urban Revenue Sharing Distribution: Options Paper.*

————. 2003a. 'Commission on Financing K–12 Education', news release, Learning/Finance 264, 2 May.

————. 2003b. 'Strengthening our K–12 Education System', mimeo.

————. 2004a. Commission on the Financing of Kindergarten to Grade 12 Education. *Finding the Balance* (Final Report).

————. 2004b. 'Government Receives Boughen Commission's Final Report', news release, Learning, 8 Jan.

————, SUMA, and SARM. 1997. *Memorandum of Understanding Project Management Plan.*

Saskatchewan Association of Rural Municipalities (SARM). 1990–2002. *Rural Councillor.*

Saskatchewan Party. 2004. 'NDP Government Should Reject Proposal for $200 Million PST Increase', media release, Learning, 8 Jan.

Saskatchewan Urban Municipalities Association (SUMA). 1995a. SUMA Task Force on Urban Government Renewal, *Renewal in Motion (Mid-Term Report).*

————. 1995b. Task Force on Urban Government Renewal. *Recommendations: The ABC's of Renewal.*

————. 1990–2002. *Urban Voice: The Newsletter of the Saskatchewan Urban Municipalities Association.*

————, Saskatchewan Association of Rural Municipalities, and Saskatchewan School Trustees Association (SUMA, SARM, SSTA). 1991. *Vision 2000: Financing Local Governments and Economic Development in the Year 2000* (Symposium Report).

Smiley, Donald V. 1960. 'Local Autonomy and Central Administrative Control in Saskatchewan', *Canadian Journal of Economics and Political Science* 26, 2: 299–313.

Stabler, Jack, and Rose Olfert. 2000. 'Functional Economic Areas in Saskatchewan: A Framework for Municipal Restructuring', paper commissioned by Saskatchewan Municipal Affairs and Housing.

CHAPTER 5

Municipal Reform in Manitoba: Homogenizing, Empowering, and Marketing Municipal Government

CHRISTOPHER LEO AND MARK PIEL

INTRODUCTION

In Manitoba there are two municipal worlds—Winnipeg and all the other municipalities. Since 1990 both worlds have been subjected to substantial reforms. These changes began in the mid-1990s when the provincial government conducted a review of the municipal legislation that applied to all municipalities other than Winnipeg.

The Municipal Act (1996) outlined the roles, responsibilities, and powers of these municipalities. A year later, the City of Winnipeg hired a consultant to review its operations and recommend changes. The broad principles of these recommendations have since been incorporated into the City of Winnipeg Act. That was only the beginning of statutory reforms related to Winnipeg. In 2002 the province proposed a complete overhaul of the City of Winnipeg Act that brought several important principles from the Municipal Act into Winnipeg's legislation.

This chapter[1] provides an overview and assessment of these reform initiatives, organized into two major sections. The first section deals with reforms that impinged on municipal governance for municipalities other than Winnipeg by focusing on the review of that portion of the municipal system undertaken by a special task force and the resulting reforms embodied in the Municipal Act (1996). The second section is devoted to reforms of Winnipeg's government, focusing on an overview and assessment of Winnipeg's internal review process, the resulting reforms, and the most recent statutory reform proposal, the City of Winnipeg Charter Act (2002).

Along the way, we hope to draw critical attention to the issues that lie at the foundation of municipal reform in Manitoba, which has followed a global trend.

Provincial governments have granted municipalities the powers and responsibilities they have sought for some time in order to adapt to what municipal representatives feel are the pressures of economic globalization.

The granting of these powers and responsibilities has resulted in the institutionalization of market mechanisms and market philosophies in the municipal legislative architecture in Manitoba. Taken on their own, these market-oriented reforms do not constitute a threat to good governance. What will be interesting to see is if, when, and how these philosophies clash with more traditional ideas of what municipal government is all about. The organizational cultures of local government and their bureaucracies, issues of democratic accountability, public and privately funded partnerships, and the ongoing relationship between the province of Manitoba and its municipalities, as well as inter-municipal relations, all are affected by this new legislative regime.

The central theme of this chapter is that the reforms indicate a shift in three directions:

- greater uniformity in the treatment of municipalities by the province;
- increased authority for municipal governments;
- a market model for service delivery.

The move towards greater uniformity is evident both in the reduction in the number of categories of municipalities and in the decision of the New Democratic government to place all municipalities, including Winnipeg, under the authority of the Department of Intergovernmental Affairs. Under the previous Progressive Conservative government, that authority was divided between the Department of Rural Development and the Department of Urban Affairs, which was responsible only for Winnipeg.

However, despite the movement towards greater uniformity in the treatment of municipalities, Winnipeg continues to occupy a unique status in the municipal system and operates under a separate statute substantially different from legislation that applies to other municipalities. Winnipeg's unique status among municipalities is understandable given its dominance in the province's political economy. In 1997 Winnipeg accounted for almost 80 per cent of the province's total economic activity, was home to 65.4 per cent of the province's labour force, and accounted for 65 per cent of the province's retail trade. In 1996, the population of the Winnipeg CMA was nearly 60 per cent of the province's total population.[2]

REFORM INITIATIVES FOR MANITOBA'S MUNICIPAL SYSTEM BEYOND WINNIPEG

Municipal renewal in Manitoba beyond Winnipeg was undertaken under the auspices of a Conservative provincial government through a process of public consultation that lasted two years. In 1993 the Minister of Rural Development appointed a five-member review panel to conduct hearings across the province in order to tap into the concerns of local residents.

A discussion paper distributed the same year to provide a focus for the hearings set out several issues for discussion. Major themes of the paper were municipal service provision, increased autonomy for municipal governments, and the necessity of statute review. Review of legislation was thought important in order to achieve greater co-ordination of service provision among the numerous boards and authorities in municipalities throughout the province. The discussion paper identified the following seven broad 'issue areas' that would serve as the basis for public consultation:

- municipal rights and provincial approvals;
- the structure of municipalities;
- elections and accountability of municipal councils;
- council practices and proceedings;
- municipal finance;
- legal proceedings;
- local service delivery.

While the seven proposed areas of discussion were quite broad, the provincial government specifically requested that the review panel gauge public opinion on municipal service delivery. Not surprisingly, therefore, the majority of recommendations made to the provincial government dealt with service delivery aspects of municipal government.

Although subsequent legislation reflected opinions expressed to the panel, it was not necessarily the public at large that was being heard. Despite the fact that 139 oral and 153 written presentations were made in the fall of 1993, very few private individuals were heard. The panel itself expressed regret at the paucity of participation by private individuals. By contrast municipal politicians, representatives from municipal school boards,[3] and the business community, including the Keystone Agricultural Producers and the Chamber of Commerce, were well represented.

Structural Reforms: Service Delivery and Inter-municipal Co-ordination
It is hardly surprising that the panel concluded that service delivery needed to be better rationalized. The review occurred during a time of fiscal stress. The tax base of many rural municipalities had decreased (Diamant, 1994: 16),[4] and the province's financial plight was such that it could provide no financial assistance. Thus, the panel determined that better co-ordination among municipalities offered a way forward.

The character of the Manitoba municipal system certainly suggested that rationalization held promise. Nearly 300 special-purpose bodies provided local services more or less independently of the 201 Manitoba municipalities beyond the boundaries of Winnipeg, which have a combined population of 440,000 (Manitoba, 1995: vi–vii; Nesbitt, 25 May 1999).[5] That adds up to some 500 separate bodies, all providing local services, but generally operating in isolation from one another, without the benefit of systematic deliberations about the many ways in which the work they do and the problems they face impinge on one another.

The review panel expressed concern over the limited mandates of these boards and commissions and the implications of those mandates for long-term planning. 'Each [special-purpose body] is limited to matters within its specific scope', the panel said in its final report. 'Long-term planning is generally conducted solely within the scope of that entity's authority . . . . There is often no long-term commitment to work with the same partners on a broad range of issues' (Manitoba, 1995: vii).

In line with the well-established municipal tradition of not saying exactly what we mean, for fear that we might be understood, the report studiously avoids the all-but-taboo phrases, 'consolidation of municipalities' and 'integration of service delivery'. Clearly a concern of both the review panel and the provincial government is fragmentation both of municipal jurisdictions and of special-purpose bodies with narrow mandates, fragmentation that may inhibit effective planning and, in some instances, produce inefficiencies.

But discussion of this issue is hampered by the shared resolve of the review panel and the provincial government to avoid anything that smacks of imposition, or, in the words of another commentator, 'the tone of the Municipal Act Review that consolidation should be gently encouraged, but not legislated' (Diamant, 1994: 16). The fortunes of the Conservative provincial government in power at the time were heavily dependent on that minority of Manitobans who live outside Winnipeg and whose local governments were the ones affected by the outcome of the review. The provincial government had every incentive to tread lightly here.

The panel's tone reflects that of the presentations in the hearings, many of which favoured greater integration of municipal services, to the accompaniment of conflicting views as to how this integration and co-ordination would be achieved. Many presenters were of the opinion that forced municipal restructuring was highly undesirable and that, whatever was done, it should be primarily locally driven, not imposed by the provincial government.

Two of the restructuring options discussed were the amalgamation of existing municipalities in order to maximize the level of service delivery over the broadest possible jurisdiction, and the establishment of an upper tier of government to act as a regional authority. Apropos of amalgamation, many submissions to the panel reflected the view that the centralization of service delivery would entail unnecessary bureaucratization. As well, it was argued that the residents of smaller municipalities find it easier to hold politicians and officials accountable. Throughout the hearings the panel was told repeatedly that any moves towards amalgamation would have to be voluntary.

As for the formation of upper-tier governments, the review panel concluded that such reorganization was undesirable, regardless of whether it were locally or centrally initiated. This conclusion revealed the panel members' doubts that the administrative costs of such a reform could be recouped, especially considering rural and small-town Manitoba's low population density and small tax base. It also reflected concerns, expressed at the hearings, that an upper tier would undermine the authority of existing municipal governments (Manitoba, 1995: ix).[6] Thus, the panel recommended that under no circumstances should a regional or county system of municipal government be considered for the province.

This recommendation carries on a well-established Manitoba tradition. Not long after the founding of the province an attempt was made to transplant Ontario's county system, but those arrangements, as Tindal and Tindal (1995: 34) observe, 'proved to be ineffective . . . because of the large areas covered, the often sparse and scattered population, and the local objections to a two-tier system.' The newly created province was not conducive to a regional government system. Years later the 1964 Michener Commission proposed a regional government scheme that was rejected (Manitoba, 1964).[7]

In short, proposals for two-tier systems of municipal government have always fared badly in Manitoba outside Winnipeg and provincial government did nothing in 1996 to change that tradition. As for consolidation of municipalities and integration of service delivery, presenters to the review panel, the panel itself, and the provincial government all seemed to view such changes as necessary. However, as we show below, the Manitoba authorities' concept of how to achieve those objectives rests on market principles rather than on conventional notions of consolidation and integration.

One of the more striking changes emanating from the review process concerned the classification of municipalities. Under the old legislation there were five municipal classifications—cities, towns, villages, rural municipalities, and local government districts—each having specific criteria for their formation based on the amount of assessable property and population. Under the new legislation, there are only two types of municipalities; urban and rural,[8] and the basis for categorizing them has been simplified. Moreover, total property assessment has been dropped as a criterion for classification purposes.

The distinction between urban and rural municipalities is based on population and population density, with municipalities that have more than 1,000 residents and a population of at least 400 per square kilometre eligible for city status. Unlike the property assessment benchmark, population densities help determine what level of service provision is needed and feasible for a given area and to what degree service co-ordination between municipalities is necessary and appropriate (Municipal Act, 1996, part 2, division 1, s. 4[2]).

The panel saw the existence of five separate categories of municipalities, with different governing arrangements for each, as an obstacle to co-ordination among neighbouring municipalities and an invitation to parochialism. The simplification of categories was therefore seen, in part, as a way of combatting parochialism and of enhancing the ability of municipalities to co-operate in promoting economic development. Or, to put it more plainly, it was helping to create favourable conditions for municipal consolidation and integration of service delivery without imposing it.

The other notable change recommended by the panel and incorporated into legislation was the dissolution of unincorporated village districts, with a new classification provided in their place: local urban districts. This designation is reserved for semi-urban growth within an existing rural municipality, and it allows the residents in the semi-urban area to establish a committee through election that represents their interests in the larger municipality. In order to bring the two bodies together, the head of the elected committee would be an appointed councillor from the greater municipality.

Jurisdictional Reforms

The government of Alberta caused a buzz in municipal circles by granting 'natural person' powers to its municipalities. Manitoba opted to grant corporate powers to its municipalities, not including Winnipeg (Municipal Act, 1996, Part 8, ss. 250–61), which sounds a great deal like the power municipalities have always had. Does that mean, as has been suggested, that Alberta, in a bold stroke, expanded the autonomy of local government, while Manitoba proceeded more cautiously?

Our position is that both the devil and the angels are in the detail, and that the labels 'natural person powers' and 'corporate powers' tell us very little about what is actually going on. Manitoba municipal officials say that they considered Alberta's approach and rejected it after concluding that, far from being too radical, it was quite simply inappropriate (Nesbitt, 17 May 1999). A number of considerations speak for their argument.

First, since municipalities more nearly resemble corporations than individuals, 'corporate powers' can be seen as providing a more straightforward path than 'person powers' towards the objective of expanded powers. Second, 'natural person' powers are expressed primarily through the language of rights, powers, and privileges, with little mention of limitations, obligations, and duties. Some of the broad categories that could be described as 'natural person' powers include: (1) contractual powers; (2) commercial powers; (3) pursuit of commerce; (4) rights of expression and philanthropy, such as selling services, goods, or land below market value; and (5) general powers, such as the right to sue or be sued, including the ability to sue and be sued for more 'personal torts' like defamation of character. By the same token, council bylaws are necessarily limited to municipal purposes, whereas 'natural person' powers are in no way subject to such limitations. Finally, individuals do not have the ability to pass legislation or collect taxes, activities of obvious importance for municipal jurisdictions.

In short, once 'natural person' powers have been granted a great deal of further legislation is needed to clarify what that means for municipalities, and this clarifying legislation, together with court decisions, determines what the original grant of power actually means. The Manitoba government has apparently concluded that the Alberta approach is as likely in practice to fatten the bank accounts of lawyers as it is to enhance the powers of municipalities. Undoubtedly Alberta authorities could respond to this argument by pointing out that municipalities, in reality, are neither persons nor corporations, and that Manitoba, too, has had to specify in legislation what the expanded powers actually consist of. This argument will not be settled by reference to the general strengths and weaknesses of competing legal concepts, and likely will persist for some time.

Two changes are at the heart of Manitoba's initiative for increasing the autonomy and powers of municipal governments. The first is the elimination of a great deal of detail from the Municipal Act. A good way of summarizing the magnitude of that change is to observe that the 589 pages of the legislation in force before the revisions have been reduced to 236. Much of that reduction takes the form of the removal of specific instructions to municipal governments, telling them not only what to do, but also specifying the circumstances in which they may do it and instructing them as to how to do it. The practical effect of such a welter of detail is often that on those rare occasions when municipal councillors work up the courage to propose an imaginative solution to a local problem the municipal solicitor will tell them they lack the authority to carry out the proposal. This can have the pernicious effect of discouraging initiative and blocking thoughtful, imaginative action. Therefore, part of the answer to the dispute over the relative merits of 'natural person' powers and corporate powers will lie in the answer, some years hence, to the question: In which province are local councils in a better position to propose a novel solution to a problem without a fearful glance in the direction of the solicitor? It will be some time before anyone can guess at the answer. The second part of Manitoba's program for freeing municipal councils from constraints is in fact found in the section on corporate powers, and takes the form of a grant of powers designed to encourage market-oriented solutions to problems of service delivery. This is discussed below.

The revised Municipal Act grants municipalities the authority to enter, by contract, into agreements with one another, within the province; with municipalities outside of Manitoba; with a person, the federal government, or one of its agencies; with the provincial government or one of its agencies; with a local authority; or with an Indian band. It also confers the ability to act as commercial entities, supplying services to one another by mutual agreement (Municipal Act, 1996, s. 250[2]), and allows municipalities to provide services to other municipalities in the province by mutual agreement. There are no restrictions on which services fall under this statute, with the exception of policing (Municipal Act, 1996, s. 271).

These changes reflect the spirit of public choice theory. The legislation recognizes that some municipalities are able to develop and subsequently provide services to other municipalities in a market-style exchange. The province anticipated that corporate optimizing of self-interest would promote rationalization of service production with attention to economies, efficiencies, and effectiveness. This logic permitted the provincial government to entertain the seemingly implausible expectation that it could induce integration of municipal services and inter-municipal co-operation without imposing it. This logic is based in neo-classical economic theory where the spontaneous workings of the marketplace achieve a natural equilibrium in which services may be provided to the point of greatest satisfaction for consumers. The end result of such a system may be the centralization of certain services in certain municipalities, agencies, or with other levels of government. If results are true to theory, the benefits of municipal consolidation, or the creation of upper-tier governments, will be realized without the mandatory provisions that were repeatedly rejected in hearings by the review panel and by the government.

Financial Reforms

In conferring the right to enter into contracts, the provincial government encourages municipalities to find innovative ways of financing joint municipal ventures in what the province cautiously hopes will be an era of municipal enterprise and co-operation. A similar intention underlies a provision that allows municipalities to make loans instead of being limited to the provision of grants (Municipal Act, 1996, part 6, division 3, s. 180[1]b). The new legislation brings the world of market discipline to municipalities by encouraging them to earn returns on their loans. In effect, the legislation encourages municipalities to act as individuals in the market as opposed to playing a philanthropic role. Perhaps a greater indication of the market orientation of the Act can be found in the revisions made to investments. Municipalities covered by the Act are now able to form investment pools with one another and the scope of where they can invest funds has been broadened (Municipal Act, 1996, part 6, division 3, s. 181[2]a–g).

While greatly increasing municipalities' freedom of action in financial matters, the Act also requires them to seek approval from the province before running an operating deficit and borrowing over a set debt limit. Municipalities are also required to seek provincial approval if they wish to spend funds from a general reserve or surplus in excess of a set formula. But the common theme of both the provisions for entering into contracts and the financial reforms is the creation of greater municipal freedom to act and co-operate in a quasi-market environment.

Municipal Organizational and Management Frameworks

One of the major thrusts of the reforms embodied in the Municipal Act of 1996 is the expanded authority of municipalities to adopt their own administrative and political structures and manage their internal affairs. Under the 1996 legislation, municipal councils must appoint a chief administrative officer (CAO) to head the administration and must appoint council committees, but are otherwise free to organize the business of their municipalities as they see fit. Specifically, the legislative provisions are that each municipality appoint a CAO (formerly known as secretary-treasurer) to head the administration and implement policy set by council; that the organizational bylaws of the municipality provide for the establishment of council committees along with other bodies of the council; and that their duties and functions be fully outlined, along with the manner in which the representatives to these bodies are to be appointed (Municipal Act, 1996, s. 148[2]).

These changes address a particularly important aspect of the problem of excessive detail in municipal legislation. As we have seen, it has long been a common feature of municipal acts and city charters that they spell out a great deal of detail—for example, the names and duties of council committees and the job descriptions of senior officials. The apparent assumption is that, although provincial governments can trust local politicians to manage municipalities, they cannot be trusted to figure out how best to do it. The practical result, insofar as it affects council appointments, may be that city councillors or the mayor, wishing to implement a policy for a perceived need, but which can best be accomplished with the help of some administrative reorganization, find themselves thwarted on learning that the municipal act or city charter does not give them the authority to proceed with their plans.

Prairie provincial governments have been somewhat less sluggish than many other provincial governments in understanding that responsibility is meaningful only when it is accompanied by authority. Thus, the commissioner system of government, variations of which were found only in major cities in Alberta, Saskatchewan, and the City of Winnipeg in Manitoba, have long given city council the authority to vary council committee and administrative assignments. The 1996 legislation brings the councils of Manitoba's rural areas, towns, and smaller cities in line with this tradition.

Another feature of the Act deals with the contentious issue of who is eligible for election to council. Two of the review panel's recommendations were that there should be restrictions on seasonal residents running for council and that ward boundaries should be 'determined by permanent population, not a balance of permanent and seasonal population.' The panel added: 'This change means that permanent residents may "control" some, but not all wards' (Manitoba, 1995: xiv). The recommendations were motivated by the predominance of summer residents in many southern Manitoba communities. The provincial government resolved this issue in favour of temporary residents. The Act was amended to allow *electors* (residents or property owners) to run for public office. The section of the Municipal Act dealing with criteria for ward boundaries in effect rejects the review panel's recommendations by making no reference to permanent and temporary residents (Municipal Act, 1996, part 3, division 2, s. 88).

AN ASSESSMENT OF MUNICIPAL REFORM INITIATIVES BEYOND WINNIPEG

The changes to the Municipal Act have an unassuming look that is characteristic of Manitoba, and that can be deceptive. At first glance, the idea that a reduction in the number of categories of municipalities will lead municipalities to undertake integration of service delivery on their own initiative sounds conservative and unduly optimistic. Likewise, the decision to refrain from granting 'natural person' powers, as Alberta did, seems to be the cautious course.

However, as we have seen, the decision not to follow Alberta's lead was not based on a desire to be more cautious. Indeed, Manitoba's unpretentious legislation could yet prove both more thoroughgoing and less troublesome than Alberta's more flamboyant initiative. Similarly, the authority to enter into contracts with other service providers does in fact provide the necessary incentive to look for more effi- cient and effective service-delivery options. The fact that this approach eschews traditional bureaucratic methods of service integration in favour of market mech- anisms is reflective both of the ideology of the provincial government that was in power and of trends across North America and around the world.

Supporters of this approach argue that a system of service competition between municipalities allows citizens to enjoy a highly pragmatic form of democracy— which entails choice that also fulfills the requirements of efficiency and accounta- bility. With such a system in place citizen action is not confined to a periodic trip to the polls to determine which candidates will comprise the council. Instead, citizens can 'vote with their feet' and take up residence in those municipalities that offer the lowest tax revenues, the best level of services, or whatever mix of services, taxes, and amenities they prefer.

This line of reasoning overlooks the fact that not all citizens are equally mobile, resulting in advantages only to those with the means to engage in the 'democratic' act of moving. The results of such 'democracy' often come in the form of spatial segregation. Those who cannot afford to move from their present surroundings are trapped in declining communities while those of greater means escape to more favoured areas.

While certainly favouring residents with a high level of income, such a system is also geared towards the highly mobile nature of capital in a globalized world economy, with municipalities competing with one another in developing services that can then be sold in the inter-municipal marketplace. This leads to competition between municipalities over external capital investment. Those municipalities that can stay 'lean and mean'—that is, lower taxes and provide efficient service delivery—stand a better chance of luring investment to their jurisdictions (Peterson, 1981). The upshot of such activity is the increase in local employment levels, commercial trade, and tax revenues.

However, those municipalities left with lower-income residents, and the attendant tax burdens in such areas as welfare, education, and policing, will not be in a good position to compete in a market environment, and many of their residents will not be in a position to vote with their feet. If this is the planning that the review panel found to be lacking under the old system, it is planning in a questionable sense. It is the sort of planning that would not prevent exurban municipalities from growing at the expense of a central city, while the inner city decays. Likewise, it would not ensure environmentally sound growth, nor would it provide equal educational opportunity for all.

It would not prevent the growth of poverty and social isolation in municipalities with relatively weak tax bases, or the development of a jobs-housing mismatch as low-wage jobs relocate from lower-income communities to communities where affordable housing is excluded by zoning and land-use regulations. It would guarantee coherent transportation systems across municipal boundaries only in the unlikely event that neighbouring municipalities always agree on appropriate transportation priorities (see Leo et al., 1998; Downs, 1994; Orfield, 1997).

In short, it is a market model, with both the strengths and weaknesses that such a model entails. On one hand the province grants constituents the wish of not having to deal with an official regional body, thereby satisfying legitimate concerns over the potential loss of accountability, but the process decided upon threatens to undermine democratic accountability in planning by throwing such matters over to the market.

The practical effects of these changes to date have been mixed. While larger municipalities have quickly adapted to new responsibilities that have come their way, smaller communities are struggling with their enhanced autonomy (Nesbitt, 26 Apr. 1999). The end result of such growing pains could be wider municipal consolidation between smaller communities in order to address the uncertainty local representatives may have in working with this new legislation, but only if it is in the interest of all communities concerned.

The provincial government did attempt to help communities that are struggling under the new legislation. The Department of Rural Development conducted educational seminars for municipal representatives in order to illustrate the enabling nature of the Act, and produced a procedural handbook to accompany such seminars. Despite the helping hand of the provincial government and civil service, the continued well-being of smaller municipalities will depend ultimately on their ability to behave in an entrepreneurial manner.

REFORM INITIATIVES FOR WINNIPEG'S MUNICIPAL SYSTEM

The Cuff Report and Structural Reform in the 1990s

Superficially, the changes in the City of Winnipeg Act (1998) were very different from those to the Municipal Act (1996). In contrast to the focus in the Municipal Act on the powers of local government, the focus in Winnipeg was on internal administrative and political reorganization. However, if we look at the changes in terms of objectives instead of procedures, similarities appear. In both cases, the intention is to achieve a government that is leaner and more oriented to market mechanisms.

Unicity, the amalgamated government of what in 1972 was Winnipeg's entire metropolitan area, was intended originally to model parliamentary-style democracy at the local level. Those intentions have long since eroded and even the name Unicity is falling into disuse. The idea of having the council elect the mayor was abandoned early on; resident advisory groups, intended as agents of neighbourhood democracy, have not remotely lived up to expectations and have never played more than a minor role; and a council of 50 members has dwindled to 15.

That much is history. The 1998 round of reforms is best understood by looking at the document, *Reshaping Our Civic Government*, adopted by city council in March 1997 (Winnipeg, 1997). The document belatedly empowered Mayor Susan Thompson, who had been swept into office in 1992 on the one-word slogan 'Change', promising a hard-nosed, cost-cutting, businesslike approach to government. She had been repeatedly thwarted in her attempts to carry out her planned reforms, but was nevertheless re-elected in 1995.

After her second election she gave up her long-cherished notion that a businesslike mayor should abstain from politics. With this transformation she developed an effective, if strong and widely resented, leadership style. The Cuff Report (George B. Cuff and Associates, 1997), a commitment to 'affordable government', marks the most significant point in her second term.

Reshaping Our Civic Government committed the city to a list of initiatives designed to reduce the size of the civic administration. The initiatives would build on the variety of contracting-out schemes that were already underway—e.g., park-mowing, transit for disabled people, and refuse collection—through privatization and alternative forms of service delivery. This set of initiatives lies at the heart of the Cuff round of reforms. The similarity between those initiatives and the market-oriented rationalization of municipal services aimed at by the 1996

Municipal Act affecting the rest of Manitoba reveals that the intentions underlying both sets of reforms are fundamentally the same.

Not surprisingly, the Board of Commissioners and the municipal public service were not enthusiastic about the contemplated reduction in the municipal public service. Thus, with the help of the Cuff Report, which spelled out the political and administrative implications of the new policies (ibid., 9), Mayor Thompson and her newly compliant council identified the Board as the main obstacle. Its elimination, and replacement by a single chief administrative officer, became the heart of the administrative reform program. Accompanying this change was a major reorganization of the administration and of the council committee structure, actions council had the authority to take on its own. These changes were accomplished with the help of golden handshakes for the Board of Commissioners and were followed by a thoroughgoing shakeup in the ranks of the public service, together with corresponding changes in the council committee system.

Under the new system, the mayor became arguably the most powerful municipal executive officer in Canada. The mayor chairs the Executive Policy Committee (EPC), the equivalent of a cabinet, and appoints its members, four of whom she simultaneously appoints as chairs of the standing committees. The mayor also has the power to suspend the CAO for up to three days, by which time the EPC must extend the suspension for 30 days, reinstate the CAO, or recommend dismissal to council. Council continued to have 15 members, elected by wards, and the terms of council and the mayor were extended from three to four years. Council has the power to appoint members of standing committees, not including the chairs. It decides how many members the EPC will have, up to a maximum of seven.

All of these changes help to ensure the accountability of the administration to council, and especially to the mayor and the EPC. However, as has been the case since the first flush of enthusiasm over Unicity died, this enthusiasm for political control and administrative potency is not matched by a similarly strong commitment to effective representation of the public in political decision-making.

Capping a long succession of reductions in the size of council—each one of which necessarily increased the cost of campaigns and the numbers that each councillor must represent[9]—the latest legislation gives council the power to abolish Community Committees. These committees of council, which were one of the more successful parts of the Unicity concept, comprise, respectively, the councillors from each of Winnipeg's five communities. The Community Committees are the first political forum for deliberation on such local issues as subdivision and demolition approvals, rezoning, snow removal issues, parking issues, construction and maintenance of recreation facilities, and so forth. These committees have been lively forums for debate, in noisy meetings that sometimes extended far into the night, whenever contentious issues arose. It is their duty to produce recommendations to Council, and the recommendations have been influential. Council has generally been reluctant to overturn a Community Committee recommendation, unless it was felt that pressing city-wide concerns justified overriding the local community's expressed will. In the original Unicity legislation, there were 13 Community Committees. As the size of council dwindled, the committees likewise dwindled to five, and now they could disappear. The replacement of Susan Thompson by Glen Murray makes their abolition appear less likely for the moment, but the legislative provision remains on the books.

The City of Winnipeg Charter Act (2002)

The 1998 revisions of the City of Winnipeg Act were legislated in the twilight of Progressive Conservative government in Manitoba. In 2002 the provincial New Democrats, who had won power in 1999, introduced legislation that provided Winnipeg with a new charter in January 2003. While the city has had its own charter since 1972, which granted Council many powers that now exist in the Municipal Act (1996), the latest effort by the provincial government sought to modernize many aspects of the old Unicity Act.

Winnipeg's Mayor Glen Murray, as mayor of one of Canada's five self-designated 'hub cities',[10] has been a vocal advocate for substantial increases in the power and independence of the governments of major cities. Murray called the new city charter an acknowledgement on the part of the province of the responsibility and accountability of Winnipeg's local government (Manitoba, 2002). Murray's comments implicitly place the changes in Winnipeg in a national and international perspective. His interest is in comparing Winnipeg with other cities in North America and around the world, and with trying to ensure that the city remains competitive, up-to-date, and if possible a leader in that arena.

In these pages, we are concerned with how the Winnipeg reforms look in a Manitoba context. For those purposes, the significance of the 2002 legislation is best understood by comparing it with the 1996 reforms affecting other municipalities in Manitoba, because both reforms focused on changes in the powers and procedures of local government, while the 1998 reforms to the City of Winnipeg Act concentrated on internal government structures. In undertaking a comparison of the 2002 reforms with those of 1996, the most significant features of the 2002 legislation were:

- a significant expansion of the city's powers to act independent of provincial control;
- provisions to increase the city's ability to buy and sell goods and services in innovative ways;
- authorization to undertake tax increment financing;
- measures billed as mandating an increase in the city government's accountability to the public.

We begin, however, by contrasting Manitoba's approach to metropolitan governance with approaches taken elsewhere in Canada.

Metropolitan Governance

The Unicity reforms of 1972 were revolutionary by Canadian municipal standards, but they were Manitoba's last revolutionary venture. Despite frequent revisions of the City of Winnipeg Act since then, there has been no far-reaching reform of the powers delegated to the city, nor a shift in municipal boundaries. Unlike Ontario, which undertook some major initiatives to 'disentangle' provincial and municipal functions and to restructure municipalities, Manitoba has not undertaken any such reform initiatives. Considering the contrast between the prudence and 'wait and see' attitude of the Manitoba Progressive Conservatives and the ideologically aggressive attitude of the neighbouring PC government then led by Mike Harris, this is hardly surprising.

The reluctance of the province to wade into deep political waters is also evident in the contrast between a number of major municipal amalgamations in metropolitan areas across the country, on one hand, and the Manitoba government's unwillingness in recent years to pursue amalgamation within the Winnipeg metropolitan region, on the other. The provincial government's efforts to reform the governance of the metropolitan area have eschewed substance in favour of appearances, abstaining not only from amalgamations but from any other actions to address regional growth issues in a significant way.

The province established a Capital Region Committee in 1989 to address regional issues affecting Winnipeg and 15 surrounding municipal jurisdictions. Each municipality is allowed one member on the committee. Thus, one person represents more than 600,000 citizens and the other 15 represent an average of about 5,000 each. Many of the 15 fringe municipalities have an incentive to build their own tax revenues through low-density urban development with minimal service levels, resulting in a very competitive tax rate. Under those circumstances, the committee of 16 will not meaningfully control exurban growth.

The highly circumscribed functions and status of the committee have been enough of an embarrassment to motivate both the previous and the current provincial governments to commission investigations into the state of regional governance. So far, however, successive governments have proved unwilling to take regional governance beyond exhortations to the 16 municipalities to co-operate, while commissioning two major investigations of the problem, the Scarth Report of 1999 and the Thomas Report of 2003 (Manitoba, 1999, 2003b).

The Scarth Report produced draft legislation that was supposed to ease obstacles to inter-municipal co-operation, but did not address problems of urban growth and was not acted upon by the provincial government. The much more thorough Thomas Report called for more meaningful regulation of metropolitan growth through provincial action, as well a program of tax-sharing in return for service-sharing, but, at this writing, the provincial government has not indicated what if any action it will take in response to these recommendations. In short, since Unicity, the Manitoba approach to metropolitan governance has been cautious almost to the point of invisibility, a marked contrast to its willingness, in both 1998 and 2002, to take serious action on the governance of the City of Winnipeg.

Spheres of Jurisdiction and 'Natural Person' Powers in Winnipeg

The current provincial government has apparently reversed the previous government's stance on the question of 'natural person' powers versus corporate powers (s. 1.4), but a closer examination suggests that, in fact, corporate powers are being granted. In the proposed City of Winnipeg Charter Act the large numbers of detailed grants of power that specify not only what powers the city has, but also how they may be wielded (ss. 1.4 and 1.7) are consolidated into 14 broad categories of powers. The 14 are:

- public convenience
- health, safety, and well-being
- activities in public places
- streets
- activities of businesses
- buildings, equipment, and materials
- floodway and floodway fringe areas

- waterways
- water
- waste
- public transportation
- ambulance services
- fire protection
- police

In the previous Act, the city had only those powers that were explicitly granted and process clauses specified exactly how these powers might be wielded. Such powers were so widely scattered throughout the Act that only a lawyer practised in municipal law could venture a meaningful interpretation. In the new legislation, everyday government actions such as joining an organization of municipalities, passing regulations, requiring licences, and taking enforcement action are permitted, provided they are taken in pursuit of the specified powers. For a city council accustomed to deferring routinely to the solicitor and going on bended knee to the provincial government, it has a dizzying potential for power, but whether it consists of 'natural person' powers is another question.

A section entitled 'Natural Person Powers', located at the beginning of the Act, states: 'The city has the capacity, rights, powers, and privileges of a natural person for the purpose of exercising its authority under this or any other Act' (Manitoba, 2003a). But that is the only mention of 'natural person' powers in the Act, while 22 sections (202–23) are devoted to corporate powers.

It seems likely, therefore, that when the dust raised by the current round of grants of 'natural person' powers to Canadian municipalities has settled, we will conclude that the term contains more politics and public relations than legal substance. Moreover, the excision of 275 pages of restrictions in the City of Winnipeg Act still leaves the Charter Act a weighty 328 pages, and Part 5, which is devoted to powers, contains many sections setting out qualifications on the powers granted.

Nevertheless, early indications are that the City of Winnipeg will enjoy significantly more authority than it has in the past and, even if there are no layoffs in the solicitor's department, perhaps the solicitors will be able to say 'yes' more often than they have in the past to queries from city councillors regarding whether the city has the power to undertake various innovative initiatives. Consequently, city council may be in a position to respond more meaningfully to the preferences of its constituents and to the needs of the city.

Procurement, Provision, and Inter-municipal Co-operation in Winnipeg City-Region

Like the Municipal Act of 1996, the City of Winnipeg Charter Act confers broad powers on the city to procure and supply goods, to enter into agreements 'with the

Government of Manitoba or the Government of Canada, or an agency of either of those governments, with a [Indian] band, . . . a school authority or another municipality either in Manitoba or in any other province, or with any person . . .' (s. 211), and to establish special service units 'to provide a commodity or service within or outside the city' (s. 215[1]). The arguments favouring the conferral of these powers are the same as those set out in section 1.5.

These provisions make it clear that some of the principles of municipal governance established in 1996 by a Progressive Conservative government are being carried forward by the current NDP government. In other respects, however, the legislation covering the City of Winnipeg breaks new ground.

Tax Increment Financing in Winnipeg

The Charter Act contains provisions that would make Winnipeg the first city in Canada authorized to adopt tax increment financing (TIF), a financial tool that has been in use in a number of American cities for some time.[11] The proposed city charter grants the City of Winnipeg the right to use TIF in order to raise funds for urban development or infrastructure projects (City of Winnipeg Charter Act, 2003, s. 222). The precise conditions of TIF programs differ from municipality to municipality, but they do share some things in common. TIF is an effort to ensure that the benefits of new development accrue to the area in which the development took place.

In effect, what is created under TIF is a revenue shelter for a geographical area within a city's limits. Property values are first assessed in the area, and then those values are frozen. Increases in tax revenue due to investment and development in the area are then channelled into a reserve fund to pay for future infrastructure projects or development subsidies in that district. Man writes: 'The creation of a TIF district assures private investors that their property taxes are used to pay for infrastructure needs and development expenditures in the district which directly benefit their businesses, rather than to pay for the general cost of local government services. In the absence of TIF, these costs would be borne by those investors' (Johnson and Man, 2001: 1151).

There are drawbacks to such a program of development financing. Should the tax revenue from development projects fall short of initial estimates, the city will have to finance the project from general tax funds, creating a 'heads-I-win-tails-you-lose' situation in which the beneficiaries of the development program get help from the rest of the city in dealing with costs, but do not have to share benefits. TIF can be used to finance infrastructure, but insofar as the benefits accrue to private investors, it may actually be little more than another subsidy 'shell game'. More positively, at its best, TIF can serve as a viable way of financing projects in inner-city redevelopment, urban revitalization, affordable housing, or other worthy projects the funding of which might otherwise prove difficult or impossible.

Increased Accountability in Winnipeg?

The City of Winnipeg Charter Act also contains some provisions designed to enhance accountability in city governance. One of the more democratically friendly aspects of the old Unicity Act was the number of individual wards that existed in the city. The numerous wards were small enough that the cost of election campaigns would not prohibit citizens from running for office. Nonetheless, critics argued that the numerous wards fostered parochialism within city limits and, axiomatically, that larger and fewer wards could ensure attention to the interests of the city as a whole.

This argument won the day, as evidenced by the progressive shrinking of council numbers, but there is little evidence to suggest that larger wards have led to a more avid pursuit of the common interest, whatever that may be. At the same time, reduced turnover rates on council do suggest that higher campaign costs and the increased salaries and administrative allowances that have come with larger wards have had the effect of entrenching incumbents more deeply than ever.

Amendments to the old Unicity Act eventually limited the number of wards in the city to 15. One of the benefits claimed for the new Charter Act is increased accountability, but this benefit may prove to be more apparent than real. The Act empowers the city to increase the number of wards by passing a bylaw independent of provincial approval (City of Winnipeg Charter Act, 2003, s. 17[1]). It is a certainty that the number of wards would never grow from the current 15 to 50, as was the case in 1972. Further, it is unlikely that council will agree to increase the number of wards beyond the current 15 because of the expense of additional council salaries and the possible jeopardy to the jobs of incumbents. In short, while council has the ability to strengthen representative democracy in Winnipeg under the new Act, it is unlikely to happen.

Another alleged accountability measure in the Act gives council the right to appoint citizens to various committees, theoretically integrating the interest of civil society actors and local government and making the latter responsive to the needs of the former (City of Winnipeg Charter Act, 2003, s. 83[2]). As good as that sounds, it is something other than democratic accountability. Since civil society is already represented on council through a mechanism called majority rule, it makes less sense to think of the appointment of extra members to council committees as an accountability measure than as a way for council to draw on additional sources of advice *at the expense to accountability* by providing double representation for those elements of society represented through the appointed positions. The most curious item in the list of alleged accountability measures is one allowing council, in the words of a government press release, 'to identify those matters it thinks are of such importance that more than the normal 50 per cent majority vote of Council is required'. Here, too, it is difficult to see how the entrenchment of questions beyond the reach of majority rule can reasonably be regarded as an accountability measure. Two other provisions, somewhat more likely to have a positive impact in the promotion of democratic governance, are one allowing council to adopt a code of conduct and one extending the jurisdiction of the provincial ombudsman to municipal government.

CONCLUSION

Manitoba is not always well governed, but, as a rule, it is not badly governed.

Long-time observers of provincial and local politics may be heard to use such terms as 'complacency' or 'sluggishness' in characterizing the provincial or a local government's stance on one issue or another, but 'chaos' and 'upheaval' are absent from the Manitoba political vocabulary, and change, while generally cautious, has been real and substantial.

In municipal governance, Manitoba has kept pace with developments elsewhere in Canada and the world, simplifying, clarifying, and paring down government, making some modest moves towards greater local autonomy, and adapting market principles to the process of governance. At the same time, for better or worse, it has avoided the upheavals of forced amalgamations and abrupt, drastic reassign-ment of responsibilities and costs from one level of government to another.

We return, then, to the themes with which we began. Despite the complications and complexities that have come with three substantial rewrites of municipal legislation in a mere seven years, the following characteristics stand out:

- greater uniformity in the treatment of municipalities by the province;
- increased authority for municipal government;
- a market model for service delivery.

Greater Uniformity

The Scarth Report (Manitoba, 1999: 51) correctly identified a tale of two types of cities in Manitoba, even if it did not contribute in a substantial way to legislative reform. In the mid-1990s the municipal world in Manitoba was one of two soli-tudes, in the report's telling phrase. Not only was the governance of Winnipeg completely different from that of the rest of Manitoba, but the communities outside Winnipeg were governed by five distinct sets of rules. Since then, there has been much convergence.

As a result of the Acts of 1996, 1998, and 2003, the number of categories of municipalities outside Winnipeg has been reduced from five to two, drastically reducing the variety of governing arrangements to be found there.

In Winnipeg, much has changed, including the abolition of the Board of Commissioners; their replacement by a CAO; a sweeping reform of the administra-tion; and changes to the organizational framework of the city, which included revamping the committee system and changing the powers of the mayor and council. After those changes Winnipeg's government remains as distinct as that of a city of more than 600,000 must be from communities numbering, at the most, in the tens of thousands. But it is not as distinct as it was before, most conspicu-ously because of the abolition of the Board of Commissioners, an institution that, in Manitoba, was unique to Winnipeg, and the establishment of a CAO system everywhere in the province.

Most significantly, however, municipalities across Manitoba, including Winnipeg, have acquired new powers that may, depending on court decisions, add up to a substantial increase in their degree of autonomy. Also, throughout Manitoba cities and smaller communities—having been granted greatly increased authority to enter into contracts, procure goods and services as they see fit, and enter into joint ventures—are finding their old habits of governance increasingly exposed to the principles and practices of the private market.

Increased Authority

Municipal statute reform, then, has left Manitoba's municipalities with noticeable increases in authority. The 'natural persons' power provision in the City of Winnipeg Charter Act (2003) is absent from the Municipal Act (1996), but, as we have noted, both Acts achieve similar goals. To reiterate, however, the inclusion of 'natural person' rather than corporate powers may lead to greater ambiguity than the kind of enabling provisions the provincial government chose to insert into the Municipal Act, and may ultimately not prove as effective. On both approaches the jury is still out.

Despite this possibly contentious matter, all municipalities in the province now have a greater ability to govern in their jurisdictions the way they see fit, and this ability has been balanced with the reality of added responsibilities. Both Winnipeg and municipalities elsewhere in the province have been freed to raise money in novel ways, including the now universal freedom to enter into contracts, procure, and undertake joint ventures, and Winnipeg's acquisition of the right to use TIF.

In all of these cases, the ability to act upon added authority at the municipal level depends on the possession of financial resources or the ability to generate them. If councils do not have the resources to administer particular responsibilities, they now have the green light from the province either to raise funds in innovative ways or to deliver services by what may have once been considered unconventional methods. The benefits of these arrangements may bypass some communities.

A Market Model

Finally, municipal reform over the past decade has been guided by market philosophies. Both the changes in Winnipeg and those in the rest of the province were part of a worldwide movement at the end of the twentieth century to reduce the size of governments and to substitute market mechanisms for bureaucratic methods of action and control. In Manitoba, as in much of the rest of the world, these reforms are barely underway, as evidenced in the service delivery and inter-municipal co-operation provisions of the Municipal Act, in the administrative cutbacks mandated by the 1998 revisions to the City of Winnipeg Act (1972), and in the procurement and special service unit provisions in the City of Winnipeg Charter Act (2003). If these reforms are to be carried through on the scale advocated by their supporters, much remains to be done. Their full impact is yet to be felt and measured.

NOTES

1.   The authors wish to acknowledge the courteous assistance of Lynne Nesbitt, who, when the research for this chapter was underway, was an official with Manitoba Rural Development, and research co-ordinator for the review panel that paved the way for revision of the Municipal Act. She bears no responsibility, however, for any mistakes we

may have made or for our interpretations and conclusions. We are also grateful to the University of Winnipeg for providing an environment conducive to academic research. Mark Piel would like to thank Professor Christopher Leo for his invaluable help and encouragement.

2. All figures are from the City of Winnipeg Web site.

3. Although the review panel had no mandate to make recommendations concerning the province's system of school boards and education, school board officials were concerned about the ramifications of possible recommendations the panel might have made.

4. The Manitoba Bureau of Statistics predicts that over the long term (until the year 2016) population levels in the southwestern region of the province, home to many of Manitoba's most prosperous farmers (and bluest Tories), will continue to decrease, with other regions showing slight population increases.

5. The total number of special-purpose bodies is 351, including 56 school divisions.

6. The report notes that presenters often used the terms 'county' and 'regional government' interchangeably to denote different things, thereby reflecting the different use of the terms in different jurisdictions.

7. The Michener Royal Commission proposed a regional government structure, arguing defensively that it would not necessarily entail the transfer of executive authority in the policy process from municipalities to a central council, but would only serve to help co-ordinate policy across municipal boundaries. That proposal, too, was rejected. Even the metropolitan government scheme that, in the 1960s, united what is now downtown Winnipeg with suburban communities was soon superseded by an amalgamation, the well-known Unicity.

8. Municipalities are still free to call themselves towns or villages as they see fit, but this has no bearing on the powers they possess.

9. The compensation for reduced intensity of representation is that councillors receive a pay increase and their positions are designated as full time. Whether they are spending their extra time in touch with and responding to constituents remains open to debate.

10. The C5 was originally conceived by renowned urbanist and economist, Jane Jacobs, and the Toronto-based businessman and philanthropist, Alan Broadbent. It first met in Winnipeg in May 2001, with Murray acting as host, in order to develop a strategy for Canada's economic hub cities. The mandate of the C5 is to push for a legislative reform agenda and to renegotiate a new relationship for municipalities with senior levels of government.

11. What follows is a cursory description of TIF. See Johnson and Man (2001) for debates on the usefulness of this municipal development financing technique from a US perspective.

References

Diamant, Peter. 1994. *The Structure of Local Government and the Small Municipality.* Brandon: Rural Development Institute.

Downs, Anthony. 1994. *New Visions for Metropolitan America.* Washington: Brookings Institution.

George B. Cuff and Associates Ltd. 1997. *Organisational Review and Performance Assessment: A Corporate Review, Final Report.* Winnipeg, Oct.

Johnson, Craig L., and Joyce Y. Man, eds. 2001. *Tax Increment Financing and Economic Development: Uses, Structures, and Impacts.* Albany: State University of New York Press.

Leo, Christopher, and Lisa Shaw, with Kenneth Gibbons and Colin Goff. 2002. 'What Causes Inner-City Decay and What Can Be Done about It?', in Katherine Graham and Caroline Andrew, eds, *Urban Affairs: Is It Back on the Policy Agenda?* Montreal and Kingston: McGill-Queen's University Press, 119-47.

Manitoba. 1995. *Meeting the Challenges of Local Government*. Final Report of the Municipal Act and Related Statutes Review Panel. Winnipeg.

————. 1996. Municipal Act.

————. 1998. City of Winnipeg Act.

————. 1999. *Final Report of the Capital Region Review Panel* (Scarth Report). Winnipeg: Department of Intergovernmental Affairs.

————. 2002. News release, 20 June. At: <www.gov.mb.ca/chc/press/top/2002/06/2002-06-20-07.html>.

————. 2003a. City of Winnipeg Charter Act, Bill 39.

————. 2003b. *A Partnership for the Future: Putting the Pieces Together in the Manitoba Capital Region* (Thomas Report). Winnipeg: Department of Intergovernmental Affairs.

Manitoba Royal Commission on Local Government Organisation and Finance. 1964. *Report*. Winnipeg: Queen's Printer.

Nesbitt, Lynne. 1999. Personal communication with Research Co-ordinator for the Review Panel, Policy and Special Projects Unit, Manitoba Rural Development, 26 Apr., 17, 25 May.

Orfield, Myron. 1997. *Metropolitics: A Regional Agenda for Community and Stability*. Washington: Brookings Institution.

Peterson, Paul. 1981. *City Limits*. Chicago: University of Chicago Press.

Tindal, C. Richard, and Susan Nobes Tindal. 1995. *Local Government in Canada*. Scarborough, Ont.: Nelson Canada.

Winnipeg, City of. 1997. *Reshaping Our Civic Government: Executive Policy Committee's Strategic Direction for City Government*. Winnipeg.

————. Web site: <www.city.winnipeg.mb.ca>.

CHAPTER 6

Municipal Reform in Ontario: Revolutionary Evolution

DAVID SIEGEL

INTRODUCTION

The history of municipal reform in Ontario is a combination of relatively short periods of frantic, politically contentious activity punctuated by lengthy periods of quietude and incremental change. There never seems to be complete satisfaction with the system of local government in Ontario, as evidenced by the fact that there is always some tinkering, but these lengthy periods of tinkering are punctuated by shorter periods of fairly fundamental change.

The broad outlines of the current system date from the Baldwin Act of 1849 that created the system of single-tier cities in urban areas and two-tier county governments in rural areas. Over the years, there have been piecemeal annexations and consolidations of a few counties, but the first major innovation was the creation of the Municipality of Metropolitan Toronto in 1954 (Rose, 1972; Colton, 1980; Frisken, 1993). This was widely regarded as a very successful initiative, but it was followed by a period of quiet contemplation until the 1967 proposal of the Ontario Committee on Taxation that the Metro experiment be repeated by the establishment of regional governments across southern Ontario (Ontario Committee on Taxation, 1967).

Following on this proposal, between 1969 and 1974, 10 regional governments were created in the Golden Horseshoe extending from Niagara to Oshawa, and in Sudbury and Ottawa-Carleton (O'Brien, 1993; Sancton, 1991). Additional regional governments were proposed but the political fallout from the initiatives caused the government to pull back.

A period of gentle persuasion followed. The County Restructuring program resulted in studies in many counties, but very little actual restructuring, all of it of a considerably less comprehensive type than the creation of regional governments

(Williams and Downey, 1999; Beecroft, 1983; Montgomery, 1990; Ontario Ministry of Intergovernmental Affairs, 1980a, 1980b).

The next flurry of activity occurred after the election of Mike Harris's Conservative government in 1995. The Conservative platform, detailed in the 'Common Sense Revolution', was a neo-conservative manifesto that promised lower taxes, less government, and streamlined bureaucracy, but said little about local government (Ibbitson, 1997). However, Al Leach, Harris's first Minister of Municipal Affairs and Housing, and the former General Manager and Chief Executive Officer of the Toronto Transit Commission, made it clear that he wanted major changes in both the provincial-municipal relationship and in the municipal system.

This chapter[1] will focus on the changes made by the Harris government in the period from its election in 1995 until 2000, when the original push for change lost steam for reasons that will be discussed later. These changes were certainly the most extensive made in the system since the Baldwin Act of 1849.

OVERVIEW OF REFORMS

The changes have been so pervasive and multi-faceted that it is difficult to trace their genesis to a single decision. Nevertheless, observers suggest that the genesis can be traced to a desire on the part of the provincial government to change the funding arrangements for school boards (Ibbitson, 1997: 221; Graham and Phillips, 1998: 187). Prior to the Common Sense Revolution, school boards in Ontario (which are entirely autonomous from municipal governments) received about half of their funding from the local property tax (imposed by the local board, but collected on its behalf by the municipality) and half in the form of provincial transfers. About half of the total property tax collected went to school boards and the other half went to municipalities. Like school boards, municipalities also received fairly significant transfers from the provincial government.

The province wanted to establish greater control over the school system and ensure better equity of funding for education across the entire province. To accomplish this, the province made school boards almost totally dependent on provincial funding by reducing considerably their access to local property taxes and instead providing most funding through provincial transfers. The province found the funds needed for this within its budget by reducing its transfers to municipalities. As compensation, municipalities were allowed to occupy the tax room vacated by school boards. The province used the words 'revenue-neutral' quite often at this time to describe the changes being made, but many municipalities were skeptical. This shift possibly was revenue-neutral for the entire system, but its impact on individual municipalities varied considerably in ways that will be discussed later.

The substantial reduction of provincial transfers to municipalities sparked a major change in the provincial-municipal relationship. Previously, there had been many provincial transfers administered by virtually every provincial ministry. Municipal Affairs and Housing Minister Leach wanted to eliminate most of these. When questioned in the legislature about how municipalities would cope with the substantial reduction in provincial transfers, he responded that they would be given considerably more autonomy to organize their affairs and they would be encouraged to amalgamate to take advantage of efficiencies he felt would be generated (Hansard, 11 Dec. 1995: 1327). Whether these statements were well-considered or were offhand statements made in the heat of battle to fend off an aggressive opposition is unclear. In any event, they have led to a number of reforms that will be discussed below under the headings of structural, functional, financial, and jurisdictional reforms.

STRUCTURAL REFORMS

The major structural reform was the encouragement (or some would say imposition) of amalgamation. When the Conservatives came to power in 1995, there were just over 800 municipalities, a number that had remained relatively stable for about two decades. By 2000, this number had declined to about 400 and was again showing signs of stabilizing. The difference was accounted for by a wave of amalgamations that were either directly imposed by the provincial government or were facilitated by changes in provincial legislation (Hollick and Siegel, 2001: 9).

In *A Guide to Municipal Restructuring*, the Ministry of Municipal Affairs and Housing (1996) set several principles to be considered as a part of restructuring (Figure 6.1). These principles reflect neo-conservative values that resonated within the Harris government's broad agenda.

Later, in 1999, when special advisors were appointed to recommend changes in the structure of four regional governments, these advisors were given terms of reference that required them to consider how best to achieve five principles:

- fewer municipal politicians;
- lower taxes;
- better, more efficient service delivery;
- less bureaucracy;
- clear lines of responsibility and better accountability at the local level (O'Brien, 1999).

While there was a long list of reasons given for amalgamation, it was clear that paramount on the list were the related goals of lower expenditure, lower taxes, and more efficient service delivery followed closely by fewer politicians. While this was seldom mentioned explicitly, it is clear that the desire for greater efficiency and lower taxes fits in with concerns about globalization and the need to make Ontario more competitive in the international environment. Well-functioning cities with reasonable levels of taxation obviously are important in attracting international business.

Several academic observers raised questions about whether the efficiency goals could be accomplished by amalgamation (Sancton, 1996, 2000; Tindal, 1996, 1997). The minister's response was to refer constantly to a provincial study (Ontario, 1995) of one relatively small category of expenditure in one small amalgamation that showed that some savings might have been achieved in this case (Sancton,

Figure 6.1 Principles for Municipal Restructuring

Less government

- fewer municipalities
- reduced municipal spending
- fewer elected representatives

Effective Representation System

- accessible
- accountable
- representative of population served
- size that permits efficient priority-setting

Best Value for Taxpayer's Dollar

- efficient service delivery
- reduced duplication and overlap
- ability to capture the costs and benefits of municipal services within the same jurisdiction
- clear delineation of responsibilities between local government bodies

Ability to Provide Municipal Services from Municipal Resources

- local self-reliance to finance municipal services
- ability to retain and attract highly qualified staff

Supportive Environment for Job Creation, Investment, and Economic Growth

- streamlined, simplified government
- high-quality services at the lowest possible cost

Source: Ontario Ministry of Municipal Affairs and Housing (1996).

2000: 136). In addition, the strategy seemed to be that the minister and his officials would simply repeat the mantra of 'amalgamation equals savings and efficiency' so often that repeating it would make it come true.

The amalgamations were accomplished in a number of different ways. The highest-profile amalgamation was in Toronto where the upper-tier Municipality of Metropolitan Toronto was combined with its six constituent municipalities to create a new single-tier City of Toronto commonly called the 'mega-city'. There was substantial vocal local opposition to this amalgamation including a court challenge, but in the end, the legislation stood and the new city became a reality on 1 January 1998 (Horak, 1999; Isin and Wolfson, 1999; Todd, 1998).

At about the same time, the province created the Greater Toronto Services Board (GTSB), a special-purpose body combining the new mega-city and its outer suburbs. The purpose of the GTSB was to co-ordinate social, transportation, and infrastructure policy in the entire greater Toronto area. This included operating GO-Transit, the commuter rail service in the greater Toronto area. The GTSB was abolished in 2002 and the province is considering taking back responsibility for GO-Transit. This indicates that while the creation of the mega-city might be seen as an improved way of organizing the core city area, there is still no clear idea of how the city should be integrated with its outer suburbs and how those suburbs should be integrated with one another.

The province handled restructuring outside Toronto in a different way. The major tool to encourage or enforce amalgamation in counties and in northern Ontario (but not in the regional governments in southern Ontario) was Bill 26 (SO 1996, ch.1, Schedule M), better known as the Savings and Restructuring Act. The Act had both permissive and mandatory elements. On the permissive side, it allowed any group of municipalities to devise its own voluntary restructuring proposal. However, there was also a mandatory aspect that permitted any municipality to ask the Minister of Municipal Affairs and Housing to appoint a commissioner, who could impose a binding settlement (Hollick and Siegel, 2001).

The minister strongly encouraged municipalities to follow the voluntary route. A proposal developed in this fashion required the approval of a triple majority, consisting of a majority of the affected municipalities containing a majority of the affected population. The third majority required was the approval of the county council. The purpose of the triple majority was to ensure that there was general agreement on the amalgamation without allowing any one unit to have a veto. The requirement for county council approval was to ensure that the new entities all would be financially viable. The minister was required by Bill 26 to accept any proposal that received the triple majority and was otherwise in order.

The mandatory route could be invoked if any municipality was dissatisfied with the progress of amalgamation discussions by this voluntary route. The disaffected municipality could ask the minister to appoint a commissioner. Only a small number of commissioners were ever appointed, and they tended to be former politicians, former public servants, and academics.

The minister was not obligated to appoint a commissioner and the minister sometimes said that he would not appoint a commissioner until it appeared that there was little hope for a voluntary agreement. If the minister decided to appoint a commissioner, there was a process established by regulation that required the commissioner to consult with local stakeholders, issue a draft report, invite further consultations, and then issue a report that was binding on all parties. If this route was pursued, the affected municipalities would lose control of the process except to advise the commissioner. The genius of the legislation was that it provided a framework for local groups to co-operate and produce a homemade solution at the same time that it kept a sword dangling over their heads in the form of a commissioner with draconian powers.

Beyond the legislation, the provincial government tried to apply as much pressure for amalgamation as possible by creating an aura of urgency (Canaran, 1996; Sancton, 2000: 139–40). Councils were generally led to believe that if they did not do it themselves, an amalgamation would be imposed on them and they would not necessarily like it. This pressure was increased when municipal governments and their ratepayers saw the result of the first appointed commissioner, who imposed a restructuring plan that was generally deemed to be the least desirable option by virtually all municipal governments involved.

The imposition of that restructuring occurred in southwestern Ontario where there had been protracted discussions involving the City of Chatham, Kent County, and its 21 constituent municipalities. When they were unable to arrive at an amalgamation plan on a voluntary basis, the province appointed a commissioner who imposed a complete amalgamation of the huge area encompassing these municipalities. While the local municipalities could not agree on much before this happened, the one thing that most of them did agree on was that they did not want a complete amalgamation. The fact that the commissioner imposed a settlement that was not supported by most municipalities sent a powerful signal to other municipalities that were dithering about what to do (Hollick and Siegel, 2001).

Most of the amalgamations were the result of voluntary negotiations, but the use of the word 'voluntary' in the circumstances described above is arguable. The amalgamations took several forms. There were several cases such as Chatham-Kent in which two-tier systems were replaced by an amalgamated one-tier system. However, the more usual arrangement was to combine two or three adjacent municipalities as one. For example, Elgin County undertook a county restructuring that resulted in 15 constituent municipalities being reduced to seven, with some shifting of responsibilities between the county and lower tiers (Hollick and Siegel, 2001).

As mentioned earlier, the amalgamation provisions in the Savings and Restructuring Act did not apply to the regional governments created in the early 1970s. However, by 1998 the province was becoming interested in restructuring the regions as well. Four regions were identified for immediate consideration (Haldimand-Norfolk, Hamilton-Wentworth, Ottawa-Carleton, and Sudbury) and several others were put on the 'B list', meaning that they were next after the first four regions were restructured.

The province appointed a special advisor for each of the four regions on the priority list. The appointees were asked to work quickly and produce recommendations to the Minister of Municipal Affairs and Housing about restructuring. They reviewed previous studies and conducted public hearings. They were able to work quickly because there had already been extensive reviews of these regions over the years.

The recommendations of the advisors, who were either current municipal staff or former public servants, were remarkably similar. In Hamilton-Wentworth, Ottawa-Carleton, and Sudbury, the advisors recommended that each of the two-tier regions be replaced by one large city similar to what had already been done in Toronto. In Haldimand-Norfolk, the advisor recommended that the lower-tier municipalities be abolished and the region be divided into two municipalities—Haldimand and Norfolk. This region was originally created by the amalgamation of Haldimand and Norfolk counties so this was a turning back of the clock to some extent.

There was little support for the restructuring in any area. Immediate reactions ranged from the pugnaciously negative to resignation to the inevitable. There were several concerns. Constituent municipalities were upset about losing their local identities, particularly if the merger involved rival municipalities. The reaction to the promise of fewer politicians was mixed. At first, people rejoiced at the idea, but as they began to understand that this could make their personal access to local politicians more difficult, this idea lost some of its attraction.

Of course, everyone was in favour of lower taxes and more efficient service delivery, but some doubted that this would occur. Some feared that more efficient service delivery would ultimately mean lower-quality services in their areas. On the tax side, some feared that combining their low tax jurisdiction with adjacent municipalities with higher taxes would result in a blending of tax rates that would benefit some and hurt others. Since one of the goals of the provincial government was 'to capture the costs and benefits of municipal services within the same juris-diction' (Figure 6.1), this blending of tax rates could be seen as a conscious strategy in areas such as Kingston, where the central city had complained for some time that the suburban municipalities had benefited from city services as free riders.

Assessment of the Structural Reforms

It is too early for a comprehensive assessment of these changes, but a few tentative remarks can be made. It is very difficult to evaluate the goals of efficiency and lower taxes because a number of other changes were made in the municipal system at the same time, including significant downloading of provincial services and a major change in the tax assessment system. For example, Chatham-Kent presented information indicating that it had saved substantial amounts as a result of amalgamation, but most of the savings were eaten up by the costs associated with downloading (Municipality of Chatham-Kent, 2000). The City of Toronto has complained of huge additional costs from the beginning (Graham and Phillips, 1998: 190; Ibbitson, 1997), but lately issues have been raised about the quality of management of the new city that suggest that some costs may have arisen more from incompetence than from amalgamation (Barber, 2001).

One significant fact is that most amalgamated municipalities have been able to avoid substantial tax increases in the years immediately following the amalgama-tion. The reason for this is subject to varying interpretations. The opponents of amalgamation point out that the promised tax decreases have not materialized. The proponents of amalgamation could counter with the argument that munici-palities have been able to withstand significant downloading without any major tax increase, which is a significant accomplishment. The truth is probably some-place in the middle. It seems that amalgamations have produced neither the catas-trophes predicted by opponents nor the windfalls promised by proponents (Kushner and Siegel, 2003a, 2003b).

One research project is tracking the results of the amalgamations in three municipalities—Central Elgin, Chatham-Kent, and Kingston. Extensive citizens' surveys undertaken in those three municipalities indicate that most respondents have not seen a major change in the quality of services since the amalgamation. In some cases, the surveys even indicate greater citizen acceptance of the amalgamation as time goes on, but this varies by area (Cornell, 2000; Kushner and Siegel, 2003a, 2001a, 2001b).

The four regional restructurings that took effect 1 January 2001 were the last high-profile amalgamations. After these amalgamations, the Conservative government seemed to lose its zeal for amalgamation. In Hamilton-Wentworth, a government member of the legislature resigned his seat in protest against the government action, and the government lost the seat in the resulting by-election. There are always a number of reasons why a party loses a particular election, but this loss, along with other rumblings, were taken as a sign that it might be better to put the amalgamation program on the back burner. It seems that Ontario has just passed through one of those periods of turbulence mentioned earlier and has embarked on another period of quietude.

However, the reverberations from this most recent round of restructurings are still being felt. The de-amalgamation movement that seems to be strong in Quebec has not caught hold in the same way in Ontario. In most places, the strong citizen opposition to amalgamation has turned into quiet acceptance. A recent survey indicates that in some areas, opposition to amalgamation has declined slightly over the years since the amalgamation (Kushner and Siegel, 2003a). The original broad-based opposition to amalgamation has changed to specific criticism of tax increases and/or service reductions. However, there is a strong de-amalgamation movement in the City of Kawartha Lakes—a municipality northwest of Peterborough that was created by amalgamation of all the municipalities in Victoria County on 1 January 2001. A referendum at the time of the November 2003 municipal election resulted in a slight majority in favour of de-amalgamation. De-amalgamation was not a major issue in the 2003 provincial election; the implication being that the new Liberal government has no interest in de-amalgamation although it was a strong opponent of amalgamation when it was in opposition. However, the new Liberal Minister of Municipal Affairs agreed to meet with the mayor of Kawartha Lakes to discuss the results of the referendum.

There are several other relatively small de-amalgamation groups in various parts of the province, but these seem to be losing steam. Most of the amalgamations have now reached the stage of passive acceptance (but certainly not enthusiasm) on the part of the general public. Even though the Liberals opposed the amalgamations when they were in opposition, they seem now to take the position that it is impossible to reverse what has been done. Most people seem to agree tacitly with a regional councillor in the early years of the Regional Municipality of Niagara who responded to calls for its dissolution by saying that 'you can't unscramble an egg.'

FUNCTIONAL REFORMS

As mentioned in the previous section, the restructuring took place in an environment of considerable provincial downloading, or in the province's preferred phrasing, 'local services realignment'. These changes took several forms. The changes in responsibilities for certain functions will be discussed in this section. The changes in provincial-municipal financial arrangements will be discussed in the next section.

The Conservative government began the process of making functional reforms with the appointment of the 'Who Does What' panel, chaired by well-respected former Toronto Mayor David Crombie. The purpose of the panel was to stream-line the provincial-municipal relationship by allocating responsibility for services clearly to one level of government, and eliminating the muddling of accountabil-ity and the administrative complications that arise when two governments share responsibility for a service (Graham and Phillips, 1998: 183; Meyboom and Richardson, 1997).

The panel consisted of a number of working groups organized on functional lines, e.g., assessment and tax reform, transportation and utilities, municipal administration. The members of the groups were a mixture of provincial public servants and municipal politicians and staff. Each group produced a report that took the form of a letter to the minister recommending changes in its sphere.

The panels tried to deal with issues in their fields on a highly rational basis, but when it came time to implement the recommendations, financial considerations became paramount. The provincial government was under considerable financial pressure because the Common Sense Revolution had promised to reduce taxes and eliminate the deficit. One of the government's first actions was to increase transfer payments to school boards, which moved it away from its goal of reduc-ing total expenditures. Therefore, it would have to reduce its expenditures even more in some other areas. At the same time, the province was aware that it provided municipalities a significant windfall by reducing the reliance of school boards on the property tax and allowing municipalities to occupy that vacated tax room. This meant that the province could download significant responsibilities to municipalities to soak up the windfall they were receiving in property taxes. This is how the 'Who Does What' exercise started as a rational method of reallocating responsibilities to the level of government best able to deliver a service, but ended up as an accounting exercise focused on making the numbers balance. There was an attempt to maintain a veneer of rationality in why certain services were trans-ferred as they were, but this rationality was always conditioned on considerations of the financial needs of both levels of government.

Table 6.1 provides a reasonably comprehensive summary of the functional changes, but it does not capture all the details related to each reform. The main functional changes will be discussed in this section, and these and other financial changes will be discussed in the next section. The plus and minus notations on the table indicate whether something was a benefit (+) or a cost (–) to municipalities. There are many more cost items than there are benefit items, but that should not be taken as an indicator of the overall financial shift. For example, the shift of a substantial portion of the education property tax generated a huge benefit for municipalities, while the costs associated with a number of the functions shifted from the province were not major. At one time, the participants tried to maintain

Table 6.1 Changes in the Provincial–Municipal Relationship

Before Common Sense Revolution	*After Common Sense Revolution*
EDUCATION PROPERTY TAX +	
Province has been funding a declining portion of total education cost.	Province will fund approximately 50 per cent of cost of education.
The major portion of education funding comes from local school boards through the property tax. Education portion of the property tax has been increasing more rapidly than the municipal portion.	School boards will reduce their residential property tax levy, which will result in rates being reduced by about 50 per cent; municipalities will be able to increase their tax rates accordingly. Province will specify uniform school tax rate for commercial and industrial properties.
FARM TAX REBATE −	
Farmer pays 100 per cent of property tax to municipality, and receives 75 per cent rebate from province.	Farmer will pay 25 per cent of residential tax rate to municipality; no provincial involvement. Municipality will bear this cost instead of province.
PROPERTY ASSESSMENT −	
Responsibility of province.	Responsibility of municipalities. Will be performed by autonomous entity funded collectively by municipalities.
SOCIAL ASSISTANCE −	
Province funds some programs 80/20, others 50/50; administration costs shared 50/50.	All programs shared 80/20; administration still shared 50/50.
SOCIAL HOUSING −	
Province funds most of the deficit through a variety of means.	Province will spend $215 million in capital upgrades, after which municipalities will be responsible for future deficits.
MUNICIPAL TRANSIT −	
Province provides some grants for both capital and operating.	Existing commitments for capital grants will be honoured, then no further grants for either capital or operating.
GO-TRANSIT −	
Province meets deficit.	Operation will be assumed by the Greater Toronto Services Board. No provincial funding.
ROADS −	
Province maintains some roads within municipalities.	Many roads switched to municipalities. One-time maintenance funding provided.
Province provides conditional grant.	Grants eliminated.

Table 6.1 Changes in the Provincial-Municipal Relationship cont.

Before Common Sense Revolution	*After Common Sense Revolution*
FERRIES AND AIRPORTS − Province provides most funding.	Most ferries and airports will be turned over to municipalities, except those in sparsely populated areas.
POLICING − OPP provides service free to small municipalities.	All municipalities will be responsible for the cost of policing. This can be handled through contracts with OPP or establishing a local police service.
PUBLIC HEALTH − Most programs funded by 80–100 per cent grants from the province.	Province will continue to fund 50 per cent of mandatory programs.
AMBULANCE SERVICE − Provided by province.	Municipalities responsible for land ambulance, province funds 50 per cent of approved expenditure; province provides air ambulance.
GROSS RECEIPTS TAX − Collected by municipalities.	Must be turned over to province.
PROVINCIAL OFFENCES REVENUE + Collected by province.	Net proceeds (after adjudication and prosecution costs) directed to municipalities.
WATER AND SEWER 0 Province provides service to smaller municipalities on a user-pay basis.	Municipalities will be responsible to service, but this was self-funding in most municipalities before anyway.
COMMUNITY REINVESTMENT FUND AND TRANSITIONAL ASSISTANCE +	Unconditional grant will be provided. Total amount has varied over time because this is the balancing figure intended to make the entire package revenue-neutral. Will be discontinued at some point to be replaced by special circumstances funding on application from municipalities each year

Note: + = municipal benefit; − = muncipal cost; 0 = no change.
Source: Hollick and Siegel (2001).

a scorecard to track the dollar value of the transfers, but this became so contentious that it was abandoned.

Property Assessment

At one time, the assessment of property for tax purposes was done by each individual municipality. This created problems of equity and comparability across municipalities and in 1970 the province took over responsibility for the assessment function. Since then, several previous provincial governments had suggested that this function be turned over to municipalities, but the municipalities always resisted because of the cost. In 1998, the province created the Municipal Property Assessment Corporation as an autonomous entity funded by the municipalities. In 2000, the total cost of its operation was $143 million, virtually all of which came from municipalities (Ontario Property Tax Assessment Corporation, 2000).

There have been several other changes in the property tax assessment system. Prior to changes made in 1998, the assessment system was terribly outdated in some areas. According to the legislation, the system was supposed to be based on fair market value, but the dates of assessments varied widely. Some municipalities had kept their assessments up-to-date by periodic reassessments, but other municipalities had not reassessed properties since the 1940s. This created a number of inequities (Niagara Region Review Commission, 1989: 113–14). For example, there were inequities within individual municipalities because it was very difficult to construct a fair assessment based on outmoded values. There was a strong presumption that newer properties were bearing a greater property tax burden than older ones.

Several attempts were made over the years to reform the system, but they all stalled on the political problem that updating such an outdated system would produce a major redistribution of the tax burden. The change would improve equity because it would force previously under-assessed properties to carry their fair share of the property tax burden. However, the fact that this would result in huge increases in taxes on some properties created a political uproar. Much of the problem was geographically concentrated in downtown Toronto, which amplified the scope of this problem.

The Conservative government approached this problem with great resolve. The initial proposals put forward by the government would have solved the problem. However, as the political protests mounted, the government lost its political will and watered down its original approach in ways that created almost as many problems as it solved. In the final analysis, a great opportunity to improve the system was lost.

The process began very simply. As of 1998, all properties were to be assessed and taxes calculated on the current value as of 30 June 1996 (Ontario Ministry of Municipal Affairs and Housing, 2000). This would be updated regularly and eventually the use of a three-year moving average, which would smooth rapid changes in property values, would be phased in.

The political problems began when it became clear that this would produce major increases in taxes imposed on some business properties, particularly in downtown Toronto. In response to the uproar, the provincial government imposed a maximum tax increase of 10–5–5, meaning a maximum increase of 10 per cent in 1998, 5 per cent in 1999, and 5 per cent in 2000. This limitation applied only to multi-residential, commercial, and industrial properties. This was beneficial to the owners of these properties, but it meant that property owners who were expecting to see reductions in their taxes because of previous over-assessment had to wait for their reductions, since municipalities could not afford to reduce those taxes as long as their maximum increases were capped. This kind of ad hoc adjustment means that one patchwork quilt has been substituted for another and a chance to improve the system has been lost.

Another distortion came about because this limitation applied only to multi-residential, commercial, and industrial properties. Therefore, the full weight of any increase would fall disproportionately on residential property-owners. In practice, this made council very reluctant to impose tax increases.

Social Assistance

The 'Who Does What' panel recommended that the province take over full responsibility for social assistance (Meyboom and Richardson, 1997: 6). This would have aligned Ontario with the other nine provinces (Haddow, 2002). It is difficult to expect local governments to fund this service because it is expensive and is better spread out over a larger area. For example, a local government can get hit with a double whammy when a local industry closes and the municipality must pay out increased social assistance benefits at the same time that its property tax take is declining. Spreading this out across an entire province makes it easier.

However, when the dust settled, the province realized that it would not have enough money to take over such a major responsibility and decided to leave it as a shared responsibility between provincial and municipal governments. Of course, this is never an equal partnership. The broad outline of the division of responsibility remained the same—the province set the rules and paid most of the cost, while municipalities administered most aspects of the program and paid a significant minority of the cost.

Of course, this broad outline obscures many of the details of such reforms. The number of different programs has significantly increased, as has the complexity of administration (Haddow, 2002). The Conservative government was very interested in encouraging claimants to re-enter the workforce and in reducing fraud. These objectives, it was believed, ought to reduce the cost of programs in the long run, but in the short run they significantly increased the administrative costs incurred by municipalities.

One senior municipal administrator stated that an initial interview with a prospective claimant that formerly required about 30 minutes now requires two hours, and this was before the implementation of a mandatory literacy test and possibly mandatory drug testing. This same administrator used expressions like 'death by a thousand programs' and 'the straw that breaks the camel's back' to suggest that the gradual accumulation of more programs and more complex rules and regulations was having a decidedly detrimental impact on municipal staff.

And it was difficult to approach council for additional funding because the case-load (as measured by number of claimants) was not increasing, although the time needed to process each one was.

Social Housing

Before the Common Sense Revolution, social housing had been predominantly a provincial responsibility, with some municipal and federal involvement through the Canada Mortgage and Housing Corporation (CMHC). For some years the federal government had been reducing its funding, which was increasing the burden on the province (Carroll, 2002).

As a result of local services realignment, the province turned over a huge number of housing units to local municipalities. The province's position has been that it is turning over a major asset to municipalities in the form of a large number of housing units. The municipalities initially objected that many of these units were in poor repair, so the province agreed to spend $215 million before they were turned over to municipalities (Graham and Phillips, 1998: 196).

This program could become very costly to municipalities in terms of immediate operating costs and longer-term capital costs when new construction or major repairs to existing buildings are needed. As with the social service programs mentioned above, there is also a significant administrative impact on municipalities.

Roads

The principle of allocation of roads has been that municipalities should be responsible for local roads and streets that carry traffic within the municipality, while the province is responsible for highways and roads that carry traffic between municipalities. In practice, this has always been a difficult distinction to make and that difficulty has been exacerbated because there have been few adjustments over the years. Almost every municipality has an example of a road that was maintained by the province because it was formerly a major highway before it was supplanted by a newer highway. It has now served only local traffic for many years, but is still classified as a provincial highway.

The province identified certain roads that it felt were more properly the responsibility of the local municipality and transferred ownership of these roads to municipalities. A significant increase in expenditure for some municipalities, this was one of the more contentious areas of downloading, particularly because these additional costs were imposed at the same time that a major conditional grant for roads was being phased out.

Policing

Prior to the Common Sense Revolution, large urban municipalities paid for their own police services, but police services were provided 'free' to smaller municipalities by the Ontario Provincial Police (OPP). In this case, of course, 'free' means that all provincial taxpayers helped to pay for policing in small towns and rural jurisdictions. This inequity was corrected by requiring all municipalities to pay for their own policing either by establishing their own police service or by contracting with the OPP. For smaller places, there was no practical alternative to contracting with the OPP, but in either case, this amounted to a major increase in expenditure for these smaller municipalities with a relatively limited tax base. Police services were one of the major incentives for some smaller municipalities to amalgamate with larger places.

Ambulance
Responsibility for land ambulance was also shifted to municipalities. It is difficult to see any rationale for this except to assist in the financial balancing discussed earlier. This required municipalities to make some difficult decisions about how to organize this service. Municipalities could provide this service on their own or they could contract it out to one or several services in the area.

Provincial Offences Courts
Since the 1960s, the provincial government has been responsible for the administration of all courts within the province, from the most senior courts of appeal down to provincial offences and small claims courts. The province has now transferred responsibility for these lower courts to the local municipalities. This has the potential to be a source of revenue for municipalities because fees are charged for filing in small claims court and municipalities will be able to keep the fines levied in provincial offences court. However, there is a substantial administrative burden for municipalities and the money to be made is not substantial.

Water and Sewers
Water provision and sewage disposal have been municipal responsibilities for some time. However, the province operated several small water treatment and sewage disposal plants generally in relatively sparsely populated areas serving a group of municipalities. Responsibility for these plants has now been shifted to the local municipalities. This will have relatively little impact on the municipalities' financial position because these services were self-funding on a user-pay basis when they were operated by the province and they should continue to operate on the same basis.

Assessment of the Functional Reforms
There were so many functional reforms that it is difficult to provide an overall assessment of their total impact. Municipalities generally reacted to specific transfers of responsibility based on their financial impact. The transfer of policing to smaller municipalities and some roads to all municipalities was heavily and loudly criticized, while the transfer of responsibility for provincial offences was seen as an opportunity to raise additional funds.

From the provincial perspective, these reforms allowed it to reduce its expenditure and pass some costs along to municipalities, although so many changes were happening simultaneously, this would be difficult to prove. However, the nature of the changes was such that the province clearly has been able to reduce the number

Table 6.2 Shift in Distribution of Property Tax

	1996	2000
Municipalities	43.2%	61.6%
School boards	56.8%	31.4%

Sources: 1996 figures: Ontario Ministry of Municipal Affairs and Housing, Municipal Financial Information 1996 (Toronto: Queen's Printer for Ontario, 1998), p. II–2; 2000 figures: Information supplied directly by Ontario Ministry of Municipal Affairs and Housing.

of its employees by transferring to municipalities such services as social housing, some aspects of social assistance, property assessment, and policing. This was likely one of its objectives (Sancton, 2000: 149).

FINANCIAL REFORMS

The main outlines of the financial reforms can be explained quite easily.

- The province has significantly increased its funding of school boards.
- In return for greater provincial funding, school boards have reduced their reliance on the property tax.
- To offset the province's increased expenditure on education, the province has significantly reduced its transfer payments to municipalities.
- To compensate municipalities for this reduction in revenue, the province has allowed them to occupy the property tax room vacated by school boards.

As mentioned at the beginning of this chapter it is presumed that the overall purpose of these reforms was to allow the province to provide more funding to school boards and therefore exercise greater control over their operation. The other steps were necessary to free up the necessary funds to accomplish this goal.

Table 6.2 demonstrates the impact of this shift. Prior to the changes discussed above, school boards received almost 57 per cent of the total property tax levy. After the changes, this was reduced to 31 per cent, creating significant tax room for municipalities.

Another reason for this shift was to focus accountability more clearly. The Conservatives wanted to reduce the complexity of provincial-municipal relations by eliminating the complex web of conditional transfers that muddled accountability. As illustrated in Table 6.1, the province terminated a number of conditional grants in areas such as roads and transit.

From the perspective of municipalities, the idea was that they would receive less funding in the form of grants, but would have greater access to the property tax and also some additional sources of revenue. Table 6.3 shows how this has occurred. Prior to these changes, municipalities collected just over two-thirds of their revenue from their own sources (property tax and user charges). After the changes, this had increased to over four-fifths. This was matched by a significant

Table 6.3 Shift in Municipal Revenue

	1996		2002	
	$ millions	% of Total Revenue	$ millions	% of Total Revenue
Real property tax	7,171.7	42.2	11,779.9	53.0
User charges	3,349.7	19.7	4,709.7	21.2
Other own-source	1,050.7	6.2	1,434.9	6.5
Total own-source revenue	**11,572.1**	**68.1**	**17,924.5**	**80.7**
Conditional grants	4,542.9	26.7	3,719.7	16.7
Unconditional grants	881.6	5.2	574.8	2.6
Total grants	**5,424.5**	**31.9**	**4,294.5**	**19.3**
Total	**16,996.5**	**100.0**	**20,495.2**	**100.0**

Source: Statistics Canada, Cansim II Table number 3850004.

decline in the percentage of total revenue obtained from provincial grants.

Throughout the earlier stages of the functional alignment initiative, the province often used the phrase 'revenue-neutral'. The stated intent was to make these shifts as close to revenue-neutral as possible and then to use a temporary program called the Community Reinvestment Fund (a fancy name for an uncon-ditional grant program) to provide the balancing amount. However, this balanc-ing exercise became very difficult because there was never agreement on the numbers. For example, expenditure on social assistance jumps around quite significantly each year. What number should be entered on the scorecard?

Assessment of the Financial Reforms

An assessment of the financial reforms would suggest that the province accom-plished its immediate goal of making municipalities more dependent on their own revenue rather than on transfers from the province. At first, municipalities raised serious concerns about these shifts and predicted dire consequences in the form of huge tax increases. A major concern was that even if the overall impact on the entire municipal system was revenue-neutral, there could still be major impacts on individual municipalities. For example, rural municipalities were particularly hard hit by the cumulative impact of the termination of the provincial farm tax rebate, the termination of the road subsidy, and the requirement to pay for policing. In fact, most municipalities were able to absorb the downloading (offset by increased tax room) without major tax increases. Many municipalities went for several years after the changes without significant tax increases. Only in about 2000 did municipalities start to increase taxes.

Municipalities complained extensively and strongly about these shifts, but a greater reliance on own-source revenue will likely give municipalities more autonomy. This autonomy will be enhanced even further by certain jurisdictional changes that came into effect in 2003.

JURISDICTIONAL REFORMS

The major jurisdictional reform in Ontario occurred as a result of the passage of a new Municipal Act that came into force on 1 January 2003. This Act replaced the previous Municipal Act, which was a patchwork quilt built up since the Baldwin Act of 1849. This legislation is consciously modelled on the Alberta legislation passed in 1994, and like that Act, it represents a major departure from its predecessor.

The previous municipal act was a highly detailed piece of legislation that was based squarely on Dillon's rule—a municipality could take no action unless it was given express authority to do so under some piece of provincial legislation. The purpose of the new Act is to provide municipalities with greater autonomy. The 'Main Policy Directions' of the legislation as stated by the provincial government were:

- enhanced flexibility for innovative municipal service delivery;
- improved accountability to the public;
- promotion of well-administered, economically healthy municipalities;
- a more comprehensive, understandable, better-organized statute;
- proposals that address key concerns raised during discussion (Ontario, Ministry of Municipal Affairs and Housing, 2001).

The general thrust of the legislation is to provide municipalities with a broader 'permissive policy framework' rather than the narrower 'restrictive regulatory framework' (Garcea, 2002). This is done by identifying 10 spheres of jurisdiction in which municipal councils have considerable latitude to operate. The spheres include: public utilities; waste management; public highways; transportation systems; culture, parks, recreation, and heritage; drainage and flood control; parking; economic development services; structures not covered by the Building Code Act, including fences and signs; and animals.

The Act also gives municipalities 'natural person' powers, meaning that they are allowed to carry out duties within these general spheres of jurisdiction without needing the kind of detailed delegation found in the previous Municipal Act. Specifically, this should provide municipalities greater flexibility in the areas of entering into contracts, suing and being sued, hiring and terminating employees, delegating administrative responsibilities to council committees and staff, entering into innovative service delivery arrangements such as public-private partnerships, and purchasing and disposing of property (Garcea, 2002).

In addition to 'natural person' powers, municipalities are also granted some governmental powers such as 'the authority to tax, to regulate or prohibit certain activities, to require individuals to do certain things, to expropriate property and to establish a system of licences, permits, approvals and registrations' (Ontario, Ministry of Municipal Affairs and Housing, 2001: 7) Many of these powers were already extant in a number of different pieces of legislation, but the new Municipal Act brings them together in one place.

There are certain limits on municipal powers. Municipalities cannot pass bylaws that would conflict with federal or provincial legislation, they must respect certain procedural requirements in making decisions, and there are some limitations on their financial activities.

This legislation was passed as a result of intense lobbying by various municipal associations that felt the previous legislation imposed undue restrictions on their ability to operate in a flexible and innovative manner. They argued that the rigid application of Dillon's rule made it difficult for them to be responsive to the new challenges they faced without being subjected to detailed judicial review. The City of Toronto in particular has argued that it should have its own charter to define its relationship with the province and provide it more autonomy (www.city.toronto.on.ca/ourcity/citycharter.htm).

Assessment of the Jurisdictional Reforms

This new legislation provides many opportunities, but it also poses some problems. One observer has suggested that these changes were made more to appease municipal governments than to empower them (Garcea, 2002). He argues that the real impact of these changes will be determined by how the municipal governments use them, how the provincial governments respond to what municipalities do, and how courts interpret the legislation.

Since this legislation took effect on 1 January 2003, it is too early to provide an assessment of the impact of the new Act either on municipal powers or on the ways that municipalities will use them. Municipalities seem to welcome the changes to the extent that they will permit them to exercise greater power without the detailed provincial controls that had frustrated them in the past. It remains to be seen whether they were unduly optimistic both about the value of these powers and about the willingness of future governments to allow them to use such powers in a relatively unfettered manner.

CONCLUSION

The reforms discussed in this chapter add up to the most significant, multi-faceted changes made in Ontario's municipal system since the current system was created by the Baldwin Act in 1849. This includes the following major changes: the number of municipalities has been cut in half; some major service responsibilities have been shifted between provincial and municipal governments; the basis of municipal finances has changed so that municipalities now rely much more on their own revenues and much less on provincial grants; and an innovative and potentially significant regime of municipal powers has been enacted in a new Municipal Act.

The first response of municipalities to these changes was negative because of what they saw as downloading without accompanying changes in their revenue. This is quite understandable because municipalities have been conditioned over the years to feel that they are the passive recipients of policies handed down from senior levels of government; they were at the end of the food chain, always having to adjust their interests and policies to respond to the interests of other levels of government.

Claims by the provincial government that the provincial-municipal realignment of functions was revenue-neutral did little to allay municipalities' concerns and complaints. The general assessment from the municipal side is that it is highly unlikely that the changes implemented have been revenue-neutral, although the changes have been so all-encompassing that that issue will likely never be agreed on to everyone's satisfaction. However, municipalities have done a remarkable job of adjusting to huge changes in the system while introducing only minimal tax increases. In the past, municipal officials tended to suffer from feelings of inferiority. Working through the catharsis of change has substantially increased the confidence of politicians and staff, creating in a short period of time a sense of much greater strength.

A longer view suggests that the future holds some significant opportunities for municipalities. The new, larger municipalities should have enhanced opportunities because they will be able to hire more highly qualified staff. The fact that they cover larger geographic areas gives them greater scope for action in the planning field. The responsibility for more services means that they must spend more money, but the broadened responsibilities will also give them broader scope for influence with other governments and in their own communities. The shift from reliance on provincial conditional grants to greater reliance on own-source revenue in the form of property tax and user charges gives municipalities more autonomy in deciding on expenditures.

The new Municipal Act will give municipalities considerably more autonomy. The establishment of 'natural person' powers releases them somewhat from the onerous burden of Dillon's rule that restricted their activity to what was expressly permitted in provincial statutes. Although it does not change the ultimate fact of provincial control over municipalities, it does mean that control is now exercised in a less detailed and cumbersome way than in the past.

Municipalities also will benefit because the status of the mayors of large cities has been enhanced. Approximately 20 per cent of the voters in the province will select the mayor of Toronto. The mayor thus gains considerably more status than any of the 28 members of the provincial legislature who represent the area and arguably becomes second in electoral status to the premier, although more people would have voted directly for the mayor than voted for the premier. This situation would also increase the power of the mayors of several other large cities so that, cumulatively, these mayors will have a great deal of electoral credibility in their dealings with Queen's Park.

This group of reforms probably closes the book on this particular period of municipal reform. I began with the assertion that the history of municipal reform has consisted of periods of rapid change punctuated by longer periods of quietude. The recent period of change now seems to have run its course so that Ontario is likely looking at a period of quiet absorption of all these changes before the next period of rapid change.

NOTE

1. The research for this chapter has been funded by a grant from the Social Sciences and Humanities Research Council.

REFERENCES

Barber, John. 2001. 'The Nasty Job of Mucking Out Megacity Stables', *Globe and Mail*, 1 Dec.

Beecroft, Eric. 1983. *Restructuring an Ontario County: The Oxford Achievement.* London, Ont.: Department of Political Science, University of Western Ontario.

Canaran, Nasreine. 1996. 'Restructure or Perish: Duet Rendering at OSUM', *Municipal World* (June): 21–2.

Carroll, Barbara Wake. 2002. 'Housing Policy in the New Millennium: The Uncompassionate Landscape', in Edmund P. Fowler and David Siegel, eds, *Urban Policy Issues: Canadian Perspectives*, 2nd edn. Toronto: Oxford University Press, 69–89.

Colton, Timothy J. 1980. *Big Daddy: Frederick G. Gardiner and the Building of Metropolitan Toronto.* Toronto: University of Toronto Press.

Cornell, Andrew. 2000. 'Restructuring: Jury Still Out on Subject', *Chatham Daily News*, 3 Nov.

Frisken, Frances. 1993. 'Planning and Servicing the Greater Toronto Area: The Interplay of Provincial and Municipal Interests', in Donald N. Rothblatt and Andrew Sancton, eds, *Metropolitan Governance: American-Canadian Intergovernmental Perspectives.* Berkeley, Calif., and Kingston, Ont.: Institute of Governmental Studies Press and Queen's University, 153–204.

Garcea, Joseph. 2002. 'Modern Municipal Statutory Frameworks in Canada', *Journal of Governance: International Review* 3, 2: 1–14.

Graham, Katherine A., and Susan D. Phillips. 1998. '"Who Does What" in Ontario: The Process of Provincial-Municipal Disentanglement', *Canadian Public Administration* 41, 2 (Summer): 175–209.

Haddow, Rodney. 2002. 'Municipal Social Security in Canada', in Edmund P. Fowler and David Siegel, eds, *Urban Policy Issues: Canadian Perspectives*, 2nd edn. Toronto: Oxford University Press, 90–107.

Hollick, Thomas R., and David Siegel. 2001. *Evolution, Revolution, Amalgamation: Restructuring in Three Ontario Municipalities.* London, Ont.: Department of Political Science, University of Western Ontario.

Horak, M. 1999. 'The Power of Local Identity: C4LD and the Anti-Amalgamation Mobilization in Toronto', Research Paper No. 145. Toronto: Centre for Urban and Community Studies, University of Toronto.

Ibbitson, John. 1997. *Promised Land: Inside the Mike Harris Revolution.* Scarborough, Ont.: Prentice-Hall Canada.

Isin, E.F., and J. Wolfson. 1999. 'The Making of the Toronto Megacity: An Introduction', Working Paper No. 21. Toronto: Urban Studies Programme, York University.

Kushner, Joseph, and David Siegel. 2001a. 'Citizens' Perceptions of Municipal Amalgamation in the City of Kingston', unpublished manuscript.

———— and ————. 2001b. 'Citizens' Perceptions of Municipal Amalgamation in the Municipality of Central Elgin', unpublished manuscript.

———— and ————. 2003a. 'Citizens' Attitudes Toward Municipal Amalgamation in Three Ontario Municipalities', *Canadian Journal of Regional Science* 26, 1: 49–59.

———— and ————. 2003b. 'Effect of Municipal Amalgamations on Political Representation and Accessibility', *Canadian Journal of Political Science* (Dec.): 1035–51.

Meyboom, Peter, and Dana Richardson. 1997. 'Changing Who-Does-What in Ontario: Ontario's Approach Towards Municipal Empowerment—Process, Results and Lessons

Learned', paper presented at conference of the International Institute of Administrative Sciences, Quebec City, 14–17 July.

Montgomery, Byron. 1990. *Annexation and Restructuring in Sarnia-Lambton: A Model for Ontario County Government.* London, Ont.: Department of Political Science, University of Western Ontario.

Municipality of Chatham-Kent. 2000, 'The Chatham-Kent Experience: A Three Year Review . . . 1998–2000', presentation to Council, 11 Jan.

Niagara Region Review Commission. 1989. *Report and Recommendations.* Toronto: Queen's Printer for Ontario.

O'Brien, Allan. 1993. *Municipal Consolidation in Canada and Its Alternatives.* Toronto: ICURR.

O'Brien, David S., Special Advisor. 1999. *Report to the Minister of Municipal Affairs and Housing: Local Government Reform for Hamilton-Wentworth*, 26 Nov.

Ontario. 1995. *New Tecumseth 4 Years After—An Interim Review of a Restructured Municipality,* Dec.

Ontario Committee on Taxation. 1967. *Report.* Toronto: Frank Fogg, Queen's Printer.

Ontario Ministry of Intergovernmental Affairs. 1980a. 'The Brantford-Brant County Local Government Project', *Municipal World* (Apr.): 87–92.

———. 1980b. *An Examination of the Brantford-Brant Local Government Pilot Project: An Alternative Annexation Process,* Aug.

Ontario Ministry of Municipal Affairs and Housing. 1996. *A Guide to Municipal Restructuring,* Aug.

———. 2000. 'A Bulletin on the New Property Tax Assessment and Taxation System in Ontario'. At: <www.mah.gov.on.ca/business/PAssmt/English/bul6_C.asp>.

———. 2001. *New Directions: A New Municipal Act for Ontario.* Toronto: Queen's Printer for Ontario.

Ontario Property Tax Assessment Corporation. 2000. Financial Statements of the Ontario Property Tax Assessment Corporation, December 31, 2000. At: <www.opac.on.ca/pdf/notestofinancials2000.pdf>.

Rose, Albert. 1972. *Governing Metropolitan Toronto: A Social and Political Analysis.* Berkeley: Institute of Governmental Studies, University of California.

Sancton, Andrew. 1991. *Local Government Reorganization in Canada Since 1975.* Toronto: Intergovernmental Committee on Urban and Regional Research.

———. 1996. 'Reducing Costs by Consolidating Municipalities: New Brunswick, Nova Scotia and Ontario', *Canadian Public Administration* 39, 3 (Fall): 267–89.

———. 2000. 'Amalgamations, Service Realignment, and Property Taxes: Did the Harris Government Have a Plan for Ontario's Municipalities?', *Canadian Journal of Regional Science* 23, 1 (Spring): 135–56.

Tindal, C. Richard. 1996. 'Municipal Restructuring: The Myth and the Reality', *Municipal World* 107, 3 (Mar.): 3–7.

———. 1997. 'Sex, Lies and Amalgamations', *Municipal World* (Feb.): 6.

Todd, Graham. 1998. 'Megacity: Globalization and Governance in Toronto', *Studies in Political Economy* 56: 196–216.

Williams, Robert J., and Terrence J. Downey. 1999. 'Reforming Rural Ontario', *Canadian Public Administration* 42, 2 (Summer): 160–92.

CHAPTER 7

Municipal Reform in Quebec: The Trade-off between Centralization and Decentralization

PIERRE HAMEL

INTRODUCTION

Quebec's municipal reform agenda at the turn of the millennium consisted of initiatives that focused primarily on the structural component of the municipal system and to a lesser extent on the functional, financial, and jurisdictional components. The structural reforms targeted the amalgamation and de-amalgamation of local municipalities as well as the reconfiguration of some of the boundaries of regional authorities in both metropolitan and non-metropolitan areas, while the functional, financial, and jurisdictional reforms focused primarily on the realignment of roles, responsibilities, resources, and jurisdictional authority both between the provincial and municipal governments and among various local and regional municipal entities. The objective of this chapter is to provide an overview and analysis of the purpose, nature and scope, politics, and effects of those reforms as well as some predictions regarding the prospects for additional reforms in the future.

THE PURPOSE OF MUNICIPAL REFORMS

The purpose of Quebec's municipal reforms during the past decade, as in the previous decades, was to modernize the municipal system in response to changes in the provincial, national, and international environments. The contemporary municipal modernization project commenced in the 1960s when the municipal system was among the first targets for provincial technocrats, who wanted to reconfigure the boundaries, functions, finances, and powers of municipalities. Municipal officials and their ratepayers viewed that particular municipal modernization effort as an attack on what they deemed to be important spaces of assembly and action for local political forces (Bissonnette, 1982). This explains, at least in part, the resistance to and failures of municipal regionalization proposed by modernizing forces in the 1960s (Meynaud and Léveillée, 1973), and the need for successive provincial governments to continue to reform various parts of the system in subsequent decades.

Forty years later modernization was still the core purpose of municipal reforms. At the turn of the millennium the provincial Minister of Municipal Affairs and the Metropolis stated that the central purpose of this particular round of municipal reforms was 'strengthening of rural communities, reinforcing of major urban regional centres, and establishing of urban and rural links' (Boisclair, 2002: 18 [my translation]; Québec, 2000a: ix). The strengthening of rural communities was thought to be crucial in improving local capacity to perform basic planning, development, and service delivery functions. In Quebec, as in other provinces, provincial officials perceived that the strengthening of rural communities required the strengthening of municipal governments in those areas through various means, including restructuring. In their view this was essential to the creation of sustainable regional and local communities and economies. The reinforcing of major urban regional centres was considered necessary in making them more competitive nationally and internationally in response to imperatives produced by globalization. The objective was to make Montreal and other major cities larger and more effective and efficient in planning, development, and service delivery so that they could be more competitive in the national, continental, and global economies. The establishment of better links between rural and urban municipalities and their communities was deemed essential to minimize problems that compromised development opportunities and equitable share of costs and benefits among neighbouring urban and rural municipalities within the various regions of the province.

Another goal of municipal reforms, which was not articulated by the minister in the statement cited above but was nonetheless very important, was to find a new balance between centralization and decentralization not only between the municipal and provincial governments but also among different levels of municipal government in Quebec. From this point of view municipal reforms were an attempt to eliminate or at least reduce the existing problematic tensions between the provincial and municipal governments throughout the system. Achieving a balance between centralization and decentralization was not merely a matter of reducing political tensions between them; more importantly, it was seen as an important stepping stone on the path towards political modernization (Smith, 1985). Such a balance is a challenging accomplishment that must be reviewed constantly in the light of the changes to the local, regional, and national societies and economies. The government rejected suggestions that some of the reforms in a major urban regional centre such as Montreal were driven primarily by political considerations related to the nature of the provincial-municipal relationship or by the political agenda of the provincial government concerning its social and linguistic policies.

STRUCTURAL REFORMS

In examining Quebec's structural reforms within the municipal sector it is important to distinguish among three major types—the amalgamation of local municipalities, the de-amalgamation of local municipalities, and the reconfiguration of the boundaries of regional municipal authorities.

During the past decade only Ontario amalgamated more municipalities than Quebec. The vast majority of those amalgamations in Quebec occurred from 1996 to 2003 under the direction of the Parti Québécois government. Only one amalgamation has occurred since the Liberal government came to power in 2003. This was the amalgamation of Drummondville and some of its neighbouring municipalities on a voluntary basis. Ironically, this amalgamation occurred just as many amalgamated municipalities were preparing to de-amalgamate.

All the amalgamations occurred as part of the long-standing objective to reduce the number of local municipalities. Traditionally, Quebec has had the most municipalities among Canadian provinces. The number of its municipalities has been particularly large in rural areas where their number increased steadily from 1841 until the early 1970s despite the fact that Quebec society became increasingly industrialized and urbanized (Bissonnette, 1982). At the turn of the twenty-first century 90 per cent of the province's municipalities were located in rural areas and accounted for 22 per cent of the population (Québec, 2001a: 5). Since the 1960s the prevailing view has been that the large number of municipalities both in urban and rural parts of Quebec is highly problematic for various facets of governance, management, planning, and development, as well as for the equitable sharing of the revenues and expenditures (Ministère des Affaires municipales et de la Métropole, 2002a: 28). Consequently, during the past four decades successive provincial governments have tried to reduce the number of municipalities through various amalgamation initiatives (Quesnel, 2000; Hamel and Rousseau, 2003; Tindal and Tindal, 2004; Fischler et al., 2004).

Notable efforts at reducing the number of municipalities started with the decision of the provincial government to enact the Voluntary Amalgamation Act of 1965. Over a period of five years approximately 100 municipalities had been amalgamated, but this fell far short of what the provincial government had anticipated (Tindal and Tindal, 2004: 117). Consequently, in 1971 it amended municipal legislation to give the minister authority to mandate amalgamations. That statutory reform did not produce the desired results either, largely because the minister was unwilling to use that authority in light of the strong opposition to its use expressed by municipal officials. Such opposition to mandatory amalgamation succeeded for approximately two decades in blocking or slowing considerably the will of provincial officials to amalgamate municipalities.

By 1990, however, the provincial government again started focusing its attention on consolidating the municipal sector. Towards that end, successive provincial governments have used a combination of voluntary and mandatory approaches with various types of incentives. The first major incentive, used by the Liberal governments of Premiers Robert Bourassa and Daniel Johnson Jr, was the downloading of financial responsibilities to the municipalities. Their hope that the resulting financial hardships would motivate many of the municipalities to amalgamate was not fulfilled. Thus, they began to explore other means to motivate municipalities to amalgamate.

To avoid a confrontation with the municipal sector, just prior to the 1994 election, which it lost, the Liberal government decided to establish a statutory policy and financial framework designed to facilitate voluntary amalgamations. This included revisions to the statute devoted to the structure of the municipal system (Loi sur l'organisation territoriale municipale, L.R.Q. c. 0–9) and a set of policy and procedural guidelines for amalgamation. It also included the promise to municipalities willing to amalgamate that they would receive special grants, and the promise to ratepayers in such municipalities that their taxes would not increase for five years. That 'carrot' approach did not produce any substantial results in the amalgamation of municipalities over the next two years.

Consequently, in 1996 Premier Lucien Bouchard's Parti Québécois government introduced a 'stick' approach—the threat to eliminate their equalization grants—for small villages, parishes, and small unorganized settlements with populations of less than 10,000 that did not opt for amalgamation. The rationale for adopting that approach was articulated by the Minister of Municipal Affairs in a position paper released in 1996 (Québec, 1996), which noted various economic and social changes during the past century that required adjustments to the municipal system. It also noted that those changes had produced not only a 'certain disjunction between decision-making centres, territories, and ways of life' (ibid., 1 [my translation]), but also an imbalance among neighbouring municipalities in terms of their fiscal and management capacities, which had to be reviewed and corrected.

The Parti Québécois government's goal of amalgamating municipalities was endorsed in the recommendations of the 1999 Bédard Commission (Québec, 1999), which had been appointed to examine municipal finances rather than municipal restructuring. The Commission recommended restructuring the municipal system through the amalgamation of local municipalities and the reconfiguration of all types of regional municipal authorities in urban, rural, and mixed urban and rural areas. The logic embodied in that document was echoed in the White Paper released by the Minister of State for Municipal Affairs and the Metropolis titled *La réorganisation municipale, changer les façons de faire, pour mieux servir les citoyens* (Québec, 2000a).

At that time the provincial government had started to focus on the amalgamation of three categories of municipal entities. The first consisted of several hundred small parish villages and small municipalities with fewer than 10,000 inhabitants that were in the vicinity of urban areas. The second involved the 700 small local communities that existed far from large urban centres and could therefore only be consolidated with other small municipalities or had to continue to operate as separate municipalities. The third category consisted of the 263 municipalities with more than 10,000 inhabitants (Collin, 2001).

In June 2000 the provincial government enacted Bill 124, the Loi modifiant la Loi sur l'organisation territoriale municipale et d'autres dispositions législatives (Québec, 2000b), which provided both for a top-down approach and a bottom-up approach to restructuring. Under the top-down approach the Minister of Municipal Affairs could, upon obtaining authorization from cabinet, order that certain local municipalities be grouped together (Québec, 2000b: 5). For that purpose the minister was authorized to ask the Municipal Commission to study the possibility of amalgamating certain municipalities and to make appropriate recommendations to the government. Under the bottom-up approach the request to the Commission would come from a group of neighbouring municipalities that decided to undertake an amalgamation initiative. If any neighbouring municipalities are not willing to amalgamate the minister can appoint a conciliator to work with the targeted municipalities to develop a plan to create a new amalgamated municipality. If the conciliator cannot produce unanimous consent of all the affected municipalities, the government has the power to authorize the amalgamation of such municipalities by decree. Those familiar with Ontario's framework for amalgamation adopted by Premier Mike Harris's government during the late 1990s will undoubtedly recognize substantial similarities between it and Quebec's framework for amalgamation.

The 'stick' approach adopted in 1996 by the Bouchard government produced some results over the subsequent four years in amalgamating municipalities, but not as much as the provincial government had hoped. By March 2000, less than half of the 407 targeted municipal entities were either amalgamated or in the process of being amalgamated. At that time the minister decided to give them an additional two more years within which to amalgamate, and indicated that if they did not amalgamate they would receive only 50 per cent of their provincial grants in 2001 and no grants at all after 2002. That 'voluntary' incentive-driven approach produced substantial results. So, too, did the provincial government's mandatory approach to amalgamation. Indeed, through the use of those two approaches, in the period from January 2001 to June 2002 a total of 228 municipal entities were amalgamated into 50 larger ones (Fischler et al., 2004: 101). The mandatory approach resulted in the amalgamation of many municipalities, including 64 in the following major cities: 28 in Montreal, 13 in Quebec City, 5 in Outaouais, 8 in Longueil, and 10 in Lévis. The provincial Parti Québécois government, headed by Premier Lucien Bouchard until March 2001 and then by Premier Bernard Landry until April 2003, proceeded with those as well as other amalgamations on a mandatory basis. It did so despite the fact that many municipalities had held plebiscites opposing its plans to impose amalgamations (Quesnel, 2000: 127–8).

The effects of amalgamation on the number of municipalities from 1993 to 2003 were significant but not dramatic, as the total number of municipalities was reduced by approximately 20 per cent. In spite of repeated efforts by the provincial government for nearly four decades to reduce their number, in March 2000 there were still 1,306 municipalities in Quebec (see Table 7.1). Over the next two years, the number of municipalities was reduced by over 200. Thus, by June 2002, not

Table 7.1   Distribution of Municipalities in Quebec by Population, 2000

Population Size	Number of Municipalities	Number of Inhabitants
Less than 1,000	552	315,029
1,000 to 1,999	296	421,988
2,000 to 4,999	251	780,360
5,000 to 9,999	82	568,166
10,000 to 24,999	76	1,200,719
25,000 to 49,999	28	985,773
50,000 to 99,999	16	1,083,551
100,000 and more	5	1,742,712
Total	**1,306**	**7,098,298**

Source: Québec (2000a: 13). Compilation by Affaires municipales et de la Métropole from population data in the 1996 census and taking account of groupings of municipalities approved by decree up to 25 March 2000.

counting the nine cities with a population of more than 100,000, Quebec still had the largest number of municipalities of any province in Canada with 1,115 municipalities grouped into 87 regional county municipalities (MRCs) (see Box 7.1).

The De-amalgamation of Local Municipalities

The ambitious municipal restructuring agenda of the Parti Québécois government became an issue in the spring 2003 election. During the election campaign the Quebec Liberal Party promised to introduce legislation that would allow municipal governments and their communities to have a say in whether the amalgamations imposed by the Parti Québécois government should be reversed. In keeping with that promise, in December 2003 the Liberal Party government enacted Bill 9 (Québec, 2003a), which gave voters of the municipalities amalgamated under the legislation enacted by the Parti Québécois government since 2000 the authority to hold a referendum on whether to de-amalgamate. The government made it clear, however, that de-amalgamation would only entail a partial reversal of what had been done because municipalities opting for de-amalgamation would still have significant policy and programmatic linkages with the existing central municipality in their agglomeration. This includes roles and responsibilities for certain functions, such as public security, social housing, public transit, and waste management that are likely to continue to be performed on an agglomeration basis by the elected municipal representatives of neighbouring municipalities within an agglomeration council.

Shortly after Bill 9 was enacted the 42 new municipalities created through the provincially mandated amalgamation of 212 municipalities throughout Quebec were informed that they would have to provide their voters with an opportunity to indicate whether they wanted to re-establish any of the former municipalities under the following four conditions outlined in Bill 9. First, the Minister of Municipal Affairs, Sport, and Leisure would commission a study of the effects of

Box 7.1 Summary of Municipal Reorganizations in Quebec as of 18 February 2002

- Creation of 9 cities with more than 100,000 inhabitants (Montreal, Quebec City, Longueuil, Laval, Gatineau, Saguenay, Sherbrooke, Lévis, and Trois-Rivières)
- Creation of medium-size cities in almost all regions
- Creation of three categories of MRCs
  - 51 rural MRCs
  - 24 rural and urban MRCs
  - 13 MRCs on the territory of metropolitan communities
  - 13 cities exercising the powers of MRCs
  - 1,147 local municipalities
- Creation of metropolitan communities (Montreal and Quebec City)

Source: Ministère des Affaires municipales et de la Métropole, Direction des politiques municipales, 'La réorganisation municipale. Changer les façons de faire pour mieux servir les citoyens' (Apr. 2001; revised Feb. 2002).

the restructuring for each of the 42 new amalgamated municipalities and their 212 old municipalities by March 2004. Second, within the 212 old municipalities a register would be open for five days in March 2004 to allow citizens to indicate whether they wanted a referendum on de-amalgamation. For a referendum to be held, it had to receive the support of at least 10 per cent of eligible voters. Third, for de-amalgamation to occur it had to be supported by at least 50 per cent of those voting in the referendum. Moreover, the 50 per cent had to constitute more than 35 per cent of registered voters. Fourth, if all of the foregoing referendum conditions were met, the provincial government was required to act according to the public will and facilitate de-amalgamation. After the referendum, communities voting in favour of de-amalgamation would establish committees both to facilitate the transition and to plan the elections in each of the re-established municipalities for mayors and councillors in November of 2005 so that they would be ready to begin governing their respective municipalities on 1 January 2006.

Of the 214 municipalities that had been amalgamated since 2000, 89 opted to hold referendums in June 2004 on whether to de-amalgamate. Although the majority of voters in 59 municipalities voted in favour of de-amalgamation, only 32 of those had the requisite voter turnout to mandate the de-amalgamation (Table 7.2). It will be interesting to see what types of administrative processes and political dynamics will be produced by the re-establishment of those municipalities and the realignment of their relationships with their former amalgamated municipalities.

Reconfiguration of Regional Municipal Authorities

In addition to the amalgamation of municipalities, the restructuring initiative in Quebec also entailed the reconfiguration of regional municipal authorities known as Municipalités régionales de comté (MRCs—regional county municipalities),

Table 7.2 Quebec Municipalities Scheduled to De-amalgamate in 2006

Cookshire–Eaton	Kirkland
Newport	L'Île-Dorval
Mandataire	Montréal-Est
	Montréal-Ouest
Les Îles-de-la-Madeleine	Mont-Royal
Cap-aux-Meules	Pointe-Claire
Grosse-Île	Sainte-Anne-de-Bellevue
	Senneville
La Tuque	Westmount
La Bostonnais	
Lac-Édouard	**Mont-Tremblant**
	Lac-Tremblant-Nord
Longueuil	
Boucherville	**Québec**
Brossard	L'Ancienne-Lorette
Saint-Bruno-de-Montarville	Saint-Augustin-de-Desmaures
Saint-Lambert	
	Rivière-Rouge
Montréal	La Macaza
Baie-d'Urfé	
Beaconsfield	**Sainte-Agathe-des-Monts**
Côte-Saint-Luc	Ivry-sur-le-Lac
Dollard-des-Ormeaux	
Dorval	**Sainte-Maguerite-Estérel**
Hampstead	Estérel

Source: Ministère des Affaires municipales Sport et Loisir, 'Réorganisation territoriale—Transition Agglomérations en transition, comités de transition et mandataires', Aug. 2004.

which were supra-municipal planning and management structures. The MRCs were the products of the reform initiatives of the late 1970s. At that time, the provincial government launched and implemented its regionalization of the municipal sector, designed to give municipal urban and regional planners the ability to implement new modes of control of municipalities and a new institutional framework better adapted to the needs of urban society. Pursuant to the enactment of Bill 125 in 1979 that established a series of regulations for urban planning, 94 MRCs were created to cover most of the province—the exceptions were the Montreal, Quebec City, and Outaouais urban communities, which had separate regional authorities. The creation of the MRCs led to the demise of the old Conseils de comté.[1] Under the 1979 legislation MRCs were able to establish contractual agreements with the cities and towns within their respective boundaries, permitting the former to provide municipal services such as property evaluation and waste management.

The MRCs were assigned three major sets of functions. The first is urban and regional planning. The MRCs were obligated to adopt and implement a planning scheme for their entire region after holding public consultations. The second is the maintenance of roads, bridges, and waterways as well as property evaluations for rural municipalities, all of which were performed by the former county councils. The third is to intervene in certain areas that were traditionally under the authority of municipalities, if endorsed by a majority vote of two-thirds of council members. Pursuant to some reforms adopted in 1988, the functions of MRCs were expanded to include other important matters such as regional economic development and environmental matters.

The MRCs are administered by a council composed of mayors from each of the member MRC municipalities. The form of representation for MRCs and the proportion of voting power of each representative are determined through consultations with the representatives and ratepayers of municipal councils that existed prior to the creation of the MRCs. At one point in the recent era the proportion of councils of which mayors had a single vote versus a weighted vote was approximately equal (Quesnel, 1990: 33). Decisions of MRC councils are made by majority vote. Each MRC is chaired by a commissioner who is elected by and from the mayors sitting on the MRC council. However, with the recent municipal reforms each MRC may decide to have its commissioner elected at large. The commissioner is allowed to vote only when there are tie votes among the other members of council. MRC council meetings take place at least once every two months. MRCs have access to two major sources of revenues. They are authorized to impose levies both on the municipalities within their boundaries and on individual ratepayers for any services that they provide to them.

The reconfiguration of regional authorities created three categories of MRC: rural MRCs (51), mixed urban and rural MRCs with more than 10,000 inhabitants (24), and MRCs within metropolitan communities (13). At the beginning of the restructuring process, the government had established the number of mixed MRCs at 26. Ultimately, however, the number was reduced by two on the recommendation of the working group established by the minister in April 2001 to examine their operation since the MRCs in question were, in its opinion, actually rural.[2]

The establishment of three distinct categories was based on the recognition of the specific role that such bodies had played both in regional planning and in the management of public-sector services since the 1980s in three relatively distinct types of regions. The reconfiguration of those regional municipal authorities was intended to produce municipal organizations with the capacity to assume additional roles and responsibilities within their respective regions that would improve the ability of local governments to deal with the service and development needs and preferences of their respective communities within the parameters of the fiscal constraints that confront them.

Each of these categories of MRCs was created through separate pieces of legislation. In 2000 legislation was introduced for the MRCs within the metropolitan centres, which came into force on 1 January 2001. For each of the cities targeted by that legislation the government of Quebec appointed a transition committee charged with the implementation of the new municipal structures (Québec, 2000b: 3). For two of those cities—Montreal and Quebec City—the existing 'urban community' councils were replaced by 'metropolitan community' councils consisting of the mayors and councillors of the largest cities and mayors of the other municipalities within the metropolitan region. Those two 'metropolitan community' councils were established pursuant to Bill 170 (Loi portant réforme de l'organisation territoriale municipale des régions métropolitaines de Montréal, Québec et de l'Outaouais).

Although all of the 30 metropolitan and urban areas throughout Quebec were within the government's restructuring sights, the first—and arguably the most important—target was Montreal, the financial problems of which had worried the province's political officials since at least the mid-1990s (Baccigalupo and Nkot, 2001). In the case of Montreal as well as in other metropolitan communities, the institutional response of using municipal mergers to resolve problems of administrative performance and equity seemed insufficient to reformers. This is why the government proposed the creation of supra-municipal regional co-ordination, planning, and development structures in the Montreal urban area. For several years, the vast majority of reviews of the problems of urban development and metropolitan governance in Montreal defended the principle of regional-level planning.[3] Although these reviews proposed the creation of regional planning and management authorities, they did not advocate a more radical solution, that is, the creation of a regional municipal government per se.

In 2001 legislation was enacted for the other two types of MRCs. Bill 29, enacted in May of that year, provided the statutory framework for the creation and operation of rural MRCs, and Bill 77, enacted in December of that year, provided for the creation and operation of MRCs that had both rural and urban communities within their boundaries. The separate pieces of legislation were enacted in recognition that the various categories of MRCs face special challenges resulting either from the nature of their urban or rural contexts or from the new spatial configuration that blends rural areas and urban functions, which is a growing trend in Quebec (Courville, 2000).

In the metropolitan areas of Montreal and Quebec City, as mentioned earlier, structural reforms involved the creation of a three-tier system that included the metropolitan community councils, the city councils, and the borough councils. The alignment of roles and responsibilities between cities and boroughs was defined in Bill 170. Each borough has a local council, the composition of which may vary from borough to borough.[4] Their responsibilities and functions include local parks and sports, cultural, and recreational facilities, social and economic development, public zoning consultations, minor exemptions from land-use planning bylaws, permit delivery, garbage collection, and local roads. The boroughs are funded by an operational allocation made by the city. These can be supplemented with revenues earned from fees for goods and services supplied to users. The boroughs may also obtain revenue from a services tax or user fee added to the property tax with a view to improving the supply of certain services. However, this measure is subject to approval by the city council (Québec, 2003b).

FUNCTIONAL REFORMS

The structural reforms discussed above were accompanied by a corresponding series of adjustments to the functions between the municipal and provincial governments as well as among various municipal governments and authorities. The adjustment of functions between the municipal and provincial governments was relatively minor in scope. The recent municipal reforms entailed the transfer of only two relatively minor functions from the provincial government to municipal governments. The first was the transfer of responsibility for policing and public security from the province to the municipal governments of municipalities with a population of at least 50,000. As part of its effort to improve the overall capacity to deal with crime in the province, the provincial government decided to require municipalities with at least 50,000 inhabitants either to supply a better or more complete police service or, starting 1 June 2002, to use the services of the Quebec provincial police force, which would supply these services for a fee. Another option for these municipalities was to institute an inter-municipal MRC-wide system of policing (Ministère de la Sécurité publique du Québec, 2001).

The other notable transfer of functions between the provincial and municipal governments was the requirement for both rural MRCs and also the new cities that were created following the mergers in the metropolitan regions of Montreal and Quebec City to assume some responsibility for social housing. In the case of the Montreal metropolitan region, for example, the regional authority at the metropolitan level is required to create a development fund—based on contributions from all the municipalities in the region—into which it must pay 'an amount at least equal to the basic contribution required to enable construction of housing allocated by the Société d'habitation du Québec on its territory' (Québec, 2000c: 96 [my translation]).

The functional reform initiative also entailed a minor realignment of functions between the various types of municipalities and municipal authorities in both the metropolitan and non-metropolitan areas. One example of this is the transfer of some functions from local municipalities to MRCs in rural areas. In this case their functions were expanded to include the creation and operation of regional parks.

Another notable example of this type of realignment of functions is what occurred between the city governments and the metropolitan councils. In Montreal, for example, the Communauté métropolitaine de Montréal (CMM) established by Bill 134, enacted on 16 June 2000 and operative as of 1 January 2001, inherited the planning and management functions on the metropolitan scale as well as the management of regional facilities. The CMM, which was established to facilitate co-ordination and co-operation within the Montreal region, covers the entire territory of the Montreal census metropolitan area (CMA) as defined by Statistics Canada in its 1996 census.[5] Since neither the MRCs nor the other co-ordination agencies in place within the metropolitan region were abolished, the CMM was required to perform some functions jointly with them and to use agreements for that purpose. The CMM was assigned planning, management, and regulatory functions for the metropolitan region. Its regional planning mandate is, among other things, to develop and adopt a 'metropolitan plan for regional planning and development' that is to take effect on 1 January 2006. Its approach involves elabo-ration of a 'strategic vision of economic, social, and environmental development aiming to facilitate the coherent use of the Community's powers' (Québec, 2000e: 29 [my translation]). In addition, the CMM is responsible for promoting economic development. This involves 'promotion of its territory to encourage growth and diversification of the economy' (ibid., 36 [my translation]). The CMM may also assume a role in matters related to facilities, infrastructure, and services of a metropolitan nature. It is responsible for management of four major regional-scale facilities.[6] It also has the power to plan public transit, manage waste, and intervene, in co-operation with municipal governments, in social housing. The CMM shares with the City of Montreal some of these planning, management, and regulatory functions related to water and waste, air quality, transportation, urban and regional planning, economic development, and social housing.

The hope was that the structural reforms would facilitate better co-ordination, co-operation, and partnerships between the principal governmental and non-governmental stakeholders in urban and regional planning and development. More specifically, the hope was that it would lead to a change of attitudes and new institutional dynamics to improve governance within the metropolitan region. This was particularly true of the three governmental entities that exist in the metropolitan region—the new city, the boroughs, and the metropolitan commu-nity.

FINANCIAL REFORMS

Financial problems and reforms have always been a major issue in relations between the provincial and municipal governments. In spite of the municipal tax reform of the 1980s designed to increase the fiscal autonomy of municipalities (Hamel and Jalbert, 1991), which contributed significantly to reducing the munic-ipalities' financial dependence on the provincial government by granting them the exclusive right to tax property, the small municipalities have remained highly dependent on various provincial programs for financial assistance. In 1999, more than 55 per cent of the budgets of municipalities with fewer than 1,000 inhabitants still came from various direct or indirect assistance programs offered by the provincial government. In the case of municipalities with fewer than 5,000 inhab-itants, this assistance amounted to more than a third of their budget (Québec, 2000a: 22).

It is not surprising, therefore, that the contemporary municipal reforms are dealing yet again with the issue of taxation. In April 1998, the government decreed the formation of the Provincial Commission on Local Finances and Taxation following an agreement reached in October 1997 between the provincial govern-ment and the Union des municipalités du Québec (UMQ, 2000). This Commission's recommendations served as the basis for establishing a new fiscal pact between the government and the associations representing the munici-palities, namely the UMQ—comprised of over 900 municipalities—and the Quebec Federation of Municipalities, comprised of representatives of various regional municipalities and representatives of several caucuses of various types of municipalities, which was established to facilitate municipal relations with the provincial and federal governments. This fiscal pact was reached in June 2000 (see Commission nationale sur les finances et la fiscalité locales, 1999).

The objective of the agreement was to 'enable municipalities to offer high-quality public services to their populations, while keeping their fiscal burden at the lowest and most equitable level possible' (Québec et l'Union des Municipalités du Québec et la Fédération Québécoise des Municipalités, 2000: 2 [my translation]). As announced in the 'Discours sur le budget 2000–2001' on 14 March 2000, the new fiscal pact between Quebec and the municipalities involved a sum of $1.5 billion to be paid to the municipalities by the Quebec government by 2005. This agreement changed two things. First, the contribution of the municipalities to the Fonds Spécial de Financement des Activités Locales (FSAL), which had been created in 1997 by the provincial government as part of its effort to fight the budget deficit, was abolished. The municipalities had been required by law to contribute to this fund, either by increasing their general property taxes or by creating a special property tax. Second, the municipalities had to cede to the government the revenues generated by taxes on telecommunications, natural gas, and electricity companies.

According to the provincial government, this agreement worked in favour of the vast majority of municipalities. The Premier felt that the pact should 'return to municipalities the means to implement their own development projects and help them return to their taxpayers a portion of the funds that were used to reach a zero deficit' (Saïdah, 2000: 5 [my translation]). However, some researchers do not share this opinion and consider, on the contrary, that the municipalities were the losers. This is clearly expressed in a recent analysis of the new fiscal pact. In fact, this new episode, quite innocuous in itself, fits perfectly in the incremental series of reforms. As far back as one can remember, these have had the effect of systematically chipping away at the municipalities' fiscal panoply by withdrawing from them, one by one, most of the fiscal tools, some of which they had developed themselves, confining them gradually to the property tax and little else (Hamel, 2002: 1).

One notable example is the changes to the provincial financial transfers to municipalities that the provincial government established as a financial assistance program to support MRCs in assuming their new responsibilities for some services (waste management, civil security, and fire security). Another notable example is the changes to the province's municipal financial assistance plan, which in the past had been used to help local municipalities whose property value was too low to provide basic services to their taxpayers. In 2001 such assistance was reduced by 50 per cent and indications suggested that it would likely be eliminated altogether in future years. Such decisions were made to encourage various types of municipalities with a weak financial base either to seek or at least to accept amalgamation as a means of meeting their financial needs. On 1 January 2002 a new municipal financial assistance program was implemented in light of the enactment of Bill 29. The modalities it introduced included a simplified formula and targeted the poorest municipalities and northern municipalities. Under the new program fewer municipalities (the number dropping from 504 to 369) would be eligible for the financial assistance from the provincial government (Ministère des Affaires municipales et de la Métropole, 2001: 1).

Another set of changes in municipal finances has been the new revenue-generating powers for the cities. Traditionally in Quebec, the municipalities' autonomous sources of revenue were property taxes, business taxes, transfer fees, and service fees. The property tax is still the main source of revenue in the municipal sector. In the context of the financial and fiscal agreement concluded in 2000 with the associations representing the municipalities, the provincial government proposed a series of measures aimed at diversifying the sources of municipal revenue. One proposal was to institute a 'program of development user fees to finance various municipal expenditures for new real estate development projects' (Saïdah, 2000: 6 [my translation]). The main objective of such fees was not only to raise additional revenues for municipalities but also to help them control urban development by having those using the new infrastructure pay for it.

At the request of municipal representatives, a variable-rate property tax program was also introduced. Under this program five general property tax categories transfer the fiscal burden from one category of buildings to another when there are fluctuations in real estate values. As part of a supplementary financial and fiscal agreement reached on 28 June 2000, the plan also called for various compensatory measures to take the place of taxes for buildings in the health and education networks. Thus, a mechanism of value adjustments for the assessment rolls of buildings belonging to the government and Crown corporations was instituted for calculating grants in lieu of taxes (Ministère des Affaires municipales et de la Métropole, 2001). As mentioned above, these measures allowed the redress of part of the financial imbalance created by the financial contributions of the municipalities that the government had required as part of its fight to reach a zero deficit. However, they did not fundamentally change the mode of funding of municipal services, as the amounts in question remained small overall (Hamel, 2002).

In the case of the CMM, the committee of elected representatives of the metropolitan region of Montreal suggested that a program be instituted for regional sharing of the growth arising from property value, known as 'tax base sharing'. However, the formula proposed did not correspond exactly to what existed in certain urban areas in the United States, such as Minneapolis–St Paul. The formula proposed in Montreal aimed to create a metropolitan development fund fed mainly by contributions from the new property value of the territory, without redistribution being made on the basis of the municipalities (Comité des élus de la Région métropolitaine de Montréal, 2000). The fund is used for projects considered a high priority by the CMM council. In addition, the CMM would fund supra-local or regional-scale facilities. The metropolitan region was required to identify its regional-scale facilities. With regard to social housing the CMM was authorized to share the financial responsibility with the member municipalities in the region. This was an innovation because before the reform, only local municipalities were responsible for social housing through their respective Municipal Housing Bureaus.

Finally, there have not been any changes in the financial responsibilities between the provincial and municipal governments for some major social service functions. In contrast to the changes brought by the municipal reforms in, for example, Ontario, there was no fundamental transformation in Quebec in the financial responsibilities of the provincial and municipal governments for public services such as education or health care. Thus, the Quebec government continues to assume exclusive financial responsibility for funding education and health care.

Jurisdictional Reforms

The municipal reforms of the most recent era have entailed only minor rather than major adjustments of jurisdictional authority between and among various orders of government. This has included the adjustments of authority between the municipal and provincial governments and those between the various types of municipal governments and authorities within a given region. In both instances the objective has been to find a new balance in matters related both to financial management and to planning and development.

The jurisdictional reforms related to financial management provided some municipal governments and agencies with slightly increased authority and autonomy in at least two areas. First, Bill 110, enacted in June 2000, provided the regional municipal agencies in the urban communities of Quebec City, Montreal, and Outaouais with the authority either to create reserve funds or to set up inter-municipal boards capable of imposing fees for municipal services (Québec, 2000f). Second, some types of municipal governments were given additional jurisdictional authority and autonomy in incurring and servicing deficits and debt. Municipalities with more than 100,000 inhabitants were granted greater authority and autonomy in entering into multi-year deficit financing for operational purposes as well as for capital projects (Ministère des Affaires municipales et de la métropole, 2002b: 2).

In exchange for increasing the authority and autonomy of municipal governments and agencies, the provincial government decided that it wanted to increase accountability to the public and encourage greater public participation in decision-making. At least two major bills contained key provisions related to these matters. The first is Bill 29, adopted by the National Assembly in June 2001 (Québec, 2001c), which modified various municipal statutes in an effort to improve the democratic operation of local institutions. This bill also dealt with several public-consultation mechanisms and with rules for transparency in granting contracts for professional services. The legislation specified the responsibilities of the borough councils in this regard. It also sanctioned a process that allows citizens to make their opinions known to municipal governmental officials through referendums on planning issues. The second is Bill 106, titled 'Tools to favour democratic life and effectiveness of municipal administrations', which was adopted in the National Assembly on 14 June 2002. This legislation was enacted by the Quebec government to establish new mechanisms for public controls of municipal councils by requiring them to operate in a more transparent manner in the management of public funds.[7]

In summary, the jurisdictional reforms had two distinct and interrelated thrusts. The first was to increase the authority and autonomy of municipal governments and agencies, and the second was to increase both the degree of their accountability to the public and the opportunities for public participation in certain decisions. These dual thrusts were clearly articulated in the provincial government's White Paper on municipal reorganization (Québec, 2000a), which stated that bolstering municipal autonomy was a primary objective of the reforms. After noting that the Quebec provincial government would accord more auton-omy to the municipalities through the current reforms, the government spokesperson added that 'more transparent management' would be expected of the municipalities (Ministère des Affaires municipales et de la Métropole, 2002b: 1 [my translation]). This orientation was similar to those of previous municipal reforms in Quebec, including the one that created the MRCs (Bissonnette, 1982) and introduced new rules for urban and regional planning in 1979, and the reform for local taxation in 1980 (Commission Nationale sur les Finances et la Fiscalité Locales, 1999a). In the latter case, the central objective was to strengthen 'local autonomy'. However, this did not mean a reduction in provincial power and an increase in municipal power. Instead, it meant that the provincial government would not interfere unduly or excessively in the functions that were assigned explicitly and exclusively to municipal governments. The jurisdictional reforms did not change the balance of power between the provincial and municipal governments. The realignment of powers between the government of Quebec and the municipal governments under recent legislation reflects the new realities to which public management must respond, in terms of effectiveness, efficiency, and accountability. Municipal management is faced with increasingly diverse and more specialized social demands than in the past, but due to the Canadian Constitution, ultimately the government of Quebec remains responsible for the efficacy of municipal governance and management and for the quality of munici-pal services that the municipalities are required to provide their residents.

The Politics of Reforms

The municipal reforms during the past decade have generated a remarkable, but not unexpected, degree of political controversy. In many respects they produced one of the most substantial political controversies of the decade and possibly even longer. Indeed, only the politics of sovereignty-association and language policy have generated more controversy. Most of that controversy surrounded the three components of the structural reforms—amalgamation, de-amalgamation, and the reconfiguration of regional authorities. The functional, financial, and jurisdic-tional reforms did not generate much controversy beyond the usual levels of disagreement between provincial and municipal officials on such matters. The most controversial were the financial reforms limiting the level of financial trans-fers from the provincial to the municipal governments, which were designed to serve the dual purpose of helping the provincial government to deal with its fiscal pressures and to encourage municipalities to opt for amalgamation.

The controversy related to the three components of the restructuring initiatives involved members of the governmental and private sectors who had different views on the merits of restructuring. In discussing the politics of restructuring it is necessary to distinguish between the politics of amalgamation and de-amalgamation. The strongest and most visible proponents of amalgamation were elected and appointed provincial government officials of the Parti Québécois governments in power between 1994 and 2003. However, they were not alone in advocating amalgamations. The mayors and influential members of the business community in many of the largest urban municipalities also supported the restructuring initiative and shared the view of the provincial officials that increasing the size of municipalities was a way to reform inefficient municipal management. This was most notably the case for Montreal and Quebec City. The mayors and influential members of the business community of both cities were fully behind the provincial government's plan of amalgamating municipalities and reconfiguring regional authorities. Indeed, they campaigned with the provincial minister to convince both their counterparts and the general public of the merits of the provincial government's reform project. The opponents of amalgamations were generally the mayors, councillors, influential community leaders, and ratepayers of the small suburban and rural municipalities. They were particularly opposed to what many of them described as the provincial government's authoritarianism in refusing to respect local democracy by imposing amalgamations. Despite their strong opposition, however, the Parti Québécois government remained resolute. Its resoluteness undoubtedly cost it some of the support it would have needed to win the 2003 election, which it lost to the Liberal Party.

De-amalgamation was also controversial. Those who favoured it and those who opposed it campaigned actively, particularly after the Liberal Party made it clear that it would allow communities in amalgamated municipalities to hold referendums on the matter if a sufficient number of eligible voters petitioned for de-amalgamation. Although the new Liberal provincial government was not necessarily in favour of de-amalgamation, it felt constrained to honour its commitment made in the years leading up to the 2003 election. Individuals and communities were quite divided on the issue and it is therefore not surprising that not all amalgamated municipalities opted for a referendum and that of those that did less than 20 per cent opted for de-amalgamation. Some of the most interesting and intense of these contests were those related to the de-amalgamation of former municipalities with a high percentage of anglophones, who felt that amalgamated municipalities compromised both their sense of belonging to distinct local linguistic communities and also their ability to deal with the service and development needs and preferences of such communities.

Assessment of Reforms

To reiterate, the general objectives of the reforms during the past decade have been to reduce the number of municipalities and to strengthen their governance capacity (Québec, 2000a). The objective here is to consider to what extent the reforms have contributed to those objectives. This is, and will likely remain, a highly debated issue. In my estimation, however, the reforms have not contributed sufficiently to those objectives. The foregoing analysis reveals that the provincial government made only modest gains in reducing the number of municipalities. They fell far short of their desired objectives. Although they reduced the number of municipalities by approximately 300 during that time, Quebec continues to have the highest number of municipalities and more than two and one-half times the number that exist in Ontario.

The reforms also fell short in strengthening governance capacity in the face of imperatives created by the national, continental, and global political economy. Part of the reason for this is that, when placed in their historical context, the changes produced by the recent reforms (Guay, 2001) were quite modest. At best, the recent reforms constitute but one small step in the transformation of municipal governance and management frameworks that is required in the context of globalization. Despite appearances and accusations that the provincial government was radical and reckless in undertaking recent reforms without paying sufficient attention to the nature of current relations between the municipal and the provincial governments, those reform initiatives suggest that the provincial government actually showed considerable restraint and timidity in structural, functional, financial, and jurisdictional reforms. The time may have come for boldness to ensure that the municipal system is organized appropriately and operates efficiently and effectively with the requisite degree of administrative and political accountability. The reason for this is that all municipalities, but particularly large municipalities in Quebec, like those in Ontario (Williams, 1999), find themselves confronted with new requirements for competitiveness and performance. Much more extensive reforms than those implemented during the past decade will be needed to maintain and improve economic competitiveness and performance.

The limited amount of restructuring and the modest scope of the functional, financial, and jurisdictional reforms are not likely to do much to enhance municipal capacity in various types of regions. At this point in time, I am skeptical about the beneficial effects of those reforms for the governance capacity of municipalities in Quebec (Hamel, 2001). Part of the reason for this is that reformers have placed undue emphasis on the importance of structural, functional, financial, and jurisdictional reforms as a means of improving such capacity. Such reforms, on their own, will not necessarily lead to improvements in governance capacity. Although those are important elements of governance capacity, equally important is the ability of local municipalities and regional authorities to co-ordinate their respective initiatives. In the case of metropolitan regions such as Montreal, for example, the questions persist regarding what the metropolitan community— whose powers remain limited—can do to orient development and planning on a region-wide scale. The current configuration of their boundaries, functions, finances, and jurisdictional authority will not suffice for them to succeed in achieving their goals. Rather, their success will depend on their ability to create a spirit of co-operation between the municipalities and the main actors of the civil society. Changes in attitudes and relations are essential for achieving their goals. This is an immense challenge that few metropolitan regions have met successfully to date.

At the time of writing the most significant question regarding the effects of municipal reforms on the governance, management, planning, and development capacity of municipal governments involves the transitional and long-term effects of the pending de-amalgamation of 32 municipalities, 15 of which are within the Montreal metropolitan region and 17 in other metropolitan and non-metropolitan regions. The most obvious effect is the loss of people and property tax base for the new amalgamated municipalities. In Montreal's case, for example, its population will shrink from 1.8 million to 1.6 million and its property tax base will shrink from $127 billion to $103 billion. Thus, the de-merger cost Montreal 200,000 inhabitants and $24 billion of its property tax base. Apart from changes to the population and tax base of municipalities such as Montreal, the de-amalgamations raise three questions that are not answerable at this time. What effect will the de-amalgamations have on the efforts of the amalgamated municipalities to continue to implement various initiatives pursuant to the goals for which they were established, given that they are losing some control over a portion of the territory and population? What effect will they have on the relations between the de-amalgamated municipalities and the ones from which they are de-amalgamating on regulatory, development, and servicing matters? Will the uncertainty created by the de-amalgamations continue to create delays in undertaking some additional reforms of potential benefit to municipal governments and their communities?

Finally, in assessing the effects of recent reforms on the governance, management, planning, and development capacity of municipal governments, it is important to note that transitional problems have emerged and that these problems should not be overlooked. Notable among such problems in Quebec's case are those arising from the amalgamations. For example, in the case of Montreal, shortly after the creation of the new city, two major problems arose—(1) labour relations involving municipal employees and (2) the allotment of financial resources in an equitable manner between the boroughs.

The harmonization of collective agreements between the former City of Montreal and the 27 municipalities of the envisaged new island municipality established pursuant to Bill 170 left open the question of the distribution of power between the trade unions, which represented workers, and the municipal administration. In the case of the blue-collar workers, whose numbers almost doubled with the creation of the new city, compromise agreements remain difficult because the new city has limited financial resources in its budget. At a union meeting on 13 November 2002, the blue-collar workers for the City of Montreal voted to support a series of measures to pressure for a full strike in their negotiations over their first collective agreement with the new municipal administration. A provision in Bill 170, which states that the harmonization of collective agreements should not occur with extra costs for 2003, limits the margin of manoeuvrability for the municipal administration, making an agreement acceptable to both parties unlikely.

The distribution of the financial resources among the amalgamated boroughs constitutes the second transitional problem for the new city. The City of Montreal was given a 10-year period to establish harmonization between taxes and services for its boroughs. In 2003, the municipal administration created equalization funds, which will make it possible to redistribute part of the financial resources coming from the former rich suburbs of the Island of Montreal to the less affluent city-centre boroughs in order to secure the overall level of services. The municipal reforms reveal the disparities that prevail between the rich suburbs of the island and the less affluent city-centre boroughs. This is evident in several facets of the system, but particularly in the substantially larger number of employed professionals working in old city suburbs than in the city-centre boroughs. It remains to be seen how much money will be needed to achieve fiscal equalization between boroughs over the next few years.

Predictions of Future Reforms

It is difficult to predict the type of structural, functional, financial, and jurisdictional reforms that are likely to be considered, proposed, and implemented in the near future. Nevertheless, based on past experience there are likely to be other rounds of reforms attempting to frame a system of municipal governance that meets the needs of the communities not only according to the perceptions of their governments and ratepayers but also those of the provincial government and its officials.

The prospects for further structural reforms in the future will depend on perceptions by provincial and municipal government officials and their ratepayers regarding the effects of the recent restructuring on various facets of municipal and provincial governance, and particularly on planning and development in metropolitan and non-metropolitan regions. More specifically, the prospects for restructuring in such regions will depend on the perceptions of the provincial government and local municipal councils regarding the efficacy of the existing system on the governance capacity of municipalities to plan and deliver public services and to foster economic and social development on an efficient and equitable basis for an entire region. Future structural reforms within such regions will also depend on the nature of interaction between local and regional municipal governing bodies, including the municipal governments that will be operating in January 2006 as a result of de-amalgamation, within their regions both with each other and with key individuals, organizations, and corporations that perform important roles in economic and social development.

The most difficult question to answer at this time regarding potential restructuring in the future is whether any of the amalgamated municipalities that did not avail themselves of the de-amalgamation option during the provincially sanctioned process in 2004 will attempt to compel the provincial government to permit them to do so in the future. That possibility leaves some uncertainty in the municipal system. Of course, restructuring of municipalities, either by local or provincial preference, has never been and will never be something in which a high degree of certainty or predictability prevails. In the future, as in the past, changing municipal boundaries is one of the means that provincial and local governments will likely use for their respective purposes. However, adverse electoral effects experienced by the Parti Québécois in the 2003 election as a result of the amalgamations it imposed will likely make provincial governments a little more careful regarding the processes they use in effecting structural changes. Imposing municipal boundaries is a politically costly reform initiative for provincial governments.

At the functional level there is reason to believe that in the years to come the roles and responsibilities of municipalities are likely to increase for several reasons. First, municipal services will become increasingly important in the framework of the current economic system, which, more than ever, is predicated on the provision of services. Another reason is the need for municipalities to be competitive in attracting human and financial capital. In light of globalization this will become increasingly important. Finally, the growing demands of citizens to obtain better-quality services and improved democratic practices in decisions regarding the provision of and fees for such services tend to increase the importance and legitimacy of municipalities. In light of the changes introduced by recent reforms, it is possible that municipalities will actually exercise their new powers to maximize decentralization of functions and possibly even the requisite jurisdictional authority and finances for the same. However, this is not the only potential scenario for the future. Whether that happens is highly contingent on the extent to which the demands of municipal governments coincide and are constant with the efforts of the provincial government to balance its functional capacity with its financial capacity.

The prospects for major financial reforms are not great, because the provincial and municipal governments seem to have achieved what might be termed a working balance in the financial arrangements between them. Notwithstanding the fact that they are not perfectly happy with that balance, neither the provincial government nor the municipal governments seem very intent or adventuresome in implementing radical changes in the near future. As in other provinces, for its part the Quebec government would like to reduce municipal dependency on provincial transfers even further, and for their part municipalities would like to increase access to alternative revenue sources that are currently under exclusive provincial and federal control. However, the prospects of either of those options materializing in Quebec in the very near future are no better than they are in any other province. Much will depend on what happens with the federal government's 'new deal for municipalities' and particularly the way that the Quebec government reacts to it in transferring any financial resources from the federal to the municipal governments.

Finally, the likelihood also is not very great that any major jurisdictional reforms will be undertaken in Quebec in the near future. Although successive Quebec provincial governments since the 1960s have introduced legislation and policies ostensibly designed to strengthen the powers of municipal governments and have made political statements favouring increased decentralization for the management of public-sector services, these did not happen to any significant degree (Hamel and Klein, 1998). The reticence exhibited by successive provincial governments to devolve jurisdictional authority to municipal governments during the past four decades indicates that we should not expect much of a change in the near future. This is particularly true of the MRCs. Despite the new regionalist discourse towards strengthening the MRCs advanced in the last few years by the government of Quebec, the control exercised at the provincial level is at no risk of being diminished. If any significant changes in jurisdictional authority are likely to occur the much greater likelihood is that they will first occur in the metropolitan regions as a result of what seems to be a growing demand on the part of city-regions, which in Canada includes Montreal, to be empowered to a greater extent than they or any other municipalities are today.

Quebec has had an interesting and arguably important series of reforms during the past decade. At this juncture the provincial and municipal governments are working diligently on implementing the de-amalgamations. In watching that process one gets the clear impression that a certain degree of 'reform fatigue' has set in and is conditioning all sides not to prepare for another major round of reforms for a few years. Of course, governments rarely have the luxury of having full control of their own agenda. Invariably, either changing conditions or new initiatives by other governments require them to act. It is only a matter of time, therefore, before such a situation arises and municipal reforms will be high on the agenda. The implementation of the federal government's 'new deal for municipalities' seems to be the most likely candidate for creating such a situation in the very near future.

CONCLUSION

To reiterate, the objective of this chapter has been to provide an overview and analysis of the purpose, nature and scope, politics, and effects of the municipal reforms in Quebec over the past 10–15 years, as well as some predictions regarding the prospects for additional reforms in the future. This analysis has revealed that the purpose of municipal reforms was to consolidate and reconfigure the municipal sector as a means to enhance the governance capacity of municipalities and regional municipal authorities in the face of imperatives created by trends towards economic globalization.

Although the reforms received considerable attention, in many respects they were relatively limited in scope. The reforms produced politics that were both partisan and non-partisan. They not only pitted provincial parties against each other, but also placed various groupings of provincial and municipal governments and ratepayers on opposing sides. The prospect for future reform is highly contingent on a plethora of factors, the most important of which are the perceptions of the governmental stakeholders regarding both the effects of this particular round of reforms and the need for additional reforms to advance their respective governance goals and objectives in the face of changing provincial, national, continental, and global economies. The hope is that any future reforms are rooted in a sounder theoretical framework regarding the nature of the problems and the best means by which to deal with them.

NOTES

1. Before Act 125 was adopted, 'The county municipalities encompassed all the municipalities ruled by the Municipal Code—that is, the local village and countryside municipalities. . . . This included a total of around 1,300 municipalities comprising 20

per cent of the population of Quebec. They covered a third of the territory of Quebec'
(Bissonnette, 1982: 29 [my translation]). On the other hand, the Loi des Cités et Villes
(Cities and Towns Act), passed in the 1870s, covered the division between rural and
urban municipalities and affected municipalities with more than 2,000 inhabitants.
After 1968, with the passage of Bill 285, the Loi des Cités et Villes no longer made a
distinction between towns and cities (Meynaud and Léveillée, 1973: 15). Finally, certain
municipalities, such as Montreal and Quebec City, are ruled by special laws.

2. These were RCM Autray and RCM Bécancouer.

3. See, in particular, the reports of the Groupe de Travail sur Montréal et sa Région (1993)
and, more recently, the Commission Nationale sur les Finances et la Fiscalité Locales
(1999a).

4. The mechanism that aims to establish equitable representation is more sophisticated. It
is difficult to summarize it in a few lines. Representation varies according to different
profiles, depending on the population and the history of the respective borough. Each
borough council has at least three elected members. Each borough with fewer than
30,000 inhabitants must elect at least one councillor to sit on the city council. For each
group of 30,000 inhabitants above this number, another councillor is elected. This was
the case in 14 boroughs in the November 2001 municipal election in Montreal. 'One or
two borough councillors [had to be elected] to attain the minimum of three. . . . Five
boroughs were exceptions to this principle, as they elected two borough councillors
even though they already had three city councillors. These boroughs were constituted
from old suburbs with a large population (Verdun, Saint-Léonard, Saint-Laurent,
Montréal-Nord, and Lasalle)' (Bruneault et al., 2002: 5 [my translation]). In principle,
borough councils have the mandate of responsibility for neighbourhood services—that
is, services for individuals. Their powers and obligations are in the following sectors:
urban planning; fire prevention; waste removal; economic, community, and social
development; culture, recreation, and borough parks; and local roadworks (Québec,
2000c: 253). They must share a certain number of powers with the city and with the
CMM. Their only exclusive power concerns waivers on interdictions to convert buildings into condos and fire prevention (Bruneault and Collin, 2002: 8). As well, the
borough council 'may formulate notices and make recommendations to the city
council on the budget, on establishment of budgetary priorities, on preparation of and
changes to the urban plan, on changes to urban planning rules, or on any other subject
that the city council submits to it' (Québec, 2000c: 101 [my translation]).

5. In the case of Quebec City, the Communauté Métropolitaine was created through
adoption of Bill 137. Like the Montreal metropolitan community, the Quebec City
metropolitan community came into effect on 1 January 2002 (Québec, 2000d).

6. These are the Montreal Botanical Garden, the Montreal Planetarium, the Biodome, and
the Cosmodome (Space Camp Canada).

7. In a press statement about the government's intentions, the Minister of Municipal
Affairs said, 'No contract will be able to be awarded in a municipality solely on a discre-
tionary basis. As a general rule, contracts will have to be submitted to public calls for
tenders, and these calls for tenders will be analyzed with all the necessary rigour, transparency, and equity so that they will be granted to the people who offer the best
quality-price ratio' (Breton and Trottier, 2002: E-1 [my translation]).

References

Baccigalupo, A., and F.P. Nkot. 2001. 'Pourquoi le gouvernement de Lucien Bouchard t-il
enfin osé?', in Côté (2001: 526–31).

Bissonnette, R. 1982. 'La régionalisation municipale au Québec (1960–1980): visées
technocratiques et résistances locales', MA thesis, University of Ottawa.

Boisclair, A. 2002. '2002: le nouveau visage du Québec', *Municipalité* 33, 1: 18–19.

Breton, P., and E. Trottier. 2002. 'Québec serre la vis aux villes', *La Presse*, 20 June, E-1.

Bruneault, F., and J.-P. Collin. 2002. 'Le partage des compétences'. Information sheet. Montréal, Service à la collectivité, UQAM.

————— et al. 2002. 'Les structures de représentation politique'. Information sheet. Montréal, Service à la collectivité, UQAM.

Collin, J.-P. 2001. 'Le milieu rural et les MRC en attente de réforme', in Côté (2001: 235–42).

Comité des élus de la Région métropolitaine de Montréal. 2000. 'Rapport portant sur la fiscalité d'agglomération'. Montréal, 29 June.

Commission Nationale sur les Finances et la Fiscalité Locales. 1999a. *Pacte 2000, Rapport de la Commission Nationale sur les Finances et la Fiscalité Locales.* Quebec City: Gouvernement du Québec.

—————. 1999b. 'Fiche d'information no 15: Les pratiques de gestion et les relations de travail dans les municipalités'. 20 Apr.

Corriveau, J. 2002. 'Les policiers craignent d'être les grands oubliés', *Le Devoir*, 5 June, A-4.

Côté, R., ed. 2001. *Québec 2002. Annuaire politique, social, économique et culturel.* Montreal: Fides.

Courville, S. 2000. *Le Québec. Genèses et mutations du territoire.* Sainte-Foy: Les Presses de l'Université Laval, L'Harmattan.

Drapeau, J. 1973. 'Étude chronologique de la constitution et du regroupement des municipalités du Québec', *Municipalités* 5, 17: 11–13.

Faure, A. 2002. 'L'agenda revisité des politiques publiques', Seminar *Les fusions de municipalités, une autre révolution tranquille?* INRS-Urbanisation, Culture et Société, Montréal, 23 May.

Fischler, Raphael, John Meligrana, and Jeanne M. Wolfe. 2004. 'Canadian Experiences of Local Government Boundary Reform: A Comparison of Quebec and Ontario', in Meligrana, ed., *Redrawing Local Government Boundaries: An International Study of Politics, Procedures, and Decisions.* Vancouver: University of British Columbia Press, 75–105.

Girard, M.-C. 2002. 'Des services municipaux paralysés', *La Presse*, 15 May, E-1.

Groupe de Travail sur Montréal et sa Région. 1993. *Montréal une ville-région: efficace, prospère et vibrante, à vocation internationale, au service des citoyens.* Montréal: Le Groupe de Travail.

Guay, L. 2001. 'La longue et tortueuse évolution de l'aménagement du territoire', in Côté (2001: 51–61).

Hamel, P. 2001. 'Enjeux métropolitains: les nouveaux défis', *International Journal of Canadian Studies/Revue internationale d'études canadiennes* 24: 106–27.

————— and L. Jalbert. 1991. 'Local power in Canada: stakes and challenges in the restructuring of the state', in C. Pickvance and E. Preteceille, eds, *State Restructuring and Local Power: A Comparative Perspective.* London and New York: Pinter, 170–96.

————— and J.-L. Klein. 1998. 'Le développement régional au Québec: enjeu de pouvoir et discours politique', in M.-U. Proulx, ed., *Le phénomène régional au Québec.* Sainte-Foy: Presses de l'Université du Québec, 293–311.

————— and Jean Rousseau. 2003. 'Revisiting Municipal Reforms in Quebec and the New Responsibilities of Local Actors in a Globalizing World', paper presented to the Municipal-Provincial-Federal Relations Conference, Institute of Intergovernmental Relations, Queen's University, 9–10 May.

Hamel, P.J. 2002. 'Le "Pacte fiscal" entre le gouvernement du Québec et les municipalités: la raison du plus fort est toujours la meilleure'. Montréal, INRS-Urbanisation, Culture et Société, Groupe de recherche sur l'innovation municipale.

Meynaud, J., and J. Léveillée. 1973. *La régionalisation municipale au Québec.* Montréal: Les Éditions Nouvelle Frontière.

Ministère de la Sécurité publique du Québec. 2001. *Vers une nouvelle carte policière.* Ministerial consultation document on policing organization. Quebec City: Ministère de la Sécurité publique du Québec.

Ministère des Affaires municipales et de la Métropole. 2001. *Muni Express* 13: 1.

———. 2002a. 'Les enjeux en matière de gouvernance et les initiatives provinciales', Working paper, 2001 provincial–territorial meeting of ministers responsible for local administrations.

———. 2002b. 'Projet de loi no 106—"Des outils favorisant la vie démocratique et l'efficacité des administrations municipales", André Boisclair', news release, 9 May.

Québec. 1996. *Le renforcement des institutions municipales. La consolidation des communautés locales.* Quebec City: Gouvernement du Québec.

———. 2000a. *La réorganisation municipale, changer les façons de faire, pour mieux servir les citoyens.* Quebec City: Gouvernement du Québec.

———. 2000b. *Projet de loi no 124 modifiant la Loi sur l'organisation territoriale municipale et d'autres dispositions législatives.* Quebec City: Éditeur officiel du Québec. Adopted 11 May 2000.

———. 2000c. *Projet de loi no 170 créant les nouvelles villes de Montréal, Québec, Longueuil, Lévis et Gatineau.* Quebec City: Éditeur officiel du Québec. Adopted 20 Dec. 2000.

———. 2000d. *Projet de loi no 134 instituant la Communauté métropolitaine de Montréal.* Quebec City: Éditeur officiel du Québec. Adopted 16 June 2000.

———. 2000e. *Projet de loi no 110 modifiant diverses dispositions legislatives concernant le domaine municipal.* Quebec City: Éditeur officiel du Québec. Adopted 11 May 2000.

———. 2000f. *Projet de loi no 137, Loi sur la Communauté métropolitaine de Québec.* Quebec City: Éditeur officiel du Québec. Adopted 2 June 2000.

———. 2001a. *Politique nationale de la ruralité.* Quebec City: Ministère des régions, Gouvernement du Québec.

———. 2001b. *Projet de loi no 77, Loi modifiant diverses dispositions legislatives concernant les municipalités régionales de comté.* Quebec City: Éditeur officiel du Québec. Tabled Dec. 2001 for adoption in spring of 2002.

———. 2001c. *Projet de loi no 29, Loi modifiant diverses dispositions législatives en matière municipale.* Quebec City: Éditeur officiel du Québec. Adopted 21 June 2001.

———. 2003a. *Projet de loi no 9, Loi concernant la consultation des citoyens sur la réorganisation territoriale de certaines municipalités.* Quebec City: Éditeur officiel du Québec. Adopted Dec. 2003.

_____. 2003b. *Municipal Reorganization in Québec.* Quebec City: Gouvernement du Québec.

——— et l'Union des Municipalités du Québec et la Fédération Québécoise des Municipalités. 2000. Entente financière et fiscale entre le Gouvernement du Québec et l'Union des Municipalités du Québec et la Fédération Québécoise des Municipalités, 20 June.

Quesnel, Louise. 1990. 'Political Control Over Planning in Quebec', *International Journal of Urban and Regional Research* 14, 1: 33.

———. 2000. 'Municipal Reorganization in Quebec', *Canadian Journal of Regional Science* 23, 1: 115–34.

Saïdah, R. 2000. 'La pacte fiscal est signé, enfin!', *Municipalité* (Oct.–Nov.): 4–6.

Sancton, A. 2000. *Merger Mania: The Assault on Local Government.* Westmount, Que.: Prince Patterson.

Smith, B.C. 1985. *Decentralization: The Territorial Dimension of the State.* London and Boston: George Allen & Unwin.

Williams, W. 1999. 'Institutional capacity and metropolitan governance: The Greater Toronto Area', *Cities* 16, 3: 171–80.

CHAPTER 8

Municipal Reform in Nova Scotia: A Long-standing Agenda for Change

DALE H. POEL

INTRODUCTION

This chapter[1] reviews and analyzes the structural, functional, financial, and juris-dictional dimensions of Nova Scotia's municipal reform agenda since the early 1990s. First, it is useful to discuss briefly the historical and contemporary context of those reforms as well as the factors that provided the impetus for and ultimately shaped them.

Any review of provincial-municipal relations, the organization of municipal government, and the nature of municipal services in Nova Scotia must begin with a reference to the Graham Commission (Nova Scotia, 1974). That Royal Commission asked most of the important questions regarding key issues and options for municipal reform in its questionnaire to the Union of Nova Scotia Municipalities (UNSM) (vol. IV, app. 10). Several of those questions remain on the provincial-municipal agenda to this day and revolve around the following issues:

- the structure and boundaries of municipal jurisdictions;
- the allocation of services between municipal governments and the provincial government and the distinction between 'general' and 'local' services;
- the financing of municipal services, property taxes, grants, and assessment;
- the nature of provincial-municipal relations and the status of municipal governments.

Nova Scotia's municipal reform initiatives in the 1990s, which are highlighted in Table 8.1, have picked up many of the unresolved aspects of those issues. These initiatives begin with the appointment of a Task Force on Local Government in 1991 and include the introduction of service exchange, two provincially driven municipal amalgamations, one municipally initiated amalgamation, and a joint review of roles and responsibilities.

The Municipal Government Act of 1999 was first of all a consolidation of most, but not all, legislation dealing with municipal government. It brought together the Planning Act, the tax collection provisions of the Assessment Act, the legislation creating the Cape Breton and Halifax regional municipalities, the towns and village service Acts, Deed Transfer Tax Act, and several others. It brought all municipal governments under one piece of legislation. It also gave more authority and autonomy in some areas to municipalities (see Appendix to this chapter). A reading of the Act, however, shows that it also brought forward the traditional and limiting specification of municipal authority that, for example, allows municipalities to remove dead, dying, or diseased trees and to spend money for snowplows.

The municipal reform initiatives of the past decade began with the creation of the Nova Scotia Local Government Task Force by the Minister of Municipal Affairs in 1991 (Vojnovic, 1997). A subsequent discussion paper produced by the department identified several factors that 'necessitated' a review of the municipal system (Nova Scotia DHMA, 1993). The most notable of these factors were the following:

- Several municipalities were either insolvent or on the verge of insolvency.
- Some private-sector groups had identified the number of municipal governments in the province as problematic (e.g., Chamber of Commerce).
- Municipal-provincial cost-shared programs and the proliferation of regional bodies were seen as diluting accountability for services and their costs.
- The Joint Task Force had identified the need for the reallocation of service responsibilities and for boundary changes as major priorities.

Other related factors that ultimately proved quite influential in driving the municipal reform agenda included challenges faced by municipal governments, challenges faced by the provincial government, and challenges in the relationship between those two orders of government. The most significant of these include the following:

- The challenges of many municipalities to provide the traditional mix of municipal services.
- The challenges of inter-municipal competition for economic development within the Halifax region.
- The challenges of the initial attempts at provincial-municipal service exchange.
- The challenges posed by the ongoing budgetary crisis of the Nova Scotia provincial government.

Structural Reforms

The structural reforms to Nova Scotia municipal government have been very visible to citizens. Reforms have produced changes in the number of municipalities,

Table 8.1 Sequence of Initiatives/Events in Nova Scotia Municipal Reform

Year		Initiatives and Events
1991		The appointment of the Task Force on Local Government by the Minister of Municipal Affairs
1992		Task Force on Local Government Report presented to government
1993		Department of Municipal Affairs produces Provincial-Municipal Service Exchange: A Discussion Paper
		Provincial election: change of government from Cameron/Progressive Conservative to Savage/Liberal government
1994		Provincial-Municipal Service Exchange—starting point for iterative process
		Cape Breton Regional Municipality Act
1995		Halifax Regional Municipality Act
		Queens Regional Municipality Act
1996	April	Halifax Regional Municipality comes into existence
		Queens Regional Municipality comes into existence
	June	Nova Scotia Municipal Legislative Review Committee: discussion paper
	Sept.	NS Municipal Government Act: A Working Paper in Legislative Form
1997		Premier's commitment to undertake, with the Union of Nova Scotia Municipalities, a Joint Review of Provincial and Municipal Roles and Responsibilities
1998		Formal memorandum commits province and UNSM to Joint Review
		Nova Scotia Department of Environment—banning organic material from landfills
		Province commits to phasing-in of provincial responsibilities for social services over a five-year period
1999	April	Municipal Government Act consolidates municipal legislation
		Municipal-Provincial Roles and Responsibilities Review produces General Work Plan and a Guide to Broad Principles for the Review (UNSM and NSHMA)
2000–1		Continued negotiations around delivery of services and responsibilities
		Provincial proposal to transfer funding of municipal equalization grants to municipal property, along with provincial take-up of corrections, social housing, and a grant in lieu of property tax for university residences
		Municipalities assume costs of assessment services provided through Service Nova Scotia and Municipal Relations
2002		The province and municipalities agree to fund a municipal equalization grant from increased taxes from Nova Scotia Power. Provincial legislation moved in this direction after rejection of the municipal suggestion to fund equalization from the deed transfer tax. The UNSM wants NSP taxes paid based on location of assets
		The provincial department (SNSMR) brings a Municipal Indicators Project on stream
2003		The province follows through with its commitment to develop a 'Guiding Principles Agreement' to formalize its working relationship with the Union of Nova Scotia Municipalities
		The province introduces legislation, Bill 40, that would place a cap on property assessment, while the UNSM opposes such a modification to the current 'market-based' assessment program.
2004		The province gives UNSM notice that a new municipally controlled agency will oversee assessment services effective 1 April 2005

the regional special-purpose bodies, the legislation to create regional municipal authorities, and also in alternative governing authorities at the local level. The amalgamations of municipal governments in the industrial Cape Breton and Halifax regions have been the most visible and, in the Halifax area, the most controversial (Poel, 2000). These two amalgamations were initiated by the provincial government. The third amalgamation, uniting the Municipality of Queens County and the town of Liverpool into the Region of Queens Municipality, was initiated at the local level. Despite those differences in approach to the creation of these regional municipalities, the legislation that applied to each of them was similar (Nova Scotia, 1994, 1995a, 1995b).

The principal reasons for the creation of these three municipalities were also similar, but not entirely the same. Improvement over the status quo was an objective in each case, but the precise focus of the improvement was different. The central objective for the creation of the Cape Breton Regional Municipality was to improve the financial viability of the nine municipalities of industrial Cape Breton, some of which could exist only with continued emergency funding from the province. Although the financial challenges provided the impetus for amalgamation (as discussed in the next section of this chapter), they did not change the overall dependency of the region on provincial assistance.

Ostensibly, the central objective for the creation of the Halifax Regional Municipality (HRM) was to achieve some cost savings (Hayward, 1993), but other issues were even more significant in the decision-making process. After all, the savings projected in the Hayward study represented less than 3 per cent of the combined municipal budgets. Even that projection was challenged as being overly optimistic in a study funded by the four municipalities (UMA, 1995). There were other possible reasons for the unilateral provincial initiative to create the HRM. The government of the day (Premier Savage, Liberal) considered the amalgamation of Halifax, Dartmouth, Bedford, and Halifax County as a solution to dysfunctional economic competition between the business and industrial parks of the separate municipalities *and* a solution to a serious political and financial problem occasioned by the provincial service exchange initiative. Amalgamation was also seen as a means to resolve the Halifax Regional Authority's impasse on the location of a new, second-generation landfill site.

The highlight of dysfunctional economic competition was seen in the expensive capturing of the first 'big box' store (Price Club/Costco) by Halifax, after the store had decided to locate in Dartmouth's generally more successful business park. The substance of service exchange will be discussed below. We note here, however, that the Halifax amalgamation brought together a rural/suburban county that was being financially 'penalized' by service exchange with three urban communities that would be 'rewarded'. By itself, the county municipality would have acquired responsibility for more than $4 million in new services in the 1995 service exchange formula. The municipalities of Halifax, Dartmouth, and Bedford together would gain by $12.9 million (Vojnovic, 1999). The HRM amalgamation brought the financial equation of service exchange into a more politically acceptable balance for the province's capital region.

Finally, the Region of Queens Municipality was created to achieve better services for the residents, possibly to achieve some economies of scale, and in recognition of a community of interest between the rural and village areas of Queens County and the town of Liverpool. Various forms of annexation and amalgamation had been discussed over a period of years. The region is dominated by the pulp and paper industry, the related forest industries, and some fisheries. It has a total population of less than 12,000. In terms of the benefits of amalgamation, this regional municipality is in a league by itself when compared to the Cape Breton (118,000) and Halifax (343,000) amalgamations, both in terms of scale and in regard to community acceptance of the change. By all accounts, this has been a 'successful' amalgamation measured by improved financial capacity, financial management, and service provision. It could serve as an example to other Nova Scotia counties that include small towns surrounded by rural areas with a more favourable tax base and lower property tax rates.

These amalgamation initiatives, particularly the negative reactions to the provincially driven Halifax amalgamation, led to the passage of the Regional Municipalities Act (1996) and ultimately the consolidation of this Act into the revised Municipal Government Act enacted in 1999. The legislation provides a mechanism for the amalgamation of municipal governments within a Nova Scotia county into a single regional municipality.

An important feature of the new legislation for existing municipalities was the promise of the provincial government not to force future amalgamation when faced with civic opposition. The new legislation calls for a study 'to determine whether a regional municipality would be in the interests of the people of the county' and requires a plebiscite in which a majority of those voting must favour the establishment of a regional municipality (Municipal Government Act, s. 372). Despite the relative success of the Queens experience, which occurred prior to the new legislation, the option for the creation of regional municipalities on a voluntary basis has not produced any further amalgamation initiatives.

In addition to the creation of regional municipalities, structural reforms in Nova Scotia have entailed both the elimination and the creation of some local authorities responsible for performing key functions in areas of transportation, waste disposal, and economic development. A notable example of the elimination of such local authorities resulted from the creation of the HRM, which led to the elimination of the Halifax Regional Authority. The Authority had been successful in fulfilling its responsibility for bus transportation, but less successful in fulfilling its responsibility for solid waste landfills.

During this era the provincial government also created several types of regional authorities for economic development and waste management. The Regional Development Authorities (RDAs) 'were established in 1994 as the coordinating bodies charged with leading economic development at the local level' (Nova Scotia, 2002). The RDAs work broadly in the area of community economic development. The 13 RDAs have governing boards with representation from the community, the private sector, and municipal governments. They receive funding from the provincial government (Economic Development and Community

Services), the federal Atlantic Canada Opportunities Agency, and the respective municipalities within the RDA. The provincial amount is relatively modest. Each RDA receives a provincial grant of $125,000. The Halifax RDA serves the rural communities of HRM while HRM Real Property Services manages five municipal business parks located within the urban areas of HRM.

Regional authorities within the provincial Department of Environment and Labour were created for solid waste resource management. The province has introduced an ambitious management plan in this program area and initial targets for diversion have been met. To foster compliance with the solid waste, compost-ing, and recycling requirements of the Nova Scotia Environment Act and 'to encourage regional cooperation', the province created the seven administrative regions that include the entire province. They came into existence with the imple-mentation of the provincial solid waste resource management regulations (NS Reg. 25/96, amended NS Reg. 24/2002). The regulations require all the municipal-ities of each region to:

- prepare and submit to the region's [provincial] Administrator a regional solid waste-resource management plan;
- implement the regional plan within time frames approved by the provincial Administrator;
- submit to the Administrator reports about the progress achieved towards 50 per cent solid waste diversion. (Nova Scotia SW-RM Regulations, s. 40[1])

One remaining local authority needs to be identified. In a small way, the initial Halifax Regional Municipality Act and now the Municipal Government Act allow for some citizen participation and decision-making comparable to community committees that existed under the former Municipality of the County of Halifax. The HRM legislation allowed for the creation of community councils whose membership would comprise at least three HRM councillors of contiguous districts—communities of interest. The HRM community councils may have significant delegated power not only to recommend levels of service and special area rates to the regional council, but also to take decisions with respect to rezon-ing within their districts (Municipal Government Act, s. 521). All municipalities now have the authority to create community committees (s. 27, part 1), but these committees have less power than the community councils of HRM.

It is important to note that no further municipal amalgamations have occurred since the 1995–6 period, the point after which the province agreed not to pursue regional governments without consent of the regions. There remain some pres-sures for boundary review from smaller towns, especially where the tax base is located or has relocated to the rural county and the property tax burden within the town is rising. The five Pictou towns and Pictou County are one example of a possible amalgamation that was discussed as early as 1967 (the 'Sanford study') and again in the 1974 Graham Royal Commission. The conditions suggesting amalgamation are informally acknowledged, but not formally 'on the table'.

Although it is too early to produce a definitive assessment of the structural reforms discussed above, it is possible to make some preliminary observations regarding the effects they had on costs, economic development, management capacity, and governance. In terms of costs, the indications are that except for the small regional municipality of Queens the other urban amalgamations have not saved any money in the short to medium term. They have not reduced the cost of municipal government and, as suggested above, were not necessarily intended to do so. This is in spite of the fact that the question about cost savings in the delivery of municipal services continues to be the most common question asked of these regional municipalities.

Assessment of the impact of structural change in economic development is difficult because the structural changes have occurred in the context of significant economic changes. These economic changes would have occurred regardless of the structural changes. Industrial Cape Breton's losses of fishing, coal mining, and a steel industry, for example, have worsened the Island's economy, regardless of changes in municipal structure. HRM, on the other hand, is experiencing a major growth period, in part because of offshore oil and gas developments, not because of amalgamation. The HRM amalgamation, however, removed the competition between municipal units for this economic growth and did so at a time when New Brunswick was considered a serious competitor at the provincial level.

In terms of management capacity, indications are that the new regional municipalities have a stronger capacity for policy analysis and management of the public sector. The CBRM saw some decrease in the number of senior-level managers, while also benefiting from more staff specialization. HRM has stronger professional resources for developing 'business planning' processes and multi-year budgeting strategy, for exploring alternative service delivery, and for developing information systems that will support activity-based costing. All this, if completed successfully, may create a performance accountability framework that can more clearly and usefully link citizens, interest groups, political leaders, and the civic service in a dialogue around the nature and directions of municipal government. The achievement of this increased capacity depends on growth within the civic service and the political leadership.

In terms of improved governance, the structural reform that produced the HRM had some beneficial effects in strengthening its political voice largely due to the size of its population and economy vis-à-vis the rest of the province. The benefits of this political strength within the provincial arena became quite clear in a public debate between the HRM's mayor and the provincial Premier over priorities in the provincial project list for the Canada Strategic Infrastructure Fund. The initial list of provincial priorities announced by the provincial government consisted only of improvements to provincial highways. It did not include the Halifax harbour cleanup initiative. After a very public exchange, the Premier rather awkwardly put the harbour cleanup back on the list, saying the province now had two priorities—highways and harbour cleanup.

FUNCTIONAL REFORMS

The alignment of functions between the provincial and municipal governments has been the perennial issue of debate in provincial-municipal relations. The debate revolves around two questions: Which order of government should provide various services? Which order of government has the requisite resources to provide those services? These questions, which were initially addressed by the 1991 Local Government Task Force, were central to the 1995 service exchange and were still on the agenda of a Municipal-Provincial Roles and Responsibilities Review that began in 1999.

The provincial government viewed the 1995 service exchange as an attempt to rationalize service delivery between municipalities and the province, as well as between different municipalities. The result was that some municipalities, especially rural municipalities and those with limited fiscal capacity, became responsible for more services (roads and policing) than they had previously. Service exchange was seen, in part, as an attempt to address the issues of sprawl and tax rate differentials between small towns and rural municipalities. An initial version of service exchange also anticipated the elimination of Nova Scotia's two-tier social services system in which municipalities had responsibility for short-term assistance and the province focused on longer-term assistance. The final version, implemented in 1995, left municipalities responsible for some administration and programs of social services and kept a larger part of roads, the cost of property assessment services, and equalization with the province.

The best description and analysis of the 1995 service exchange policy can be found in research by Igor Vojnovic. This research is important for giving referenced public visibility to the perverse financial consequences Nova Scotia's service exchange had for individual municipalities. The 1995 version, while planned as revenue-neutral between the province and the municipalities in the aggregate, generated significant costs to the Nova Scotia municipalities with the weakest economic base in terms of per capita taxable assessment. Vojnovic (1999: 529) notes:

> While the province of Nova Scotia argued in its 1993 discussion paper that one of the aims of the service exchange was to alleviate the fiscal pressures on the financially weak municipalities, it was the fiscally weakest grouping [of municipalities] that faced the most significant fiscal burden after the exchange.

Service exchange was phased in over four years to enable municipalities to adjust to their new fiscal situation. As well, there were occasional ad hoc responses in the minister's office to requests from individual municipalities that were disadvantaged in this exchange. We noted above that the HRM amalgamation solved this disparity between service exchange costs to the more rural and less affluent Halifax County and the service exchange benefits to the urban, more affluent cities of Halifax, Dartmouth, and Bedford.

The attempt to initiate a service exchange that was revenue-neutral in the aggregate was a political, administrative, and financial reform. Ultimately, the impact on individual municipalities created ongoing political and policy problems and led to the legislative correction shown in Box 8.1.

A background paper for the 1999 Roles and Responsibilities Review provides an overview of the 1995 service exchange, the goals of which were:

Box 8.1   Adjusting for the Impact of Service Exchange

Effect of service exchange

40 (1) Each municipality that gains from the exchange of service responsibilities between municipalities and the Province shall pay to the Province three quarters of the gain in the year commencing April 1, 1995, one half of the gain in the year commencing April 1, 1996, and one quarter of the gain in the year commencing April 1, 1997.

(2) Each municipality that loses from the exchange of service responsibilities between municipalities and the Province shall be paid by the Province three quarters of the loss in the year commencing April 1, 1995, one half of the loss in the year commencing April 1, 1996, and one quarter of the loss in the year commencing April 1, 1997.

(3) The amount that each municipality gains or loses from the exchange of service responsibilities between municipalities and the Province shall be determined by the Minister.

Source: Nova Scotia (1989: ch. 302, s. 40, as amended 1994–5).

- to create strong, financially viable local governments;
- to develop a clearer, fairer provincial-municipal partnership; and
- to rationalize service provision by all governments. (UNSM and NSHMA, 1999: 8–9)

This exchange of services was to be guided by the principle that:

> Municipal units should be responsible for providing local services of primary concern to a community rather than the province as a whole. The Province should be responsible for the provision of services in which the entire province is concerned. Dual responsibilities [were] to be avoided wherever possible. (Ibid., 9)

The application of these principles gave the provincial government responsibility for:

- all municipal cost-sharing on child welfare;
- nursing homes and homes for the aged;
- probate court and the registry of deeds;
- home care and boards of health.

The municipalities took responsibility for police and suburban roads. This 1999 description of the 1995 service exchange seemed straightforward. These service areas would be exchanged and provincial grants for public transit, planning, building inspection, recreation, and emergency funding would be eliminated. In retrospect, however, the exchange was not straightforward. The transfer of suburban (j-class) roads to municipalities was a bigger burden to rural counties than to urban regions and included bridges. But some bridges were too expensive and beyond the technical competence of municipalities. After a year of experience, revisions were made to distinguish between small and 'big' bridges. The province resumed responsibility for the big bridges and the Department of Transportation continued responsibility for most roads at a fixed cost to the municipalities.

The largest area left unresolved in the earlier years of service exchange was the area of social services. Early in 1998 the province and the Union of Nova Scotia Municipalities signed a memorandum of understanding (MOU) in which both committed to the 'Roles and Responsibilities Review'. The MOU also laid out the process beginning in the 1998–9 budget year and ending in 2002–3 by which municipal contributions to social services would be reduced. This was an 'uploading' into a one-tier social service system of staff and programs and a budget amount of approximately $45 million. This move to one provincial system eliminated the variations in social service benefits found in municipal social assistance.

The policy to avoid dual responsibilities for services was questioned in the Joint Roles and Responsibilities Review. The development of provincial solid waste resource regions across the province is an interesting recent example of the difficulty of defining services as general or local.[2] The regulations and the role of the provincial regional administrator define a shared jurisdiction in which the province sets the policies and performance targets while the operational component is left to the municipalities. The development of new province-wide regulations for solid waste and resource management is probably the most important and visible functional reform during this period. The Solid Waste-Resource Management Regulations were in place by 1996 and were amended in 2002.[3] They are a good example of the interest the province and municipal governments share in most areas of importance to Nova Scotians and the difficulty of sorting general from 'local' services.

Property assessment has been another area under review. While not a service in the sense of social housing, parks, or recreation, it is an important aspect of municipal governance. Assessment services are provided by the province through the Service Nova Scotia and Municipal Relations Department but the service is now paid for by the municipalities. There has been provincial interest in creating a special operating agency to remove the function from the provincial department for a number of years. The municipalities are concerned that they are paying $12 million annually for a service and have no influence over its management. At the beginning of 2004, the province gave the UNSM notice that a new municipally controlled agency would oversee assessment services. The new Conservative minority government has continued in this direction. A Transition Board is proposed to anticipate the establishment of the agency with its board of directors as of April 2005.

Although the 1995 service exchange agreement was a single event, it was implemented and adapted over a period of time. Some services were caught in the middle because municipal governments with limited financial resources could not assume new responsibilities and maintain existing responsibilities without provincial cost-sharing and emergency grants. Services also became caught in the middle because a new provincial government (the Cameron Progressive Conservative government) faced continued budget deficits following campaign promises to move towards a balanced budget. The ongoing nature of this debate is highlighted by the fact that the decade began with a major task force on the responsibilities of local governments and ended with the Union of Nova Scotia Municipalities and the provincial government joining to undertake a major Municipal-Provincial Roles and Responsibilities Review exercise. The provincial commitment in 1997 to this joint review followed two years of adjustments to the 1995 service exchange. Both the province and the UNSM recognized that a number of issues were left unresolved or not addressed by the service exchange initiatives.

The subcommittees of the Review's Working Group show the breadth of the mandate and the extent to which provincial and municipal policy and program areas are intermingled. The subcommittees were: governance, revenue structure, general services, economic development, protective services, transportation, environment, land management, and recreation. The specifics of the subcommittees' work suggest that provincial and municipal interests are linked in each of the service areas, by regulation, cost-sharing, or related but separate programming. The Review began by characterizing the current (1999) state of provincial-municipal relations as one in which:

- Nova Scotia municipalities were frustrated by increased provincial regulations, which lead to increased costs and reduced autonomy.
- There remained mandatory funding of provincial programs.
- Municipalities were increasing their demands for provincial funding.
- Small towns faced fiscal challenges.
- The province continued to face fiscal challenges in the areas of health care, education, social programs, debt servicing, and infrastructure costs.
- Both levels of government faced financial constraints coupled with increased public expectations.

This description is a reminder of the continuing nature of this agenda and the link between programs, services, and the financial capacity to deliver the programs and services.

The foregoing overview of functional reforms focused primarily on Nova Scotia's service exchange initiative. The overview reveals that the nature and scope of the functional reforms were significant. However, the reforms were not as ambitious as had been envisioned either by the Task Force on Local Government during the early 1990s or by the Working Group of the Provincial-Municipal Roles and Responsibilities Review. Instead, the reforms initially were more limited in scope because of the financial constraints on the municipal and provincial governments and particularly because of the different financial capacities of various municipal governments. Such considerations limited the scope of service exchanges between the provincial and municipal governments. Consequently the provincial-municipal discussions and negotiations focused largely on which order of government would have financial responsibility under the existing alignment of functions.

One exception was the alignment of functions for solid waste and resource management. Both orders of government have key roles in performing these two important functions effectively, efficiently, and equitably. Although the removal of domestic solid waste is a local service, what is sorted and where it goes are policy and regulatory questions of importance to the entire province. This has been a significant initiative and leadership has been shown at both the municipal and provincial levels of government as Nova Scotians move to more environmentally sustainable practices of recycling, composting, and solid waste management.

Financial Reforms

The provincial-municipal negotiations on financial reforms revolved largely around the issue of which order of government would be responsible for paying for a particular service as part of the service exchange initiative. There was considerably less discussion about new or alternative sources of revenue. Such discussion was limited largely to the municipalities' calls for access to the provincial gasoline tax, especially in light of increased responsibilities for roads. The most important debates and negotiations on this matter, however, were not related to new sources of municipal revenue, but to a new use for a traditional revenue source—the property tax. The provincial government provides 'equalization' funding to the municipalities to establish a financial floor with which all Nova Scotia municipalities can provide an appropriate level of service. This equalization payment came from the province's Consolidated Fund. It is based on a formula that includes a standardized household expenditure estimate in relationship to the property tax capacity of the municipality.[4] It attempts to take into account municipal expenditure need and municipal ability to pay for its services.

In the spring of 2001 the province and HRM were taking out newspaper advertisements to attack each other on alternative ways of paying for municipal equalization. The province suggested that equalization could be funded with contributions from the municipal property tax, and HRM suggested that it should be funded from the provincial treasury. HRM was not alone in its opposition to the provincial plan. However, the membership of the Union of Nova Scotia Municipalities was seriously divided on the issue. The division was more or less along the lines of those which relied on the equalization grant and those which did not. The UNSM pledged to help find a 'mutually acceptable solution' because, to some extent, this issue had the potential to threaten its organizational viability.

By February 2001 the mode of funding equalization was eventually linked with the service exchange discussion. The province's renewed service exchange offer came with a proposal to fund the municipal equalization grant from the municipal property tax.[5] The UNSM had no difficulty supporting the service exchange, stood strongly in favour of the equalization funding, but preferred to pursue other funding strategies. The provincial proposal (see Table 8.2) would:

- change the equalization grant;
- have the province assume municipal contributions to public housing and corrections;

Table 8.2   The Balance between Savings and Costs

Proposal	Municipalities	Province
1. Corrections	$14.6 million	($14.6 million)
2. Public housing	6.0	(6.0)
3. Grants-in-lieu/residences	1.3	(1.3)
4. Foundation grant to towns	2.3	(2.3)
5. Equalization	(22.2)	22.2
Subtotal	**Zero**	**Zero**
6. Cost of assessment	($12.0 million)	$12.0 million
7. Social services	17.6	(17.6)
Total	**$5.5 million**	**($5.5 million)**

- have the province pay full grants in lieu of property taxes to municipalities for university residences;
- have the province create a 'foundation grant' to assist towns with the upkeep of roads;
- have the equalization grant funded by municipalities with the property tax.

To reiterate, HRM and other municipalities were opposed to the proposal because the projected 'cost' for equalization to the provincial government would come from the property tax rather than from provincial revenue sources. The UNSM, in consultation with its membership, proposed an interesting alternative— that the equalization funding be fully supported through the deed transfer tax. The argument was that this tax, while still a tax on property, at least reflects economic activity and was more appropriate than the general property tax to support equalization. The problem for the provincial government was that not all Nova Scotia counties have a deed transfer tax. The government did not want to have a new tax in these counties attributed to them.

The provincial government ultimately adopted an alternative, removing some of the property tax concessions that had been granted to the private Nova Scotia Power Corporation. These concessions had been granted when Nova Scotia's electrical generation was converted from a Crown corporation to a private-sector company. Neither the Crown corporation nor the private company paid very much in the way of property taxes. The new property taxes from the Power Corporation go to the provincial government, which then funds the municipal equalization grants with those monies. Whatever the reaction from the private corporation, it was not very public or sustained because the change only brought the corporation closer to the norm in other provinces.

Provincial government figures on municipal finances indicate that as of September 2002 there was a total equalization payment of $29.5 million, revenue of $14.1 from NSPI, foundation grants of $1.5 million, and an increase to municipal revenues of $9.2 million.[6] The largest single recipient of equalization is the Cape Breton Regional Municipality, which received an estimated $15.7 million in

2002–3. No other municipality receives more than $1 million. HRM and 12 other municipalities do not receive any equalization funds because of their capacity to generate revenue from their property tax assessment bases.

It is difficult to assess the dynamics of the functional and financial areas when the suspicion is that the provincial government's budgetary deficit and campaign commitments to eliminate it are driving decision-making more than questions of service content or quality. This assessment reflects on politics more than on administration. The Progressive Conservative government under Premier Hamm began its term with a $600 million annual deficit and produced a 'balanced' budget by the end of its term. By 2002 the provincial government analysis showed that decreases in municipal expenditures for social services plus provincial contributions for equalization less charges to the municipal governments for assessment services brought the municipal governments, in the aggregate, $30 million ahead of their position in the fiscal year 1997–8 (correspondence from the minister to the president of the UNSM). The province also considers that Nova Scotia, of all provinces, has the lowest portion of education costs funded by property taxes (17 per cent). The municipalities, on the other hand, see this as a financial cost that could have been assumed completely by the province in the service exchange agreement.

Within the provincial civil service there are people working with a professional perspective of municipal government who can see beyond the financial necessities of the day. Evidence of this can be seen in the municipal benchmarking project that provides each Nova Scotia municipality performance measures against which to assess the delivery of services. Benchmark measures will be revealed in terms of both costs and quality of service.[7] This initiative puts comparative information on Nova Scotia municipalities in the public domain and offers municipalities the opportunity to assess their relative performance on a number of indicators. The overall state of provincial-municipal relations, however, causes some municipalities to see the municipal benchmarking project as a strategy for future municipal amalgamation rather than an example of best practices.

Nova Scotia municipalities and the province do not get high marks for financial reforms. The service exchange dialogue and decisions represented the pushing of dollars around between the two levels of government, rather than truly substantial reforms. The debate about funding the municipal equalization process and assessment exhibited that same quality. These were essentially administrative reforms that may have simplified the financial exchanges between the municipalities and the province, but they have not changed substantially the fundamental features of municipal finances in Nova Scotia—the reliance on the property tax for revenue and the necessity for equalization.

JURISDICTIONAL REFORMS

In Nova Scotia, as in other provinces, some interesting jurisdictional reforms were undertaken. The question is whether those reforms were important either in empowering or disempowering municipal governments or in altering the relationship between them and the provincial government. Some changes in the area of municipal jurisdiction that can be noted are:

- the removal of the requirement for ministerial approval for most of the bylaws municipalities can pass (Municipal Government Act, 1998, ch. 18, s. 186) and a more general expression of the areas of bylaw powers;
- the option of using a chief administrative officer with significant management responsibilities—most municipalities may use a CAO rather than a clerk, although the regional municipalities must use the CAO model;
- clearer authority and encouragement to pursue public-private partnerships in the delivery of municipal services;
- the option for rural counties of electing an 'at-large' mayor to head their council, rather than appointing a 'warden' from the elected councillors;
- the move to a four-year term of office for municipal councillors.

Nova Scotia has not moved towards the introduction of 'natural person' powers for municipal government. One response to questions about this possible reform pointed to section 2 of the MGA (Box 8.2). The section reads well and could be used to justify a more broadly focused, ambitious, independent municipal decision-making were it not balanced by the more traditional restrictions and enumeration of specific tasks in the rest of the legislation. The contrast between section 2 and the section that enumerates in minute detail the processes, services, and facilities for which councils 'may expend money' (Municipal Government Act, 1998, ch. 18, s. 65) is considerable and brings one back into the traditional, centralized authority model that has characterized provincial-municipal relations in the past.[8]

Although the jurisdictional changes have been useful reforms for municipal governance, a question remains of whether the changes represent fine-tuning or broad municipal legislative reform. The suggestion of broader municipal powers under section 2 of the MGA and the changes in authority are undercut by a history of centralized, provincial control and micro-managing. It remains to be seen whether municipalities and the province will take hold of the broader framework of municipal powers.

The promotion of the CAO model represents an important step towards a management capacity not present in the clerkship model. It will be interesting to observe the performance of municipalities working with CAOs, including the capacity of the elected councillors to work through the policy/administration dichotomy that is explicit in the legislation.

The new municipal legislation had some implications for the jurisdictional authority of municipal government over their finances. While some of those provisions are restrictive, others are permissive. Some of the more notable provisions are those related to the following:

- Most municipalities can, and the Halifax Regional Municipality must, have urban, suburban, and rural tax rates.
- All municipalities have discretion to set area rates to fund specific services.

Box 8.2   A Broad Definition of the Purpose of the Municipal Government Act

2 The purpose of this Act is to

(a) give broad authority to councils, including broad authority to pass by-laws, and respect their right to govern municipalities in whatever ways the councils consider appropriate within the jurisdiction given to them;
(b) enhance the ability of councils to respond to present and future issues in their municipalities; and
(c) recognize that the functions of the municipality are to
  (i)   provide good government,
  (ii)   provide services, facilities and other things that, in the opinion of the council, are necessary or desirable for all or part of the municipality, and
  (iii) develop and maintain safe and viable communities. (Municipal Government Act, 1998, ch. 18, s. 2)

• Nova Scotia municipalities may not enter special tax agreements or use tax concessions as economic development incentives.

Another jurisdictional reform was directed at providing rural municipal governments with a slightly broadened scope of authority over the mode of selecting their mayors. The 1998 MGA gives rural municipalities the option to elect a mayor at-large rather than choose a warden from the elected council members. This change was suggested in UNSM annual resolutions, but only one rural municipality has opted for this change to date. The theory is that communities should determine whether they want voters to have a direct say in who becomes mayor, rather than leaving that decision in the hands of their elected representatives. The election of an at-large mayor as chair of the rural municipal councils warrants watching. It may change the dynamics of political leadership.

One reform anticipated the level of co-operation between the UNSM and the province throughout the Roles and Responsibilities Review. The MGA was amended in 1998 to include the section shown in Box 8.3, which says the 'Minister shall consult' with the Union before amending the MGA. The Union's enthusiasm for this commitment was challenged recently when the province added about $1 million to municipal expenditures by removing municipal governments' right to restricted licence plates. The Union executive was not consulted, nor was 12-month notice given. The provincial government kept the letter of the law by making this change through legislation other than the Municipal Government Act and argued that this was appropriate since the change applied to all restricted licences, not just municipalities.

At this point, the jurisdictional changes consolidated in the Municipal Government Act represent a capacity for reform, but their impact remains uncertain. Will recognizing municipalities as an 'order of government' accorded a

Box 8.3   Legislated Requirements To Consult and Notify

Requirement to consult with Union (MGA)
518   The Minister shall consult with the executive of the Union of Nova Scotia Municipalities respecting any proposed amendment to this Act. (Municipal Government Act, 1998, ch. 18, s. 518)

Requirement to notify Union
519   (1) The Minister shall notify the Union of Nova Scotia Municipalities at least one year prior to the effective date of any legislation, regulation or administrative action undertaken by or on behalf of the Government of the Province that would have the effect of decreasing the revenue received by municipalities in Nova Scotia or increasing the required expenditures of municipalities in Nova Scotia.

(2) Subsection (1) does not apply with respect to any legislation, regulation or administrative action applying to the Province generally and not mainly to municipalities. (Municipal Government Act, 1998, ch. 18, s. 519)

broader section 2 mandate, electing councils for four-year terms with a clearer capacity for public-private partnerships, and allowing more general bylaw powers requiring fewer ministerial approvals flow through to changes in municipal government performance in service delivery that is visible to the general public? It will be difficult to sort out the impact of these jurisdictional changes from the impact of Nova Scotia's economic development, especially the development of offshore natural gas. The impact of a pipeline on the property tax base of some municipalities will be significant. Will subsequent changes be attributed to jurisdictional or economic changes? Hopefully, these jurisdictional changes will increase municipalities' capacity to make decisions in a new economic environment.

CONCLUSIONS

The purpose of reforms may be patently obvious—'to improve the capacity and performance of municipal government'—or may be buried in the motivations and leadership of provincial and municipal politicians. Within the broad, shared hope of improved municipal services, financial sustainability, and governance several themes of purpose may be identified. The foregoing review of this period in Nova Scotia's provincial-municipal relations suggests the following efforts:

- an attempt to distinguish 'general' from 'local' services when most services represent a shared interest along some continuum of policy, regulation, and operations;
- an attempt at administrative realignment of financial responsibility for services so that financial responsibility is more closely aligned with operational responsibility and/or ability to pay;
- an attempt to offer increased policy, management, and economic development capacity through the option of regional municipal government

and a broadening of the legislative language defining municipal powers;
- an ongoing attempt to adjust the provincial financial role in municipal government to sustain those municipal governments without the financial capacity to provide necessary services.

All of this is said without reference to 'provincial downloading' as a possible financially driven purpose of municipal reform. This is so because the numbers provided by the province show that, in the aggregate, municipal governments are better off financially today than they were five years ago. That does not mean that all municipal officials would concur.

What has been the impact of these reforms? In spite of the reforms reviewed above, interviews with key governmental stakeholders produced the following list of outstanding issues:

- provincial equalization grant to municipalities;
- completion of transfer of responsibilities from the municipalities for corrections and housing;
- grants-in lieu of taxation for university residences;
- funding of education;
- responsibilities for roads;
- cost recovery for assessment services provided to municipalities by province;
- financial viability of small towns;
- rural/urban tax rates and service disparities.

These issues represent a continuation of provincial-municipal consultations that has been ongoing in one form or another since the Graham Commission. Most of these issues involve money rather than questions of substantive vision for municipal government. The agenda will continue to be defined in these terms until the provincial budget remains out of deficit range, the economy of the province and its municipalities improves, and/or the federal government follows through with its recent interests in urban Canada.

The boldest reform in Nova Scotia, certainly, has been the legislation of regional municipal government. The bold stroke was driven by financial necessity (Cape Breton), politics and governance (Halifax), and a community of interest (Queens). The legislation remains 'on the books' as an opportunity for a number of Nova Scotia communities to strengthen their capacity for governance, planning, and development.

The functional and financial reform that has an impact on large numbers of Nova Scotians and removes a substantial program area from municipal governments is the provincial takeover of social services and the elimination of the previous two-tier system. Social services were the largest financial component of a service exchange idea that began in 1994 and concluded in 2003. It may have a two-sided quality. Social service clients will now received the same benefits regardless of where they live in the province, but all will experience the same cutbacks when the province implements budgetary restraints.

An important functional change noted above is the development of a solid waste resource management policy, regulation, and operations framework. This area of shared responsibility represents significant leadership and accomplishment for both levels of government. It is recognized as such both within professional circles (GPI, 2004) and also by citizens (Poel, 2000).

The impact of municipal reform on provincial-municipal relations in Nova Scotia has been mixed. The unilateral provincial initiatives in municipal amalgamation were softened by a reversal of field that assured popular support for any future changes. The experiences of both the first Task Force and the Joint Review of Roles and Responsibility gave further, positive experience of working together. The transfer of the costs of property assessment to the municipalities reinforced the sense of provincial downloading in municipal politicians, regardless of the overall financial balance.

The changes in finance, jurisdiction, and governance offer the potential for increased capacity in political leadership and decision-making. The potential represented in a legislative framework can only be taken up with the addition of political leadership and decision-making. A Municipal Government Act creates a framework for political decision-making and leadership. We have noted above that the Nova Scotia legislative framework is a curious blend of broad statement of local government powers (e.g., section 2) and a very detailed delegated mandate. The legislative framework contributes in a small way to the quality of political leadership at the municipal level—that is, who runs for local office and what they do once in office. This is a limitation to a discussion of municipal reform that focuses primarily on the legislative content.

APPENDIX:
SUMMARY OF PROVISIONS IN THE 1998 MUNICIPAL GOVERNMENT ACT[9]

Governance

- Municipalities recognized as 'a responsible order of government'.
- Municipal councillors to have a four-year term of office effective at next municipal election, October 2000—to help councillors deal with greater complexity of municipal government.
- An option for rural municipalities to have an at-large, elected council head (mayor).
- Voting procedures standardized requiring all to vote, including chair, and counting abstentions as negative votes.
- Limits on the use of private council meetings (e.g., to deal with property transactions, personnel matters, labour relations, contract negotiations, legal matters, and public security).
- Subject areas of bylaws expressed in more general terms to broaden powers.
- Fewer ministerial approval requirements by eliminating the requirement for municipalities to obtain approval for most bylaws and for withdrawal from capital reserve accounts.
- Approval process for planning documents has been 'streamlined'.

- Disclosure of municipal election campaign contributions over $50 and an auditing of campaigns costing more than $10,000.
- Requiring Canadian citizenship for nomination for municipal office.
- Village power 'modernized'—new bylaw powers, election procedures, honoraria.

Service Delivery
- Explicit authority to enter into partnerships with the private sector to provide municipal services. Also allows partnerships with other municipalities.
- New planning tools—site plan approval and the ability to protect transportation corridors, greater land-use bylaw authority to deal with environmental matters during construction.
- Ability to levy off-site development charges to recover costs of providing services (sewer and water) resulting from subdivision development.
- Volunteer fire and emergency services can be registered to clarify liability—corporate, not individual.

Taxation
- Councils given authority to set different tax rates for urban, suburban, and rural areas.
- Councils have discretion to levy area rates on all types of assessed property or one or more types (commercial, residential, resource, occupancy).
- Tax exemption for the property of 'the Legion'.

Consultation and Co-operation
- Requires the provincial government to consult with the UNSM before making future amendments to the Municipal Government Act—the province 'shall consult' and 'shall give prior notice'.
- Freedom of information similar to that required by provincial government.
- Municipal planning must be consistent with a provincial interest in use and development of land.

NOTES
1. This work is part of a larger study of the Halifax Regional Municipality amalgamation project, which was funded by the Donner Canadian Foundation. Help with this chapter was received from Jane Fraser and Nancy Flam (Nova Scotia Department of Finance), Nathan Goral, John Cameron, Shingai Nyajeka, Robert Houlihan, John Mesereau (Service Nova Scotia and Municipal Relations), Ken Simpson (Union of Nova Scotia Municipalities), Mark Gilbert (Nova Scotia Municipal Finance Corporation), and David Cameron (Dalhousie University). Only the author, however, is responsible for any omissions or errors.
2. Igor Vojnovic refines these notions of general versus local services by developing a framework that distinguishes point-specific from non-point-specific service characteristics and juxtaposes that distinction with a service's externality versus non-externality generating qualities. His work represents new light on an old issue. See Vojnovic (2000).

3. See <www.gov.ns.ca/regulations/regs/envsolid.htm> for these details.
4. Details of the formula are in the Municipal Grants Act. R.S., ch. 302, s.17.
5. UNSM press release, 30 March 2001, at: <www.unsm.ca/prev-med.htm>.
6. This information came from the Service Nova Scotia and Municipal Relations departmental Web site: <www.gov.ns.ca/snsmr/muns/info/impact.stm> as of July 2002.
7. The Municipal Indicators Project database was publicly available at the writing of this chapter. The initial data focus on more readily available financial information and population demographics. See <www.gov.ns.ca/snsmr/muns/indicators/>.
8. Writing this chapter has reminded the author of an earlier experience that symbolizes the provincial-municipal relationship. He and a graduate student were asked to leave a municipal social service officers' annual meeting because they mistakenly arrived without having received permission to observe the meeting from the provincial Deputy Minister of Social Services. But that was many years ago.
9. These are the categories within which the department organized its assessment of the Municipal Government Act. Most of these provisions fall broadly within the theme of jurisdiction as discussed in this book. The remaining provisions refer to financial changes.

REFERENCES

Genuine Progress Index (GPI). 2004. Measuring Sustainable Development: The Nova Scotia GPI Solid Waste-Resource Accounts. Halifax: Genuine Progress Index for Atlantic Canada. At: <www.gpiatlantic.org/pdy/solidwaste/solidwaste.pdf>.

Hayward, William. 1993. Interim Report of the Municipal Reform Commissioner. Halifax: Halifax Metro Region.

Nova Scotia. 1989. Municipal Grants Act, Revised Statutes.

———. 1994. An Act to Incorporate the Cape Breton Regional Municipality.

———. 1995a. An Act to Incorporate the Halifax Regional Municipality.

———. 1995b. An Act to Incorporate the Queens Regional Municipality.

———. 1996. An Act Respecting Regional Municipalities Acts.

———. 1998. Municipal Government Act.

———, Department of Housing and Municipal Affairs. 1993. Provincial-Municipal Service Exchange: A Discussion Paper. Halifax: NSHMA

———, ———. 1998. Memorandum of Understanding Respecting Short Term Policy Initiatives and Comprehensive Review of Roles and Responsibilities.

———, ———, and Union of Nova Scotia Municipalities. 1998. Municipal-Provincial Roles and Responsibilities Review.

———, Economic Development 2002. 'RDA Backgrounder', at: <www.gov.ns.ca/econ/links/rda_backgrounder.asp>.

———, Ministry of Municipal Affairs. Task Force on Local Government. 1992. Report and Briefing Book to the Government of Nova Scotia. Halifax: NSMA.

———, Royal Commission on Education, Public Services, and Provincial-Municipal Relations (Graham Commission). 1974. Report, 4 vols. Halifax: Government of Nova Scotia.

Poel, Dale H. 2000. 'Amalgamation Perspectives: Citizen Responses to Municipal Consolidation', Canadian Journal of Regional Science/Revue canadienne des sciences régionales 23, 1: 31–48.

UMA. 1995. Analysis of Municipal Amalgamation. Halifax: The UMA Group in association with Doane Raymond.

Union of Nova Scotia Municipalities and Nova Scotia Housing and Municipal Affairs. 1999. 'Introduction to the review'. Halifax: Roles and Responsibilities Review Working Group.

Vojnovic, Igor. 1997. Municipal Consolidation in the 1990s: An Analysis of Five Canadian Municipalities. Toronto: ICURR Press.

————. 1999. 'The Fiscal Distribution of the Provincial-Municipal Service Exchange in Nova Scotia', *Canadian Public Administration* 42, 4: 512–41.

————. 2000. 'Municipal Consolidation, Regional Planning and Fiscal Accountability: The Recent Experience in Two Maritime Provinces', *Canadian Journal of Regional Science/Revue canadienne des sciences régionales* 23, 1: 49–72.

CHAPTER 9

Municipal Renewal in Newfoundland and Labrador: A Tradition of Cautious Evolution

PETER G. BOSWELL

INTRODUCTION

Although there have been a number of initiatives to reform municipal govern-ment in the province of Newfoundland and Labrador since the late 1980s, the structures, operations, and financial arrangements are little changed from the system that has been in place since the major reforms of the late 1970s. This chapter[1] will outline the extent and limits of recent changes in the structural, func-tional, financial, and jurisdictional role of municipal government in the province in light of amalgamation, regionalization, and legislative initiatives. The argument will be made that, despite some extensive recommended and contemplated changes, a tradition of cautious evolution towards municipal reform has devel-oped and is likely to continue into the foreseeable future.

STRUCTURAL REFORMS

While the number of municipalities has increased substantially since Newfoundland and Labrador entered Confederation in 1949, the basic structure of local government in the province has changed relatively little. Indeed, the only structural change of note has been the conversion of rural districts, local improve-ment districts, and local government communities into towns. The most recent efforts on the part of the provincial government at a restructuring initiative designed to foster regionalization were met with considerable resistance, as was an earlier attempt at extensive amalgamation.

Emergence and Evolution of Municipal Structures

Compared with the rest of Canada, local government in Newfoundland and Labrador is still in an early stage of development. In central Canada and the

Maritimes, municipal institutions were well established before Confederation in 1867. In Newfoundland and Labrador, however, beyond the creation of a few water companies and local roads boards, no steps were taken towards the development of municipal government. St John's was incorporated as a town in 1888 but did not obtain city status until 1921.

The incorporation of Windsor in 1938 was the first of about 20 incorporations of municipalities outside of St John's that occurred during the Commission of Government years. Although the first Local Government Act had been passed in 1933, it was not until the Commission of Government passed the Local Administration Act in 1937 and, more importantly, adopted the policy in 1942 of passing a special Act for each municipality, that municipal incorporations began a slow growth (see Long, 1999).

Following Confederation with Canada in 1949, a Local Government Act was passed, followed in 1952 by a Community Councils Act. By 1955, a total of 53 municipal units had been incorporated. The real explosion in growth occurred over the next 15 years, and by the time the Royal Commission on Municipal Government in Newfoundland and Labrador (the Whalen Commission) was established in 1972, the number of municipalities had risen to nearly 300.

The Whalen Commission was appointed, in part, because of the problems that had accompanied the rapid growth of municipalities. Among its findings, the Commission noted that many of the smaller municipalities had insufficient resources to finance the desired services and that the existing system of government grants was inadequate. To deal with these deficiencies, the Commission included among its many recommendations: the introduction of mandatory real property tax in certain circumstances; a restructured system of provincial grants to municipalities; and the introduction of a series of regional governments across the province. The Commission's recommendations were widely discussed following the report's release in 1974, and many of the recommendations were included in new legislation that evolved from the study, namely, the Municipalities Act (1979) and the Municipal Grants Act.

The Commission's recommendations also had an effect on the structure of the municipal system through the reduction of the types of municipalities, although not on the numbers. Immediately before the Municipalities Act came into being, there were 295 municipalities in the province with five separate forms of structure. Table 9.1 provides a summary with current numbers for comparison.

Prior to 1979, the fivefold classification of municipalities included cities, towns, rural districts, local improvement districts, and local government communities. Cities and towns were essentially the same as their counterparts in other provinces in terms of their purposes, functions, and powers and need no further explanation here. A brief explanation of the other three types of municipal authorities is useful for the purposes of this chapter.

Rural districts, despite their name, were merely neighbouring towns joined together in one municipality. They originated from a desire to provide one municipal government to two or more contiguous communities, while avoiding the political repercussions of an attempted amalgamation. The political compromises

Table 9.1 Forms of Municipal Government in Newfoundland, 1979–2004

Type of Municipality	Number (1979)	Number (2004)
Cities	2	3
Towns	118	286
Rural districts	14	0
Local improvement districts	32	0
Local government communities	129	0
Total	**295**	**289**

of this type of structure often were evident in the names of rural districts, such as Badger's Quay–Valleyfield–Pool's Island. Rural districts had the same powers and responsibilities as towns, with elected councils and, occasionally, even had a ward system. Rural districts were converted gradually into towns after the passage of the Municipalities Act (1979).

Local improvement districts were quasi-municipalities that possessed all the powers and duties of a town, but they were governed by a provincially appointed board of trustees, which acted in all respects like an elected council.[2] These quasi-municipalities were used in communities where the provincial government felt a municipal government was necessary, but could not find enough people to stand for election, or in places such as Labrador City where the province deemed it in the best interests of the community not to have an elected council that, presumably, might create a conflict between the citizens and the community's major employer. Most local improvement districts were converted into towns in the early 1980s.

A further form of municipal government was introduced in 1952. Designed for populations of less than 500, the Community Councils Act provided for elected municipal councils with somewhat more restrictive powers and more limited taxing ability than the other forms of local government in the province. One of the unique features of these community councils was the requirement that they hold annual meetings of all electors in the community to discuss the previous year's business and to approve the next year's budget. Elections to the two-year terms were frequently held during these annual meetings. Community councils were converted into towns as of 31 December 1996 (Municipalities Act, 1979, s. 7.1 as amended 1996).

In effect, the structure of local government in the province had changed little since 1949, other than the conversion of rural districts, local improvement districts, and local government communities into towns. Specific problems had been dealt with by ad hoc solutions, the primary concern having been to encourage the growth of municipal government. The structures themselves were causing few problems; however, many of the province's municipalities were encountering severe financial difficulties. As a partial response to the recurring financial problems encountered by numerous small municipalities, the solution of amalgamation was attempted in the early 1990s.

The Amalgamation Initiative of 1989

The newly elected 1989 Liberal government was aware that Newfoundland's ratio of municipal governments to population was one of the highest in Canada and, being convinced that municipal government would be less expensive if there were fewer municipalities, determined to reduce the number of municipalities in the province. While many municipalities, because of their geographic location, could not readily be joined with any other nearby community, 108 municipalities were identified as reducible to 43. For a variety of reasons, including local opposition, most of the proposed amalgamations were abandoned. By the end of the amalgamation initiative, 33 municipalities had been reduced to 13, leaving the total number of municipalities in the province only slightly reduced. Although the forced amalgamation approach was abandoned, efforts to encourage neighbouring municipalities to voluntarily amalgamate continue through the use of financial incentives, including the debt restructuring program as outlined later in this chapter.

Amalgamation/Regionalization in St John's Metropolitan Area

The City of St John's and the Northeast Avalon region represent a special case, insofar as St John's has been agitating strongly and persistently for the past few years for the provincial government to amalgamate it with the City of Mount Pearl and the urbanized portion of the Town of Paradise. The question of how the municipalities in the capital city region could best be organized has been an issue of long standing.

Regional government was initially proposed for the St John's area in a 1957 report (Canadian British Engineering Consultants, 1957). Most of the report's recommendations were ignored by the provincial government, except for the creation in 1963 of the St John's Metropolitan Area Board. One of the main functions envisaged for this Board was the co-ordination of regional planning. In reality, however, the Metro Board served primarily as a means of delivering municipal services to unincorporated areas in the region. Its limited effectiveness as a regional planning body was weakened by the gradual transfer of large areas of undeveloped territory from its jurisdiction to those of newly created municipalities.[3]

In 1971, the provincial government appointed two consulting firms to conduct a comprehensive study of regional planning, control, development, and local government structure in the St John's metropolitan area (Proctor & Redfern et al., 1973). The *Urban Regional Study* offered three alternative forms of municipal government: an independent city-county system; a two-tier regional system with the City of St John's, and five enlarged towns comprising the lower tier and a regional council providing the upper tier; or a regional city with four subordinate sub-regions.

Before selecting one of the options, the provincial government appointed another commission to determine public opinion on the matter and to make specific recommendations on the best option for the area (Newfoundland and Labrador, 1976). The report of this commission, chaired by Alex Henley, recommended that a two-tier structure of regional government be established along with an expanded City of St John's. While the form and powers of the proposed regional government were not significantly different from those found elsewhere in Canada, the recommended membership scheme was unique: a chairman and four members to be appointed by the provincial government; six members from an enlarged City of St John's; and four members selected from four clusters of lower-tier municipalities and unincorporated areas called sub-regions.

The public release of the Henley report in January 1977 produced considerable debate and controversy, but the provincial government acted on it by introducing Bill 101, An Act to Establish the St John's Urban Region. This bill was withdrawn and replaced in May 1978 by Bill 50, An Act to Establish the Northeast Avalon Urban Region. The provisions of Bill 50 differed from the Henley report's recommendations in two significant areas. First, the composition of the upper-tier regional council was changed to give the city only four seats, while representation from the surrounding area was increased to six. Second, there was no provision to extend the city's boundaries.

Bill 50 was met with strong opposition. The City of St John's attacked the failure to extend its boundaries, minority representation on the regional council, the potential acquisition of city assets without compensation, and the possibility of higher taxes. Residents and leaders of 11 area communities formed the Association of Northeast Avalon Communities to spearhead their objections to the bill, and the opposition Liberal Party pursued the attack in the House of Assembly. The opposition Liberals eventually succeeded in having the bill deferred for a period of six months, which effectively killed the proposed legislation. Despite indications that a new bill would be introduced, regional government for the St John's area stalled at that point.[4]

Since that time, several other smaller commissions and studies have examined municipal organization in the St John's region, and several minor boundary changes have occurred. But it was not until the Liberal government's amalgamation initiative in 1989 and the Regional Service Boards legislation in 1990 that serious thought was again given to reorganization of municipal government in the St John's area. Following months of discussion and study, the boundaries of the City of St John's were extended in 1991 to take in some surrounding communities. At the same time, some amalgamation of the remaining communities took place, reducing the 19 existing municipalities to 11. However, the only body of regional co-ordination, the St John's Metropolitan Area Board, was disbanded because municipal boundaries in the Northeast Avalon had been expanded to be contiguous and the Board's primary role of providing municipal services to unorganized areas was no longer necessary. Only two limited forms of regional co-operation remain: a Regional Fire Committee and a Regional Water Board. An ad hoc committee, the Avalon Waste Management Community Consultative Committee, was appointed by the provincial government in November 2001 to review waste-management practices in the region and make recommendations for improvement. This committee, which is composed of municipal and community representatives from Clarenville to St John's, recently recommended a $40 million waste-management facility to serve the entire Avalon Peninsula (*Evening Telegram,* 14 Nov. 2002).

While it is unlikely that the current situation will continue to exist indefinitely, municipal reorganization in the St John's region does not seem to be a high priority with the provincial government. Evidence of this can be found in the government's reaction to a May 2001 amalgamation study undertaken for the City of St John's (ATI Consulting, 2001). While the study argued that amalgamation would result in substantial economic and financial benefits for the region and became an issue in the 2001 municipal elections, then-Premier Roger Grimes and various provincial government ministers reiterated their position that municipalities will not be forced to amalgamate against their will.[5] This was a similar position to that which effectively blocked the province-wide regionalization scheme initiated by the provincial government a few years earlier.

The Time for Regionalization Initiative

With the general failure of the 1989 amalgamation initiative, the perceived problem remained of too many small municipalities, each with its own council, plans, and priorities. In 1996, the provincial government began actively to consider the process of province-wide regionalization. The Whalen Commission's recommendation—that up to 20 two-tier regional authorities be established across the province—had been provided for in Part III of the Municipalities Act (1979), but only one regional council (that of Fogo Island) had been established in the province. In early 1996, the Minister of Municipal and Provincial Affairs issued the document *The Time for Regionalization,* which discussed the issues and concept of regional government and outlined two potential options: regional councils and regional service authorities (Newfoundland and Labrador, Department of Municipal and Provincial Affairs, 1996: 6–8).

The regional council option was based on the model set out in the Whalen Commission report and subsequently incorporated into the Municipalities Act (1979). It would have provided for 'a mix of appointed/elected representatives to coordinate regional servicing initiatives among municipalities; to extend municipal servicing and taxation to neighbouring unincorporated areas; and to explore the need for further regional servicing' (ibid., 7). Under the regional council option, existing municipalities would remain as they were while a second-tier regional structure would co-ordinate regional servicing among municipalities and provide municipal services to unincorporated areas.

The regional service authority option would 'formalize ad hoc arrangements', which currently existed or had 'the potential to exist between municipalities to provide or coordinate a service or services to two or more municipalities within a specific grouping' (ibid., 8). This option was based on concepts contained in the Regional Service Boards Act (passed in 1990, but not proclaimed until 2004).[6] The thinking behind this Act was that an appointed board could be established to provide certain services to municipalities within designated regions. The board would be appointed by the minister from councillors of municipalities within the region, and could provide potential services including: regional water supply systems, regional sewage disposal systems, regional storm drainage systems, and regional solid waste disposal sites; regional police and ambulance services; animal and dog control; a regional public transportation system; street and road names; regional recreational facilities; regional fire protection services; other facilities or services of a regional nature; and 'the charging of user fees on municipal authorities, areas under development control or unincorporated areas benefited by a regional facility' (Regional Services Board Act, s. 9).

Following release of *The Time for Regionalization* document, a brief tour of major centres in the province by the minister and department officials was undertaken to introduce the regionalization initiative. As promised, an independent Task Force was appointed in January 1997 to undertake a province-wide public consultation process.[7] The Task Force conducted its hearings between February and June 1997 and issued its report on 10 September 1997.

During its hearings, the Task Force found that municipalities generally were opposed to the concept of regionalization, especially the regional council option outlined in the policy paper. Their greatest concern was that another level of government was not needed and that regional government would only drive up costs as provincial grants were going down. Despite this opposition, it was often stated that many communities in close proximity to others were being run inefficiently and that survival could only be ensured through reform, sharing, and by the residents of unincorporated areas starting to pay for the services that government now provides free of charge (such as road construction, maintenance, and snow clearing).

With regard to the unincorporated areas, many municipalities suggested that they lacked the financial capacity to take control of unincorporated communities in close proximity and to provide basic services to them; the amounts collected in taxes would not cover the cost of providing the services.[8] While municipalities may have been reluctant to assume additional servicing costs for nearby unincorporated areas, they felt that residents of these areas should be contributing to their costs of operating recreation facilities. Hockey arenas, swimming pools, arts and culture centres, curling rinks, and many other facilities built and paid for by residents of a particular municipality often are used by all residents of the region. While many of the facilities have been constructed with the help of provincial and federal funding, the greater portion of operational and maintenance dollars frequently is provided by residents of a single municipality through municipal taxation rather than by the residents of the region.

Concerns about municipal regionalization were expressed in a number of areas. Some saw regionalization as providing the provincial government with an opportunity to download government services to the municipal level. Others expressed the concern that the regional economic zone boundaries were so large as to eliminate the possibility of significant efficiencies in service delivery or the elimination of duplication of services. Not surprisingly, a number considered the regionalization initiative as a serious threat to the autonomy of individual towns. On the positive side, however, regionalization was seen as enabling communities to have a stronger voice in lobbying the provincial government for infrastructure funding. In addition, regionalization received support insofar as it would mean that individuals and businesses that deliberately move just outside municipal boundaries to avoid taxation would then be subject to municipal taxation.

The Task Force found considerable controversy over the question of sharing. Many municipal representatives argued that they were already sharing all the services that were feasible or desirable and that if the need for further sharing or co-operation became evident, they would pursue such arrangements themselves. Some argued that the distances between their own municipality and neighbouring towns was too great for any sharing of services. Many made the assumption that it was possible to share services only with immediately adjacent communities. Others stated that they could not share with neighbouring communities because a river or bridge separated their community from the next community.

The Task Force found this perception of distance as an obstacle to sharing to be rather perplexing, since in many other provinces, such as Ontario and British Columbia, services are successfully shared among communities within a large geographical area, many of them separated by significant distances. Further, the Task Force found that many presenters who stated that they were already sharing services to their full potential seemed to have overestimated the degree of sharing and underestimated the potential and benefits for increased sharing. It often became clear during subsequent discussion that many areas of sharing, such as accounting, tax billing and collecting, animal control, tendering for materials and services, and even staffing, had never been considered. Further, there was some indication that services such as animal control, engineering and financial services, and garbage collection could be done under contract by larger towns in the area more cheaply and more efficiently than existing service provisions.

The Task Force encountered an angry response from representatives of many of the province's 328 unincorporated areas. Most of those making both formal presentations and informal remarks indicated strong opposition to any form of regionalization. Further, many of those from unincorporated areas were staunchly opposed to being brought under municipal authority. While the Task Force found a high degree of support from the residents of unincorporated areas for paying their fair share for services received, considerable suspicion was expressed about regionalization being a way to force residents of unincorporated areas to help pay the debts of financially troubled municipalities.

Related to this, the Task Force found a strongly expressed resentment towards the categorization of those who live in rural and unincorporated areas as 'free-loaders' or people who are getting away without paying their fair share. It was repeatedly pointed out to the Task Force that people living in unincorporated areas pay their own way, sometimes at greater expense than those living in larger towns. The one area where unincorporated communities might be considered to be 'getting a free ride' is that of road maintenance and snow clearing. The Task Force was presented with overwhelming evidence that provincial policy in this area is highly inconsistent. In some communities, the Department of Works,

Services, and Transportation plows only the main highway; in others, all side streets are plowed. Where cost recovery is in effect, the amounts per kilometre appear to vary.

In sum, people from unincorporated areas in the province told the Task Force quite clearly that while there may be some benefits to regionalization, such benefits would have to be demonstrated before the concept would receive any support. Further, people living in rural and unincorporated areas of the province overwhelmingly felt that the existing local service district system was adequate for their needs and ability to pay.[9] A typical comment was that 'the system we have works and it works well. Leave it alone.' While the sentiment of 'go away and leave us alone' was the predominant one the Task Force heard from residents of unincorporated communities, there were a number of submissions indicating residents would be willing to take part in a regionalization process that allowed for their input.

In assessing the government's proposals to bring about municipal regionalization as a means of improving services while reducing costs, the Task Force evaluated a number of alternatives. In addition to the two models set out in *The Time for Regionalization*, the Task Force considered the alternatives of the status quo, amalgamation, and mass incorporation. After examining the regional models proposed by the government, and after listening to many briefs and presentations, the Task Force concluded that a middle ground was needed between the two proposed models, one that would provide a legal structure, allow for regional taxation or service fee collection, and provide a democratically elected forum for decision-making. While it might have been possible for the government to amend either of the two models to bring them into line with the Task Force's thinking, it was felt that a totally new approach was better, while using the best features from each of the proposed models. In particular, the Task Force saw the need to formalize existing regional services and to expand them to a greater population base with an open and democratically controlled decision-making process.

While some cost savings may be realized by greater sharing of services, these were not the primary aims. More important was to bring a sense of equity between incorporated municipalities and unincorporated areas and to provide the framework for a regional approach to solving common problems and adjusting to new environmental and financial realities. As part of this process, the Task Force argued that it was necessary to bring the unincorporated areas into the regional structure while retaining the maximum amount of independence and autonomy for both unincorporated communities and existing municipalities. For this reason, the Task Force believed it was essential to allow a high degree of flexibility in opting in and out of services commensurate with sufficient rigidity to allow stability.

The Task Force recommended that a Regional County Services Board (RCSB) be established in each regional economic zone with sub-zones for shared municipal services being established as deemed necessary by each RCSB and adjustments between zonal boundaries being made as necessary. Each RCSB would be composed of elected directors from municipalities and unincorporated areas according to a formula that roughly provided for one director from each municipality

with a weighted vote proportional to the municipality's population and one director from each electoral area to be created in the unincorporated areas based on a
combination of area and population.[10] In an effort to prevent either the unincorporated areas or a few municipalities from being able to dominate the Board's
decisions, the Task Force recommended that a triple two-thirds formula be
mandatory for all votes.[11] The Task Force also recommended that all directors be
subject to recall and limited to two consecutive terms.

The powers recommended by the Task Force for the Regional County Services
Boards included mandatory responsibility for solid waste management and land-
use planning (including Crown lands) within the county outside of municipal
boundaries.[12] Once established, the Boards could choose to undertake a wide
range of additional powers, including such things as building and occupancy
permits, fire protection, regional economic development, regional recreation,
animal control, emergency 911 services, regional water and sewer construction and
operation, tendering, bulk purchasing, levying and collecting of taxes, airport
management and operation, and any other powers available to municipalities
under general legislation. Each municipality by resolution and each unincorporated community by majority vote would have the option of availing itself of
regional services provided by the Regional County Services Board. With the
exception of solid waste management and land-use planning, municipalities and
unincorporated communities could withdraw from regional services on a two-
thirds majority vote of their councils or electors, respectively.

The Task Force recognized that the level of staffing would vary between
Regional County Services Boards depending on the number of services each
Board decided to undertake. At a minimum, however, the Task Force recommended that each RCSB be required to appoint a clerk with duties equivalent to
those of a municipal clerk. It also recommended that, where feasible, staff of the
existing municipalities in a region be utilized to serve the Board.

Since the financing of the Regional County Services Boards was likely to be a
controversial matter, the Task Force began from the assumption that all residents
who benefit from any of the services should pay their fair share of the costs. To this
end, the Task Force recommended that all property throughout the province be
assessed and that a minimum property tax be levied by each RCSB on property
owners living outside municipal boundaries. This was based on the assumption
that those living within municipal boundaries would be paying their share of the
Board's costs through their municipal taxes. The Task Force also recommended
that all capital expenditures requiring long-term financing must have the prior
approval of a majority of voters, and that the Boards not be allowed to exceed a
maximum 25 per cent ratio of debt payments to locally raised revenue. Regional
County Services Boards would have no responsibility for purely local services
unless specifically requested by a municipality. In that case, the service would be
provided on a cost-recovery basis by contract. Regional County Services Boards
would have responsibility for regional matters as agreed on by the boards of directors. However, municipalities and electoral areas would have the prerogative of
opting in or out of specific services that are offered.

As indicated earlier, the Task Force met with almost universal opposition from unincorporated areas to any form of regional government. The recommended Regional County Services Board model was created, at least in part, to minimize the impact of a regional structure on unincorporated areas. In this context it is important to emphasize that the Task Force recommended that RCSBs would provide municipal services to unincorporated areas only when requested to do so by a majority vote of a community. In no circumstances would a Regional County Services Board be permitted to undertake the provision of municipal services in an unincorporated community without the approval of that community's residents. Existing service-sharing arrangements that some unincorporated communities have with other unincorporated communities or with nearby municipalities could continue unchanged.

It was expected that one of the most politically controversial recommendations of the Task Force's report would concern the province's 20 Regional Economic Development (RED) Boards, which had been created in 1995 to foster economic development as successors to the 59 Regional Development Associations (see House, 1999: 180–201). At the time of the report, the RED Boards were trying to formulate and formalize their own roles. Some were in the process of becoming quite powerful entities with visionary schemes for economic development, while others had not yet become organized well enough to prepare a workable action plan. Most were in the early stages of organization and planning. While municipalities are represented on all of the RED Boards, and in many cases hold a majority position, the Task Force was concerned that competition between two regional bodies could lead to political struggles for scarce funding and squabbles over jurisdiction and roles. In addition, since RED Board representation is through an interest group selection process rather than by direct democratic elections, the Task Force was troubled by a lack of accountability.

The Task Force believed that the functions of the Regional Economic Development Boards could be maintained and indeed strengthened by aligning them more closely with an elected and accountable regional government. Accordingly, the Task Force recommended that the Regional County Services Boards become the umbrella organization over the Regional Economic Development Boards through their establishment as a standing subcommittee of each Regional County Services Board. In addition to strengthening the democratic nature of the Regional Economic Development Boards, bringing them under municipal authority through the Regional County Services Boards would aid coordination of economic development in each region of the province.

The Task Force handed its report to the Minister of Municipal and Provincial Affairs in early September 1997 and presented its recommendations to the Social Policy Committee of cabinet the following month. Although the provincial government did not act on the Task Force's recommendations, a provision for regional structures was maintained in the new Municipalities Act (part II, ss. 26–52). The Act contains two major statutory provisions for the future restructuring of municipalities in Newfoundland. First, section 3 allows the provincial cabinet, on the recommendation of the minister and subject to a feasibility study, to incorporate a town, amalgamate towns and annex areas to towns, establish and alter the boundaries of towns, and de-incorporate towns. The minister can set the number of councillors between five and nine (Municipalities Act, s. 13). Second, section 26 allows the provincial cabinet, on the recommendation of the minister and subject to a feasibility study, to establish an area as a region, to amalgamate regions and annex areas to regions, to establish and alter boundaries of regions, and to disestablish a region. Cabinet may establish, by order, a regional council with an unspecified number of members, some of whom may be elected at large or to represent wards, while some may be appointed by the councils of cities and towns within the region (ss. 41–4). The chairperson of the region is to be elected by the regional councillors at their first meeting (s. 45). The province's current position with regard to regional structures is that it will assist any group of communities that wants to pursue either amalgamation or regional co-operation, but will not take the initiative in trying to bring about either.[13]

Why Structural Change Has Not Occurred

Although several studies have recommended significant structural changes for municipal government in Newfoundland,[14] none has occurred. Certainly, the legislation governing municipalities has been simplified and updated; municipalities have been given a few more powers with the concomitant reduction in provincial supervision (or 'tutelage', as Whalen called it); the peculiar collection of municipal structures has evolved into the two forms of towns and cities; and municipalities have become more self-reliant. The two most controversial changes in the last 50 years were the introduction of mandatory real property tax (in certain circumstances) and enabling legislation for regional government contained in the 1979 Municipalities Act. The mandatory aspect of real property tax was removed in the 1999 Municipalities Act, and while only one regional government was established under the Municipalities Act provisions, the enabling legislation was retained in the new Act. As discussed above, the mass amalgamation initiative of the early 1990s was quickly abandoned in the face of concerted opposition from affected municipalities.

Why have none of the recommended structural changes occurred? It could be argued that the lack of change reflects a lack of political will, and that any outcry from rural Newfoundland—which not only has a history of economic depression, but also retains the status of being essential for winning a majority government—will quickly kill any attempt at municipal structural reform. It may also be true that the need for widespread municipal reform is not as great in Newfoundland as in other parts of Canada. Many of the nearly 300 Newfoundland municipalities are very small and frequently operate quite efficiently with minimum staff and expense. Some voluntary sharing of resources already occurs and there are several communities currently considering more formal joint arrangements. The new Urban and Rural Planning Act strengthens the province's capability to develop regional planning without formal regional municipal structures.

In sum, although no comprehensive province-wide study of municipal structures and finances has recently been undertaken,[15] it is possible that the existing multiplicity of small municipal units may be the most cost-effective way of delivering municipal services while providing democratic representation. Perhaps as a practical realization of this, the provincial government recently signed a comprehensive training and development agreement with the province's Federation of Municipalities and Association of Municipal Administrators (Municipal Training and Development Partnership, 1999). The mandate of the new training initiative is to identify training needs for elected and appointed officials and to develop and deliver the necessary training services. By assisting in the development of better-trained councillors and staff, the provincial government is providing support, at least implicitly, for the existing network of many small municipalities while simultaneously encouraging greater sharing of resources and, where sought, facilitating structural mergers. Not exciting, but eminently practical.

FUNCTIONAL REFORM

Since Newfoundland's entry into Confederation in 1949 few changes have occurred in the core functions of municipal governments. Unlike the situation in some other provinces, no major functions have been transferred from the province to the municipalities. Further, since Newfoundland municipalities have never been responsible for any portion of the costs or activities of delivering health care, administering justice, or providing social services or education, while there have been significant changes in the organization and management of these functions, municipalities have not been directly involved. Similarly, municipal functions have not generally been transferred to other local authorities. Indeed, the only notable exception to this has been the transfer of the City of Mount Pearl's firefighting function to the St John's Regional Fire Services Committee in 1996.

Functional responsibility for programs and services has been shifted from the provincial to the municipal level only in the areas of assessment, auditing, and planning. Prior to the mid-1980s, the provincial government conducted real property assessment on behalf of municipalities that requested it. Partially as a consequence of long wait times for municipalities seeking assessment, and partially as a result of increased pressure on the province's finances, the province announced in 1996 that subsidies of assessments would be ended. A Crown corporation, the Municipal Assessment Agency, was created in 1997. Initially, the Agency received a $500,000 annual grant from the provincial government, but by the year 2000 it was required to be self-supporting, based on the collection of assessment fees from municipalities. The City of St John's continues to do its own real property assessment.

Although falling outside this work's primary period for analysis of reforms, another function transferred from the province to municipalities has been that of auditing. While the larger centres had always arranged and paid for financial audits on their own, many smaller municipalities relied on the province to undertake annual audits at nominal charge by the Auditor General's staff of the provincial government. In the mid-1980s, the province began to require municipalities to hire and pay for their own annual audits, a process that still causes financial problems for smaller municipalities whose records often require considerable work prior to the actual audit.

Similarly, until the mid-1980s, most municipal planning was undertaken by the provincial government on behalf of municipalities requesting it. Now, although a council must apply to the minister before starting a municipal plan in order to have the planning area defined, and must submit the final plan for ministerial review and registry, the hiring of a planner and the development of the plan itself are entirely within municipal powers. The minister can decline to register a municipal plan only if it is contrary to a provincial law or policy, although the minister may make regulations on a wide variety of development matters.

FINANCIAL REFORMS

Since 1990 there have been some interesting and important reforms to the system of municipal finances. The reforms have been part of an ongoing effort to reduce the level of financial dependence on the provincial government for operational and capital funding and to increase the self-sufficiency of municipal governments. Towards that end the provincial government rationalized its granting formulae and limited the amount of transfers through grants. A full appreciation of the reforms since 1990 requires a brief overview of the financial reforms implemented during the previous two decades. This is particularly true of the changes to the province's system of grants to municipalities.

Prior to the changes instituted based on recommendations of the Whalen Commission, the grant system was composed of a revenue grant based on a percentage of locally raised revenue (the percentage decreased as local revenue increased!), a per capita road grant, a water and sewerage subsidy, special or emergency grants, and capital projects grants. There were also special grants for the cities (since most of the preceding grants did not apply to them) and various miscellaneous grants, which were fairly specific in nature. Only the revenue and road grants were based on any formula, the rest being subject to ministerial discretion. And while the water and sewerage subsidies did have some guidelines that were occasionally adhered to, the special and emergency grants had none and were given for a variety of reasons, largely based on political considerations.

It was not surprising, then, that the Commission found that not only were municipalities raising an increasingly smaller percentage of their total budgets from their own revenue sources, but that in many cases the amount paid on debt service charges was greater than the revenue raised from all forms of local taxation.[16] This lack of fiscal responsibility was encouraged by the relatively unstructured and political nature of the provincial system of grants to municipalities.[17]

By the early 1970s, the system of provincial grants to municipalities was in disarray, with little relationship between real need and grants received and with little coherence in the overall pattern of grants. Some municipalities were receiving far more than their share while others were receiving much less. The challenge for the Commission was to recommend a revision that would be considered fair by all municipalities yet would be affordable to the province.

The starting point for the Commission's recommendations was an 'equity principle', which took into consideration local needs, tax capacity, and a degree of fiscal equalization. A three-part grant system was recommended consisting of: a general municipal assistance grant with a basic allocation scaled to population, a social assistance component related to the incidence of social assistance in a municipality, and a local road mileage supplement based on the mileage of roads within a municipality; a municipal tax incentive grant consisting of an amount equal to a municipality's yield from real property tax the previous year; and a municipal capital projects grant to assist in cost-sharing capital projects other than water and sewerage facilities.

A regional incentive grant equal to one-half the annual cost of a regional authority's general legislative and administrative functions and delivery of area-wide services also was recommended, along with the abolition of existing water and sewerage subsidy grants and other 'special' assistance (Newfoundland and Labrador, 1974: 344–9, 354–68).

The province implemented, in principle, most of the Commission's recommendations in the Municipal Grants Act (1977), although a water and sewer subsidy was included and the operational regulations were not. When the latter were released in 1980, there were some important differences between the Commission's recommendations and the province's formulae. The most important difference was the reduction of the tax incentive grant from the recommended fully matching subsidy to $0.50 for every $1.00 raised in real property taxes up to a maximum of $2 million, then a subsidy of $0.25 per $1.00 thereafter. The new grant system was phased in over a five-year period to make the adjustment easier for those municipalities that had been receiving more than their fair share.

Not all municipalities were happy with the new grants system, especially those that saw their grants reduced, and many felt that the tax incentive component was unfair to those municipalities that had a relatively low assessment base. Shortly after the election of a Liberal government in 1989, the Minister of Municipal and Provincial Affairs announced a major review of the municipal grant programs. At the same time, he reiterated that municipalities must become more fiscally responsible by forcing their taxpayers rather than the provincial government to pay for services. A new grant system was announced in December 1990 and came into effect on 1 January 1991. It contained two major sections: municipal operating grants and water and sewer subsidies.

The municipal operating grant (MOG) consisted of four components. The first was that of equalization. This component had two parts, one for municipalities that imposed a real property tax and one for those that did not. For those municipalities that imposed the real property tax, the province would contribute to the municipality an amount based on the percentage by which its assessed property value fell below the provincial average. Municipalities that did not impose the property tax would receive $40 per household. The second component of the MOG was the local revenue incentive component. The purpose of this component was to encourage municipal councils to raise more revenue by rewarding those that would do so. The total amount of local revenue would be divided by the number of households in the community. That amount would then be applied to a sliding scale from which the total grant for this component was calculated. The third component of the MOG was a household subsidy consisting of a flat rate subsidy of $85 per household. The final component of the MOG was the road grant based on an amount per kilometre of roads in the municipality, but the precise amount was not announced. As with the previous changeover to the Municipal Grants Act, provision was made for the new system to be phased in over a three-year period.

The second major section of the new grant system concerned water and sewer subsidies. The underlying rationale of the revised water and sewer subsidy was that municipalities should be paying a greater share of their water and sewerage installation costs, while help should be provided to those municipalities whose costs were significantly greater due to unusual rock formation or extensive distance from the water supply. The precise amount of the subsidy depended on whether the debt had already been debentured or whether it was still covered by a guaranteed bank loan. In any case, the maximum contribution that a municipality was required to make towards its total water and sewer debt charges was $300 per household. As with the municipal operating grant, changes were phased in over a three-year period.

Increased financial pressures experienced by the provincial government in the mid-1990s resulted in a re-evaluation of the municipal grants system. Ever since the Whalen report, a succession of ministers had proclaimed the need for municipalities to become more self-sufficient and reduce their reliance on the province for funding. Partially as a step in this direction and partially as a consequence of an economic downturn, the MOG was capped at $41,500,000. This was a reduction of $4,000,000 from the 1991 level of funding. Following the 1996 provincial election[18] and the appointment of a new minister, the cutbacks began in earnest. The 1996 cap was set at $31,850,000 and the 1997 cap at $28,130,000 (NLFM, 1997). Stating that 'municipalities must become more self-reliant', the Minister of Finance announced in his 1997–8 budget speech that the MOGs would be reduced a further 20 per cent in each of the next three years. With the 1998 MOG cap set at $21,500,000, the municipalities were receiving less than half the amount they had received in operating grants at the beginning of the decade. Four days before the 18 January 1999 provincial election call, the new Minister of Municipal and Provincial Affairs announced that the planned further MOG reductions would not be implemented and that the MOG cap would remain at $21,500,000 for 1999 and 2000.[19] This level of funding continued into the 2002–3 fiscal year.

In conjunction with the reductions in the MOG, the provincial government has undertaken a program of restructuring municipal debt. The program began in 1996 with the aim of encouraging municipalities to consolidate their long-term debt and take advantage of lower interest rates at commercial institutions. The province has provided funding to 'buy out' existing debt and simultaneously provide some debt reduction for municipalities unable to meet existing debt payments. In the first year of operation, 1996–7, the debt reduction program cost $6,430,000; this gradually fell to just over $5,000,000 for the 2000–1 fiscal year,[20] although this was increased to $12 million for 2002–3. Total debt relief since 1996 has been $47 million (Minister of Municipal and Provincial Affairs, 2002). The debt restructuring program has been carried out on a case-by-case basis with the primary criteria for participation being the municipality's need, ability to repay, and willingness to shoulder a greater proportion of debt repayment through increases in locally raised revenue. The province has recently begun to link greater debt restructuring with a willingness of municipalities to undertake voluntary amalgamation where feasible.

A final component of provincial funding to municipalities is the water and sewer subsidy program. The province enters into individual cost-sharing agreements for each project. Since 1997, all water and sewer loans have been based on a specific cost-sharing ratio. Pre-1997 water and sewer debt payments are determined by a formula designed to have a municipality pay 100 per cent of the debt charges until its maximum annual contribution is the greater of $500 per household, the municipality's contribution of the previous year, or 25 per cent of the local revenues and MOG in the previous year.[21]

JURISDICTIONAL REFORMS

Newfoundland is among the provinces that have enacted a new general municipal statute during this reform era with some implications for the jurisdictional authority and autonomy of municipal governments. The objective in this section is to discuss key provisions related to the jurisdictional authority and autonomy of municipalities contained in the new Municipalities Act.

Jurisdictional Reforms in the Municipalities Act, 1999

On 6 July 1999, the provincial government enacted a new Municipalities Act, which came into force on 1 January 2000. This new Act not only consolidated the numerous amendments made to the 1979 legislation, but removed many restrictive provisions, expanded municipal authority, and permitted a greater degree of local decision-making. The Act also provided increased municipal autonomy in the areas of taxation, administration, and financial management, new authority for economic development, and new and expanded authority for service delivery and municipal controls. Several provisions of the new Act have implications for jurisdictional authority and autonomy in the areas of taxation, financial and human resources management, asset management, and economic development.

The new Municipalities Act included some minor provisions regarding the authority and autonomy of municipal governments in various types of taxation. Under the old Act, municipalities that imposed a real property tax could set only one minimum tax, which applied both to residential and to commercial properties. The new Act (s. 114) allows councils to establish a separate minimum tax for residential and commercial properties. Municipalities continue to be required to impose a business tax and a new power to impose taxes on transient businesses has been added (ss. 121–2). A provision in the old Act that allowed councils to impose a poll tax on a spouse who was not considered to be a joint owner of a property where the designated owner paid real property tax has been removed (s. 112). Under the previous Act, councils were required to impose a real property tax if 50 per cent or more of the municipality was serviced by water and sewer or if provincial assistance for water and sewer facilities to 50 per cent of the municipality was applied for. This provision has now been removed, leaving the imposition of real property tax optional.

One of the most significant reforms that has implications for the jurisdictional authority and autonomy of municipal governments focused on the management of their financial resources. Perhaps the most important of these reforms concerns the degree of provincial oversight for municipal financial management. Until the 1999 Municipalities Act, municipalities were required to have their budgets approved by the minister prior to their coming into effect. This requirement has now been removed, except for any regional councils that may be established. Similarly, amended budgets can now be passed by municipal councils without ministerial approval, although the requirement for balanced budgets remains. Councils may also now adopt a two- or three-year budget instead of the previous one-year limit. The establishment of capital reserves and transfers of funds into reserves still requires the approval of the minister, although councils may now transfer any operating surplus into reserves rather than having them applied to the following year's budget. The Municipalities Act, 1999 also extended the limits to municipal managers' spending without the prior approval of council from $500 to whatever limit a council sets. The same limit applies to the amount of money councils are permitted to spend without receiving the prior recommendation of the manager.

The human resources management powers of councils remained virtually unchanged until 2000. Under the provisions of the Municipalities Act, 1999, the old schedule of statutory duties for senior municipal officials was removed, provision was made for a delegate to attend all meetings of council if the manager was unable to do so, the clerk was given the right to speak at council meetings if there is no manager or if the manager is absent, the provision stipulating that senior employees hold office 'at the pleasure of council' was removed, mandatory salary guidelines were abolished, and the procedures for suspension of senior employees was made more flexible.

The only significant change to asset-management powers has been the provision in the Municipalities Act permitting councils, with ministerial approval, to assume ownership of assets for any purpose, not only those necessary for the operations of council. This new provision allows municipal councils to take over assets such as fish plants, wharves, or community airstrips that may be in danger of being abandoned by their current owners or operators. A few additional powers have been granted to municipal councils, such as the ability to pursue economic development, wider discretion in appointing auditors, and additional powers to sell property for tax arrears.

One of the most potentially important powers now available to councils under the new Municipalities Act is that of pursuing economic development through 'an agreement with another municipality, local service district, agency, person or the government of the province' (s. 203). Prior to this, councils had no power to engage in any form of economic development, although many did so either directly or through representation on privately incorporated economic development committees.

Several other changes related to internal council operations were contained in the new Act, including new conflict of interest guidelines and voting procedures. A new Urban and Regional Planning Act (2000) and Municipal Elections Act (2001) have also been passed.

Conclusion

Newfoundland's municipal reform agenda since 1990 has been relatively ambitious in each of the four dimensions examined in this chapter. However, the nature and scope of the actual reforms has been evolutionary rather than revolutionary. In most areas of reform, the provincial government has proceeded with caution and has been prepared to back off in the face of opposition. The amalgamation and regionalization initiatives were effectively abandoned in the face of concerted opposition, although the province remains committed to assisting and encouraging municipalities who wish to pursue either of these options. Functional reforms have been minor, with no major transfers of responsibility between the province and municipalities. In the area of financial reforms, the province has proceeded cautiously with relatively minor adjustments to municipal legislative powers on taxation and budgets along with debt restructuring. The possible exceptions to this were the cutbacks in municipal operating grants, which were driven by the province's own precarious financial position, and even here the province backed away from its avowed intent to eliminate the grants entirely. The jurisdictional reforms largely reflected an evolutionary elimination of legislative provisions that were generally unworkable, together with adjustments and clarifications sought by municipalities.

Looking to the immediate future, it is unlikely that any major reforms in municipal structure, functions, finances, or jurisdiction are on the horizon. Some minor amalgamations may take place if rural communities continue to lose population and as urban communities expand, but such restructuring likely will be voluntary, albeit encouraged by the province. Formal regionalization is not likely to occur, although informal regional co-operation may well be seen. Unless the province's financial situation changes drastically, it is unlikely that further financial reforms will take place, although tinkering with the existing formulae is quite possible. Major legislative or jurisdictional changes are not likely in the near future, although it is possible that a Cities Act may someday replace the existing separate legislation for each city. This, however, is not a current priority for the provincial government and would be initiated only if one or more of the larger towns actively seek city status.[22]

Municipal reform in Newfoundland and Labrador during the last decade has been much less than anticipated considering the initiatives that have been proposed. The tradition of cautious evolution is likely to continue. Despite the experience in other Canadian provinces where a change in government has quickly brought about a new perspective on municipal reform, the new

Progressive Conservative government has given no indication that reforming municipal government in the province is a high priority.

Notes

1. Parts of this chapter are based on a paper presented at the annual meeting of the Canadian Political Science Association, Quebec City, 28 May 2001, and on a paper presented at the annual meeting of the Canadian Political Science Association, Sherbrooke, Que., 7 June 1999.

2. The members of the board of trustees were appointed by the Lieutenant-Governor in Council for unlimited terms, although any or all members could be dismissed at any time. The Act also gave cabinet the power to convert a local improvement district into an incorporated municipality.

3. In 1957, there were only four municipalities in the region.

4. Further details of the history of these bills and the events leading to their demise can be found in Boswell (1978, 1979).

5. The Liberal government was defeated in the provincial general election of 21 October 2003. The new Progressive Conservative government of Danny Williams has given no indication that its position on amalgamation in the St John's region will differ from that of the previous government. The appointment of the strongly anti-amalgamation former mayor of Mount Pearl, Dave Denine, as Parliamentary Secretary to the Minister of Municipal and Provincial Affairs is indicative that the desire of St John's to take over Mount Pearl is not likely to happen soon.

6. The rationale behind the government's adoption of new regionalization provisions seemed to be that the existing regionalization legislation was too cumbersome for the model of regional co-operation as opposed to regional governance, which was desired, together with the fact that the 1979 Act had been amended so many times that it had become quite unwieldy and a further set of major amendments was not desirable.

7. Members of the Task Force included the author of this chapter; Sam Synard, then president of the Newfoundland and Labrador Federation of Municipalities; and Freida Faour, a community activist from Corner Brook.

8. The Town of Marystown, for example, noted that the cost of providing basic infrastructure to three nearby unincorporated communities 'would add upwards of $10,000,000 to the debt load of our town. If this is to happen, then we simply could not financially afford to support the funding of these additional projects.'

9. Local service districts are 'quasi-municipalities' created under the Municipalities Act to provide basic services in rural areas. In theory, the 178 local service districts are governed by a committee elected by the residents of a community. In practice, a volunteer or group of volunteers emerges from the community without formal elections being held.

10. The precise composition of each Board would be determined during the pre-incorporation facilitative study process.

11. Each motion would require the support of two-thirds of the directors' weighted votes representing two-thirds of the communities having two-thirds of the population.

12. The term 'county' was deliberately used by the Task Force as a relatively neutral term to avoid using either 'municipality' or 'government'. Since the county form of government has never been used in Newfoundland, it was also felt that this designation would avoid any confusion with existing structures of government.

13. Recent discussions with officials in the Department of Municipal and Provincial Affairs indicate that the new Progressive Conservative government has not yet expressed any indication of changing this policy.

14. The most significant of these have been the Whalen Commission in 1974, which recommended a number of two-tier regional governments; the Henley Commission of 1977,

which recommended a two-tier regional government for the St John's metropolitan area; and the Task Force on Municipal Regionalization in 1987, which recommended 20 regional county services boards to cover the entire province.

15. The Newfoundland and Labrador Federation of Municipalities called for a Royal Commission on Municipal Governance in its pre-election policy statement and asked each of the provincial parties to respond to a questionnaire that included the question, 'Will your party support the Federation's call for a Royal Commission on the Future of Municipal Governance?' (NLFM, 2003).

16. The ratio of debt charges as a percentage of total taxes was as high as 199.9 in some communities; the ratio of debt charges as a percentage of total local revenue was as high as 178.0; and the ratio of debt charges as a percentage of total disposable revenue reached 50.9. Without provincial assistance, many municipalities would have been bankrupt. See Newfoundland and Labrador (1974: 217, 379–80).

17. 'No province . . . has evolved a system of municipal grants based to such a large measure upon the discretion of the central government . . . only the revenue and road grants are allocated strictly in accordance with any fixed formula. And these latter contributions, we emphasize, have in recent years constituted a declining share of the total grants allocated to local authorities.' (Newfoundland and Labrador, 1974: 79).

18. The Liberals won an increased majority of seats (37 Liberals to a combined opposition of 11) with 55 per cent of the popular vote, their best showing in nearly 40 years.

19. Statement by Lloyd Matthews, 14 January 1999. The Liberals still lost five seats in the 1999 provincial election.

20. Personal interview with the Director of Municipal Finance, 17 May 2001.

21. The funding level for 2001–2 is $42,650,000.

22. The City of Mount Pearl has been actively seeking a new Cities Act and has even gone so far as to have a consultant prepare a draft. The initiative, however, is not supported by the City of St John's, which is more interested in pursuing the amalgamation of Mount Pearl.

References

ATI Consulting. 2001. *City of St John's, St John's Amalgamation Review*. Halifax: ATI Consulting.

Boswell, Peter G. 1978. 'Strike Two for Regional Government', *City Magazine* 3 (Oct.): 1–2.

———. 1979. 'Regional Government for St John's?', *Urban Focus* 7 (Jan.–Feb.): 1–2.

Canadian British Engineering Consultants. 1957. *Report on the Planning, Utility, Services and Metropolitan Administration of an Area Embracing the City of St John's, the Town of Mount Pearl Park-Glendale, and the Surrounding Areas*. St John's.

House, J.D. 1999. *Against the Tide: Battling for Economic Renewal in Newfoundland and Labrador*. Toronto: University of Toronto Press.

Long, Gene. 1999. *Suspended State: Newfoundland Before Canada*. St John's: Breakwater Books.

Minister of Municipal and Provincial Affairs. 2002. Press release, 21 Mar.

Municipal Training and Development Partnership. 1999. *Memorandum of Understanding*. 6 Nov. (The name was recently changed to Municipal Training and Development Corporation.)

Newfoundland and Labrador. 1974. *Royal Commission on Municipal Government in Newfoundland and Labrador*. St John's: Queen's Printer.

Newfoundland and Labrador. 1976. *Commission of Enquiry into the St John's Urban Region Study* (Henley Commission). St John's: Queen's Printer.

Newfoundland and Labrador, Department of Municipal and Provincial Affairs. 1979. Municipalities Act, 1979.

————. 1990. Regional Services Boards Act.

————. 1996. *The Time for Regionalization: Reforming Municipal Government in Newfoundland and Labrador.*

————. 1999. Municipalities Act.

————. 2000. Urban and Rural Planning Act, 2000.

————. 2001. Municipal Elections Act.

Newfoundland and Labrador Federation of Municipalities (NLFM). 1997. *Pre-Budget Submission.* St John's: NLFM.

————. 2003. *Where We Stand: Municipal Voices and the Provincial Election 2003.* St John's: NLFM.

Proctor & Redfern Limited and Paterson Planning and Research Limited. 1973. *St John's Urban Regional Study*, 4 vols. St John's and Toronto.

CHAPTER 10

Municipal Reform in Prince Edward Island: Uneven Capacity and Reforms

JOHN CROSSLEY

INTRODUCTION

In his classic work *The Government of Prince Edward Island*, published in 1951, Frank MacKinnon told us that 'the history of municipal government on the Island has been uneventful, for there have been no great issues of municipal reform and no significant struggles for local democracy' (MacKinnon, 1951: 274). Half a century later, MacKinnon's assessment remains partly true. The fundamental democratic issues of municipal government remain largely irrelevant to most Islanders and, with the exception of the amalgamation of municipalities in the Charlottetown and Summerside areas in 1994, municipal government reform excites few debates and motivates few political actors. However, the history of municipal government in the last 50 years has not been uneventful. Its history is made interesting by the creation and recreation of a variety of local, municipal, and regional governments and agencies; by the struggle to find ways to organize and finance municipal governments in rapidly growing urban centres; and by attempts to justify and maintain local rural government in a province in which rural identity remains important, but in which the provincial government and its agencies provide many municipal-type services directly to citizens.

This chapter examines the eventful recent history of municipal government reform in Prince Edward Island by looking at the formation and reformation of municipal structures, functions, finances, and jurisdiction. In each section, the paper provides brief historical context, summarizes the nature of changes, and analyzes the causes and effects of the changes. A concluding section summarizes the analyses presented in each section and examines the potential for future reforms.

Structural Reform

The municipal structure in Prince Edward Island has long been a mixture of 'actual municipalities' (Higgins, 1986: 43), quasi-municipal—or, at least, community-based—authorities, and provincially established regional agencies. Until 1995, the core *municipal government* structure comprised one city (Charlottetown) and a small handful of towns (eight in 1995). There are now two cities and seven towns. However, the broader *local governing* structure has, at various times, included up to 488 local school boards, 30 villages, and from 50 to 66 community-based authorities called Community Improvement Councils (or Committees) (CICs), communities, or, simply, municipalities. Superimposed on this array of municipal governments and local authorities are various special-purpose regional and local agencies created by the province, the jurisdictional boundaries of which generally do not coincide with the boundaries of municipal, local, or other regional bodies. In addition, in 1990 it was calculated that about 30 per cent of the province's residents lived in unincorporated areas, a proportion that is unlikely to have changed (PEI, Royal Commission on the Land, 1990: 106). In fact, incorporated municipalities account for well under half the land in Prince Edward Island (Cousins, 1999: appended maps).

In sum, the province has developed a rich variety of municipal, local, and regional government and, therefore, an equally rich history of municipal-level governance and reform. A brief review of that history reveals at least three recurring themes in municipal formation and reform. First, municipal governments have been created and reformed as a direct consequence of the urbanization and modernization of the province. Much of the story of municipal reform, particularly in recent years, is intimately related to the emergence of Charlottetown and, more recently, Summerside as significant urban and economic centres. Second, Islanders and their governments have struggled and continue to struggle to find municipal government structures appropriate for dozens of non-urban communities in which very small populations live a short automobile drive from a dominating urban centre within a province that itself has a population smaller than 18 (according to 2001 census data) or 21 (according to current population projections) Canadian cities (Statistics Canada, 2001b, 2003). Third, reforms to municipal government structures have been driven from the centre. There has been little public pressure for reform of municipal governments, either in urban or rural settings. Rather, reforms to the structure of urban governments have resulted from provincial governments' desire for urban areas to have appropriately formed and financed administrations capable of delivering typical municipal services efficiently. Reforms to the structure of governments in rural communities have resulted from decisions made by provincial governments with ambiguous purposes: there has been a clear desire, for cultural, democratic, and administrative reasons, to decentralize delivery of various services, but no provincial government has acted on the belief that the local rural community is the appropriate mechanism for delivering most of these services.

Municipal government in the modestly urban areas of Prince Edward Island emerged between 1855 and 1920 with the incorporation of the City of

Charlottetown in 1855, the town of Summerside in 1877, and the towns of Alberton, Borden, Georgetown, Kensington, Montague, and Souris between 1910 and 1917. In each of these cases, incorporation occurred when the concentration of population and businesses reached the point at which local services were required, such as fire control and police protection, and when locality-specific regulations were required to preserve public health and supervise public amusements and markets (MacKinnon, 1951: 275). In spite of the early emergence of towns and a city, for most of the province's political history, municipal government formation and reform have concentrated on *rural* communities. Indeed, from 1920 until 1983, several attempts were made to provide a viable rural municipal government structure, while scant attention was paid to the need to reform municipal government in urban areas. Thus, in 1950, the provincial government, convinced that emerging social, economic, technological, and demographic changes would create public demand for local government and services in small rural communities (Smith Green and Associates, 1991: 9), passed the Village Services Act, creating very limited municipal government for communities thought to be too small for actual incorporation but large enough to require basic local services, such as sidewalks, sewers, and fire protection (MacKinnon, 1951: 280). By the mid-1960s, the provincial government had concluded that the Village Services Act was not serving the rural population well and a Community Improvement Act was passed and proclaimed in 1967, making it possible to create a new type of municipal government, the Community Improvement Council in small rural communities. The powers of the CIC were to be quite limited, even more than was the case with towns and villages: 'fire protection, garbage collection and disposal, street lighting, and general administration' (Smith Green and Associates, 1991: 10) were the only functions of the CICs. Finally, in 1983, the newly elected Conservative government of J. Angus MacLean attempted to effect a 'rural renaissance', which included a firm ideological commitment to local communities and traditional rural economic activities (MacDonald, 2000: 348–51). A new Municipalities Act replaced the Town Act, Village Services Act, and Community Improvement Act; it prohibited changes in municipal boundaries except upon application from residents in all of the municipalities affected and provided no incentives for amalgamation of adjacent communities or consolidation of municipal services.

Two points about the historical focus on rural municipal governments are relevant to our understanding of modern municipal reform. First, rural municipal government has always been of more interest to provincial decision-makers than to the residents of the communities. Elected and appointed provincial officials often have sought the planning, regulatory, and administrative benefits that might be derived from a system of municipal government in rural communities, and have been smitten frequently by the appeal of the pastoral culture of the Island's history. Rural residents, however, have generally recognized that the services they have needed were delivered by the province (as in the case of road maintenance and police protection), or could be purchased from neighbouring municipalities and paid for by the provincial government's property tax system (as in the case of fire protection), or could be purchased from private enterprises that relied on provincially operated infrastructure (as in the case of garbage collection and delivery to provincial waste disposal sites), or were provided by the homeowners themselves (as in the case of water from individual, but provincially regulated, wells and waste disposal in private, but provincially regulated, septic systems). Thus, municipal government has often appeared redundant, perhaps even irrelevant, to rural Islanders.

Second, the growing problems of municipal governance associated with urbanization were not only ignored but actually exacerbated. As population shifted during the 1960s and 1970s to the areas around Charlottetown and Summerside, the province refused to adjust the boundaries of the urban centres to include new subdivisions or to amalgamate communities that were once rural but now abutted the city or the town. Rather, the province continued to create villages and CICs. As a result, to the effects of urbanization were added the inefficiencies and inequities associated with having several small municipalities in a single urban area. By the early 1990s, the problems with municipal government structure, especially in the urban areas around Summerside and Charlottetown, could no longer be ignored. Reform of municipal government structures became a significant public policy issue when Royal Commissioner Douglas Boylan made it a central recommendation in the 1990 *Report* of the Royal Commission on Land Ownership, Land Use, and the Landscape.

This Royal Commission, known widely as the Royal Commission on the Land, was struck by Premier Joe Ghiz in 1988 to consider all aspects of landownership, use, and regulation in Prince Edward Island. It produced an enormous report that touched on many issues. Its central thesis, however, 'was the necessity for comprehensive land management—voluntary if possible, legislated where necessary—for the entire province' (MacDonald, 2000: 362). This focus on land management led the Commission to produce a thorough critique of the structure of municipal government in the province and to call for municipal government reform to produce a structure capable of planning and managing land use.

The Royal Commission addressed both of the province's fundamental and traditional municipal reform concerns: the organization of effective and efficient urban governments and the best way to govern and provide services for rural communities. The latter—rural municipal reform—was clearly the more important matter for the Royal Commission because of the large amount of rural land needing management. The Commission produced a scathing indictment of rural municipal government (PEI, 1990: 103–17), pointing out that few of the rural municipalities, whether towns, villages, CICs, or 'communities', had actually pursued or shown any interest in self-government. Most had never developed an official plan, many exercised only a few of the municipal powers available to them, and some had never made a bylaw or levied a tax. In addition, most rural municipalities were so tiny that they had neither the human nor fiscal resources to manage municipal functions and services. The Commission argued that the rural municipal structure 'is a waste of human resources and, at the same time, it is a system without sufficient capacity to be effective as a proper management tool in the administration of land use plans and other services' (ibid., 112). It argued that small municipalities adjacent to the province's two urban centres should be absorbed by the urban municipalities and that most of the rural communities (but not the towns and larger villages) should be abolished and replaced by county-level governing authorities. (This was a radical recommendation. Although the province has been divided into three counties since it was first surveyed by the British in 1764, no county-level government has ever existed and no administrative jurisdiction has ever been defined by county boundaries (Cousins, 1999: 2.)

The Royal Commission also addressed the need to restructure government in the Charlottetown area (ibid., 119–31). Besides its recommendation for expanding the boundaries of Summerside and Charlottetown, the Commission pointed out the inequitable municipal finance system that drove up expenses and tax rates in Charlottetown and allowed adjacent communities to maintain low tax rates while enjoying many of the services provided by the city. Of greater importance to the Commission, however, was the adverse effect that the fragmented municipal government structure had on the quality of life in the Charlottetown area. Its *Report* pointed to a number of instances where decisions by municipalities adjacent to Charlottetown had adversely affected traffic flow in the capital city area, or had been in direct opposition to the city's zoning regulations, and had encircled Charlottetown with strip development. Perhaps most significantly, the Commission's *Report* devoted an entire chapter (ibid., 411–30) to the threats posed to the water supply in the Charlottetown area by the unco-ordinated and largely unregulated development of industries and residential subdivisions in the municipalities adjacent to the city. The Commission presented three alternatives for the restructuring of municipal governments in the Charlottetown area: maintaining the status quo, superimposing a level of regional government on existing municipal governments to force co-operation and planning, or amalgamating the various municipal governments into a single municipality. It argued strongly for amalgamation.

The *Report* of the Royal Commission helped set an agenda for debate about municipal reform. However, it is ironic, perhaps, that the reform of most importance to the Royal Commission—restructuring rural municipal government—was largely ignored in the debate over municipal reform that ensued during the four years following the publication of the *Report*. Indeed, the recommended reforms to the structure of rural municipal government have not been addressed to this day. Almost from the time the *Report* was released, public and political attention focused on the question of amalgamation of the municipalities around Charlottetown and Summerside.

In fact, the *Report* was neither the first nor the only source of arguments for municipal amalgamation in the urban centres, although it did popularize and legitimize the issue and lay out the arguments in favour of amalgamation in a complete and palatable way. In 1998, the Institute of Island Studies at the University of Prince Edward Island had been commissioned by the Federation of PEI Municipalities and the Department of Community Affairs to review the structure of local and regional government in the province, and the resulting publication, *The Geography of Governance* (Cousins, 1999), argued that the province was over-governed and needed to rethink its municipal structures, including in the Charlottetown and Summerside areas. At roughly the same time, the Department of Community and Cultural Affairs commissioned a local consulting firm, Smith Green and Associates, to undertake a thorough review of municipal finance and recommend improvements. The Smith Green *Municipal Study Report* argued that 'a major factor underlying perceived inequities in the property tax and municipal grants regime is the structure of municipal government in the province' (Smith Green and Associates, 1991: 23). Of particular concern to the consultants was the proliferation of municipalities in the Charlottetown and Summerside (and, to a lesser extent, the Montague) areas: 'within five "crow-flight" kilometers of the City of Charlottetown population growth has resulted in a new metropolitan area consisting of sixteen municipalities' (ibid., 25).

By the early 1990s, then, a consensus was emerging around the need for amalgamation of the several municipalities in the Charlottetown and Summerside urban areas. This consensus was catalyzed into government action in early 1993 by the selection of Catherine Callbeck to succeeded Joe Ghiz as leader of the Liberal Party and, therefore, Premier of the province. Callbeck proved to be a committed and bold reformer and she made urban municipal amalgamation a top priority. On 29 March 1993, Callbeck led the Liberal Party to a substantial victory in a provincial general election and immediately set her sights on amalgamation. She appointed Jeannie Lea to her cabinet as Minister without Portfolio with special responsibility for Municipal Reform. On 25 June 1993, Lea tabled a White Paper on Municipal Reform in the Legislative Assembly, in which she announced the government's intention to proceed with significant reform of municipal structures in the Charlottetown and Summerside areas. At the same time, the government appointed a highly respected, recently retired senior public servant, Lorne Moase, as a one-person Commission on Municipal Reform, charging him to recommend the most appropriate model for reform and to make recommendations concerning various practical issues involved in reform. Moase reported in December 1993, presenting a case and a framework for amalgamation, and on 31 March 1994 Lea tabled a position paper, *New Cities . . . New Towns*, setting out the government's final decisions concerning urban municipal amalgamation. These decisions became effective with the proclamation of the Charlottetown Area Municipalities Act on 28 July 1994 and the City of Summerside Act on 24 August 1994. On 3 October 1994, voters in four newly created municipalities, three in the Charlottetown area and one in Summerside, elected councillors to their new municipal governments. Within 18 months of the creation of the Government Reform Office, the task of urban municipal amalgamation was complete.

Debate over municipal amalgamation was vigorous and focused on the need for reform, the model most appropriate to achieve the required reforms, and the extent of reform (number of municipalities to be amalgamated). Ancillary discussions and debates, carried on primarily among those most directly involved and interested in municipal government, addressed various implementation issues, such as the need for a ward system for municipal representation and creation of single municipal service agencies where several existed before amalgamation. Because the intent of this chapter is to look at the broad factors that have shaped the restructuring of municipal governments, little attention is given below to these issues of implementation.

Debate over the prudence of and necessity for amalgamation was not encouraged by the provincial government, which made it clear from the outset that it had decided that urban municipal reform was required and desirable. The 25 June 1993 *White Paper on Municipal Reform* started from the assumption that reform was necessary and went on to explain how the province would benefit from it. It pointed out in some detail that the existing boundaries of urban municipalities were antiquated and artificial and failed to reflect the patterns of settlement and population growth. It decried inequities in the delivery of municipal services and the level and distribution of property and commercial taxes. It argued that duplication of services led to inefficiencies and was probably wasteful of tax dollars. Similarly, it suggested that public funds and democratic energy were squandered on an unnecessarily large number of elected officials in the Island's urban areas. In the Summerside area there were 25 elected officials for every 10,000 residents, while in the Charlottetown area the ratio was 20 for every 10,000. In Halifax, Fredericton, Sydney, and Moncton, the numbers were, respectively, 1.1, 3, 4.5, and 1.9 elected representatives per 10,000 residents (PEI, Government Reform Office, 1993: 10). Finally, the White Paper pointed out that Prince Edward Island lagged significantly behind all the other provinces when it came to rationalizing and modernizing urban municipal government.

The White Paper asserted that all of these deficiencies, problems, and inefficiencies could be addressed by restructuring municipal government in the two urban areas. In addition, such reform would strengthen the two urban centres, making them more self-reliant, politically relevant and powerful, competitive with urban centres elsewhere, and attractive for economic development. The capacity to plan and the ability to make good decisions would be improved. Most importantly, said the White Paper, in acknowledgement of the influence of the Royal Commission on the Land, urban municipal reform would facilitate the implementation of sound land-use planning (ibid., 30–1).

In spite of the government's insistence that the fundamental decision had been taken to go ahead with some sort of urban municipal reform, some arguments were made in defence of the status quo. Not surprisingly, the Charlottetown Area Co-operation Council, an organization that had been formed to promote co-operation among various municipalities, argued that municipal reform was unnecessary (*The Guardian*, 26 June 1993: 2) and a number of the smaller municipalities that would be affected by municipal reform, such as Parkdale in the Charlottetown area and St Eleanors in the Summerside area, opposed the idea of municipal reform on the grounds of their historical existence as communities (ibid.). But as the provincial government had anticipated, public sentiment, as articulated by the print and broadcast media, political parties, and academics, was very much in favour of urban municipal reform and those opposed to the idea were not able to mobilize support or organize an effective opposition. Some, like the Federation of Prince Edward Island Municipalities and the Town of Parkdale (adjacent to Charlottetown, incorporated in 1973, population about 2,000), criticized the process used by the government as insufficiently consultative and heavy-handed (*The Guardian*, 9 July 1993: 23; 30 June 1993: 2.) and called for further consultation or a plebiscite. However, these arguments also failed to gain much support and debate quickly began to address the model to be followed for urban municipal reform and the optimal geographical extent of reform.

The *White Paper on Municipal Reform* had identified three models that might be used to effect urban municipal reform: annexation of small municipalities by their dominant urban neighbour, the introduction of a two-tier regional government, or the amalgamation of territory and people into completely new municipal governments governed by new legislation. The White Paper itself rejected annexation, although it gave few reasons for doing so; indeed, it pointed out that annexation would allow a smooth incremental transition to larger urban governments (PEI, Government Reform Office, 1993: 34–5). Presumably, the government was concerned that annexation would make Charlottetown and Summerside appear predatory and thus would intensify opposition to urban municipal reform and create potentially long-lasting bitterness in the annexed communities. In any event, the rejection of the annexation option was never raised as an issue, either during the Commission consultation process or during public debate. The White Paper directed the Commission on Municipal Reform to assess the two-tier regional government option and the amalgamation option and to recommend the more appropriate and effective model for the circumstances.

As it turned out—and as the provincial government might have expected—the two-tier regional government approach to urban municipal reform was never a serious option. The White Paper had suggested that under such a model 'Area Municipal Authorities' might be created in the Charlottetown and Summerside areas, with responsibility for land-use planning and the development of regional plans, sewers, water, policing, street maintenance, solid waste disposal, and regional economic development and promotion. The existing municipalities would remain in place and might be responsible for such matters as residential land-use planning, fire protection, recreation, parks, sidewalks, storm sewers, and animal control (ibid., 35–7). A review of newspaper reports from the date that the White Paper was released until the first elections under the new urban municipal regime shows no one arguing for the creation of a second-tier regional government, and the *Report* of the Commission on Municipal Reform points out that none of the municipalities, individuals, or groups consulted by the Commissioner favoured this model (PEI, Commission on Municipal Reform, 1993: 45). The prime benefit of the model was thought to be the preservation of local, often historic, communities, but this benefit was not thought sufficient to offset its major deficiency, i.e., the creation of yet another and potentially costly and inefficient level of government. When the comparative cost-benefit analysis of the various models of municipal reform, commissioned by the Commission on Municipal Reform, was made public one month after the Commission's *Report* had been tabled, public suspicion about second-tier regional governments proved to be justified. The cost-benefit analysis looked at three different approaches to amalgamation, all of which promised savings in expenditures by urban municipal governments. The creation of second-tier regional governments, however, promised to increase municipal government expenditures by significant amounts (Porter Dillon, 1994: 97).

From the beginning of the reform process, then, a consensus formed in favour of amalgamation as the most appropriate model for urban municipal reform. The Commission on Municipal Reform reported almost unanimous support for amalgamation among the individuals and municipal representatives who made presentations to the Commission. Indeed, even the community of Wilmot (adjacent to Summerside), which favoured no form of municipal reform, spoke approvingly of the amalgamation model (PEI, Commission on Municipal Reform, 1993: 48). Perhaps surprisingly, a consensus emerged almost as quickly and easily about exactly which communities were to be amalgamated and into how many new municipalities.

In the Summerside area there was never any doubt that amalgamation would lead to a single urban municipality. Nor was there any doubt that the new municipality would be an incorporated city rather than a town. There was only ever a short list of communities that might be amalgamated, and there were few ambiguities. The Summerside urban area clearly included the following tightly adjacent communities: Summerside (town, incorporated 1877, population about 8,000), Sherbrooke (CIC, created in 1972, population just under 600), St Eleanors (village, incorporated in 1956, population just under 4,000), and Wilmot (village, incorporated in 1965, population just under 2,000). In addition, there was an economically important unincorporated area within the Summerside urban area called Slemon Park, an industrial park created on land that was, until the mid-1980s, CFB Summerside. If amalgamation was to take place at all, it had to include these four communities and Slemon Park. Thus, even though St Eleanors, Wilmot, and Sherbrooke resisted amalgamation, the Municipal Reform Commission recommended that a City of Summerside be created by amalgamating the four municipalities and Slemon Park, a recommendation that the provincial government accepted and implemented with the City of Summerside Act, proclaimed on 24 August 1994.

In the Charlottetown area, it was not obvious which communities should be amalgamated; nor was it obvious that the result should be a single urban municipality. In total, there were 16 candidates for amalgamation and because the Charlottetown urban area is divided into three parts by the Hillsborough River and Charlottetown harbour to the southeast of historic Charlottetown and the North River to the west, the 16 communities were not adjacent. The list below shows the distribution of the municipalities that were potential candidates for amalgamation.

Municipalities adjacent to the historic City of Charlottetown:
• Charlottetown: city, incorporated 1855, population about 16,000

- East Royalty: village, incorporated 1977, population about 2,000
- Hillsborough Park: village, incorporated 1976, population about 1,000
- Parkdale: town, incorporated 1973, population about 2,000
- Sherwood: village, incorporated 1960, population about 6,000
- West Royalty: village, incorporated 1980, population about 2,000
- Winsloe: CIC, created 1971, population about 1,200

Municipalities southeast of the Hillsborough River and south of the harbour:
- Battery Point: an unincorporated residential area
- Bunbury: village, incorporated 1969, population about 1,000
- Cross Roads: CIC, created 1972, population about 2,000
- Keppoch-Kinlock: CIC, created 1983, population about 450
- Southport: village, incorporated 1972, population about 1,500

Municipalities west of the North River:
- Clyde River: CIC, created 1974, population about 550
- Cornwall: village incorporated 1966, population about 2,000
- Elliot River: CIC, created 1975, population about 1,000
- North River: CIC, created 1974, population about 2,000

One obvious option was to amalgamate all of these municipalities into one city. Such grand-scale amalgamation would provide optimal opportunities for planning and regulation, would certainly eliminate over-government in the Charlottetown area, and would resolve inequities in municipal finance. Moreover, as the cost-benefit analysis of municipal reform showed, amalgamation into a single city provided by far the greatest economies of scale and promised the greatest savings over time (Porter Dillon, 1994). In spite of these advantages, only the Greater Charlottetown Area Chamber of Commerce argued in favour of amalgamation into a single city (*The Guardian*, 17 Sept. 1993). Not one of the 16 municipalities affected spoke in favour of amalgamation into a single city (PEI, Commission on Municipal Reform, 1993: 54).

The possibility of amalgamating all of the municipalities except those in the North River–Cornwall area also received no support, even though this, too, was arguably advantageous from the perspective of municipal planning and clearly would provide significant economies of scale and savings. In the end, the Commission on Municipal Reform and the Government Reform Office were faced with a nearly unanimous position from the affected municipalities: if there had to be amalgamation, it should result in three municipalities in the Charlottetown area and the boundaries between those municipalities should be dictated by the geography of the harbour and rivers that cut through the greater Charlottetown urban area. Although the Commission on Municipal Reform recognized this as the least desirable of the three approaches to amalgamation, it accepted the practicalities of the situation and recommended the creation of one city (Charlottetown) and two towns, which it gave the working names of Charlottetown West and Charlottetown South.

The recommendations of the Commission on Municipal Reform were accepted by the provincial government and implemented with the City of Summerside Act and the Charlottetown Area Municipalities Act. The residents of what the Commission on Municipal Reform called Charlottetown South chose to call their new town Stratford and those in Charlottetown West chose to retain the name Cornwall. Where there had been 18 municipalities and two unincorporated areas, there were now two cities and two towns after the amalgamations in Summerside and Charlottetown.

The reorganization of municipal government in the province's two urban areas in 1994 ended structural reform of municipal government, at least temporarily. Although the Charlottetown *Guardian* speculated in the fall of 1994 (30 Sept. and 28 Nov.) that the province would embark on a second round of municipal government reform, possibly leading to amalgamation of communities in the Montague–Cardigan area, there has been little but silence with respect to further municipal reform. The province has had three general elections since amalgamating the urban municipalities, and in none of them was municipal reform—or, for that matter, municipal government—an issue. However, significant structural problems remain and it is likely that some future government will want to address them. Municipal restructuring in the urban areas was left incomplete in 1994. By creating three municipalities in the Charlottetown urban area, the province left unresolved the issues of effective urban planning and service delivery. Stratford, with a population of fewer than 6,500, and Cornwall, with a population of fewer than 4,500, are relatively small and, therefore, pressure for further rationalization of municipal government is likely to arise.

The municipal restructuring issues that are more likely to arise in the near future, however, are those that address municipal government in the province's rural areas. The critique of rural municipal government developed by the Royal Commission on the Land in 1990 has never been addressed by provincial decision-makers. The 66 'communities' that continue to provide varying degrees of municipal and quasi-municipal government remain ineffective and, arguably, a waste of time and money, and a significant number of Islanders and most of the land remain beyond the bounds of all municipal government. Unless an effective rural governing structure is found, the provincial government will continue to provide municipal-type services in much of the province. This, however, offends many Islanders, who, like Angus MacLean in the 1980s, believe in the virtues of rural life and hope for a 'rural renaissance'. These Islanders continue to search for a model of rural municipal government in which all rural areas have local governments with meaningful responsibilities, sufficient resources, and appropriate capacity to address local needs. In 1998, an Employment Summit Panel struck by the provincial government to consider some aspects of economic development in the province argued that reform of rural municipal government is an essential prerequisite for economic development in the province's rural areas. A year later a Population Strategy Panel struck by the provincial government to consult with Islanders issued a similar call for a thorough review of rural municipal government (Institute of Island Studies, 2000: 35). In 2002, the director of the Institute of

Island Studies at the University of Prince Edward Island argued before the Federation of PEI Municipalities for a comprehensive review of the structure of municipal government outside the province's urban areas (Baglole, 2002). Eventually such a review will occur because it so obviously is needed.

FUNCTIONAL REFORM

The functions of municipal governments in Prince Edward Island have varied by type of municipality and over time. In general, the functions of rural municipal governments have been restricted by legislation and even more restricted in practice. The provincial government has adopted many of the functions normally carried out by municipal governments. Only cities and the larger towns have carried out significant municipal functions. Over time, the tendency has been for functions to move from the municipal level to the provincial level. Where there have been pressures or incentives for functions to be decentralized away from the province, the tendency has been for the provincial government to create special-purpose regional agencies under provincial control, rather than to devolve functions onto municipal governments.

If we examine the various statutes that have created and empowered municipal governments over the years (City of Charlottetown Act, Town of Summerside Act, Towns Act, Village Services Act, Community Improvement Act, Municipalities Act, Charlottetown Area Municipalities Act, and the City of Summerside Act), we find that, on paper, there is a fairly standard list of municipal functions. For CICs, the list includes fire protection, garbage and refuse collection and disposal, street lighting, recreation, and tree preservation and protection. For cities, towns, and villages, the list is longer: administration of the municipality, fire protection, garbage and refuse collection and disposal, street lighting, recreation, drainage, sewage collection and treatment, sidewalks, roads, parking, regulation of traffic, police protection, parks, community economic and commercial development, housing development, local libraries, animal control, building and standards control, regulation of real property maintenance, regulation of business practices, and public transportation. However, both these lists are deceptive.

In practice, few of the municipalities in Prince Edward Island have acted in any of these areas of responsibility. Rather, for the vast majority of towns, villages, CICs, and 'communities', the province exercises these responsibilities or the responsibilities are simply not met or required. Thus, the province maintains roads in all municipalities except the cities of Charlottetown and Summerside and the town of Stratford. Similarly, only the cities of Charlottetown and Summerside, the town of Kensington, and the community of Bordon–Carleton maintain their own police forces. All other municipalities are policed by the RCMP, which serves as the provincial police force under the Police Act (Statutes of PEI, 1988: ch. P-11). Similarly, only a few municipalities maintain libraries; the rest benefit from the provincial library system, which circulates material throughout the province. With respect to water and sewage, most rural municipalities encompass areas where private wells and septic systems are the norm, and both are provincially regulated. Of the major municipal functions, it is fair to say that only fire protection has consistently been delivered by municipal governments. Thirty-five municipalities maintain volunteer fire departments and each of the municipalities without a fire department contracts with a neighbouring municipality for fire protection services.

In sum, then, to understand tendencies in the reform of municipal functions, we must understand, first, that most municipalities do very little and, second, that the province has always been the effective deliverer of many municipal services. Against this backdrop, we can identify three trends in the reform of municipal functions. First, as we have already seen, the province has attempted to create municipalities in the two urban areas that can effectively carry out the more sophisticated functions of municipal government. Thus, one of the motivations for the reform of urban municipal government in the 1990s was the creation of governments that could engage in urban planning, regulation of businesses, and local economic development with a minimum of direction and supervision from the province. Indeed, the 1990s municipal government reforms have allowed the province to devolve significant administrative, planning, and regulatory functions onto the cities of Charlottetown and Summerside and, to a lesser extent, onto the towns of Stratford and Cornwall.

The second trend in the functional reform, or evolution, of municipal governance in Prince Edward Island has been the movement of some important functions from the municipal level to the province (in addition to those municipal-type functions that have always been exercised by the province). The most famous example of this movement of functions to the senior government occurred with the reform of public education in 1971 and the abolition of hundreds of local school boards. What had been, arguably, the single most important function of local-level government became immediately a provincial function. Initially, the province made some effort to maintain local input into the educational system by creating five regional school boards with elected trustees, but the trend to centralization of this function continued and now there are two regional school boards (Eastern and Western) and one French-language school board.

A more recent instance of the movement of functions from municipalities to the province is solid waste collection and disposal. Until 1994, garbage collection was unambiguously a municipal responsibility—or, in many villages, CICs, and unincorporated areas, an individual responsibility—while the province provided the infrastructure necessary for garbage disposal, including collection sites, landfills, and 'energy-from-waste' incinerators. By the early 1990s, however, Prince Edward Island was facing a developing crisis in managing solid waste. Landfills were becoming full and the quantity of waste requiring disposal continued to grow each year. In 1992, the province decided to implement a comprehensive waste sorting and recycling program. It created a new provincial East Prince Waste Management Commission and, in 1994, initiated the new provincial waste management regime on a pilot basis in the eastern Prince County region (which includes Summerside). In East Prince, regulations made it mandatory for residences, business, and institutions to sort their garbage into compostables, various types of recyclables, and garbage. The Commission built centralized composting and sorting facilities, published regulations for sorting waste, and took over collection of all waste in the East Prince area. The pilot project proved successful, with up to 65 per cent of the waste in the region being diverted away from landfills. Consequently, the province created the Island Waste Management Corporation and began the process of extending the regime to all parts of the province. Among much 'not-in-my-backyard' controversy, a site was selected close to Charlottetown for a second centralized composting facility and bids were invited from private companies interested in handling collection and sorting of recyclables. By the end of 2002, the provincial government had taken over all aspects of waste collection and disposal from all municipalities in the province.

The movement of responsibility for schools and garbage from municipalities to the province (or to agencies created for these purposes by the province) is explainable by the nature of the changes required and by the smallness of Prince Edward Island. In both cases, the province concluded that significant public good could be achieved if centralized services were provided. However, because the province has so few people living in such proximity to one another, centralization of these services quickly became provincialization, with some regionalized aspects.

In no other areas of public policy has the pursuit of provincial policy objectives led to the taking over of functions from municipalities. During the amalgamation of urban municipalities in 1993–4, it was suggested that the two new towns and two cities could save money if they allowed the province to take responsibility for maintaining their roads and streets. (The province would retain a larger share of property tax collected to cover its additional expenses, but the savings to the municipalities would be greater than the loss in revenue.) With respect to the municipalities that became the towns of Stratford and Cornwall, this was seen as a continuation of the status quo ante, not the taking over of a municipal function by the province, because none of the municipalities that were amalgamated to create Stratford and Cornwall had previously been responsible for their own streets and roads. In the case of Charlottetown and Summerside, this would have been a significant movement of function from the municipal to the provincial level (PEI, Commission on Municipal Reform, 1993: 74–8). In any event, neither of the cities opted to transfer this function to the province, and Stratford decided to maintain its own streets. It is significant that the sole reason for considering transferring this function to the province was to save money. Unlike the management of schools or disposal of waste, there were no larger public policy goals or general good sought. Therefore, the provincial government was not enormously enthusiastic about taking on the function and the municipalities were inclined to incur relatively small additional expenses in order to retain (or create) autonomy.

The third trend in the reform agenda of municipal functions in Prince Edward Island has to do with the movement of functions from provincial to municipal jurisdiction. In fact, there have been no such transfers of function. However, the province has, from time to time, wanted to decentralize functions that might, in some circumstances, have become municipal functions. In each instance the province created new special-purpose agencies, at least in part because the structure of municipal government has been too weak and incomplete to implement new functions.

Two brief examples illustrate the tendency for provincial governments to devolve authority to local agencies other than municipal governments. The first example is in the area of local economic development. At least twice during the 1970s when faced with geographically specific problems of economic development, the province created special-purpose local development agencies rather than delegate economic development functions to municipal governments. In the mid-1970s, it created the Charlottetown Area Development Corporation to manage development projects that would revitalize downtown Charlottetown and encourage economic growth in the greater Charlottetown area (Lea, 1987). In 1977, it created the West Prince Industrial Commission to tackle serious problems of underdevelopment and economic hardship in the westernmost parts of the province (MacKinnon, 1989). Each of these initiatives illustrates one of the two fundamental weaknesses of the province's municipal government structure. Had the Charlottetown urban area not, at the time, included over a dozen municipalities, the province could have helped the City of Charlottetown to create its own economic development capacity. Similarly, if the province had developed an effective structure for governing rural communities, the West Prince Industrial Commission may not have been necessary.

A similar picture emerges when we look at local planning, a function that the provincial ministry responsible for municipal affairs had dominated since at least 1966 when the first municipal planner was hired by the province (PEI, Department of Municipal Affairs, 1967). Because of the fragmented nature of urban municipal government before 1994, the province facilitated the creation of the Charlottetown Area Regional Planning Board to do the local-level urban planning that the individual municipalities could not do and that the province no longer wanted to do. Also, because of the continued weakness of rural municipal governments, the province has created a number of 'Special Planning Areas' that allow provincial government planners to work with committees of officials from a number of municipalities to develop land-use and economic development plans. Again, had the structures of municipal government been adequate it is likely that these planning functions would have devolved directly onto municipal authorities.

In conclusion, there have been relatively few reforms to the functions of municipal governments in Prince Edward Island. The structural weaknesses of the municipal government system have made it difficult for the province to devolve functions onto municipal governments, while the same weaknesses and the province's small population and territory have sometimes made it easy and prudent for the province to take over municipal functions to effect important public policy objectives. It is possible, however, that the restructuring of urban municipal government in 1994 will make it easier in the future for the province to transfer some functions to municipal government. In fact, in 1999 the Department of Community and Cultural Affairs, the City of Charlottetown, the City of Summerside, and the Town of Stratford agreed to review and discuss the delivery of specific services by municipal and provincial governments (PEI, 2001) and reforms are possible. However, with respect to other municipalities, until the rural municipal government structure is reformed and made effective, any further functional reforms are likely to involve the continued movement of functions from the municipal level to the provincial level.

FINANCIAL REFORM

Effective and equitable financing of urban municipal governments has been a significant issue in municipal government in Prince Edward Island since at least the mid-1960s. Reviews of municipal finance (particularly the grants system) were conducted in 1967, 1971, 1975, 1976, 1978, 1983, 1986, and 1991, and one of the strong reasons suggested by the 1993 *White Paper on Municipal Reform* for restructuring the urban municipal system was to create a structure that would allow for equitable municipal finance. The underlying theme of the long discussion of municipal financial reform has been the attempt to find a financing regime appropriate to a situation in which the provincial government provides municipal services for many communities while some municipal governments provide extensive services and others provide practically no services at all.

Municipalities in Prince Edward Island are funded by property tax revenues, grants from the province, grants in lieu of property taxes from the provincial and federal governments, and miscellaneous fees. Neither grants in lieu nor user fees have been particularly controversial and have not been the subject of reform initiatives. However, both the property tax and municipal grants regimes have been the subject of much thought and some reform. The modern era of property taxation in Prince Edward Island began in 1971. Prior to that year, various municipalities and the hundreds of school boards had the authority to assess property within their boundaries and levy property taxes, poll taxes, school taxes, sidewalk taxes, automobile taxes, and other special taxes (Novack, 1990: 36). A review of municipal finance conducted for the provincial government in 1967 had been critical of this tax regime (Touche, Ross, Bailey, and Smart, 1967), but the catalyst for property tax reform was the decision to abolish the local school boards and have the province take direct responsibility for maintaining and managing schools. When the province took over the schools, it also took over the property taxation that had supported the schools. With the entry of the provincial government into the property tax field in 1971, the property tax system was rationalized and centralized. The province abolished all of the smaller specialized taxes, took over responsibility for land valuation, imposed a uniform property tax regime in the province, and assumed sole responsibility for collecting property tax. In marked contrast to most other provinces, then, since 1971 the provincial government has levied a provincial property tax and collected municipal property taxes on behalf of all municipalities. Revenue from property taxes has come to provide approximately 70 per cent of the total revenue of municipal governments and just under 10 per cent of the revenue generated by the provincial government from its own sources (Novack, 1990: 36; PEI, Department of the Provincial Treasury, 2002: 76). As in many other jurisdictions, the property tax has been criticized and arguments are often made for property tax reform.

Uniquely Island arguments for reform of the property tax system address both the provincial property tax and the municipal property tax. Since at least the early 1980s, the provincial property tax has been criticized on several grounds, most relating to the difficulties caused for municipal governments by the province's occupation of this tax field (see Smith Green and Associates, 1991: 33–5, for a summary of these criticisms). Municipal officials have tended to begin their criticism from the assumption that property tax is essentially a way to fund municipal services and so should not be used to fund general-purpose provincial services. Thus, municipal officials from Charlottetown and Summerside have argued that it is unfair for the province to collect property tax in municipalities where it does not provide municipal-type services. In addition, municipal officials argue that because the provincial government levies a uniform tax on all property in the province, regardless of the services delivered, ratepayers in municipalities that must themselves levy significant property taxes to maintain municipal services end up paying an unfairly large amount of tax. With respect to the municipal property tax regime, criticisms over the past 30 years have emphasized the inequities of a system in which residents of some communities pay lower property taxes than do citizens in other communities simply because in some locations municipal services are delivered by the province and in others by the municipalities. In addition, several municipalities have argued that it is unfair for residents of some communities to pay higher taxes for the delivery of recreational and other services that are available at no similar cost to residents of neighbouring communities.

The criticisms of the property tax regime in place since 1971 have led to relatively few reforms to the system. The province has repeatedly rejected the argument that it is occupying a tax field that should be used for uniquely municipal purposes. Rather, it points out that the original reason for the introduction of the provincial property tax was to finance schools and argues that this remains sufficient reason for it to levy a property tax and for that tax to be uniform across the province. This position was supported both by the Smith Green and Associates review of municipal finance (ibid., 40) and by the Commission on Municipal Reform (PEI, Commission on Municipal Reform, 1993: 91–2).

Arguments about the perceived and actual inequities of the property tax system have been taken more seriously. In 1991, Smith Green and Associates undertook a quantitative analysis to determine whether or not the property tax system did lead to inequities in the levels of taxation and the generation of municipal government revenue. It found that inequities were measurable and recommended that the province 'establish differential property tax rates for residents living in areas where it continues to provide municipal type services, compared to municipalities where such services are not provided by the province or are provided at municipal expense' (Smith Green and Associates, 1991: 74). Since municipal amalgamation in 1994, the province has indeed introduced some differentiation in its effective property tax rates, but it has done so not by setting different rates for property located in different types of municipality, but by turning over a share of its property tax revenue to municipalities that deliver more expensive municipal services. In effect, it has begun to transfer property-tax points to Charlottetown and Summerside.

The reform issues with respect to provincial grants to municipalities have been similar to those relating to property tax: equitable funding for municipalities that deliver significantly different levels of service to their citizens. The modern municipal grant system began in 1975. Prior to that year, the province had provided special-purpose conditional grants to municipalities for a variety of programs, such as laying sidewalks, paving streets, police protection, and firefighting. In addition, the province provided per capita unconditional grants to support municipal administration and other services. The use of conditional grants allowed the financing system to respond appropriately to the functions actually exercised by municipalities, so the large majority of municipalities for which the province maintained the streets and provided police protection would not receive funding for those functions. However, the unconditional grant system was not sensitive to the variation in municipal functions across the province, and inequities quickly set in. When the unconditional grants were begun in 1947 they were a uniform one dollar per capita (Touche, Ross, Bailey, and Smart, 1967: 117). However, by the early 1960s, the unfairness of such flat-rate funding had caused the province to introduce different levels of funding for different types of municipality. Thus, in 1963, unconditional grants were set at $10 per capita for Charlottetown and the seven towns, but for villages the grants matched revenue from other sources, with a floor of $1.25 per capita and a ceiling of $4.75 per capita (Canadian Tax Foundation, 1963: 53–4). By 1967, the grant was set at $12 per capita for Charlottetown and $7 per capita for the towns, while villages continued to receive grants that matched their revenue from other sources, although the ceiling on provincial grants to villages had been raised to $6 per capita (Canadian Tax Foundation, 1967: 84).

In spite of the attempt to make the unconditional grants match the differing requirements of different municipalities, inequities remained for the simple reason that some of the villages were larger and provided more services than some of the towns. After extensive review of the granting system, the province introduced a radically new approach in 1975. At the heart of the new approach to municipal grants was a *weighted* unconditional per capita transfer, which was supposed to replace the previous conditional and unconditional grants. The single unconditional grant system was proposed by Touche Ross & Company, which had been hired by the province to review the grant system. Touche Ross recommended, and the province accepted, a per capita grant system that attempted to recognize the fact that some types of municipalities provided more services than other types of municipalities. Thus, in calculating grants, towns were given a weight of 1.0, while villages were given a weight of 0.66. Charlottetown and Summerside were given weights of 1.7 and 1.3 respectively (Touche Ross, 1975: 4).

In addition to the weighted per capita unconditional grant, the 1975 grants formula introduced for the first time the principal of equalization. Municipalities with a relatively low tax base would qualify for supplementary equalization grants to bring them up to the provincial average revenue. The Touche Ross report argued that no grants other than the unconditional per capita and equalization grants should be necessary to fund municipal governments. The 1975 granting formula did not solve the problem of inequitable municipal funding. It was almost immediately clear that the granting regime did not adequately reflect the fact that a few municipalities delivered a significant quantity of relatively expensive services. In 1976, the province changed the per capita grant weights for Charlottetown and Summerside, increasing Charlottetown's from 1.7 to 2.3 and Summerside's from 1.3 to 2.0 (PEI, Department of Municipal Affairs, 1976: 2–3), but the inequities remained. By 1977, the province was once again making conditional grants to municipalities to support police, transportation, and recreational services in a few larger municipalities (Canadian Tax Foundation, 1977: 160–1).

The municipal grant system continued to fail to meet the needs of the province and the larger municipalities and was under almost constant review and study (Smith Green and Associates, 1991: 20). In 1978, a joint provincial-municipal committee proposed a radical solution to the problem: remove the financial inequities by ending the inequities in municipal functions. Specifically, the joint committee recommended that all towns and villages become responsible for street maintenance and policing, expenditures that appeared to be responsible for most of the inequity in the municipal grant system (PEI, Department of Municipal Affairs, 1978). However, neither the province nor many of the towns and villages were ready for such a radical reform to municipal government. A similar proposal was made and rejected in 1983 (Smith Green and Associates, 1991: 20).

After more than a decade of review and discussion, a new municipal grant system was introduced in 1986. In fact, this system was a tidying up and rationalization of the system that had developed after 1975. Unconditional per capita grants and equalization grants remained at the core of the granting system. However, rather than attempt to weight the grants to reflect the fact that some municipalities did more than others, the 1986 grant system introduced unconditional funding based on the obviously expensive services provided by larger municipalities. Thus, in 1986, in addition to unconditional per capita and equalization grants, municipalities might receive from the province $25 per capita if the municipality provided its own police service, $6,250 per kilometre of road maintained by the municipality, and Community Recreational Support grants if the municipality maintained and operated arenas or other recreational facilities (ibid., 21).

Although the 1986 grant system remains problematic, it is essentially still in effect today. In 1991, Smith Green and Associates pointed out continued inequities resulting from the municipal grant system and recommended some reforms, but no radical changes were made. In fact, fiscal restraint and provincial government expenditure reductions led to across-the-board reductions in provincial grants to municipalities in the early and mid-1990s. For the same reasons, the equalization component of the municipal grants was frozen in 1995 and began to grow again only in 2002 (PEI, Department of Community and Cultural Affairs, 2002). Meanwhile, in 1998 the Federation of PEI Municipalities and the Department of Community and Cultural Affairs began once again to review the municipal grant program (Cousins, 1999: 7).

The solution to the outstanding issues of municipal financial reform is undoubtedly intimately connected to the solution to the outstanding issues of municipal government structure and function. Almost every proposal for reform of municipal finance attempts to do one of two things. Either it tries to divide the Island's municipalities into various categories and connects funding levels to those categories, or it seeks to estimate the real cost of delivering specific municipal services and connects funding to the existence of those services. Until the province reorganizes the rural municipal system or imposes a standard series of functions on municipal governments, any proposed funding formula will be perceived as problematic by at least some municipalities.

JURISDICTIONAL REFORM

Generally speaking, the jurisdictional regime established by the early 1980s continues with little debate or challenge. There are some variations in jurisdiction depending on the size and type of municipality involved, but the effective variations in jurisdiction depend on whether or not municipalities have chosen to exercise the jurisdiction available to them. In recent years there have been few calls for reallocation of jurisdiction and no amendments to municipal legislation have addressed fundamental issues of jurisdiction.

Jurisdiction in the very small municipalities—villages and communities—has remained quite limited since the passing of the first Village Services Act in 1950, under which village commissioners could be appointed by the Lieutenant-Governor-in-Council to tend to matters such as sidewalks, sewers, and fire protection. Under the Municipalities Act, originally passed in 1983 and consolidated in 1988, the jurisdiction of municipalities with Community Improvement Committees is not much larger than that envisioned in 1950: administration of the municipality, fire protection, street lighting, recreation, and 'tree preservation and protection' (Municipalities Act, s. 31) To effect these purposes, municipalities with Community Improvement Committees have the authority necessary to tax property at rates 'sufficient to raise the sum required to defray projected municipal expenditures' (Municipalities Act, s. 37[1] [b]), to borrow money (up to a total debt no more than 10 per cent of the assessed value of real property in the municipality; ss. 43 and 44), to pass bylaws, including bylaws that create offences and prescribe penalties not exceeding $1,500 (s. 58), to employ municipal workers, and to purchase, lease, license, or expropriate land (s. 51). In addition, such municipalities are authorized by the Planning Act of 1988 to create official plans, employ staff to develop and implement the plans, and make bylaws to enforce the plans. Although only 18 of these municipalities have developed such plans, those that have done so have ended up with jurisdiction similar to towns and villages, particularly with respect to community, tourist, and industrial development.

Municipalities with legal status as towns or villages have jurisdiction over significantly more activities. In addition to the short list of powers of municipalities with Community Improvement Committees, towns and villages have jurisdiction over matters such as drainage; sewerage; sidewalks, roads, and streets; parking and the regulation of traffic; police protection; water distribution and purification; parks; community, tourist, and industrial development; housing; libraries; animal control; signage; building standards; regulation of business practices; and public transportation (Municipalities Act, s. 30). Again, this jurisdiction is similar to that provided by legislation throughout the twentieth century. Towns and villages have the same jurisdiction with respect to bylaws, administration, taxation, and planning as do municipalities with Community Improvement Committees.

The three municipalities governed by the Charlottetown Area Municipalities Act (Charlottetown, Stratford, and Cornwall) and the City of Summerside have statutory jurisdiction that is very similar to towns and villages under the Municipalities Act. They have broader authority over economic development, including the authority to create and administer development commissions, and somewhat broader regulatory jurisdiction over property and heritage sites. In addition, these municipalities can make bylaws that create offences and prescribe penalties up to $5,000.

The jurisdiction of all municipalities is limited by moderate provincial oversight. Generally, municipalities are able to act within their jurisdiction without provincial approval, but they must report taxes and bylaws to the minister responsible for municipal affairs. However, the province retains, with respect to all municipalities, the authority to dismiss a municipal council and appoint a special administrator 'where a Council has become inoperative or in the opinion of the Minister functions in a manner contrary to the best interests of the residents' (Municipalities Act, s. 10). Also, the province quite properly has authority over municipal status, boundaries, dissolution, and amalgamation (Municipalities Act, part IV). Only with respect to planning does the province directly supervise and approve the actions of municipal governments. The Planning Act allows the Lieutenant-Governor-in-Council to make regulations with respect to planning, including regulations that might supersede or suspend municipal bylaws (Planning Act, s. 8.1). In addition, a municipality's official plan, once it is approved at the municipal level, must be submitted to the minister responsible for municipal affairs for approval and any bylaw made under the authority of the Planning Act or the official plan must be approved by the minister before it comes into effect (ss. 14[2] [b] and 17).

In summation, the large majority of municipal governments in Prince Edward Island have very limited jurisdiction, while a handful of larger municipalities enjoy jurisdiction similar to municipalities in many other parts of Canada. Very little political energy has been expended debating municipal jurisdiction and the basic statutory lists of powers have remained similar for at least two decades. Indeed, a review of amendments to municipal legislation since 1988 (the date of the last consolidation of statutes) shows that jurisdiction has not been on the agenda.

CONCLUSIONS

In spite of the irrelevance of municipal government to most Islanders, Prince Edward Island has a long history of municipal reform. This history has been marked by tensions between the need to govern an increasingly urban society effectively and a cultural and ideological desire to preserve the province's rural heritage. For most of the past half-century, municipal reform has focused on attempts to build municipal structures for small rural communities. These attempts have clearly failed and the province continues to have an ineffective rural municipal system. Furthermore, the emphasis on reform of rural municipal governments led the province to ignore for almost 25 years pressing needs for urban municipal reform. Because of the weaknesses of both rural and urban municipal governments, the province delivers a large number of services of the type most Canadians would think of as municipal services.

There can be no doubt that municipal reform will remain a public policy and political issue in Prince Edward Island, although it is unlikely often to be near the top of the provincial policy agenda. The fundamental issues of rural municipal organization that have bothered the province since 1950 have not been resolved. Indeed, Islanders appear not to have decided whether they even want rural municipal government or, rather, are satisfied with provincial delivery of municipal services. Nor has an effective and publicly acceptable approach to financing municipal government been found. Even where municipal reform has been most successful, as in the restructuring of urban municipal governments, compromises were made that left three municipal governments in an urban centre that should probably have had only one. These may not be great issues of municipal reform and local democracy, but they are important practical issues of effective governance and public administration and, as such, will continue to demand attention.

REFERENCES

Baglole, Harry. 2002. 'Land Use Issues on Prince Edward Island', an address to the semi-annual meeting of the Federation of Prince Edward Island Municipalities, 27 Oct.

Brittain, Horace L. 1951. *Local Government in Canada.* Toronto: Ryerson Press.

Canadian Tax Foundation. 1963. *Provincial Finances 1963.* Toronto.

———. 1967. *Provincial Finances 1967.* Toronto.

———. 1977. *Provincial and Municipal Finances 1977.* Toronto.

Cousins, J.A. 1999. *The Geography of Governance: An Overview of Boundaries, Powers, and Responsibilities on Prince Edward Island.* Charlottetown: University of Prince Edward Island, Institute of Island Studies.

Federation of Prince Edward Island Municipalities. 2002. Municipalities with Official Plans, Feb. At: <www.fpeim.ca/official.htm>.

Guardian, The. Various issues. Charlottetown.

Higgins, Donald J.H. 1977. *Urban Canada, Its Government and Politics.* Toronto: Macmillan of Canada.

———. 1986. *Local and Urban Politics in Canada.* Toronto: Gage.

Institute of Island Studies. 2000. *A Place to Stay? Report of the PEI Population Strategy '99 Panel.* Charlottetown: Institute of Island Studies, University of Prince Edward Island, Mar.

Lea, William. 1987. *Report on the Charlottetown Area Development Corporation, 27 April 1987.* Charlottetown: Prince Edward Island Department of Justice.

MacDonald, Edward. 1985. *A Community of Schools.* Charlottetown: Institute of Island Studies, University of Prince Edward Island.

———. 2000. *If You're Stronghearted: Prince Edward Island in the Twentieth Century.* Charlottetown: Prince Edward Island Museum and Heritage Foundation.

MacDonald, Kenneth Stirling. 1990. 'The Decline of Public Participation in Rural Prince Edward Island', MA thesis, Acadia University.

MacKinnon, Frank. 1951. *The Government of Prince Edward Island*. Toronto: University of Toronto Press.

MacKinnon, Wayne. 1989. *The West Prince Industrial Commission: A Case Study*. Local Development Paper No. 7. Ottawa: Economic Council of Canada, Oct.

Milne, David. 1982. 'Politics in a Beleaguered Garden', in Verner Smitheram, David Milne, and Satadal Dasgupta, *The Garden Transformed: Prince Edward Island, 1945–1980*. Charlottetown: Ragweed Press.

Nemetz, Donald. 1982. 'Managing Development', in Smitheram, Milne, and Dasgupta, *The Garden Transformed*.

Novack, Jack, ed. 1990. *A Guide to Local Government in Prince Edward Island*, 3rd edn. Halifax: Maritime Municipal Training and Development Board.

Porter Dillon Limited. 1994. *Comparative Cost-Benefit Analysis, PEI Municipal Reform. Final Report*. Halifax: Prepared for the PEI Commission on Municipal Reform, Jan.

Prince Edward Island (PEI). 2003. *Statutes of Prince Edward Island*. Charlottetown Area Municipalities Act (Chapter C-4.1); City of Summerside Act (Chapter S-9.1); Municipalities Act (Chapter M-13); Planning Act (Chapter P-8). Consolidated to 1 Nov. 2003. Charlottetown: Queen's Printer.

———, Department of Community and Cultural Affairs. 2001. 'Department Releases Final Report on the Most Appropriate Level of Government to Deliver Specific Services', news release, 17 Jan.

———, ———. 2002. 'Province Reinstates Equalization Component of the Municipal Support Grant Program', news release, 29 Apr.

———, Department of Community Services. 1971. *Report on the Proposed Municipal Grants System*. Charlottetown, Dec.

———, Department of Municipal Affairs. 1967. *Annual Report*.

———, ———. 1976. *An Evaluation of the Municipal Grant System*. Charlottetown, Oct.

———, ———. 1978. *Interim Report of the Provincial/Municipal Steering Committee on Provincial/Municipal Relations*. Charlottetown, Sept.

———, Department of the Provincial Treasury, Statistics and Federal Fiscal Relations Division. 2002. *28th Annual Statistical Review 2001*. May.

———, Government Reform Office. 1993. *White Paper on Municipal Reform*. Charlottetown, 25 June.

———, Royal Commission on Land Ownership and Land Use. 1973. *Report*. Charlottetown: Queen's Printer.

———, Royal Commission on the Land [formally, Royal Commission on Land Ownership, Land Use and the Landscape]. 1990. *'Everything Before Us': Volume 1 of the Report of the Royal Commission on the Land*. Charlottetown: Queen's Printer, Oct.

Smith Green and Associates Inc., the ARA Consulting Group, and Kell Antoft. 1991. *Municipal Study Report*. Charlottetown: Department of Community and Cultural Affairs, May.

Statistics Canada. 2001a. 2001 Census, Geographic Units: Census Metropolitan Area (CMA) and Census Agglomeration (CA). At: <http://www.statcan.ca/english/census2001/dict/geo009.htm>.

———. 2001b. 2001 Census, Population, Dwellings and Geography, Tables: Canada, Provinces, and Territories; Urban Areas; Urban and Rural; and Statistical Area Classification (SAC)—CMAs, CAs, CMA and CA Influenced Zones (MIZ), and Territories. At: <http://www12.statcan.ca/english/census01/products/standard/popdwell/tables.cfm>.

———. 2003. *The Daily*, 25 June, 'Demographic Statistics'. At: <http://www.statcan.ca/Daily/English/030625/d030625e.htm>.

Touche Ross & Company. 1975. *Province of Prince Edward Island: An Effective Municipal Grants Program for the Future.* Prepared for the Province of Prince Edward Island, Jan.

Touche, Ross, Bailey, and Smart, 1967. *Provincial-Municipal Fiscal Study.* Prepared for the Province of Prince Edward Island, Aug.

Chapter 11

Municipal Reforms in New Brunswick: To Decentralize or Not To Decentralize?

Daniel Bourgeois

Introduction

For 40 years, municipal reform has been an ongoing process in New Brunswick. The latest round of reforms, undertaken in 1992 yet nowhere near completion, has sought the appropriate structural, functional, financial, and jurisdictional arrangements between provincial departments and municipalities. The four sections of this chapter illustrate how the provincial government has tried yet failed to forge an ideal balance. The first outlines the historical context of municipal reforms in New Brunswick. The second describes the structural, functional, financial, and jurisdictional reforms launched in 1992. The third assesses the reforms and draws four lessons from two case studies. Finally, the conclusion presents prospects for municipal governance and reform in New Brunswick.[1]

Historical Antecedents

In March 1962, the Robichaud Liberals established the (Byrne) Royal Commission on Finance and Municipal Taxation (New Brunswick, 1963). It recommended the abolition of the 15 county councils and their replacement by approximately 250 local service districts (LSDs). It also recommended that 'services to people' (education, health, social assistance, justice) be centralized from municipalities and counties to technocratic provincial commissions, in order to standardize services between poor and rich, rural and urban, and Acadian and anglophone areas.[2] In 1966–7, the Robichaud government implemented the Equal Opportunities Program (EOP). Standardization and centralization of services were maintained as the principal means to ensure equality, but technocratic commissions were rejected in favour of bureaucratic structures easier to control—ministerial departments (see Young, 1987; Krueger, 1970; d'Entremont, 1985).

However, the centralization efforts left a regional vacuum: there were no structures to deal with the regional issues that largely stemmed from increasing suburbanization. To fill that void, the Hatfield Conservatives decentralized some provincial authorities in the 1970s and 1980s by establishing 12 land-use planning commissions, 13 economic development commissions, 12 solid waste commissions, 51 hospital corporations, and 42 school boards, among others.[3] The nearly 300 regional agencies, boards, and commissions (ABCs), however, did not solve all the problems created by urban sprawl and linear development. Also, those special-purpose bodies created other problems, as did the creation of 291 unelected local service districts to provide services to the unincorporated areas of the province, previously serviced by counties.

During their second mandate, the McKenna Liberals launched the most significant municipal reforms since 1966. Although they also targeted municipal finances, functions, and jurisdictions, their major focus beginning in 1992 was amalgamating municipal structures.[4] But this centralization effort was too incoherent to solve the problems addressed. Indeed, the McKenna reforms were too sectoral (they isolated the four dimensions of municipal governance), diachronous (they reformed one dimension at a time), and geo-distinct (they dealt with one type of governance structure at a time).

The incoherence of the McKenna era reforms, amplified by the government's high-handed implementation, was one of the reasons why Conservatives regained power in June 1999. Faithful to their electoral promises, the Tories favoured decentralization. The re-establishment of school boards in 2001 is the most obvious example. And although it happened by accident, the Lord government is headed towards a holistic, synchronous, and geo-synchronous reform of local governance in New Brunswick. But the government's procrastinations on municipal issues suggest any solution also may occur by accident.

The McKenna Reforms, 1992–9

In December 1992, the McKenna government launched the most significant municipal reforms in 25 years. The initiative was related to similar structural modifications in other provincial services that were launched simultaneously to reduce public expenditures. In addition to seeking municipal consolidations, the government reduced the number of health corporations from 51 to 8, and school boards from 42 to 18, then from 18 to two (Bourgeois, 1995). Municipal restructuring was complemented by reforms in land-use planning and police services (Bourgeois, 2001). The government's Commission on Land Use and the Rural Environment (CLURE) identified the absence of local governance in the rural areas and the fragmentation of authority in the urban areas as the main causes of urban sprawl and linear developments. Concluding that this fragmentation in the urban areas produced small police forces unable to meet modern standards, the Grant report recommended regional police forces in the same urban areas targeted by the municipal consolidations. Moreover, New Brunswick reforms were almost identical to those initiated by Nova Scotia and Prince Edward Island at almost the same time and for the same fundamental reason: to combat suburbanization (Bourgeois, 2001).

The 1992 round of municipal restructuring was related to reforming municipal finances, functions, and jurisdictions, but structural reforms were given priority and chronological preference over the other dimensions. Our review of the latest reforms will start with the structural aspects then proceed with the functional, financial, and jurisdictional ones.

Structural Reforms: Amalgamation or Regionalization?

Structural reforms were initiated on three distinct fronts, yet all three were concerned by the negative effects of suburbanization. Environmental groups wanted to stop urban sprawl and linear development because they eroded natural resources. Cities wanted to stop the erosion of their populations and tax bases, which were being bled off to the contiguous suburbs and unincorporated areas. Furthermore, the province was unable to rationalize local services or to improve some regional services, such as land use and policing, without structural modifications. Because a significant opposition arose from suburbanites in many targeted areas, the government eventually implemented only part of its structural reforms.

The structural reform was explained in a White Paper published by the Department of Municipalities, Culture and Housing.[5] *Strengthening Municipal Government in New Brunswick's Urban Centres* proposed two solutions—amalgamation of contiguous municipalities or formal regionalization of their services—to the many problems created by suburbanization.[6] The White Paper presented a list of such problems. Urban sprawl and linear development were damaging the environment: developments in unincorporated (non-governed) areas depleted water, animal habitat, and natural resources. The creation and expansion of bedroom communities, at the demographic and economic expense of cities, were decreasing the efficiency of allocating local services in the cities. The document noted that most cities lost taxpayers to the suburbs between 1971 and 1991, but had to maintain their infrastructure.[7] Suburbanites were using the infrastructure when they went to work, but did not pay for their maintenance. Empire-building and turf wars between growing suburban communities and the cash-strapped cities were said to promote duplication of services. Finally, the contiguous municipalities did not always plan their expansions in regard to each other until problems arose—in municipal parlance, 'streets didn't meet.' As the White Paper concluded, 'traditional municipal structures and boundaries, in many cases, may not be the most appropriate' (New Brunswick, 1992: 3). It suggested that structural reforms were needed 'to strengthen the municipal urban centres by amalgamating or integrating their municipal units in order to provide cost effective services, in a manner that retains maximum accountability to the elected municipal councils' (ibid., iv).

Urban sprawl and linear development are widespread social phenomena, and the ensuing problems outlined in the previous paragraph are typical throughout the world, but they are more significant for municipal governance in New

Brunswick because of the regional vacuum left by the abolition of counties. The Round Table on Local Governance best expressed this problem: 'Regional issues most often require regional responses, and there are no structures or tools in place to allow this to happen' (New Brunswick, 2001a: 23). In fact, there are regional commissions in place for land use, economic development and solid waste, among others, but they were unable to prevent suburbanization or solve its problems. Many of these ABCs are single-function units that operate within their respective silos. Land use and economic development often go hand in hand, but the respective commissions did not adequately co-ordinate their services. In some areas, the boundaries of the land-use and economic development commissions did not coincide. Other areas had no commissions. Those that did exist exhibited another problem: they were not sufficiently accountable to the citizens. This is especially the case for New Brunswickers living in most local service districts, where local services are managed by advisory boards that have little say in the workings of unelected regional commissions. However, granting representation on regional boards to sparsely populated rural areas would increase the number of board members to an unmanageable total or inequitably decrease the number of board representatives of heavily populated cities on a per capita basis.

The absence of counties facilitated suburbanization and, consequently, the abuse of the environment, the inefficient allocation of municipal services, conflicts between cities and their suburbs, the inability of LSDs to control development, and the lack of accountability and co-ordination of single-function regional commissions. These five major problems[8] were interrelated, just as municipal structures, finances, functions, and jurisdictions were. Yet the McKenna government applied different reforms—land use, police services, structures, jurisdictions, finances— managed by distinct departments in a separate, chronological order. Local restructuring was considered a more urgent solution, followed by reforms on the other dimensions, albeit paralleled by reforms in the other functions. This piecemeal approach, as we will see, would prove confusing and counterproductive.

The CLURE was established in January 1992 to study four major land-use issues in the province: natural resources, environmental risks, rural planning processes and structures, and settlement patterns. In its report, published in April 1993, the Commission came to the same conclusion as the White Paper's authors in blaming suburbanization for the land-use problems. In its opinion, urban sprawl and ribbon developments occurred because the unincorporated areas offered lower dwelling expenses (lot prices, property taxes, road maintenance) and minimal negative externalities (planning regulations, traffic, pollution). The Commission proposed five solutions, including increasing rural property taxes and 'annexing built-up areas bordering municipal boundaries' (New Brunswick, 1993a: 7–9). Thus, the CLURE and the White Paper proposed somewhat different solutions to combat suburbanization (Bourgeois, 1994). In fact, the government's response to the CLURE report significantly downplayed rural property tax increases,[9] arguably because it would have cost many votes and seats in a rural-dominated legislature, and it chose formal regionalization as the alternative to amalgamation in spite of regionalization's limited ability to combat suburbanization.

The Grant report, published in March 1992, argued that most police forces in New Brunswick were too small to meet the modern standards for police services. Alan Grant, the author of this report, recommended a new Police Act and new regulations to ensure all police forces in the province met such standards. This would imply combining police forces in the urban centres and hiring the RCMP to service the rest of the province. Grant added that these changes would require the collaboration of the departments of Municipal Affairs, Public Safety, and Finance, especially in the light of possible municipal restructuring.

The White Paper recognized the interdependence of municipal restructuring and reforms in land use and police services (New Brunswick, 1992: 3, 11) and assured that the reforms would eventually coincide. To that end, the government appointed local panels to study whether amalgamation or regionalization was the best structural solution to the suburbanization problems found in each of the province's seven urban areas, taking into consideration land use and police reforms when reaching that conclusion. Panels were struck in Miramichi, Campbellton, Moncton, Saint John, and Edmundston.

Amalgamation was recommended and implemented in three of the four urban areas scrutinized (for Miramichi, see Vojnovic, 1998; Sancton, 2000). Moncton avoided amalgamation because of the symbiotic relation between language, terri-tory, and municipal identity and services in Canada's only officially bilingual province (Bourgeois, 1995). In short, the Acadian minority identifies with and seeks control over the local institutions serving an area where it is the majority (Bourgeois and Bourgeois, 2004; Clarke, 2000). The Moncton panel noted the presence of 'seven special purpose agencies' and 'a remarkable record of coopera-tion' between Moncton, Dieppe, and Riverview; and it applauded the fact that the relative segregation geographically of Acadians in the east and anglophones in the west 'has not prevented the two founding partners of the area from working and playing together and, consequently, enjoying each other's rich cultural and artistic heritage', but it ultimately rejected amalgamation in favour of regionalizing many municipal services for cultural reasons: 'it is only at the municipal level that Acadians can hold majority political power in New Brunswick' (Malenfant and Robison, 1994: 30, 20, 26, 34).

The McKenna government accepted the panel's conclusion and recommenda-tion, and asked the municipal councils of Moncton, Dieppe, and Riverview to create a joint board to regionalize common services, as recommended by the panel (Duffie, 1994). These included fire, water treatment, cultural facilities, tourism promotion, industrial parks, economic development, urban planning, public transportation, solid waste, pest control, and emergency measures. However, the government contradicted itself by ordering the three councils to establish a regional police force, as recommended by the Grant report but rejected by the panel, and to establish a regional 911 emergency dispatch centre for fire, police, and ambulance calls, contrary to the Robison-Malenfant panel's recommended provincial dispatch centre.

The regional board created by the three municipalities would have difficulty with such provincial inconsistencies that stemmed mostly from departmental turf wars. Police and dispatch services, as we will see, provided the best examples of provincial incoherence. Another example was provided when the provincial department responsible for economic development contradicted the department responsible for municipal affairs by rejecting the panel's recommendation to centralize the management of the three industrial parks under the regional economic development commission (CTC, 1999: app. 4, 12). In defence of the province, the three councils refused to let the regional authority 'assume responsibility'[10] for many services, arguably because of provincial incoherence but also because of municipal turf wars. In this they refused either to share common police services like fingerprinting or to combine their respective police forces, thereby forcing the province to do it for them. It established a single RCMP detachment for the entire urban area in January 1998.

In short, in spite of limited empirical data supporting municipal amalgamations (Sancton, 1991; Fox, 1980), the provincial government created the City of Miramichi out of 11 communities in 1995, amalgamated eight Saint John suburbs into three municipalities (the city remained intact, but a regional commission was established to share the costs of regional facilities and services) in 1998, and annexed four communities to Edmundston in 1998. It also asked the municipalities of Moncton, Dieppe, and Riverview to regionalize many of their local services. The municipal restructuring effectively ended after the Conservatives gained power in June 1999. The elections thus put a premature end to the structural reform launched in December 1992. Indeed, the government did not follow up on the Campbellton study and avoided Bathurst and Fredericton altogether over the seven-year period. The present government does not have any plans to reconsider structural reforms. In fact, if anything, the Lord government wants to 'let the dust settle'.[11]

Structural reforms were nevertheless resuscitated indirectly in December 2000 when the Minister of Municipal Affairs asked her Round Table on Local Governance to study 'provincial fiscal transfers to municipalities; local representation, land use planning, and property taxation in the unincorporated areas . . . and the relationship between municipalities and surrounding unincorporated areas' (New Brunswick, 2001a: 1). As had the previous McKenna government, the Lord government was also forced to recognize that 'these issues are interconnected' (ibid.). But, contrary to the Liberals' efforts, it asked the Round Table to study them holistically; therefore, the Round Table could not avoid structural considerations.

The Round Table gathered representatives from municipalities, regional commissions, LSDs, and provincial departments (Municipal Affairs, Finance, Transportation, Public Safety, and Natural Resources and Energy). It concluded that 'the status quo is no longer an appropriate option' in the unincorporated areas (ibid., 15) and that 'the entire New Brunswick population [should] have access to a governance system that provides for elected representation' (ibid.). In other words, the 270 LSDs should be replaced by elected bodies with real authority and autonomy.[12] It did not, however, recommend any specific governance model in unincorporated areas. Instead, it suggested the issue be resolved through 'discussion and comment by a larger audience', in respect of seven key principles:

(1) Taxation warrants local representation.
(2) New Brunswickers should be governed by an elected local body.
(3) The local body should have decision-making autonomy.
(4) Communities should be proactive in seeking local governance.
(5) The local body should be accountable to the citizens.
(6) Differences between communities require that local bodies have particular authority.
(7) Communities should be able to choose among various governance models to meet their particular needs. (Ibid., 32)

The Round Table nevertheless limited this choice by rejecting three-tier governance for fear it could add a layer of bureaucracy and 'undermine or reduce the role of existing municipalities' (ibid., 27).

The Round Table also rejected the status quo in regional governance. It recommended 'a multi-service body . . . in each region of the province' to manage land use, solid waste, economic development, and any other public services and infrastructures on a regional basis (ibid., 37). To that end, it suggested Quebec's Municipalités régionales de comté, British Columbia's regional districts, and the co-operative model as structural options. Such a regional body would 'achieve cost savings through economies of scale', increase 'effectiveness in dealing with issues that cross jurisdictions', improve 'cooperation among the various administrative units', increase 'accountability to communities served', and improve 'land use planning at the local and regional levels' (ibid., 37–8). Formal regionalization was thus a better structural mechanism than amalgamation to combat suburbanization. The reform had returned to its starting point after nine years. Indeed, the White Paper had categorically rejected the BC model because it was a 'regional government' (New Brunswick, 1992: 28).

In spite of this confusion, the Round Table adopted a coherent bottom-up, community-based approach to any regionalization of services. First example: 'It would be up to the local governments, working with their [regional body], to determine which services are best delivered on a regional basis' (ibid., 36). Second example: the regional body 'would serve as an agent of municipalities' (ibid., 35). Third example: 'Local governments could choose to offer a service on their own . . . if they had the capacity to do so' (ibid.). The principle of subsidiarity would replace the province's top-down, big brother approach followed since 1992.

Finally, the Round Table added that some forms of regional collaboration would lead to additional restructuring. Most obviously, the existing single-function commissions would be eliminated in favour of a single multi-purpose service agency in the region. The new structure would also lead to 'annexation' of LSDs to the neighbouring urban cities (ibid., 34). The Lord government 'accepted in principle' the Round Table's report (New Brunswick, 2001c), yet simultaneously blocked its most significant recommendation of regional multi-function bodies by creating, for instance, single-function economic development agencies (New Brunswick, 2002a). It subsequently established a special committee of the Legislative Assembly to study, through public consultations, those recommendations pertaining to local governance and regional collaboration. The all-party Select Committee on Local Governance and Regional Collaboration held 13 public hearings throughout the province in the winter of 2002. Its report, published in January 2003, noted that 'The Multi-Service Body recommended by the Round Table did not receive much support' and, save nine minor recommendations intended to 'gradually improve' local governance, it unequivocally favoured the status quo, that is, to 'enable unincorporated communities to gradually acquire the powers they need and desire in order to facilitate the exercise of community governance for the building of sustainable communities' (Select Committee, 2003: 11, 10). The government's response was 'entirely consistent' with the unanimous recommendations made by the Select Committee (New Brunswick, 2003a, 2003b), thus contradicting its earlier acceptance in principle of the Round Table's report. More importantly, the government did not act in the year following its April 2003 response.

Functional Reforms: The Weakest Link?

The White Paper indicated that reforming municipal structures could entail the transfer of additional functions to municipal councils, but it did not go into details. Ten years later, the Lord government delegated additional responsibilities to municipalities, but these were relatively insignificant. There was talk of downloading road maintenance to municipal councils, but that particular functional decentralization has been put on hold.[13] The McKenna government also indicated that its new Municipalities Act would let municipalities manage 'spheres of jurisdiction', but it never tabled the legislation and never explained if the concept meant 'more functions' or 'more authority in regards to existing functions'. The Lord government tried to ignore the issue since 1999 by repeatedly promising new legislation before the May 2004 municipal elections (*Acadie Nouvelle*, 2003: 3). The 1966 EOP separation between 'services to people' and 'services to property', however, does not seem to be on the agenda;[14] it is a separation that has become somewhat a sacred cow.

Financial Reforms: Should Those Who Pay the Piper Call the Tune?

The White Paper indicated that urban municipal finances were suffering because of an increase in suburban free riders since 1971. It added that provincial finances also were suffering the consequences of suburbanization. In fact, the provincial government covers the $22 million annual deficit between the property taxes it collects in unincorporated areas and the costs of policing services and road maintenance it provides in these areas. Since 40 per cent of New Brunswickers live in LSDs yet control 60 per cent of the legislature and would oppose tax increases, the provincial government has maintained a 65-cent mill rate since 1984. Also, the CLURE report recommended increasing property taxes in suburbs, especially in the LSDs where low provincial tax rates had encouraged urban sprawl and ribbon development. The Liberal government officially put the rural property tax increase on the back burner: it launched a study of the 65-cent mill rate, but could not (or refused to) complete this endeavour before the June 1999 elections. The McKenna government nevertheless increased taxes and fees for specific services in the rural areas it governed.[15] The Lord government resuscitated the review of property taxes, in parallel with municipal finance reforms, but the Finance Minister quickly put the review on hold once he realized that financial reforms could not proceed coherently without consideration of structural and jurisdictional reforms. The Round Table on Local Governance was then asked to study the issue in its holistic complexity. It concluded that the existing financial system should be changed to respect the four basic principles of a sound system: (1) communities should pay for what they get but also get what they pay for; (2) taxation warrants local representation; (3) all property owners should share the costs of police and transportation services; and (4) grant funding should continue. It recommended a blend of per capita grants, provincial transfers, and tax expenditures, and equalization of fiscal capacity, translated into a new funding formula, to buttress the municipal funding system (New Brunswick, 2001a: 43).

The Finance Department established two committees to study the issue (New Brunswick, 2001c). The Technical Working Group on Municipal Finances, comprised of officials from LSDs, municipalities, and the departments of Finance and Municipal Affairs, analyzed the costs and benefits of unconditional grants and additional tax sources and funds for municipalities, while the Committee on Property Taxation, comprised of staff from Finance and the Auditor General, determined what changes were required to the 65-cent mill rate to ensure an efficient allocation of police services and road maintenance in unincorporated areas. Established in March 2002, both committees took into consideration the Select Committee's report and the Lord government's response. But the process was somewhat reversed to let the government delay its response until the working groups completed their effort: 'The work of these groups is complex and it is interrelated, and the government needs to know the recommendations from all three committees before it can make informed decisions' (New Brunswick, 2002b). The Working Group's report was ready for cabinet in January 2003 but there has been no action on the issue since. There is no word on a report from the Committee on Property Taxation. The government extended the municipal grant formula for 2002 and again for 2003 (New Brunswick, 2001b, 2002b), before reducing the total grants by 10 per cent for 2004 (*Moncton Times & Transcript*, 2003b). The issue is thus unresolved and a slim majority in the legislature suggests it will remain so.

Jurisdictional Reforms: Permissive or Prescriptive Legislation?

The distinct reforms of municipal dimensions undertaken in December 1992 were to culminate in a revised and consolidated Municipalities Act. Indeed, after the municipal institutions serving the seven urban areas had been restructured, hopefully with added functions and an alternative funding mechanism, the McKenna government promised to modify the legislation to enable all municipalities to meet the internal needs and external requirements of the future. The new statute was supposed to abandon the 'prescriptive' philosophy in favour of a 'permissive' philosophy in order to provide municipal councils 'with the full legislative latitude requested and required to exercise their powers' (New Brunswick, 1998: 4). It was the only effort undertaken by the Liberals to decentralize municipal jurisdictions.

A committee of six municipal and three departmental representatives was established in August 1995 to review the Municipalities Act, modified on more than 20 occasions since it was adopted in 1966. The committee surveyed the municipalities in the fall of 1995, deliberated between February 1996 and March 1997, and produced a report in October 1998 containing 234 recommendations. The recommendations dealt with the fundamental requirements of the legislation, such as municipal elections, decision-making processes, legal actions against and by municipalities, access to information, powers, services, and financial operations. In all cases, the committee members sought to 'liberate municipalities from the confines of the express authority doctrine' (ibid., 51). In other words, the 'spheres of jurisdiction' approach should delineate municipal powers in broad and permissive terms, albeit 'subject to all applicable provincial legislation' and regulations as well as national (fire, building) codes (ibid., 54). The committee also recommended that the revised legislation consolidate the various statutes that frame municipal governance.[16] Finally, it recommended that the new Act 'be drafted in plain language so that it may easily be understood by members of the public' (ibid., 4).

The government also published its internal *Review of Local Service District Legislation* (New Brunswick, 1999a) in January 1999. It outlined 33 proposals intended to enhance governance in the LSDs.[17] Municipalities and LSDs were thus segregated for legislative purposes. The government then established a Municipalities Act Review Panel to consult the public on the 234 recommendations and the 33 proposals. After 25 public hearings in the spring of 1999, the panel concluded that 'the status quo is not acceptable' and that the new statute 'must allow for divergent governance requirements' (New Brunswick, 1999b: 165). It also recommended a significant reduction in the number of LSDs and their replacement by regional rural districts (ibid., 169, 177).

The legislative review was put on hold after the June 1999 elections and again before the 2003 elections. It has nevertheless proceeded piecemeal.[18] The new statute is ready for tabling. Our sources indicate a blend of the 'permissive' and 'prescriptive' approaches. If true, the Lord Conservatives will provide the first significant modification to the 1966 Municipalities Act, but the degree of significance will probably be relatively minor.

An Initial Assessment: Lessons Learned (and Others Not Learned)

From this brief overview of the four sets of reforms, we draw four lessons for future municipal governance and reform. All four lessons could have been drawn from the academic literature, thereby indicating a fifth lesson: provincial governments either do not read the academic contributions or ignore them when reforming municipal structures, functions, finances, and jurisdictions. Lack of space prohibits further discussion on this last lesson. To draw these four lessons more clearly, we will highlight two specific municipal services that were significant targets of the reform in the Moncton area: police and emergency dispatch. It is here that the provincial reform rubber hit the municipal road.

First Case Study: Police Regionalization

The idea of a single, regional police force in the Moncton area came from the Grant report in March 1992 (Grant, 1992: 63). The White Paper of December 1992 replicated this idea (New Brunswick, 1992: 11). The Malenfant-Robison report, however, rejected the idea in April 1994, arguing that combining the three municipal forces would not ensure adequate bilingual services. Instead, the panel recommended that the Moncton Police Force 'take immediate steps to enhance its bilingual capabilities' and that the regional board created to assume responsibility over all regional services 'determine the conditions that should be met prior to the regionalization of police services' (Malenfant and Robison, 1994: 52). The McKenna government asked the three municipalities to implement the panel's recommendations, but it also reaffirmed 'its commitment to the implementation of the Grant report and . . . a single police force' in the area (Duffie, 1994). In other words, the government both accepted and rejected the panel's recommendations. It added that the three councils had two years to regionalize their police forces (and implement a regional central dispatch centre) or face amalgamation.

On 2 April 1996, the ministers responsible for Public Safety and Municipal Affairs met with representatives of the regional board—the Commission of Three Communities (CTC)—to eliminate the confusion. The CTC had asked the two ministers to get their signals straight because the three police chiefs had refused to 'work in close cooperation and harmony' (Malenfant and Robison, 1994: 52). The chiefs of the Dieppe and Riverview forces dismissed the provincial government's threat to regionalize police services and to amalgamate the communities. They wanted to 'call the Province's bluff' (CTC, 1999: app. 4, 4). With the threat of amalgamation hanging over its head like the sword of Damocles, the CTC had little time and patience to let the chiefs hide behind their dual accountability.[19] The two ministers agreed to co-sponsor a cost-benefit analysis of a regional municipal police force and the sharing of common services to determine the best option for the three municipalities. A third option (a regional urban RCMP detachment) was later added at the request of the Town of Riverview. The initial study was conducted under the auspices of the Department of Public Safety, but proved incomplete.[20] The CTC then conducted its own study (CTC, 1996a).

On 11 December 1996, the CTC recommended that 'the three options be prioritized as follows: (1) the Codiac Police Force, pending successful collective bargaining negotiations with the union(s), which facilitate the cost-effectiveness forecast in option; (2) the regional agreement on the sharing of specialized services; and (3) the RCMP' (CTC, 1999: app. 4, 5). The union representing the members of the Moncton Police Force initially refused to make concessions because it scoffed at McKenna's threat to impose a regional RCMP force.[21] The three municipal councils then agreed to disagree. Moncton accepted the CTC's recommendation, but Dieppe opted for option 2 and Riverview favoured option 3. On 17 April 1997, Public Safety Minister Jane Barry announced that the provincial government would break the deadlock by creating a regional RCMP detachment (option 3). On 18 January 1998, the Moncton Police Force and the Dieppe Police Force were disbanded and replaced by the regional Codiac RCMP detachment.

The RCMP detachment is managed by the Codiac Regional Police Authority, the seventh single-function regional commission in the greater Moncton area. The City of Moncton, on the hook for millions of dollars in benefits paid to its former police officers because of the imposed takeover, initially refused to sign on. The city subsequently accepted the takeover when the Lord government allocated funds to offset some of the start-up costs. No formal efforts have been undertaken to replace the RCMP, although the idea has been resuscitated during recent cost-sharing disagreements between the three councils (*Moncton Times & Transcript*, 2004a).

Second Case Study: Central Dispatch

Improving the allocation of emergency 911 central dispatch services in the Moncton area was 'the most frustrating experience' in the CTC's four-year endeavour (CTC, 1999: 4). The provincial government was again blamed for the confusion. On the one hand, the province modified the panel's recommendation: instead of a single, provincial dispatch service, the McKenna government opted for seven regional systems to handle and co-ordinate police, fire, and ambulance emergency calls. On the other hand, provincial departments played turf wars: the Department of Health decided to establish a provincial dispatch centre for ambulance calls; the decision by the Minister of Public Safety to establish a regional RCMP detachment in the area would let 'J' Division handle all police calls from its provincial dispatch centre; and officials of the Department of Municipal Affairs, responsible for fire dispatch, were unable to convince their colleagues to integrate the three systems. Instead of a single dispatch centre for the entire province or seven integrated regional dispatch centres, the government settled for a more complicated arrangement: two provincial dispatch centres handle ambulance and police calls, respectively, six regional emergency call dispatch centres handle fire calls and transfer all other calls by 'hot-button' links to the two provincial dispatch centres, and one regional dispatch centre in the Saint John area handles all regional 911 calls.

In spite of requests from the CTC as early as February 1996 to act 'coherently' in the matter (ibid., 8), the McKenna government insisted the three municipalities follow 'plan A'. On 2 April 1996, two months after the Minister of Health announced the establishment of a provincial dispatch centre for ambulance calls, the Ministers of Municipal Affairs and Public Safety repeated the threat of amalgamation if the three councils did not establish a single, integrated dispatch centre for the region. When confronted by the CTC with their government's incoherence, both ministers agreed to fund a feasibility study, which ultimately warned the province that the final decision depended on the policing option (Andersen, 1996). On 9 May 1997, the Minister of Health reiterated his intention to 'consolidate ambulance service dispatch into one site' (King, 1997). The CTC again asked the Minister of Municipal Affairs to 'liaise with her Cabinet colleague' to sort out the 'three contradictory directions coming from the Province of New Brunswick'

(CTC, 1999: app. 4, 8). She initially replied that the CTC 'should pursue the estab-lishment of a single communications centre' since 'there is no intention that any of these initiatives should stall . . . the establishment of a single shared communica-tions centre' (Breault, 1997a). But after her deputy minister accepted the CTC's request but failed to co-ordinate the three departments' efforts before imposing any solution on the three municipalities (Bourgeois, 1997), the minister finally admitted that her government 'should have recognized this [mistake] and possibly avoided some of the ensuing frustrations' (Breault, 1997b). She nevertheless insisted that the CTC keep striving for an integrated, regional centre.

The CTC then chastised the McKenna government for its incoherence and silo mentality: 'The Province finally admitted, 18 months after it forced the CTC to do something impossible, that it made a mistake [by] giving contradictory directives to the CTC. However, the Province never apologized nor explained its incoherence. Common courtesy should have dictated the Province apologize and explain its incoherence' (CTC, 1999: app. 4, 8). In other words, 'The Province's right hand did not know what its left hand was doing, and the CTC was stuck in the middle of incoherent directives for more than two years' (ibid.).

The Lord government has not been able to resolve the issue, either. In fact, it maintains its predecessor's penchant for confusion and incoherence. A recent tragedy in Riverview, as happened on earlier occasions, has indeed reignited the debate and departmental turf wars (*Moncton Times & Transcript*, 2002a, 2002b). The Lord government responded by striking a panel to study the issue over the next two years (New Brunswick, 2002c).

First Lesson: Municipal Reforms Should Be
Couched in Coherent Political Philosophies

In general, the Liberals pursued individual-liberal reforms while the Conservatives pursued communitarian-liberal reforms. The Liberals under Robichaud and McKenna believed that (1) 'there are too many governments in New Brunswick',[22] (2) the individual citizen should be in direct contact with his provincial govern-ment, and (3) regional and municipal institutions are mere administrative units that should be created, reformed, or eliminated from time to time by the provin-cial government to ensure the most efficient and effective allocation of local serv-ices to individual citizens. The Liberals believed that local democracy was a myth since municipalities cannot ensure majority rule, uniformity, and equality (Langrod, 1953). They thus shared the Lockean individual strand of liberalism. Finally, the Liberals shared the centralist approach to public goods and services (Vié, 1986). Provinces should thus exercise their constitutional obligations to manage provincial institutions effectively and efficiently. In short, New Brunswick Liberals believed that municipalities should be motivated by the stick.

For their part, the Conservatives under Hatfield and Lord argued that (1) local democracy was an important element of the provincial fabric, (2) communities have an important role to play between the provincial government and citizens, and (3) municipal institutions, in particular, are community-based organizations that should be multiplied and protected to ensure greater public choice yet encouraged by local circumstances to collaborate with their neighbouring communities to improve the local allocation of municipal services. They believed that local democracy is possible because municipalities can ensure citizen participation and the accommodation of divergences, which are greater democratic values than uniformity (Panter-Brick, 1953). The Conservatives thus shared the communitarian political philosophy (Walzer, 1983; Taylor, 1992; Sandel, 1982). Finally, they shared the public choice approach to the allocation of public goods and services (Cornes and Sandler, 1986; Ostrom et al., 1988). Municipalities should thus be motivated by the carrot.

Espousing different political values and philosophies is a necessary competitive feature of democratic states, but it does create problems for local governance. First, it confuses citizens. Many citizens throughout the province opposed the structural reforms, believing that the 'myth of local democracy' (Bourgeois, 1995: 87) would protect their municipal council from the provincial 'big brother'. Their confusion is understandable because the McKenna government, on the one hand, argued that municipalities 'are a responsible, autonomous and elected form of government' (New Brunswick, 1992: iv), but on the other hand, single-handedly removed any autonomy this level of 'government' supposedly had. The multitude of public hearings on local governance since 1993 also demonstrated public confusion and apathy, albeit many recent submissions demonstrate an increased awareness of the complexity of the issue. Second, all four reforms argued that they would improve local democracy, thereby presenting either opposite conceptions of (local) democracy or opposite solutions to local democratic limits. It is too early to tell if public participation in municipal elections and policy-making processes has increased as a result of the recent reforms. Then again, one would have to assess the democratic value of each reform according to different definitions of local democracy and the respective evaluation criteria. And third, political philosophies are inappropriate practical guides to the allocation of municipal services. Water extraction and treatment, sewers, street lights, and sidewalks have, at best, a minimal link with democracy. Also, decentralizing 'services to people' from provincial departments to municipalities, in order to render municipalities politically meaningful (Sancton, 1992), has been considered an anachronism in New Brunswick since 1966.

The lesson learned can be summarized as follows: either (1) adopt a clear and consistent political philosophy—municipalities are administrative units governed by the province with the advice of locally elected councils and/or community organizations best able to determine and meet the communal needs as determined by autonomous councils—or (2) abandon divergent political philosophies when weaving through the complexities of daily local governance. The central dispatch fiasco demonstrates what can go wrong when provincial departments treat municipalities as mere administrative units charged with implementing provincial policy, rather than as multi-functional spheres of public governance and co-ordination at the local level. Municipalities should not be expected to be, *simultaneously*, corporations responsible for the efficient and effective allocation of provincial services and democratic institutions responsible for allocating and co-ordinating various services within a single community (Tindal and Tindal, 2000: 368). Nor should municipalities be expected to be both *alternatively*, when different parties gain power.

Divergent provincial political philosophies may also lead to strategic behaviour on the local front. It is no coincidence that the 'spirit of co-operation' between the three municipalities in the Moncton area, an argument presented by the panel to reject amalgamation (Malenfant and Robison, 1994: 34), disappeared once the Lord government came to power. Dieppe wants its own water treatment facility, downtown business district, economic commission, and urban planning commission (*Moncton Times & Transcript*, 2002f, 2003a, 2002e, 2002d),[23] and Moncton City Council again proposed amalgamation (Moncton, 2002b: 2).[24] The inaction of the Lord government since 1999 has pushed the pendulum to the municipalities' side.

However, the police regionalization demonstrates that political philosophies have limited value if they are not followed through in practice. The Lord government erased the provincial statute that forcibly created the Codiac RCMP detachment and gave Moncton, Dieppe, and Riverview the possibility to re-establish their own police forces,[25] but it did not fund the prohibitive costs of re-establishing these forces. The provincial measure is thus purely symbolic. The RCMP has since established a quasi-monopoly over policing services in New Brunswick, thereby increasing its comparative advantages over municipal police forces in the province—more bilingual capacity, more specialized services, easy access to national and international forces, lower number of officers required—and minimizing its limitations—higher salary and benefits, decisions made in Ottawa and Fredericton, less responsive to community needs (CTC, 1996a: 17–18). The fact that federal subsidies tilt the playing field in favour of the RCMP also reduces the options of municipal councils. Communitarian principles limited by individual-liberal premises became individual-liberal principles.

Even if the lesson is learned, however, it may not be applied. Differing political values and philosophies will endure. Indeed, differences may be amplified in the future (Castells, 1997). It may thus be illusory to hope for a single conception of the role of municipal institutions in our global and postmodern public governance in the age of information. Similar differences exist in academe, where municipal councils and regional ABCs are often perceived as, simultaneously, democratic and legitimate spheres of governance and mere administrative units of the (provincial) state (see Hill, 1974; Langrod, 1953; Panter-Brick, 1953). And there may be no solution to the dilemma. The appropriate degree of decentralization may thus depend as much on particular partisan political philosophies as on administrative criteria, such as the efficient and effective allocation of municipal services, as well as the myth of local democracy.

Second Lesson: Provincial and Local Governments
Do Not Learn from Past Experiences

The province has conducted no cost-benefit analysis to determine if the amalgamations in Miramichi,[26] Saint John, and Edmundston produced economies of scale, improved the quality of local services, increased the co-ordination between regional commissions, or provided democratic governance in LSDs. Nor does it plan to. Neither does it plan to evaluate the regionalization efforts in the Moncton area. The province sought similar solutions (formal regionalization) to solve the same urban and rural problems and their same cause (suburbanization), but it produced few, if any, empirical data to substantiate its claims and recommendations and to reject alternatives (three-tier governance). The province still proceeds with reforms, albeit modified by political philosophies, not having learned to 'refrain from intervening in municipal governance until it can prove its efforts will undoubtedly provide scale economies, improve services and/or increase public accountability' (CTC, 1999: 8). It does not heed the CTC's stinging critique: 'we hope the Provincial Government intervenes honestly (proves its assumptions beforehand), patiently (recognizes that implementation of provincial policies is already difficult enough at the provincial level and that it is even more so when other organizations are ordered to do it) and coherently (avoids contradictory directives)' (ibid.). The more things change . . . .

To its credit, the Lord government learned to study municipal governance in its holistic complexity. But it did so after trying, in vain, to separate financial and structural reforms. And although our data point to 'an integrated package deal' and a revised, consolidated, and permissive Municipalities Act, it is more probable that structural, financial, and jurisdictional reforms will not be completed simultaneously. The Lord government did not learn from its predecessor that municipalities behave strategically and will thus take advantage of Lord's carrot approach. Naming municipal representatives to the Round Table may have enabled it to 'learn much from the aggregate expertise and knowledge that exists' in the heads of 'seasoned management staff' within municipalities,[27] but relying *only* on such representatives runs the danger of biased reports in favour of vested stakeholders (LSDs, municipal councils). The McKenna government at least named 'independent and objective citizens' to study some aspects of its reforms.[28]

Municipal councils have also failed to learn any lesson from the reforms. Indeed, although the Moncton, Dieppe, and Riverview councils learned the hard way that their lack of co-operation in police services prompted the McKenna government to impose its police preference—the 'mayors and councillors acknowledge[d] that cooperation was not very tangible at the CTC table until the Provincial Government imposed a regional RCMP police force' (CTC, 1999: 8)— they did not increase co-operation afterwards. In the words of the volunteer CTC chair, the councils did not 'put up' (CTC, 1996b: 4). Then again, maybe the councils learned a valuable lesson: resist provincial intervention patiently until a more congenial party gains power. This is, in fact, what happened in June 1999 and co-operation between the three municipal councils has never been worse, as recent disputes over the RCMP cost-sharing formula attest (*Moncton Times & Transcript*, 2004b). Only time will tell if the councils learned the right lesson. If not, the provincial 'big brother' may have to intervene. The communitarian and indecisive Lord government may provide only short-term respite.

Third Lesson: Municipal Reforms Should
Be Internally and Externally Coherent

Internal coherence implies that municipal reforms will be instrumentally rational: the means (amalgamation or regionalization), objectives (economies of scale, co-ordination and accountability of regional services, improved local democracy), and societal ends (economic prosperity and balanced budgets) will be logically consequential. External coherence implies that municipal reforms will not contradict other related reforms (land use, regional police forces, provincial ambulance dispatch centre). As we demonstrated elsewhere (Bourgeois, 2001), the McKenna municipal reforms were rather internally and externally irrational. Our analysis indicated that amalgamations in Edmundston will not reduce suburbanization because they will encourage urban sprawl and linear development beyond the new city's borders. Amalgamation will probably reduce suburbanization in Miramichi, since it includes an extensive territory, but this vast size will probably not provide scale economies. Here, scale economies and amalgamation opposed each other. More importantly, the municipal reform did not match the land-use, police, and central dispatch reforms. It did not even respect its own logic: instead of integrating the regional services, police regionalization in Moncton created another, distinct regional layer of bureaucracy (the Police Authority). And both the McKenna and Lord governments failed to realize that the Department of Transportation's construction of a new, expanded bridge between Moncton and Riverview will encourage further suburbanization to the south. The Lord government tried but has thus far failed to perform the necessary balancing act between the various departmental initiatives related to urban sprawl and governance.

As the CTC's effort and report demonstrated, the provincial departments failed to 'think outside their box'. This is understandable from the perspective of the departments responsible for Public Safety, Health, and Transportation, who have only sporadic relations with municipal councils. But it is difficult to understand how Municipal Affairs officials could forget that municipal governance is framed by a multitude of statutes and departments. Municipalities may be provincial institutions, but unlike school boards and health corporations, they implement numerous departmental policies, manage numerous functions, and co-ordinate these policies and functions within the same community. Municipalities are territorially decentralized administrative units that manage multiple functions simultaneously (Lemieux, 1986; Page and Goldsmith, 1987). The CTC may have exaggerated its claim that provincial civil servants were 'out of their league' when they defended the provincial reforms and the panel's recommendations, but it did not exaggerate its claim that the officials 'often disappointed' them during their mandate (CTC, 1999: 8).

To their defence, Municipal Affairs officials indeed know that municipalities are multi-functional units. They did not have the ability to force their colleagues to integrate their respective reforms. That ability lies solely in the Premier's Office. Since the reforms were initiated by the Premier himself, Frank McKenna is ultimately responsible for their lack of internal and external rationality (Bourgeois, 2001). Not only must municipal reforms integrate structural, financial, functional, and jurisdictional considerations, but they must also integrate the various links between local and provincial institutions. If a provincial government can argue that municipalities are local administrative institutions, it must assume responsibility for the lack of provincial horizontal management. It cannot expect the municipal units to force provincial departments to collaborate. If, on the other hand, it believes that municipalities are 'governments' (Cooper, 1996), supported by the myth of local democracy, it should act coherently when initiating municipal reforms.

Fourth Lesson: There Is No One-Best-Way To Reform Local Governance
New Brunswick offers lessons on municipal reforms and governance, but these lessons may be inapplicable elsewhere because of characteristics that make the province too particular for generalizations. The White Paper recognized that New Brunswick had a small, dispersed, rural, and bilingual population (New Brunswick, 1992: 17). The dispersed, rural population severely limited the provincial government's courage to increase rural tax rates. Also, the linguistic composition limited the recourse to amalgamation in the Moncton area. The Round Table also concluded that there was too much of a 'significant diversity amongst municipalities' to adopt a single solution (New Brunswick, 2001a: 20). The Advisory Committee that reviewed the Municipalities Act, for its part, concluded that the seven cities, 112 towns and villages, and 270 LSDs had 'differing legislative needs' (New Brunswick, 1998: 1). Provincial officials conceded that there were 'significant differences in the province' between municipalities: urban or rural, rich or poor, big or small, and densely or sparsely populated.[29] The relative popularity of the 'myth of local democracy' in different areas and the distinct political philosophies espoused by different parties in power may also hinder uniform initiatives. The recognition of divergences in local characteristics, in particular, suggests that municipal reforms should either adopt (1) a permissive legislation, thereby letting each municipality adopt bylaws and policies to meet its particular needs according to its financial abilities, or (2) distinct legislation for each type of municipality (municipalities, LSDs, rural communities) to match the variety of structures, functions, financial ability, and jurisdictions. Thus, provinces should legislate to produce varying degrees of decentralization rather than creating polar extremes that lead to sporadic and confusing modifications.

If internal characteristics render lessons inapplicable elsewhere, the same could be said for external factors. Globalization, information technology, and the service economy will incur not only different impacts on municipalities throughout Canada, but also different impacts on New Brunswick municipalities (Lamarche, 1994; Vincent and Villeneuve, 1994; Higgins, 1994). Industrial Saint John has lost its status as the province's first urban centre to a more diversified Moncton. And the difficult resource-based economy of the northern areas is leading to significant southbound migrations. Consequently, differences in urban population movements will jeopardize standard provincial initiatives. For instance, since the northern areas of the province are losing population to the southern areas, and since the economic stagnation of Saint John has resulted in a reduced population and tax base, suburbanization may be limited to the Moncton area in the future. This could make amalgamation, sooner or later, an attractive solution in that area, *but only* in that area.

Conclusion

The quest for the appropriate level of centralization or decentralization in New Brunswick depends on internal characteristics, including differing (and partisan) political philosophies, as much as on changing contextual factors. Judging four decades of activity, it is probable that every new government will shuffle the municipal cards and put its stamp on local governance. This will be the case whether it is for ideological or partisan purposes. Add to this the certainty that social and economic trends will push the provincial government to act as the 'big brother' of local governance from time to time. One can thus predict that municipal governance in New Brunswick will experience more reforms in the future as internal and external variables change. And change they will. How much change will determine the scope of the next round of reforms, and how fast it occurs will determine the timing.

The reforms undertaken over the past decade have led to incremental rather than radical changes, and nothing suggests they will alter the foundations of municipal governance in the province any time soon. They probably will not establish the appropriate balance between provincial departments and municipal councils, so additional reforms will be needed in the near future. On the other hand, 'reform fatigue' may set in (OECD, 2000). This may explain the Lord government's procrastination, but our data suggest otherwise.

In fact, radical ideas like a three-tier (provincial, regional, municipal) elected governance model are rejected without any empirical or rational argument. This is in part because the opponents of such ideas are biased in favour of provincial or municipal stakeholders.[30] The second part is that it goes against the sacrosanct New Brunswick Equal Opportunities Program. Indeed, the most popular argument presented against three-tier governance is that 'it goes against the Byrne report' and the ensuing EOP.[31] According to this argument, New Brunswickers are unable to think outside the 'Byrne box'. They are able to understand a governance model containing three formal 'levels' of government (federal, provincial, and municipal), complemented by a variety of regional ABCs that may or may not overlap, but they are somehow unable to understand a model that would formalize the regional level and integrate overlapping regional services under a fourth 'level'. This argument is strictly ideological. Those who have no valid empirical objection use it to ward off heresy. If they are right, they have yet to prove it.

The only empirical objection presented against an elected regional level is that of 'limited area and population': 'New Brunswick is simply too small' (New Brunswick, 1992: 31). But this argument is flawed: neighbouring Nova Scotia has almost identical geographic and demographic characteristics, yet has elected, multi-functional, regional governments (county councils). In New Brunswick, therefore, despite the persistence of the 'myth of local democracy' and the belief that municipalities are a third 'level of government', the balance is tilted heavily in favour of provincial centralization. Integrating, overlapping, and electing regional commissions would tilt it the other way. Ironically, municipal councils who seek greater decentralization often are also those who oppose regional councils for fear of losing their own power. Present structural, functional, financial, and jurisdictional arrangements will thus prevail.

However, a greater irony may lead to greater decentralization. As a consequence of the EOP, New Brunswick became Canada's only officially bilingual province in 1969. That status was then inserted in the Canadian Constitution in 1993. That insertion, interpreted liberally by the New Brunswick Court of Appeal (*Charlebois v. Mowat and City of Moncton* [2001], NBCA 117), forced the Legislative Assembly to adopt a new Official Languages Act in June 2002. The new Act obliges all cities and municipalities (plus waste management and economic development commissions) where the minority represents at least 20 per cent of the population to provide bilingual services.

In this way New Brunswick became a distinct society when it comes to municipal institutional autonomy. Moreover, there are elements of the Canadian Constitution that lead some Acadians and scholars to believe that 'Acadian' municipal institutions cannot be easily restructured by the provincial government. According to this argument, municipalities in New Brunswick that contain a francophone majority are protected by section 16.1(1) of the Constitution; it guarantees to francophone citizens the right to 'distinct cultural institutions as are necessary for the preservation and promotion' of their society. It is argued that municipal rationalizations cannot go as far as the amalgamation of Acadian-controlled municipalities if Acadians become a minority within the new municipality[32] because 'their' municipalities are 'cultural institutions' that need protection against excessive provincial intervention. Consequently, New Brunswick municipalities play by a different set of democratic rules than do their counterparts in other provinces and other countries.

The irony lies in the fact that the EOP significantly centralized local governance, in great part to help the 'poor and rural' Acadian communities survive and prosper; but the subsequent legislative modifications and constitutional guarantees that stemmed from the EOP probably will decentralize local governance. In other words, the constitutional protection may not only prevent future provincial 'big brother' efforts, but also force the government to delegate more authority to Acadian municipalities. And since anglophone municipalities can obtain equal treatment for their 'municipal "cultural" institutions' via section 16.1(1), they will be able to obtain the same delegated authority. Therefore, New Brunswick's quest for the appropriate level of (de)centralization is far from over. Indeed, it may never end.

NOTES

1. The author thanks Michael Sullivan, former Assistant Manager, City of Moncton, for his valuable comments on the draft version of this chapter.
2. This is the gist of the conclusions presented in the collection edited by Ouellette (2001).
3. To be precise, school boards and health corporations existed well before 1966. The EOP

consolidated most of these ABCs along regional lines. Since then, school boards were reduced from 42 to 2 by the McKenna government in 1996, but increased from 2 to 14 by the Lord government in 2001. The McKenna regime also reduced the number of health authorities from 51 to 8. The exact number of regional economic development, land-use planning, and solid waste commissions has varied over the years. While these regional commissions have changed names, functions, and boundaries, they have usually numbered between 10 and 13.

4. According to the *Terms of Reference for Feasibility Studies* (New Brunswick, 1993b: 10), the panels were asked to consider 'as a first pass, the advisability and acceptability of municipal amalgamations in the subject areas.'

5. The official names of the provincial departments have changed since the reforms began in 1992. For example, Municipalities, Culture and Housing is now Environment and Local Government, Solicitor General is now Public Safety, Health and Community Services is now Health and Wellness, and Transportation and Public Works is now Transportation. For the sake of simplicity, we will reduce the terminology to the departments' basic function in relation to municipal governance. Consequently, we will speak of the departments of Municipal Affairs, Public Safety, Health, and Transportation, except in the notes and references.

6. New Brunswick is the only known jurisdiction to lose its urban status. Indeed, while 51 per cent of New Brunswickers lived in urban areas in 1971, only 48 per cent were urban dwellers in 1991. As in many other jurisdictions, both rural and urban areas lost dwellers to suburban areas. Except for Moncton and Fredericton, where the population increased because of annexations, every urban city of the province decreased between 1971 and 1991 while suburbs increased by almost 50 per cent.

7. According to the decennial census, New Brunswick's six cities lost a combined 6.2 per cent of their population between 1971 and 1991, while their incorporated suburbs increased their numbers by 48 per cent, and their unincorporated suburbs doubled their population. If not for annexations in Fredericton and Moncton, the net loss in the six cities would have surpassed 15 per cent in 20 years.

8. The 1992 White Paper (New Brunswick, 1992: 3–4, 47) argued that amalgamation or regionalization, through economies of scale and better integration of regional and municipal services, would also prepare the urban areas to compete in the new global economy. The White Paper thus assumed that municipal restructuring would improve the cities' comparative advantages in the global economy.

9. The McKenna government supported 'the principle of an equitable tax treatment for all residents in the Province and that the tax system should clearly link services to taxation', but stated it was 'reluctant to propose significant changes without a full review of all relevant tax measures' (New Brunswick, 1993c: 27).

10. The Malenfant-Robison panel recommended that the Board 'assume responsibility' for the sewerage commission (p. 60), the economic development commission (p. 67), the public transit authority (p. 71), the solid waste commission (p. 73), the pest control authority (p. 74), and the emergency planning committee (p. 75). The Board was supposed to 'provide coordination, liaison, and financial control over those special purpose agencies providing municipal services' in the area (p. 41). The panel also recommended that the Board 'oversee' co-operative efforts in police services (p. 52), fire services (p. 56), water treatment (p. 60), cultural facilities (p. 63), tourism promotion (p. 65), and industrial parks (p. 67), the latter two through the regional economic commission. Finally, it recommended that the planning and inspection activities performed by the regional urban planning commission be 'unified' and 'harmonized with economic development', thus suggesting that these services also be 'assumed' by the Board.

11. Interview with provincial official, Fredericton, 16 Apr. 2002.

12. Municipal amalgamations in Miramichi, Saint John, and Edmundston, and the creation of a 'regional community' in Memramcook in 1995, reduced the number of LSDs from 291 to 270.

13. The Department of Transportation oversees the construction and maintenance (repairs, snow removal) of provincial roads and shares with the respective municipal council the costs of 'regional' roads running through the municipalities. Municipal councils and taxpayers are responsible for municipal roads. The discussions thus far have revolved around the designation of the cost-shared 'regional' roads, but they have been put on hold until the completion of the studies related to municipal taxation and finances and property tax rates and assessments.

14. Scholars have argued that the separation between services to people and services to property is 'misguided and unsustainable' because municipalities are better able than provincial departments to adapt to divergent social service needs (Graham et al., 1998: 279). Sancton (1992) adds that municipalities that get out of social services risk becoming irrelevant.

15. The provincial government increased the fees for land-use planning services (1995), solid waste (1998), and property assessment (1998) in rural areas under its supervision. Land-use planning and solid waste services were already available in some rural areas, but many rural property owners did not pay for non-existent services until the provincial impositions.

16. Officially, the Department of Environment and Local Government, and the municipal institutions under its supervision according to section 92(8) of the Canadian Constitution, oversees only nine typically municipal statutes: (1) the Municipalities Act, (2) the Control of Municipalities Act, (3) the Municipal Assistance Act, (4) the Municipal Capital Borrowing Act, (5) the Municipal Debentures Act, (6), the Municipal Thoroughfare Easements Act, (7) the New Brunswick Municipal Finance Corporation Act, (8) the Municipal Heritage Preservation Act, and (9) the Municipal Elections Act. However, the department also oversees another handful of statutes that have a direct bearing on municipal governance: (10) the Business Improvement Areas Act, (11) the Community Planning Act, (12) the Days of Rest Act, (13) the Pesticides Control Act, (14) the Fire Prevention Act, and (15) the Unsightly Premises Act. Moreover, other departments oversee statutes that frame municipal governance. Among the most important, the Department of Finance oversees (16) the Real Property Tax Act, Public Safety oversees (17) the Police Act, the Department of Natural Resources and Energy oversees (18) the Parks Act, and the Department of Justice oversees (19) the Limitation of Actions Act. The Review Advisory Committee (New Brunswick, 1998: 100–4) recommended that only statutes 2–8 and 10, listed above, be incorporated into a revised Municipalities Act.

17. The most significant problem with local governance in LSDs is the lack of authority and democratic accountability. In the first case, the local members of the advisory committee do not make any decisions; decisions are made by the minister, often after a direct popular consultation with local residents. In the second, only 168 (62 per cent) of the 271 LSDs had, in 1999, an elected advisory committee to oversee local services (New Brunswick, 1999b: 163).

18. The Lord government adopted An Act to Amend the Municipalities Act in April 2003 (52 Elizabeth II, chapter 27). See also New Brunswick (2003c).

19. The police chiefs claimed that police work fell under the Police Act administered by the Minister of Public Safety, rather than the Municipalities Act administered by the Minister of Municipal Affairs and the municipal councils. Consequently, they did not have to follow the municipal councils' desire to regionalize police services, as outlined

in the panel's report, or police forces, as ordered by the Minister of Municipal Affairs, until they were ordered to do so by the Minister of Public Safety. This is why the CTC asked both ministers to make sure the police chiefs could not hide behind the accountability that suited their structural preferences.

20. The initial study presented three major limits. First, it did not present any costs for option 2 (regionalization of common services) yet concluded that the savings it could provide 'would not be as significant as a regional police service' (New Brunswick and CTC, 1996: 98). Second, although it presented a detailed analysis of option 1 (a single municipal police force), it simply photocopied the RCMP's proposal as option 3, without analyzing its advantages and disadvantages. Finally, it did not specify the start-up costs for the three options. The CTC's Supplementary Report to 'Policing Review' (CTC, 1996a) was necessary to 'fill the initial report's voids' (CTC, 1999: 4).

21. The administrative head of the CUPE local representing Moncton Police Force officers, Bill Whelan, turned down the CTC chairperson's request that his union make major concessions on benefits and bilingualism. In his opinion, no concessions were needed since 'McKenna doesn't have the balls to impose a regional RCMP in the Moncton area.' This was because 'McKenna can't break the law' that guaranteed unionized positions. The McKenna government did impose the RCMP in the greater Moncton area a few months later and CUPE lost 158 members.

22. Interview with school board official, Moncton, 22 Oct. 2000. McKenna uttered that conclusion when explaining to school board officials, in January 1993, why he was going to reduce the number of school boards from 42 to 18. In public, however, McKenna explained that the consolidations in school boards and health corporations, for instance, were necessary to do more with less and spend public funds in programs and activities rather than administrative fees.

23. The province eventually rejected Dieppe's request.

24. The mayor was supported in great part by the Strategic Economic Development Plan for the Greater Moncton Area (Moncton, 2002a: 39). See Dieppe's strategic opposition to amalgamation and greater integration of municipal services in Moncton Times & Transcript (2002b).

25. The Act to Amend the Police Act (48–9 Elizabeth II [2000], ch. 38) eliminated the Act to Amend the Police Act (45–6 Elizabeth II [1997], ch. 55) and thus re-established each of the three councils' full autonomy in establishing the police forces of their preference.

26. In their assessment of the Miramichi amalgamation, both Kitchen (1995) and Sancton (2000) demonstrate that it produced scale diseconomies. This was predictable since all things were not equal: the action amalgamated rural and urban communities with significantly different tax rates and service levels within a huge and mostly rural territory. Amalgamating three contiguous and significant cities with similar tax rates and service levels within a clearly urban area, as is the case in the Moncton area, may produce scale economies. Contextual variables are determinant.

27. Interview with provincial official, Fredericton, 16 Apr. 2002.

28. We obtained 'independent and objective citizens' from 'It was considered appropriate to appoint a citizen panel independent of government that could interpret the input that was provided during the public consultations in an objective manner that reflected the concerns of all stakeholders' (New Brunswick, 1999b: 2).

29. Interview with provincial official, Fredericton, 16 Apr. 2002.

30. I do not claim that counties should be re-established in New Brunswick or are the ideal solution, but opponents should not be allowed to easily discard empirical support for regional governance. Fiscal equalization between regions is an alternative.

31. Interview with provincial official, Fredericton, 16 Apr. 2002; interview with provincial official, Fredericton, 28 Mar. 2002; interview with cabinet minister, Fredericton, 10 May

1993. I have heard similar arguments from dozens of provincial officials over the years. I am not suggesting the Byrne reforms were unwarranted or erroneous. A thorough assessment is necessary. None exists. But I do argue that the Byrne reforms have been unduly reified in the provincial political culture. A recent uncritical academic collection by Ouellette (2001) is a case in point. I also claim that automatic refusals to 'reconsider Byrne' amount to ideology. Using 'the Byrne defence' without critical assessment is irrational.

32. Acadians in Dieppe threatened court action against the province in 1993 if it amalgamated their town with Moncton. They dropped their threat when the province chose regionalization.

REFERENCES

Acadie Nouvelle (Caraquet). 2003. 'Un projet de loi sur la gouvernance locale sera déposé ce printemps', 1 Dec., 3.

Andersen Consultants. 1996. *Central Dispatch Business Case.* Moncton, 17 Oct.

Bird, Richard, and Enid Slack. 1993. *Urban Public Finance in Canada.* Toronto: John Wiley & Sons.

Bourgeois, Daniel. 1994. 'Rationality in Policy Analysis', Final Report of the Third Conference of the International Consortium for the Study of Environmental Security, 31 May–4 June, Tufts University, Boston, published in *Population/Environment Equation* (special issue): 37–8.

———. 1995. 'La décentralisation administrative de 1992 au Nouveau-Brunswick et le contrôle du territoire', *Égalité* 38 (automne): 59–97.

———. 1997. 'Chairperson's Report on Meeting with Officials of the Department of Municipalities, Culture and Housing on June 12, 1997'. Moncton: CTC, 13 June.

———. 2001. 'La réforme municipale dans les provinces maritimes: (ir)rationalités néo-brunswickoises', paper presented at the Colloque de l'Association canadienne-française pour l'avancement des sciences, Sherbrooke, 15 May.

——— and Yves Bourgeois. 2004. 'Frontières stratégiques ou stratégies frontalières? Intégration et ségrégation territoriale chez les Francophones du Grand Moncton en 2002', *Francophonie d'Amérique* (forthcoming).

Breault, Ann. 1997a. Letter to Daniel Bourgeois, Chair of the Commission of the Three Communities. Fredericton: Department of Municipalities, Culture and Housing, 5 June.

———. 1997b. Letter to Daniel Bourgeois, Chair of the Commission of the Three Communities. Fredericton: Department of Municipalities, Culture and Housing, 8 Oct.

Castells, Manuel. 1997. *The Power of Identity.* Oxford: Basil Blackwell.

Commission of the Three Communities (CTC). 1996a. *Supplementary Report to 'Policing Review'* (Daniel Bourgeois and Laurann Hanson, authors). Moncton: CTC, 11 Dec.

———. 1996b. *Chairman's Discussion Paper on the Codiac Police Force.* Moncton: CTC, Dec.

———. 1999. *Final Report of the Commission of the Three Communities on the Implementation of the 27 Recommendations made by the Robison-Malenfant Panel.* Moncton, Dieppe, and Riverview: CTC, 17 Sept.

Cooper, Reid. 1998. 'Municipal law, delegated legislation and democracy', *Canadian Public Administration* 39, 3 (Fall): 290–313.

Cornes, Richard, and Todd Sandler. 1986. *The Theory of Externalities, Public Goods, and Club Goods.* Cambridge: Cambridge University Press.

d'Entremont, Harley. 1985. 'Provincial Restructuring of Municipal Government: A Comparative Analysis of New Brunswick and Nova Scotia', Ph.D. dissertation, University of Western Ontario.

Duffie, Paul. 1994. Letter to the mayors of Moncton, Dieppe, and Riverview. Fredericton: Department of Municipalities, Culture and Housing, 31 Aug.

Fox, William F. 1980. *Size Economies in Local Government Services: A Review*. Washington: United States Department of Agriculture, Economic Statistics and Cooperative Services, Rural Development Research Report no. 22, Aug.

Graham, Katherine A., Susan D. Phillips, and Allan M. Maslove. 1998. *Urban Governance in Canada: Representation, Resources, and Restructuring*. Toronto: Harcourt Brace & Co.

Grant, Alan. 1992. *Policing Arrangements in New Brunswick: 2000 and Beyond*. Fredericton: Solicitor General, Mar.

Higgins, Benjamin. 1994. 'Restructuring without Tears in a Free Trade Environment', in George J. DeBenedetti and Rodolphe H. Lamarche, eds, *Shock Waves: The Maritime Urban System in the New Economy*. Moncton: Canadian Institute for Research on Regional Development, 101–20.

Hill, Dilys M. 1974. *Democratic Theory and Local Government*. London: Allen & Unwin.

King, Russell. 1997. Letter to Daniel Bourgeois, CTC Chairperson. Fredericton: Department of Health and Social Services, 9 May.

Kitchen, Harry. 1995. Presentation to Municipal Government Officials of Brant County on Municipal Restructuring, 21 Dec., p. 11, quoted in Sancton (1996: 274).

Krueger, Ralph. 1970. 'The Provincial-Municipal Government Revolution in New Brunswick', *Canadian Public Administration* 13, 1 (Spring): 50–99.

Lamarche, Rodolphe H. 1994. 'A Changing Maritime Urban System: Facing Restructuring and Integration', in George J. DeBenedetti and Rodolphe H. Lamarche, eds, *Shock Waves: The Maritime Urban System in the New Economy*. Moncton: Canadian Institute for Research on Regional Development, 43–74.

Langrod, Georges. 1953. 'Local Government and Democracy', *Public Administration* 31 (Spring): 26–31.

Lemieux, Vincent. 1986. 'Deconcentration and decentralization: a question of terminology?', *Canadian Public Administration* 29, 2 (Summer): 318–23.

Malenfant, J.E. Louis, and John C. Robison. 1994. *Strength Through Cooperation*. Fredericton, Apr.

Moncton, City of. 2002a. *Strategic Economic Development Plan for the Greater Moncton Area*. Moncton: Grant Thornton, Jan.

———. 2002b. *Presentation by the City of Moncton to the Select Committee on Local Governance & Regional Collaboration*. Moncton: City Council, 22 Mar.

Moncton Times & Transcript. 2002a. 'Revise 911 system: fire chief', 10 Apr., A-1.

———. 2002b. 'Mayor, council criticize merger talk', 10 Apr., A-2.

———. 2002c. 'More join call for 911 review', 11 Apr., A-1.

———. 2002d. 'Dieppe needs gov't OK to leave Moncton planning commission', 4 Dec., A-1.

———. 2002e. 'Dieppe questions benefits of membership in economic commission', 13 Dec., A-1.

———. 2002f. 'Dieppe hires consultants to evaluate water source', 20 Dec., A-1.

———. 2003a. 'It was year of transition for Dieppe', 1 Jan., A-5.

———. 2003b. 'NB cuts cash for cities', 25 Nov., A-1.

———. 2004a. 'Moncton to shop for own police force', 6 Jan., A-1.

———. 2004b. 'Deal reached to end RCMP funding feud', 28 July, A-3.

New Brunswick. 1963. *Report of the Royal Commission on Finance and Municipal Taxation in New Brunswick*. Fredericton: Queen's Printer, Nov.

———. 1992. *Strengthening Municipal Government in New Brunswick's Urban Centres*. Fredericton: Department of Municipalities, Culture and Housing, Dec.

———. 1993a. *Final Report*. Fredericton: Commission on Land Use and Rural Environment, Apr.

———. 1993b. *Terms of Reference for Feasibility Studies on Local Government Restructuring in Selected Urban Centre Regions.* Fredericton: Department of Municipalities, Culture and Housing, June.

———. 1993c. *Government Response to the Final Report of the Commission on Land Use and the Rural Environment.* Fredericton, Nov.

———. 1998. *Report of the Municipalities Act Review Advisory Committee.* Fredericton: Department of Municipalities, Culture and Housing, Oct.

———. 1999a. *A Review of Local Service District Legislation.* Fredericton: Department of Municipalities, Culture and Housing, Jan.

———. 1999b. *Opportunities for Improving Local Governance in New Brunswick.* Fredericton: Municipalities Act Review Panel, Sept.

———. 2001a. *A Vision for Local Governance in New Brunswick.* Fredericton: Round Table on Local Governance, Department of Environment and Local Government, June.

———. 2001b. 'Municipal grant formula, funding levels to remain in place until 2002', press release NB 567, 14 June.

———. 2001c. 'Government responds to report of Round Table on Local Governance', press release NB 991, 11 Oct.

———. 2002a. 'Enterprise Network Launched', press release NB 737, 2 July.

———. 2002b. 'Freeze in unconditional grants to municipalities', press release NB 963, 2 Oct.

———. 2002c. 'Review of NB 911 services and dispatch systems', press release NB 889, 11 Sept.

———. 2003a. 'Response to Local Governance and Regional Collaboration report', press release NB 341, 8 Apr.

———. 2003b. *Local Governance and Regional Collaboration for New Brunswick— Government Response to the Final Report of the Select Committee on Local Governance and Regional Collaboration.* Fredericton: Environment and Local Government, Apr.

———. 2003c. 'Amendments to Municipalities Act introduced', press release NB 340, 8 Apr.

——— and CTC. 1996. *Policing Review.* Fredericton: Solicitor General and CTC, 27 Sept.

Organization for Economic Co-operation and Development. 2000. *Government of the Future.* Paris: OECD.

Ostrom, Vincent, Robert Bish, and Elinor Ostrom. 1988. *Local Government in the United States.* San Francisco: Institute for Contemporary Studies Press.

Ouellette, Roger, ed. 2001. *The Robichaud Era, 1960–70.* Moncton: Canadian Institute for Research on Regional Development.

Page, Edward C., and Michael J. Goldsmith, eds. 1987. *Central and Local Government Relations.* London: Sage.

Panter-Brick, Keith. 1953. 'Local Government and Democracy: A Rejoinder', *Public Administration* 31 (Spring): 344–7.

Sancton, Andrew. 1991. *Local Government Reorganization in Canada Since 1975.* Toronto: Intergovernmental Committee on Urban and Regional Research.

———. 1992. 'Provincial-Municipal Entanglement in Ontario: A Dissent', *Municipal World* 107, 2 (July): 23–4.

———. 1996. 'Reducing costs by consolidating municipalities: New Brunswick, Nova Scotia and Ontario', *Canadian Public Administration* 39, 3 (Fall): 267–89.

———. 2000. *Merger Mania: The Assault on Local Government.* Montreal and Kingston: McGill-Queen's University Press.

Sandel, Michael. 1982. *Liberalism and the Limits of Justice.* Cambridge: Cambridge University Press.

Select Committee on Local Governance and Regional Collaboration. 2003. *Local Governance and Regional Collaboration for New Brunswick.* Fredericton, Jan.

Taylor, Charles. 1992. *Multiculturalism and 'The Politics of Recognition'*. Princeton, NJ: Princeton University Press.

Tindal, C. Richard, and Susan Nobes Tindal. 2000. *Local Government in Canada*. Toronto: Nelson.

Vié, Jean-Émile. 1986. *Les sept plaies de la décentralisation*. Paris: Économica.

Vincent, Guy, and Paul Villeneuve. 1994. 'Maritime Cities as a Part of the North American Urban System', in George J. DeBenedetti and Rodolphe H. Lamarche, eds, *Shock Waves: The Maritime Urban System in the New Economy*. Moncton: Canadian Institute for Research on Regional Development, 75–100.

Vojnovic, Igor. 1998. 'Municipal consolidation in the 1990s: an analysis of British Columbia, New Brunswick, and Nova Scotia', *Canadian Public Administration* 41, 2 (Summer): 239–83.

Walzer, Michael. 1983. *Spheres of Justice*. Oxford: Basil Blackwell.

Young, Robert A. 1987. 'Remembering Equal Opportunity: Clearing the Undergrowth in New Brunswick', *Canadian Public Administration* 31, 1 (Spring): 88–102.

CHAPTER 12

Municipal Reform in the Northern Territories: Now for Something Different

KATHERINE A.H. GRAHAM

INTRODUCTION

This chapter reviews recent and anticipated municipal reforms in Yukon, the Northwest Territories (NWT), and Nunavut. Although it deals with the same dimensions of reform as previous chapters—structural, functional, financial, and jurisdictional—the context in which these reforms have been undertaken in the three territories is very different from the provincial context. The uniqueness of the territorial context compared to the provincial scene is one of the main themes of this chapter. A second major theme is that in recent years the three territorial governments have had different priorities for and approaches to municipal reform. The Yukon government, in collaboration with the Association of Yukon Communities, has made revisions to the Municipal Act a priority. In the NWT, the emphasis is on community capacity-building. In Nunavut, municipal reform is closely linked to building the new territory. One size does not fit all in the territorial North. The third theme that emerges from this review is that local governance is central to community development and sustainability in the North. Nonetheless, municipal government is very fragile in each of the territories. In some cases, this fragility results from common challenges, such as financial constraints and the needs to develop local political and administrative capacity and retain good people. It also stems from the different ways in which each territorial government, the federal government, and Aboriginal groups are dealing with land claims and self-government issues in each territory.

The following five sections of this chapter are devoted, respectively, to the context of municipal government in the North, reforms in Yukon, reforms in the Northwest Territories, the reforms in Nunavut, and some concluding observations regarding the current and future challenges for municipal reformers in the northern territories.

The Context of Municipal Government in the North

Four important ways in which the context of municipal government in the territorial North differs from southern Canada are: the number and size of municipalities in each of the three territories; the absence of conurbations; the nature of the land regime in the territorial North; and the evolution of municipal government in the context of Aboriginal claims.

The geographic area of Canada's northern territories exceeds that of the Indian subcontinent. This vast terrain is, however, very sparsely populated. The total population of each territory, as of the 2001 census, was: Yukon 29,000 people, a decline of 6.8 per cent from the 1996 census; Northwest Territories 37,000 people, a decline of 5.8 per cent from the 1996 census; and Nunavut 27,000 people, an increase of 8.1 per cent since 1996 (Statistics Canada, 2002).[1] In each case, the territorial capital is home to a large portion of the territorial population. Whitehorse has 66 per cent of Yukon's population, with a 2001 total of 19,058. Yellowknife had a 2001 population of 16,541 or 45 per cent of the NWT total. In the case of Nunavut, the population dominance of Iqaluit was somewhat less. Its 2001 population of 5,236 constituted 19 per cent of the territory's total population.

While the capitals are major population magnets, they would not be classed as major population centres in the broad Canadian context. They are, however, very large in comparison to other municipalities in each territory. For example, Dawson is the second largest municipality in Yukon. It had a 2001 population of 1,251. In the NWT, Inuvik is the second largest, with a population of 2,894 in 2001. Rankin Inlet is the second largest Nunavut municipality, with 2,177 residents, as of the 2001 census (ibid.). The remainder of the population in each territory is resident 'on the land' or in municipalities that are very small indeed by Canadian standards. Many municipalities have only a few hundred people. Although compared to various provinces there are relatively few municipalities in each territory, considering the relatively small size of the population of each territory they have a relatively high number of communities. Yukon has a total of eight municipal governments, the NWT has 33 recognized 'communities', and Nunavut has 28 municipalities.

Their second distinguishing characteristic is that municipalities in all three of Canada's territories are geographically isolated from each other. Every province has at least one conurbation, a major node of population. Very often, the urban boundaries of these major centres do not correspond to municipal boundaries. In major Canadian urban centres boundaries make candidates for structural reform. Think, for example, of the greater Toronto area, the Lower Mainland of British Columbia, or the greater Montreal area. Even allowing for the vast differences in scale, there is no parallel pattern of conurbations in any of the territories. Municipalities are separated from each other by large distances, often measuring hundreds of kilometres. Furthermore, the movement of people and goods among them is often a significant challenge—exacerbated by the weather and the challenges of maintaining a road network. Indeed, within Nunavut there is not even an inter-municipal road network to maintain.

The land regime in Canada's territories also shapes the development and prospects for municipalities. Each territory and its government are creations of federal statute. As a result, territorial lands remain federal Crown lands. Some of these lands, specifically lands within community settlements, have been delegated to territorial responsibility as 'Commissioner's lands'. To a very large degree, these lands, even in municipalities, remain in public ownership. One outcome of this is that the municipal planning process is driven by a different dynamic than in the south. There is no land 'development industry' in any territory that is contributing to a push for municipal reform. A second important outcome is that the property tax is largely inappropriate as a source of municipal revenue. For example, of the 33 municipalities in the NWT, only six have a sufficiently developed market of private or leased property to allow for a property tax system. All northern municipalities rely significantly on territorial transfers and user fees, primarily for water delivery and the collection of household waste, for revenues.

The final aspect of the context of municipal governments in the North is the influence of Aboriginal claims on the evolution of land regimes and governance in the territories. As will be discussed in more detail in the treatment of each territory, the specific aspirations of different claimant groups have varied from claim to claim. But the most significant common factor is that, in the territorial North, Aboriginal claims negotiations are relatively advanced or completed. In each case, the claim has or will have a very specific impact on the development of municipal government. This impact is related to the disposition of lands under the terms of land claims agreements and to the plan of Aboriginal governance that emerges for lands and other matters through the negotiations.

With this context in mind, we can now proceed to consider the course of recent municipal reforms in each of the three territories, as well as prospects for the future.

Municipal Reform in Yukon

The Context

The development and reform of the eight municipalities of Yukon occurs in the context of a much larger governmental tableau. In addition to the eight communities that fall under the purview of the Yukon Municipal Act, the government of Yukon recognizes 13 unincorporated communities and nine rural areas that have some form of community association—largely to organize social and recreational activities (Municipal Act Review Committee, 1998: 5). Of all the municipalities in Yukon, the capital city, Whitehorse, overwhelmingly predominates in population. Combined, Whitehorse and the second-most populous centre, Dawson, contain 70 per cent of the territory's population.

All of these municipal and community entities coexist with increasingly important First Nations governments. In 1993, the government of Canada signed an Umbrella Claims Agreement with the Council for Yukon Indians (CYI), which negotiated on behalf of 14 Yukon First Nations. Although formally signed between the Council and the federal Crown, the Yukon Umbrella Claims Agreement has had a fundamental impact on the Yukon territorial government and on municipalities. Subsequent to the signing of the Umbrella Agreement, negotiations between Canada, Yukon, and the 14 individual First Nations moved into high gear to conclude a self-government agreement for each First Nation. The territory's largest municipalities were directly affected, with Whitehorse having a direct interest in two of the First Nations' agreements and Dawson being affected by another. Smaller municipalities also have interests. In some cases, First Nation governments in Yukon have jurisdiction comparable to municipalities—for example, in areas such as public works. In other cases, their jurisdiction is coincident with territorial jurisdiction for the non-Aboriginal population—for example, in education and health. Under the terms of the Umbrella Agreement, Yukon First Nations also participate, as equals, in a number of territory-wide land-use planning and management bodies (Abele, 2002: 13). This has brought about an evolutionary process of fundamental change in the Yukon government and has been an important catalyst inducing municipal reform (Abele and Graham, 2003).

One specific reason why the negotiation of First Nation self-government agreements has spurred municipal reform in Yukon is the need to deal with the challenges of scale. Generally, First Nations governments in the territory have small resident populations. The coexistence of this population with a relatively small non-Aboriginal population necessitates practical approaches for sharing local and territorial resources.

Contemporary Municipal Reform in Yukon
The cornerstone of contemporary municipal reform efforts in Yukon has been an overhaul of the Yukon Municipal Act. This has been undertaken through a collaborative process involving representatives from the Association of Yukon Communities and staff from the then Yukon Department of Community and Transportation Services.[2] From 1996 until release of a discussion paper containing proposals for a new Municipal Act in 1998, the Joint Municipal Act Review Committee engaged in consultations and in a fundamental and clause-by-clause review of the existing municipal legislation. The Committee met monthly for two years. Its work was influenced by commentary within Yukon and by municipal reform initiatives in other provinces. The 1994 Alberta Municipal Government Act, which removed the requirement for specific provincial delegation to municipalities in favour of assigning to municipal governments 'natural person' powers over broad functional areas and jurisdictions, was particularly influential. New models of accountability, specifically the enhanced use of plebiscites in Roslyn, BC, were also the subject of considerable interest.

Following additional public and legislative debate, the revamped Yukon Municipal Act was passed in late 1998. It has a fundamental impact on the structures, functions, financial authorities, and jurisdiction of Yukon municipalities. In some cases, specifically in the functional and financial aspects of the new legislation, the new Municipal Act is important because it provides the potential for change—an important requirement given the evolving Yukon political landscape. In other cases, specifically in terms of structure and jurisdiction, the legislation provides for new public accountability for municipal government and the potential to engage in new governmental structures with other governments on a local or regional basis. This is important in view of the challenge of scale discussed earlier and of the emergence of First Nations governments.

The 1998 Municipal Act contains three major initiatives regarding the structure of municipal government in Yukon. First, it streamlined the classification of municipalities. Whereas formerly there had been a three-tier classification of incorporated municipalities—villages, towns, and cities—the new legislation provides for two. There are now provisions for cities, with a minimum population of 2,500, and incorporated municipalities that have the freedom to call themselves a village or town, depending on local wishes. There are no distinctions in the responsibilities and authorities granted to any incorporated municipality. The only difference between Yukon's one city, Whitehorse, and the rest of the municipalities is in the number of councillors. Whitehorse has six councillors, plus a mayor. The rest have four members, plus a mayor (s. 169).[3]

The 1998 legislation also deals with the establishment of government structures in rural areas in a more comprehensive manner than its predecessor (Municipal Act Review Committee, 1998: 14–15). It lays out a procedure for petitioning the Minister of Municipal Affairs, including the requirement that the name of any nearby municipality or First Nation government that might have an interest in the formation of a rural government structure be submitted with the application (s. 29[3]). The new rural government structures are conceived as taking on municipal types of responsibilities gradually, not having to assume the full basket of powers and duties given to incorporated municipalities.

Restructuring of municipal government has not been a major item on the reform agenda. Interestingly, although the legislation does deal with how to form, dissolve, or alter the boundaries of a municipality (s. 17), the words 'annexation' and 'amalgamation' are notably absent. As indicated earlier, the geographic dispersion of Yukon municipalities makes these undertakings irrelevant. One important structural innovation that the 1998 legislation does provide for is the establishment of common administration or planning structures with First Nations governments (ss. 27, 28). The Act is permissive in this regard. A municipality could join with one or more First Nations governments for these purposes. Equally important, municipalities have the capacity to initiate common structures for these purposes that also involve the government of Canada and the government of Yukon. This addresses the Association of Yukon Communities' desire to be a full player in the changing governance regime in the territory. Municipalities can both initiate and participate in new common structures with First Nations government.

Notably absent from Yukon's municipal reform agenda is any realignment of functions either between the territorial and municipal governments or between the latter and any other type of government or governing authority. Although discussions regarding municipal reform in Yukon occurred in the aftermath of major realignment of responsibilities between the provincial and municipal governments in some parts of Canada, this was not a major part of the reform agenda in this territory. There are likely a number of reasons for this. First, the

Yukon government itself has a strategic stake in key areas that have been the subject of transfer from one level of government to another in southern jurisdictions. The central role of social services, education, and maintenance of the territorial road network in serving the entire non-Aboriginal population of the territory (and, in the case of roads, everyone) provides a substantial justification for the continuing existence of the territorial government, in the post-claims-settlement era. Furthermore, without any significant tax base, municipalities would have no capacity to finance these costly services with any degree of independence or, likely, to any degree of acceptable standard. Finally, the specialized talent and equipment required to manage and provide technical/professional support in these areas would be extremely difficult for municipalities to acquire and maintain. One of the critical challenges facing Yukon municipal governments is attracting and retaining staff, especially at senior levels. Most come from other parts of Canada and other countries. If they do stay in the territory, many are soon lured away by the higher salary levels offered by the Yukon and federal governments.

Recent financial reforms have focused on making municipal councils more publicly accountable for their budget decisions, their debt, and even the expansion of the scope of activities that municipalities can undertake that are funded by user fees. The 1998 Municipal Act empowers incorporated municipalities to levy real property tax (s. 246). With the possible exception of Whitehorse, however, all municipalities rely on a block grant from the Yukon government as their main source of revenue. The principle that a block grant, rather than conditional transfers, should be the basis of municipal revenue seems firmly established in the territory.

Municipalities are required to pass an annual operating budget bylaw and a capital expenditure bylaw that reflect a multi-year capital plan. One significant reform in the 1998 Municipal Act is that decisions around specific financial choices can now be subject to direct popular will. The legislation provides for binding referendums on individual capital projects if 25 per cent of eligible voters petition for a referendum. This approach has been adapted from similar provisions in place in Roslyn, BC. The entire operating and capital budget bylaws are, however, exempt from this provision (ss. 153, 154).

The 1998 reforms raise the debt limits for incorporated municipalities from 2 to 3 per cent of the total assessed value of property. This increase had been recommended by the Municipal Advisory Committee (Municipal Advisory Committee, 1998: 59). Under the 1998 legislation, municipalities may exceed this limit only with approval of the minister, who may require a local referendum on the matter. This reform, then, simultaneously gives municipalities more financial capacity and direct accountability.

Finally, the 1998 reform enables municipalities to become involved in a broader range of activities than could be funded through user fees. The legislation recognizes that the small size of Yukon's private sector may require municipalities to offer a 'for-profit' service that would normally be outside the realm of local government. The largest potential for expansion is their new ability to become involved in utilities. The extent to which this occurs in the future will depend on many factors, including the overall state of Yukon's economy and the existence of appropriate technology. It is also conceivable that utility ventures involving Yukon municipalities would emerge out of joint interest and in partnership with First Nations and/or other governments.

As has already been stated, the fundamental jurisdictional reform to municipal government in Yukon in recent times has been to vest municipalities with 'natural person' powers. Although the Minister of Community Services still retains a broad supervisory role for municipalities, they have more freedom to manoeuvre. This includes their ability to enter into agreements with First Nations governments. Coincident with this and the broader changes wrought in Yukon governance since 1993, the composition of Yukon's Municipal Board has been changed. In addition to a chair and deputy chair, the Board now has constituent membership representing the minister, the Association of Yukon Communities, and the Council for Yukon First Nations (s. 329). This model is unique in Canada. The fact that this approach was recommended by the Municipal Advisory Committee (1998: 71) suggests an emerging and healthy dynamic between Yukon municipalities and First Nations governments. The fact that this recommendation was adopted by the Yukon government suggests a broader political consensus that new models of collaboration within the territory will be the way of the future.

The 1998 Municipal Act has been in place for six years. It is legitimate to ask what real difference it has made and how it might shape the future. In some municipalities, ongoing issues exceed the scope and importance of municipal reform. Chief among these are population loss and economic survival in the face of the decline of Yukon's mining economy. In other cases, municipalities have struggled to hire and retain competent staff. This challenge has sometimes led to the requirement that elected officials become directly involved in administration, a practice that is limited under the Act (s. 174). The fact is that these are real struggles in Yukon because of the size and fragility of communities and their municipal governments. Yukon municipal governments have not become hotbeds of populism since the 1998 reforms, nor have they gained a lot of new capacity. Nonetheless, these reforms set in place the potential for innovative practices in Yukon municipal government. In the near and distant future the development of municipal government in Yukon will be increasingly linked to the creation and evolution of First Nations governments in the territory and to resulting changes in the Yukon government.

Municipal Reform in the Northwest Territories
The Context
The nature and scope of municipal reform in the Northwest Territories in recent years have been significantly different from what has transpired in Yukon. A full appreciation of those reforms requires some understanding of the creation and evolution of municipal governance in the NWT.

In contrast with Yukon, where the prospect of gold caused rapid development of settlements at the turn of the twentieth century, permanent settlements in the

NWT were established over an extended period, beginning roughly in the 1930s and extending into the latter part of the twentieth century. NWT communities were often not 'natural' settlements. Some, including the current NWT capital, Yellowknife, owe their roots to the establishment of mines. Others, such as Cambridge Bay (now in Nunavut), were chosen by Ottawa as appropriate sites for community settlement, in part because of the location of a military installation nearby. Beginning in the post-World War II period, many settlements in the central and eastern Arctic (now Nunavut) were established to provide essential health care, education, and other government services by bringing people 'off the land'. The NWT's second largest municipality, Inuvik, was established in the early 1960s as a showcase for new northern technology (the above-ground construction of piped services, known as the 'utilidor', and multi-storey buildings on the permafrost) and to relocate the population of Aklavik, which was thought to be sinking into the Mackenzie Delta.[4]

The role of the federal government in northern development has been dealt with extensively elsewhere (see, for example, Dacks, 1981; Grant, 1988; RCAP, 1996). The important point in the contemporary municipal context is that, until less than 50 years ago, virtually every aspect of government in the NWT, including the decisions to establish communities and operate them, was done from Ottawa. This began to change in the late 1960s. In 1962, the Royal Commission on Government Organization (the Glassco Commission) recommended devolution of more authority from the federal bureaucracy to territorial commissioners and the creation of a separate civil service for the NWT (Clancy, 1990: 27). This idea took full form three years later with the report of the federally appointed Advisory Commission on the Future Government of the Northwest Territories (the Carrothers Commission). The commissioner, Alfred Carrothers, travelled the NWT in the course of his work. He concluded that the establishment of a system of municipal government was an important element of the political development of the NWT. He maintained that providing northerners with an opportunity to experience civic life in their own communities would serve an important training ground for further participation and political development (Graham, 1990).

The government of the Northwest Territories began the move to the new NWT capital, Yellowknife, in 1967. Three years later, it had almost 1,300 personnel in Yellowknife and in the outlying regions of the NWT, up from less than 100 public officials when the activist Commissioner, Stuart Hodgson, began the transfer. A Department of Local Government (now the Department of Municipal and Community Affairs—MACA) was one of the original NWT departments.

In many respects, contemporary municipal reform in the NWT has its roots in community experience and frustration stemming from these early days. The first 'system' of municipal government in the NWT was a classic case of the 'hyper-fractionalized quasi-subordination' observed by Stefan Dupré, when he studied the Ontario system of local government in the mid-1960s (Dupré, 1968). The NWT government put in place a five-level hierarchy of municipalities. Communities would begin as settlements. These had a locally elected council but were essentially administered by territorial personnel. The idea was that a community would 'advance' from settlement status to hamlet, through village and town status, ultimately to achieve 'city' status, including operation with a property tax base. Election practices and council procedures were prescribed using southern models of debate and voting, rather than deliberation to achieve consensus, as would be the traditional Aboriginal way. Emphasis was on the municipal operation of services to property. Social services and education were tightly controlled by the Departments of Social Services and Education. These departments, along with others, such as Natural Resources, had their own tentacles into each community through separately established committees. In 16 communities in the Mackenzie Valley and South Slave region, municipal councils coexisted with Indian band councils, but operated with little interaction between them. Moreover, neither of them had the requisite human and financial resources to operate effectively and efficiently.

As of the late 1970s, the need for reform was evident. There were two specific catalysts to reform. The first, and ultimately the most significant, were the various Aboriginal claims that covered the entire territory. Contrary to federal policy at the time, claims groups insisted that governance arrangements be included in the negotiations, as well as land and compensation packages. The second catalyst was the Drury Report (1980). Former federal cabinet minister C.M. Drury was appointed by Pierre Trudeau as the Special Representative on Constitutional Development in the Northwest Territories in 1977.

In many respects, the interplay between the local government reforms stimulated by Drury and the claims negotiations in various regions of the NWT have shaped contemporary municipal reform in the NWT. In order to elaborate, we will deal first with the local government reforms undertaken by the NWT government until the division of the territory on 1 April 1999. We will then see how these initiatives have interacted with the governance proposals of different Aboriginal groups and what has emerged as a result.

Drury's work was undertaken in the context of two important movements within the NWT. The first, as has already been discussed, was the desire by Aboriginal organizations representing claimants to include political arrangements in the negotiation of their claim. At the time, the NWT was subject to claims by four groups: the Inuvialuit of the Western Arctic/Beaufort area; the Dene Nation and Métis Association of the Northwest Territories, who had separate claims covering roughly the same area of the Mackenzie Valley and South Slave; and the Inuit of the central and eastern Arctic. Each had their own evolving visions of governance associated with their claim, involving local as well as regional governance for their respective claim areas. The Inuit had a unique and ultimately very important foundation for their governance proposal. Beginning in 1976, they advocated the formal division of the Northwest Territories and the creation of public government in what would eventually become the new territory of Nunavut.

Drury's mandate included consideration of division,[5] but not the merits of expanding claims negotiations to include governance issues. This limitation was the source of a certain amount of tension during his mandate. This tension extended beyond Drury's report in 1980, as claimant groups eyed local government reforms initiated by the NWT government as potentially frustrating their political aspirations.

Much of Drury's report dealt with the inappropriate character of the local government system that had been implemented in the NWT over the previous 13 years. He reaffirmed Carrothers's view that local government was an important element in the NWT political system. He recommended that the hierarchical system be streamlined and that municipalities become the focal point of local governance, eliminating the plethora of committees that coexisted with municipalities. He also noted various proposals for the establishment of regional councils. At that time, some government-appointed regional directors had established forums consisting of all of the communities in their respective regions. The Baffin regional organization was particularly advanced. Also, the Inuvialuit of the Western Arctic and Beaufort were proposing the establishment of the Western Arctic Regional Municipality (WARM). Drury took the view that regional councils should be allowed to emerge where there was local will and should not be imposed uniformly across the NWT.

Contemporary Municipal Reform in the Northwest Territories

Beginning in 1980, the territorial government has undertaken municipal reforms that have attempted to respond to Drury, to the winding course of various constitutional reform processes within the NWT (principally focused on the question of division), and to claims negotiations. From 1980 until the creation of Nunavut in 1999, these reforms were aimed at 61 municipalities throughout the territory, seven of which had a tax base. Since 1999, the orbit of NWT municipal reform has been 33 communities in the new NWT, six of which have a property tax base.

For the purposes of this review, the watershed of municipal reform in the NWT is the 1997–8 period. It marks the culmination of initiatives launched post-Drury and sets the stage for division. The main thrust of reform has been on the structure and jurisdiction of municipal governments. More specifically, the main thrust has been on consolidating the responsibilities of municipal councils, developing new ways of linking First Nations governments to municipalities, and dealing with different approaches to regional government that emerged through the claims process. All of these initiatives have occurred in the context of increasingly scarce financial resources at the territorial level that, in turn, had a direct impact on local funding. The challenges of developing administrative and technical capacity at the municipal level, as well as building civic involvement, have been ongoing.

Coincident with Drury's work, the NWT Department of Local Government developed a new model of municipal structure that identified the municipality as the 'prime public authority'. This concept was intended to convey the idea and reality that local councils were to be pre-eminent in providing the overall direction for communities. The issue of relations between municipal and First Nations band councils was dealt with by developing the concept of 'charter communities', allowing communities with coexisting Aboriginal and public governments to create their own charters to meet specific local needs and interests. A 1990 review of the progress made in implementing these concepts described the situation as 'tangled and difficult' (Graham, 1990: 209). This was attributed to bureaucratic politics between the Department of Local Government and other government departments and agencies, a focus on the Aboriginal claims agendas in communities, and the lack of capacity in municipal governments. The department (now MACA) persevered, however. The context for this type of reform changed significantly in 1982, when the federal government changed its policy and began to discuss political arrangements in claims negotiations. This opened a channel to discuss the creation of Nunavut, as well as a variety of regional and local arrangements that might emerge out of other claims.

By 1996, the NWT government had modified its concept of prime public authority to focus on a more flexible model of community empowerment. The idea behind this model is that municipal governments move at their own pace to assume responsibilities, in light of community priorities and capacity. A 1997 review of progress regarding community empowerment indicates a range of initiatives in different communities. Many were still at the stage of municipal capacity needs assessment. In other cases, the document acknowledges that 'At times, Community Empowerment activities are taking a back seat to political negotiations and GNWT consultations involving constitutional discussion' (Municipal and Community Affairs, 1997). Over five years later, the initiative was still underway in the 'new' NWT. The community of Holman has taken on the most extensive range of responsibilities, assuming a role in every function except education and health.

A second reform initiative began in the late 1990s when MACA and the NWT Association of Municipalities embarked on a review of all municipal legislation in the territory.

Municipalities, Aboriginal organizations, and the interested public were initially informed about possible directions for reform in a preliminary discussion paper. This paper was the basis for formal focus group discussions involving municipal officials and Aboriginal leaders. The discussion paper was also an important agenda item at the 1997 annual general meeting of the Northwest Territories Association of Municipalities. Considerable effort was invested in a clause-by-clause review of the Charter Communities Act, Cities, Towns and Villages Act, Hamlets Act, Settlements Act, Local Authorities Elections Act, and Property Assessment and Taxation Act.

This review culminated in two 1998 reports, one for the western NWT and one for Nunavut. Impending division was one reason for this approach. It was thought, too, that other key differences in the two territories were germane. Land claims and self-government negotiations were continuing in the west, while the model of public government and terms of the agreement between Canada and the Inuit of the central and eastern Arctic had been accepted by their respective representatives in 1993. An additional reason for producing two separate reports was that there were some significant differences in the nature of the municipal systems in the eastern and western parts of the territory. One such notable difference is that there were no settlements or charter communities in Nunavut (Municipal Legislation Review Committee, 1998: Letter of Transmittal).

Consultation concerning the recommendations of this review were extensive. There are some interesting recommendations. Instead of 'natural person' powers, the Municipal Legislation Review Committee recommended expanding the explicit list of corporate powers for municipalities. In contrast to Yukon, where the classification of municipalities was streamlined, it proposes to retain the five-tier structure of municipal governments in the NWT (four-tier in Nunavut). Similar to Yukon's reforms, however, the Committee advocated permitting municipalities to enter into joint agreements with Aboriginal organizations and governments. Also similar to Yukon's reforms, the Committee considered the question of whether or not municipalities should be permitted to engage in new businesses. Unlike its Yukon counterpart, the Committee urged careful consideration before proceeding. Finally, the Committee advocated the development of protocols for including youth on municipal councils. This interesting recommendation is a reflection of the demographics of the NWT and Nunavut communities, as well as the desperate need to involve and train as many people as possible for purposes of developing local government capacity.

Municipal Reform and the New Political Landscape in the NWT

The municipal reform initiatives discussed above, which were undertaken at the behest of MACA and the NWT Association of Municipalities, were paralleled by proposals by various Aboriginal organizations in the context of their claims. In discussing those proposals and their relevance for municipal reforms it is useful to distinguish between the reform initiatives in the new Northwest Territories and in Nunavut.

The process of Aboriginal claim negotiation in the NWT was altered by the 1982 shift in federal policy to permit discussion of governance arrangements. In the current NWT, it was also changed by the evolving dynamics of claimant groups. When Drury undertook his review, there were, broadly speaking, three groups of Aboriginal claimants in what is now the NWT. These were the Inuvialuit, concentrated in the Beaufort and Mackenzie Delta, the Dene, and the Métis.

The Inuvialuit signed the first comprehensive claims agreement in the territorial North in 1984. This agreement did not provide for any specific forms of local or regional government but indicated that Inuvialuit should not be treated differently from any other Aboriginal groups in terms of developing models of self-government (RCAP, 1996: IV, 434). As stated earlier, the organization representing Inuvialuit claimants in the negotiations had developed the broad outlines of a model for a Western Arctic Regional Municipality, but this was set aside in the initial focus on implementation of other aspects of the claims agreement.

The Dene, by no means a monolithic group in terms of kinship and history of relations with the federal and territorial governments, and the Métis had attempted to negotiate a common claim agreement with the Crown, with the latest attempt beginning in 1984. A draft final agreement for this comprehensive claim, reached in 1990, was ultimately rejected through referendums held for potential beneficiaries. Subsequently, the claims negotiation process has been regionalized. Three agreements have been finalized. The Gwich'in, who coexist with the Inuvialuit in the Mackenzie Delta, have concluded an agreement, as have the Sahtu Dene and Métis in the Mackenzie Valley. Most recently, the Dogrib of the North Slave area have achieved a land claim and self-government agreement, as of August 2003. These agreements in the Mackenzie Delta/Beaufort and the Dogrib agreement likely will have significant impacts on municipal reform.

In the Mackenzie Delta/Beaufort region, a Beaufort-Delta Regional Council has been established, led by area mayors and chiefs. It is examining the possible devolution of responsibilities from the territorial government, which is anticipated to involve a gradual process. Community governments may also continue to emerge in this region. As was noted, Holman, which is located in this region, is considered a model of a community that has taken on broad responsibilities.

In the Dogrib area, a Dogrib First Nation government has been established with jurisdiction over Dogrib lands and citizens. It is also intended that there be public governments in three communities, established by territorial legislation. These have been designated 'Dogrib community governments' and have jurisdiction over municipal matters. These governments would be effectively controlled by Dogrib (who are the majority in the region), as the intention is that the chief be Dogrib in each community and that at least half the members of council be Dogrib (Indian and Northern Affairs Canada, 2002). In practical terms, the current Dogrib plan is to constitute the Dogrib First Nation government as a regional council, with each community government having two representatives. The Grand Chief will be elected at large. As in the Mackenzie Delta/Beaufort, an evolving relationship between the regional council and community governments is envisioned.

Aside from these potential reforms, some ongoing challenges remain for municipal governments in the new Northwest Territories. The first is human resource capacity. The NWT government has established a School of Community Government to build capacity in the municipal sector. The school works in collaboration with municipalities and professional/trades organizations to provide in-class and Internet learning programs for the skills and trades required in northern municipalities. The goal, through this process of collaboration and through the guidance of a Human Resource Sector Council, is to achieve a major improvement in recruitment, retention, and skill levels of northerners as municipal employees.

The funding regime for NWT municipal governments also represents a continuing challenge. The six tax-based municipalities are finding it difficult to maintain services, given their current funding regime. The tax base is fragile at best, with payments in lieu of taxes from other governments being the single largest component of the tax base. User fees are increasing. Unlike the south, there is scant potential to explore public-private partnerships for the development of new facilities. Other municipalities rely almost completely on territorial grants. The NWT Association of Municipalities is advocating a move to a block grant system but, as of now, there is continuing reliance on conditional grants. The challenge of writing proposals for grants for capital facilities is particularly onerous on municipalities. Applications frequently must be directed to multiple sources, with different application, monitoring, and reporting requirements. For some NWT communities, the highest priority in recent years has been to get support to hire a proposal writer.

Finally, there is the very real and immediate problem of housing shortages in communities and of developing and maintaining sound municipal infrastructure. Growth pressures, as a result of either high birth rates or resource development, are placing strains on some NWT communities. Geography and climate raise particular problems in terms of the cost of construction and maintenance. In concluding its report in 1998, the Municipal Legislation Review Committee (1998: 26) identified a number of challenges for the future. These centre on the question of whether it is appropriate to further simplify the legislative base and hierarchical structure of municipal government in the NWT. The Committee also signalled the need to address issues related to the system of municipal finance, including a major review of the property tax system. At the time of writing, efforts to deal with these challenges are 'on hold'. Instead, the government of the Northwest Territories and municipalities in the NWT are focusing on the impact of division, the challenges of potential resource development, and the changing *realpolitik* of regional and local government arrangements in the context of Aboriginal claims.

MUNICIPAL REFORM IN NUNAVUT

The Context

For the Inuit of the central and eastern Arctic, the creation of Nunavut on 1 April 1999 was a remarkable achievement. It took only 17 years from their first formal proposal for a new territory coincident with their land claim until 1993, when Parliament passed the Nunavut Land Claims Agreement Act and the Nunavut Act. Over that relatively short time, the Inuit and their claimant organization, the Tungavik Federation of Nunavut,[6] and members of the NWT legislature from the region convinced the majority of eligible voters in the NWT and the federal government to agree to division. The year 1982 was an important one in this project for two major reasons. It was the year when the majority of eligible voters in the NWT who voted in a plebiscite expressed their support for the division of the territory, and when the federal government revised its land claims policy to consider governmental arrangements as part of negotiations.

The creation of Nunavut is even more remarkable when one considers that the central and eastern Arctic has the shortest history of civic government of any part of the territorial North. Virtually all government and public administration, aside from policing and military activities, had been put in place since the 1950s. Communities were established to feed, house, educate, and otherwise care for people in an efficient way. As discussed earlier, municipal government was introduced in order to expose Inuit to democratic practice. There are 28 recognized communities in Nunavut, with only the capital, Iqaluit, having a property tax base.

The period from 1993 to 1999 was one of intense activity as the citizens of the new territory prepared for their new government. There were several streams of activity. The Tungavik Federation of Nunavut (now Nunavut Tungavik Inc.) was preoccupied with establishing the various resource management and planning boards for settlement lands under the land claim agreement. The Nunavut

Implementation Commission was charged with responsibility for creating a new territorial government from scratch. It considered everything from the size and representation base of the legislative assembly to the administrative structure of the territorial government. A number of implementation proposals had been put forward in the negotiations around creation of the territory, but the challenge was now a real one of maintaining public services, while adapting government to the needs and interests of Nunavut residents.

One consequence of this sea change in territorial politics and government is that municipal reform per se has been less of a focus in Nunavut than in the other two territories. As has already been discussed, some of the NWT reform initiatives of the 1980s and 1990s did have potential for Nunavut municipalities. These include the prime public authority and community empowerment initiatives. An overview of municipal political leaders' reaction to these reforms suggests that they were focused on the prospect of division and the new territorial and claims structures that were emerging (Northwest Territories Municipal and Community Affairs, 1997).

Contemporary Municipal Reform in Nunavut
The stage for future reform developments has been set within the Nunavut government by the creation of a Department of Community Government and Transportation as one of the 10 territorial departments. It is responsible for 16 Acts, ranging from the All Terrain Vehicles Act and the Dog Act (dog control is a major and serious issue in communities in all three territories) to the Cities, Towns and Villages Act. The first minister responsible for this department was formerly Minister of Community and Municipal Affairs in the NWT government. In fact, she was the minister who signed off on the 1998 reports of the Municipal Legislation Review Committee that are still under consideration.

In recent years the nature and scope of municipal governance in Nunavut have not been shaped by any special municipal reform initiatives comparable to those of other territories or provinces. Instead, it has been shaped primarily by some major policy choices that have been made in light of some major challenges associated with setting the new territorial government on a firm footing. One of the fundamental decisions made early on was to develop a highly decentralized model of territorial government. Various government departments and units within departments would be dispersed among Nunavut communities, both as a means of making government responsive and also for distributing employment opportunities and other economic benefits associated with government activity to as many communities as possible.

Communities appear to be highly supportive of this approach. It has, however, created some short-term challenges. First, is the challenge of housing. In many communities, high natural population growth has created pressure on the housing stock and government is constrained from responding due to financial pressures. As indicated earlier, there is only a minuscule private development industry in the territory; government is the major provider of housing. This shortage has been exacerbated by decentralization. Although the goal is to develop indigenous employment in communities through decentralization, there has been a short-term requirement to recruit from outside. These people need accommodation. Interestingly, the capital, Iqaluit, has also been severely affected by a housing shortage. Even with a decentralized model of public administration, the shift of central government functions from Yellowknife, the expansion of activities of Nunavut Tungavik Inc., and other parapublic developments have contributed to a 24.1 per cent growth in Iqaluit's population between 1996 and 2001 (Statistics Canada, 2002).

The second challenge faced by municipalities is that of attracting and retaining staff. The issue of human resource capacity is a common one across the three territories. The decentralized model of territorial administration places a premium on attracting good talent within communities. In times past, many of the trained people would have been municipal employees. Further, the Nunavut government is itself facing stiff competition for staffing from Nunavut Tungavik Inc. and the various planning and management bodies set up to administer the land claim. Aside from the inherent attraction of these jobs, these organizations are paying salaries higher than those found in the public sector.

Finally, there is the challenge of financing municipal government in Nunavut. With the partial exception of Iqaluit, Nunavut municipalities are almost completely dependent on the territorial government for their finances. The Nunavut government is, in turn, virtually dependent on federal transfers, which it argues are inadequate. In short, the system of public finance in Nunavut is under stress and the serious consequences of this not only for the operation of municipal governments but also for the very safety of communities is a matter of concern. This situation is illustrated by an incident in the early years of the new territory when the Nunavut government accidentally distributed tainted fuel to various communities for the operation of heating and power systems. This placed considerable pressures on the finances of the territorial government because not only did it have to pay for the initial shipment of fuel, but it then had to pay for the remedial actions that were required to deal with the tainted fuel. Such incidents reveal that the future of municipal reform in Nunavut will be very much tied to the development of the territorial government.

Conclusions

Our review of municipal reform in the three northern territories has shown the importance of the overall context of northern political development in shaping the role and character of municipal government. Although they share some common challenges, the most important of which are inadequate financial resources and the development and retention of staff, the specific characteristics of municipal government in the three territories are different. Municipalities in the three territories have different historical origins. We also see differences in the extent to which municipal governments have been engaged with Aboriginal governments and organizations. Regardless of those differences, dealing with the emergence and evolution of Aboriginal governments across all three territories will be a common challenge for municipal governments. In a part of Canada where conditions are rugged, if not harsh, development of a sense of community is integral to survival. The extent to which 'community' is embodied in the municipal government system is a work in progress.

Looking across Canada, one of the themes in municipal reform has been the appetite (or lack of appetite) of provincial government to encourage or initiate change. Looking at the three territories, we can conclude that territorial governments have undertaken municipal reform in two contexts. The first is the need for reviewing basic municipal legislation. This was the subject of attention and action in the Yukon and of deliberation in the NWT prior to division. It is reasonable to think that territorial governments will continue to engage in periodic consultative processes for this purpose. The second context for territorial government action is to engage in municipal reform as part of 'territory-building'. Looking at history and at the current challenges faced by each of the territorial governments, this may be the more important source of change in the role and place of municipal governments in the future.

NOTES

1. Statistics Canada began to collect separate population counts for the area now established as the Nunavut Territory in 1991, even though the territory itself did not come into existence until 1 April 1999. Thus, the population decline in the Northwest Territories is a real decline, not the result of the establishment of Nunavut.

2. The Department of Community and Transportation Services has since been split. Municipal matters now fall under the purview of the Yukon Department of Community Services. This department also has the mandate to lead initiatives providing better access to territorial government services for Yukoners, another reflection of the changing context for governance in Yukon.

3. This and similar citations refer to the relevant section of the Municipal Act.

4. Aklavik exists to this day. Some relocation occurred, but Inuvik owes its existence to government (it is a regional centre for the government of the Northwest Territories) and to resource development in the Mackenzie Delta and Beaufort Sea.

5. Drury did not pronounce on the merits of division. Instead, he recommended a constituent assembly in the NWT to consider the matter.

6. The original claims organization was the Inuit Tapirisat of Canada. In the 1980s, Inuit across Canada made the decision that ITC should focus on national issues and cultural development, rather than claims negotiations. This led to the establishment of Tungavik Federation of Nunavut as the claimant organization in the central and eastern Arctic.

REFERENCES

Abele, Frances. 2002. 'Aboriginal Peoples in Northern Canada: The Peaceful Revolution Meets Global Capital', *CRIC Papers #6: The Canadian North: Embracing Change.* Montreal: Centre for Research and Information on Canada.

———— and Katherine A.H. Graham. 2003. *Serving the Public North of 60.* Toronto: Institute of Public Administration of Canada.

Clancy, Peter. 1990. 'Politics by Remote Control: Historical Perspectives on Devolution in Canada's North', in Gurston Dacks, ed., *Devolution and Constitutional Development in Canada's North.* Ottawa: Carleton University Press.

Dacks, Gurston. 1981. *A Choice of Futures: Politics in the Canadian North.* Toronto: Methuen.

Dogrib Agreement-in-Principle. 2002. Highlights. At: <www.ainc-inac.gc.ca/pr/agr/dogrib/hil_e.html>.

Drury, C.M. 1980. *Constitutional Development in the Northwest Territories.* Ottawa: Minister of Supply and Services Canada.

Dupré, J. Stefan. 1968. *Intergovernmental Finance in Ontario: A Provincial-Local Perspective.* Toronto: Queen's Printer.

Graham, Katherine A.H. 1990. 'Devolution and Local Government', in Gurston Dacks, ed., *Devolution and Constitutional Development in Canada's North.* Ottawa: Carleton University Press.

Grant, Shelagh D. 1988. *Sovereignty or Security: Government Policy in the Canadian North 1936–1950.* Vancouver: University of British Columbia Press.

Northwest Territories, Municipal and Community Affairs. 1997. *Focusing on Our Future: Community Empowerment Summary Report.* Yellowknife.

———, Municipal Legislation Review Committee. 1998. *Empowerment Through Community Government Legislation.* Yellowknife.

Royal Commission on Aboriginal Peoples (RCAP). 1996. *Report,* 5 vols. Ottawa: Canada Communications Group.

Statistics Canada. 2002. Census Geography—Highlights and Analysis. At: <http://geopot2.statcan.ca/Diss/Highlights/Page3/Table2_e.cfm>.

Yukon. 1998. *Statutes of the Yukon,* Chapter 19: Municipal Act.

———, Municipal Act Review Committee. 1998. *Proposals for a New Municipal Act: A Discussion Paper.* Whitehorse.

PART III

COMPARATIVE

OVERVIEW

Reflections on Municipal Reform: Reconfiguration or Reinvention?

EDWARD C. LESAGE JR AND JOSEPH GARCEA

INTRODUCTION

The objectives of this chapter are threefold. The first objective is to provide an overview and an analysis of the results, politics, and processes of recent municipal reform, based largely on the case studies in the previous chapters and on some of the extant literature. The second objective is to look to the near future in regard to the prospects for and the nature and scope of further municipal reform agendas and initiatives. The third objective is to provide some suggestions for additional research on current and future municipal reforms.

PURPOSES OF MUNICIPAL REFORMS

The purpose of municipal reforms during the turn-of-the-millennium reform period was improved governance at the municipal, provincial, and territorial levels (Frisken, 1994; Graham et al., 1998; Tindal and Tindal, 2004). To that end, reform initiatives were undertaken with three broad objectives that were declared, undeclared, or ascribed: improving governance capacity, improving intergovernmental relations, and improving municipal-community relations. Although those objectives had some prominence or importance in all municipal reform agendas, differences existed in precisely how important they were for governmental and non-governmental stakeholders in conjunction with various reform initiatives. Moreover, although substantial consensus existed on those objectives, there was considerable disagreement on the means by which to advance them.

Improving Governance Capacity

The most commonly stated objective for municipal reform in recent years was the need to improve the governance capacity of the municipal, provincial, and territorial levels of government. Improving governance capacity refers to the ability of those levels of government to perform their respective governance and management functions.

Improving Municipal Governance Capacity

Arguably, the first and most important objective of municipal reforms undertaken during the last 15 years was to improve municipal governance capacity. The municipal reform agenda was rooted in a strong and widely shared belief in the need to improve the governance capacity of all types of municipalities to ensure that they could perform their core functions effectively in light of the existing and emerging challenges (Lightbody, 1995; Martin, 1996; Frisken, 1997; Andrew, 1997; Thomas, 1997; Tindal and Tindal, 2004). Despite the consensus on the merits of improving municipal governance capacity, there were substantial differences on what should be done and also on the means by which to do it. Generally, two major means for improving municipal governance capacity—the empowerment of municipal governments and the restructuring of the municipal system—were proposed and in some cases implemented.

Empowerment as a means of improving municipal governance capacity was strongly favoured by the vast majority of elected and appointed municipal officials. Indeed, they viewed this as the *sine qua non* of improved municipal governance (Canadian Federation of Municipalities, 1998). They argued that only with such empowerment in the form of increased jurisdictional authority and autonomy and increased access to financial resources could municipal governments perform their respective governance and management functions effectively and efficiently. Municipal officials generally wanted a combination of constitutional recognition as 'orders of government' and enabling and permissive statutory provisions that protected them from intrusions by other orders of government. More specifically, they wanted constitutional and statutory provisions that provided them with greater scope for independent action in performing their functions and conducting their internal organizational affairs unencumbered by the policies and regulations of the provincial, territorial, or federal governments. Representatives of large and small municipalities alike argued that the existing provincial and territorial statutory and regulatory frameworks were unduly limiting and restrictive. This was especially true of officials from larger municipalities, who argued that, among other things, those frameworks hampered their ability to be more entrepreneurial in providing the requisite municipal infrastructure and services to their residents and in managing their financial and capital assets (Toronto, 2000a, 2000b, 2000c, 2000d, 2000e). Such arguments were particularly pronounced in light of provincial and territorial expectations that all municipal governments become more entrepreneurial in such matters. Some municipal officials argued that particularly problematic from their perspective were provincial and territorial statutory provisions mandating some of the roles and responsibilities of some elected and appointed municipal officials. Those arguments were echoed in many of the reports produced during the turn-of-the-millennium reform period, which recommended that the scope of municipal jurisdictional authority and autonomy should be expanded either for all or at least for some types of municipalities. The argument commonly made by advocates of increased municipal authority and autonomy was that 'Dillon's rule', which stipulates that municipalities can do only what is explicitly and clearly prescribed in legislation, was inappropriate for municipalities operating in a mature modern municipal system. In effect, they wanted a level of authority and autonomy at least comparable to what is afforded to some American municipalities pursuant to the principle of 'home rule' (Tindal and Tindal, 2004: 195–6). As discussed in more detail in a subsequent section of this chapter, the general response of provincial and territorial governments was to expand the jurisdictional authority and autonomy of municipal governments in the legislation. However, they were reticent to go very far in that direction, and their concessions usually fell somewhat short of what many municipal officials envisioned and demanded.

The restructuring of municipalities was also proposed as a means to enhance the governance capacity of municipal governments. This was advocated by many, if not all, provincial and territorial governments, albeit not to the same extent. The restructuring that they advocated for this particular purpose was regional governance through amalgamation of neighbouring municipalities and/or the creation of regional authorities to perform various municipal planning, development, and service delivery functions (Tindal, 1996). The result was the creation of one-tier or two-tier regional governance (Sancton, 2002a, 2002c).

The proponents of municipal restructuring made several key arguments regarding its benefits for enhancing governance capacity (Siegel, 1993; Saskatchewan, 2000; Tindal and Tindal, 2004: 150–71). First, they claimed it would provide municipal governments with a greater ability to deal effectively, efficiently, and equitably with matters such as growth management, land use, and transportation planning. Second, restructuring was seen as providing municipal governments with a greater ability to eliminate or at least minimize the negative effects of inter-municipal competition and conflict as well as spillover and free-rider problems among neighbouring municipalities. Third, proponents claimed that restructuring would provide municipal governments with a greater ability to engage in more rational and substantial economic planning and development initiatives as well as various related marketing initiatives to ensure that they were competitive in the continental and global economic development sweepstakes (Blais, 1994; Coffey, 1994a, 1994b; Gertler, 1996).

This rationale for restructuring as a means of increasing municipal governance capacity was criticized by various governmental and non-governmental stakeholders and academic analysts (Sancton, 1994, 1999, 2000a, 2000d; McFarlane, 2001). The strongest critique was aimed at suggestions that one particular form of restructuring—amalgamation—would enhance governance capacity. Some of those who advanced such a critique maintained that there was no evidence to suggest that amalgamation would have a positive effect on governance capacity or on any other objectives of reform, such as greater efficiency, effectiveness, and responsiveness in service delivery or greater accessibility and accountability (Sancton 1994, 1996a, 2000a, 2000b, 2000c, 2002a; Kitchen, 1995; Tindal, 1996; Bish, 2000, 2001).

Improving Provincial/Territorial Governance Capacity
Improving the governance capacity of provincial and territorial governments was also an objective related to municipal reforms during the period under discussion. In many if not most jurisdictions, there was a strong, albeit often a muted, belief that reforms producing improved governance capacity in the municipal sector would contribute to improved governance capacity in the provincial and territorial sector. The major reason that this particular belief was muted is that provincial and territorial governments did not want to exacerbate complaints that their municipal reform initiatives were designed primarily with their own needs in mind, rather than those of the municipal governments. It was not uncommon to hear municipal officials and other protagonists in reform debates arguing that various reforms initiated or supported by provincial and territorial governments were designed primarily to serve at least two needs or interests of the upper-level government—to reduce the municipal dependency on provincial and territorial financial transfers, and to facilitate the development and implementation of provincial and territorial policies or programs that either impinged upon or could be influenced by municipal governments. Such a critique was not entirely unfounded. Provincial and territorial governments generally admitted, however reluctantly in some cases, that although the bulk of the benefits of municipal reforms would accrue to municipal governments, some benefits would also accrue to them and to various other levels of government (e.g., federal and Aboriginal) and governing authorities (e.g., education and health) that either directly or indirectly were affected by the nature and scope of governance in the municipal sector.

Improving Intergovernmental Relations
The second most commonly cited objective of municipal reforms throughout the turn-of-the-millennium reform period was improved intergovernmental relations. This included both provincial/territorial-municipal relations and inter-municipal relations (Graham et al., 1998: 171–201; Tindal and Tindal, 2004: 179–219).

Improving Provincial/Territorial-Municipal Relations
Improving provincial-municipal relations was a shared objective among various governmental and non-governmental stakeholders involved in municipal reforms across the country. There was a consensus among provincial and municipal officials that such relations were adversely affected by several controversial issues between them, the most notable of which were the alignment of their respective functions, finances, and powers. Generally, officials from both levels of government recognized a misalignment in each of these areas that not only hampered their ability to perform their respective governance functions efficiently and effectively, but also contributed to persistent problems of co-ordination and conflict between them (Andrew, 1995; Boswell, 1996; Graham and Phillips, 1999). Consequently, in recent years both levels of government have sought ways to produce a more appropriate and balanced alignment of functions, finances, and powers. Although they generally agreed that reforms were required, they often

disagreed about the precise nature and scope of such reforms and the means by which to develop and implement them.

There were three interrelated sets of such disagreements. The first set focused on which level of government should perform various governance and service delivery functions. Such disagreements occurred on a vast array of functions, ranging from the relatively more circumscribed and less expensive ones, such as assessments for property taxes, to the relatively broader and more expensive functions, such as public health services, community services, and income support services. It is difficult to make generalizations regarding the precise preferences of municipal governments and their respective provincial and territorial governments on such matters. About all that can be said with some confidence is that their preferences were based on the actual and potential financial and political costs that a particular alignment of functions would have for them.

The second set of disagreements, and closely related to the first, focused on the level of financial transfers from provincial and territorial governments to municipal governments, and on the ability of municipal governments to access alternative taxation bases controlled by provincial and territorial governments. For their part, municipal governments demanded increased transfers and/or increased access to alternative taxation bases. The provincial and territorial governments, however, were generally quite reticent to comply with such demands. Indeed, they wanted to reduce the level of their financial transfers to municipal governments (Graham et al., 1998: 203–26; Tindal and Tindal, 2004: 221–56; Siegel, 2002).

The third set of disagreements dealt with the need to balance jurisdictional authority between the municipal governments and their respective provincial and territorial governments. This issue had been on the reform agenda for many years (Kitchen and McMillan, 1985). Municipal governments demanded that provincial and territorial governments should enact statutory and even constitutional amendments that recognized them as an 'order of government' and granted them greater jurisdictional authority to perform their functions. In making their demands, municipal governments pointed to restrictive legislation, inadequate consultations prior to major reforms, insensitivity by provincial and territorial governments to the positions advanced by municipalities within such consultations, and policy initiatives that they perceived to serve provincial and territorial, rather than municipal, purposes. Although the upper-level governments were not receptive to municipal demands for constitutional recognition of municipal governments as 'orders of government', some of them acceded to municipal demands for such recognition in statutes and policies, and others acceded to municipal demands for greater jurisdictional authority to perform their functions.

Improving Inter-Municipal Relations
Improving inter-municipal relations among neighbouring municipalities was another major shared objective of governmental and non-governmental protagonists involved in municipal reform initiatives. There was a general recognition that while some competition and conflict among neighbouring municipal governments in metropolitan and non-metropolitan regions was inevitable, and in some

cases beneficial, an excessive amount could be counterproductive. This belief led protagonists involved in various reform initiatives to call on the provincial, territorial, and municipal governments to find ways to eliminate counterproductive competition and conflict between neighbouring municipal governments. As discussed in other sections of this chapter, various types of structural, functional, and financial reforms were advocated and in some cases implemented for the purpose of minimizing counterproductive inter-municipal competition and conflict. By far the most common of these were structural: the amalgamation of neighbouring municipalities, the creation of regional governance frameworks in the form of second-tier regional municipalities, and the creation of regional special-purpose authorities (Richmond and Siegel, 1994; Artibise, 1998; Bish, 2000, 2001). Much less common were functional and financial reforms, such as the transfer of some functions to existing regional governments or authorities or the sharing of costs and revenues among existing neighbouring municipalities. This is so despite the fact that enabling legislation in some jurisdictions permitted inter-municipal collaboration for performing and financing various municipal functions.

Improving Municipal-Community Relations

The third most commonly cited objective for municipal reform was improved municipal-community relations (Graham et al., 1998: 125–47; Tindal and Tindal, 2004: 299–340). Although attention was given to this particular objective in the rhetoric of various reform debates, it was not the most significant objective in the actual reform initiatives. Efforts to improve municipal-community relations focused on two key governance matters: greater responsiveness to community preferences, and increased transparency and accountability.

Significant measures designed to foster responsiveness to community preferences included: providing more opportunities for public consultations, plebiscites, and referendums; the direct election of heads of municipal councils such as occurred for rural municipalities in Nova Scotia and Alberta; the institutionalization of the ward system in British Columbia for various types of municipalities; and the creation of various sub-municipal community-based administrative and advisory bodies. The creation of such bodies was most pronounced in Ontario, Quebec, and Nova Scotia in conjunction with their major restructuring initiatives that led to the creation of new 'megacity structures' in Toronto, Montreal, and Halifax, and the creation of regional municipal governments through the amalgamation of smaller urban and rural municipalities and any adjacent unincorporated areas. The central purpose of such bodies was to minimize what were viewed as the undesirable effects of the extra distance being created between ratepayers and their city or regional councils as a result of the consolidation of neighbouring municipalities. A related purpose in select cases was to soften the political transition to mega-structures by retaining rough approximations of the replaced municipal structures in these sub-municipal bodies.

Important measures designed to increase transparency and accountability included additional requirements for more frequent use of open committee meetings, mandatory reporting on a wider range of their activities, mandatory distribution of any such reports, and conflict of interest guidelines. Although British Columbia was arguably the leader in adopting these types of measures, other provincial and territorial governments also adopted measures to encourage greater transparency and accountability (Smith and Stewart, 1998).

In summary, the overarching goal of municipal reforms during this period was improved governance at the municipal and provincial and territorial levels. Notwithstanding the centrality of one or more of three broad objectives in various reform initiatives—improving governance capacity, improving intergovernmental relations, and improving municipal-community relations—there was considerable disagreement as to which objective(s) should have primacy and on the means of achieving the desired change. Considerable disagreement also prevailed on what were the true objectives of various reform initiatives. Municipal governments and their ratepayers were often suspicious and in some instances overtly cynical of initiatives favoured by provincial and territorial governments, believing that the senior governments hid ulterior or undeclared objectives.

Products of the Municipal Reform Initiatives: The Outputs

The objective in this section is to provide a comparative overview of four types of reform—structural, functional, financial, and jurisdictional—implemented in the provinces and territories during the past 10–15 years. This section presents a comparative overview of the nature and scope of the reform initiatives for each of these four pillars of the reform agenda.

Overview of the Structural Reform Initiatives

Major structural reforms were considered in most provinces and territories. However, extensive restructuring was achieved only in Ontario, Quebec, and to a much lesser extent in the four Atlantic provinces (Vojnovic, 1997; Graham et al., 1998: 65–92; Vojnovic and Poel, 2000; Sancton, 1991, 2000c; Tindal and Tindal, 2004: 85–178). No comparable substantial structural reforms were undertaken in the four western provinces or in the three northern territories. In the six eastern provinces these structural reforms involved the amalgamation of various types of municipalities in rural, urban, and metropolitan regions.

Although it is beyond the scope of this chapter to provide a highly detailed comparative analysis of the precise nature of structural reforms in each of the six provinces that implemented such reforms, two observations are in order. First, regarding the main features of the restructured municipal systems, it is noteworthy that they relied on a combination of the two classic approaches to regional governance: one-tier and two-tier (O'Brien, 1993; Smith, 1996; Artibise, 1998; Bish, 2000, 2001; Sancton, 2002c). Creation of one-tier regional municipal governments was evident in the restructuring initiatives in Ontario, Quebec, Nova Scotia, New Brunswick, Prince Edward Island, and Newfoundland. Although a substantial part of the structural reforms in Ontario and Quebec consisted of changing two-tier systems to one-tier systems, there were also some adjustments to the existing two-tier systems and the creation of a few new ones (Sancton, 2002c).

The second observation is that a major challenge in the restructuring initiatives in those provinces, but particularly in Ontario, Quebec, and Nova Scotia, was to find the appropriate representational framework for various communities within the newly created regional municipalities (Tindal and Tindal, 2004: 125–6). For example, the architects of the new Toronto, Montreal and Quebec's other major cities, and Halifax metropolitan municipalities introduced new sub-municipal structures. In Toronto and Halifax these councils were established as city council advisory committees mandated to provide forums for local community input into the decision-making process. In Montreal, Quebec City, Longueuil, Levis, Saguenay, and Sherbrooke, the sub-municipal entities have taken the form of boroughs responsible for administering several basic services, including garbage collection, road repair, sport and recreation, and the issuance of building permits. Boroughs have no powers of taxation per se and apparently no substantial powers over policy. They are essentially administrative agents that draw revenues from user fees for services they provide and from budget allocations from city council.

Ontario's structural reforms were comprehensive and controversial both in metropolitan and non-metropolitan areas. In metropolitan areas this included the restructuring of several major city regions—Toronto, Ottawa, Hamilton, and Sudbury—in which two-tier regional structures were replaced by consolidated one-tier entities through amalgamations. The most ambitious and controversial of these structural reforms was the creation of the Toronto 'megacity', a single municipality with a population of nearly 2.8 million. Many regional government structures created in the late 1960s and the 1970s were also restructured, thereby eliminating the two-tier arrangements and resulting in larger municipal authorities. Other major restructuring initiatives in Ontario entailed amalgamations within the province's long-enduring county system that in combination with amalgamations within large urban centres reduced the number of municipalities by more than 200 (Downey and Williams, 1998; Williams and Downey, 1999; Sancton, 2000c). Within four years of commencing its restructuring initiative, the Ontario provincial government had consolidated its municipal system substantially with the number of municipalities reduced from over 800 to about 400. What is notable about all of the Ontario amalgamations is that they were initiated by the provincial department rather than by local preference (Graham et al., 1998: 74–9; Sancton, 1996b, 2000c: 136–47; Tindal and Tindal, 2004: 109). In all cases the provincial government either compelled or mandated municipalities to amalgamate. It compelled them by informing them that the local preference option was only open in making some choices regarding the precise configuration of the amalgamated municipalities if a consensus prevailed in a given region. In the event that they could not agree on the configuration of the amalgamated municipality, however, the province would mandate a configuration based on recommendations from provincially appointed commissioners. The threat of forced amalgamation proved to be a significant motivator for the majority of municipalities to become involved in facilitating their own amalgamation. Consequently of the 230 municipalities that were restructured by May 2001, approximately 85 per cent exercised their local preference option, but the boundaries for the others were mandated by the provincial government regardless of local preference (Fischler et al., 2004: 92–6).

Although there was a fledgling de-amalgamation movement in Ontario in the first few years following amalgamation, it quickly lost steam in most communities as people started to accept the impossibility of reversing amalgamation. The only notable concerted effort at de-amalgamation occurred in the amalgamated City of Kawartha Lakes. In the referendum held in conjunction with that city's 2003 municipal election, de-amalgamation was supported by 51.6 per cent of the voters. However, shortly thereafter the new Liberal government told the mayor and council that it was not willing to authorize a de-amalgamation because it was not financially prudent to proceed at that particular juncture (Ontario, 2004). In opposition the Liberals had indicated that they would honour the results of such referendums. The position of the Liberal government took most of the wind out of the sails of regionally based de-amalgamation movements throughout the province as their protagonists recognized that de-amalgamations would not likely to be facilitated or approved by the government even if economic circumstances change.

Quebec's structural reforms were comparable to Ontario's both in nature and scope, involving not only the amalgamation of many small municipalities but also adjustments to the boundaries of some regional authorities (Quesnel, 2000: 122–4; Tindal and Tindal, 2004: 124, Fischler et al., 2004: 96–104). The fundamental difference, of course, is that Quebec achieved not only amalgamations but also de-amalgamations during this period. Quebec's restructuring strategies involved a combination of the voluntary approach driven by the positive and negative financial incentives established by the provincial government and the mandatory approach by provincial fiat. Both approaches produced substantial results in reducing the number of Quebec's municipalities, although Quebec continues to be the leader among provinces in the number of municipalities. Quebec's restructuring reforms involved three major sets of initiatives. The first involved extensive amalgamations of municipalities of various sizes in metropolitan, urban, and rural regions throughout the province. In some places only a few municipalities were amalgamated to form a new municipality; in other cases at least two dozen municipalities were amalgamated. The result of those amalgamations was the reduction in the total number of municipalities by approximately 300 over the decade.

The second set of Quebec's restructuring initiatives involved the reconfiguration of regional municipal authorities. Quebec's restructuring initiatives also included the creation of regional authorities in metropolitan and non-metropolitan regions. In the Montreal, Quebec City, and Outaouais metropolitan regions, the provincial government established metropolitan regional councils to facilitate the co-ordination of planning and regional infrastructure, facilities, and services management among the various communities therein. In the Montreal region, a super-regional authority—the Communauté métropolitaine de Montréal (CMM)—was established to perform the various planning and management functions on a metropolitan scale for over 100 Montreal-area municipalities (Fischler and Wolfe, 2000). It exists in tandem with the MRCs (Municipalités régionales de comté) of the region. Quebec also overhauled the MRC system and established three separate categories of regional counties: rural, mixed rural and urban, and metropolitan. The MRCs were reconfigured in light of roughly two decades' experience that made it clear that the regional organizations performed somewhat different roles in these three contexts.

The third set of Quebec's restructuring initiatives involved the de-amalgamation of municipalities. This occurred following the 2003 provincial election when Premier Charest's Liberal government honoured its election promise of providing the local preference option to all municipalities amalgamated between 2000 and 2003 (Séguin, 2003, 2004). In December 2003 it enacted a statute that outlined the process for de-amalgamation. Of the 212 former municipalities eligible for such de-amalgamation, 89 collected the requisite signatures of 10 per cent of eligible voters needed to trigger the referendums that were held in June 2004. The majority of voters in 59 of those former municipalities voted in favour of de-amalgamation. However, only 32 of those had the requisite voter turnout of at least 35 per cent of eligible voters to sanction the de-amalgamation. The de-amalgamation of those municipalities will be facilitated by a special committee established in each of those communities to co-ordinate the elections to be held in November 2005 to elect mayors and councils who will commence governing their respective municipalities in January 2006. Undoubtedly, both the processes and effects of those de-amalgamations will be closely monitored by academics and by stakeholders in the municipal sector inside and outside Quebec. The focus will be on three matters: first, to see how they progress and whether the provincial government attempts either to influence or even to pre-empt them in any way; second, the effects that the de-amalgamations will have on the capacity, costs, and quality of governance in the municipalities as well as in the municipalities from which they are de-amalgamated; and third, the likely effects on relations between neighbouring de-amalgamated and amalgamated municipalities.

Structural reforms in the Atlantic provinces were somewhat less encompassing than those implemented in Ontario and Quebec (Tindal and Tindal, 2004: 127–40). Nova Scotia's most dramatic structural reforms involved the creation of the geographically extensive Halifax Regional Municipality and the Cape Breton Regional Municipality (Vojnovic, 1997, 1998). Following on these initiatives, the province established permissive legislation that enabled municipalities to amalgamate voluntarily. One voluntary amalgamation completed prior to the coming into force of the new enabling legislation was the Region of Queens Municipality. To date it has been the only voluntary amalgamation. Nova Scotia reformers also made changes to special-purpose authorities. Thirteen regional development authorities were established in 1994 with mandates to foster economic development within their respective regions. The province also established seven regional authorities for solid waste resource management that blanketed the province.

New Brunswick pursued structural reform by seeking to consolidate municipal units in most of its major urban areas. Structural reform included the complete or partial amalgamation of municipalities in the Saint John, Edmundston, and Miramichi regions and selected boundary expansions elsewhere. Amalgamation in the Moncton region was also studied but a proposal to create a single municipality was rejected in light of strong opposition from the local Acadian population. As an alternative a regional services board was proposed. An amalgamation study for the Campbellton region was not followed up and action in the Fredericton and Bathurst regions was simply avoided. Proposals by a provincial Round Table that envisioned the creation of multi-functional regional bodies to replace single-function bodies operating in rural areas and to facilitate urban-rural collaboration lost steam because these proposals did not generate much enthusiasm in subsequent consultations and the provincial government's subsequent creation of a network of regional economic development agencies confounded the proposal for a multi-functional agency. Similarly, efforts to replace the province's 270 local service district committees with some form of elected representative municipal governments do not appear to have been pursued wholesale. Instead, the province has favoured the gradual implementation of a system of empowered community representation.

In Newfoundland the provincial government launched an amalgamation drive in 1989 seeking to reduce the number of municipalities from more than 100 to just over 40. This initiative ended with the consolidation of 33 municipalities into 13, thereby reducing the total number of municipalities by only 20. The boundaries of the City of St John's were expanded in 1991 to take in some surrounding communities and, concomitantly, area-wide amalgamations reduced the number of municipalities in the region to 11 from 19. These particular reforms also eliminated the existing region-wide service board as St John's assumed responsibility for some of the functions previously performed by that board. In 1991 the provincial government passed regional service board legislation but this was never proclaimed. Newfoundland created 20 Regional Economic Development boards (REDs) in 1995. Proposals to establish Regional County Services Boards were advanced by a provincial task force in 1997, but this idea was abandoned in the face of considerable controversy.

In Prince Edward Island structural reforms were considered and recommended by four major reports produced between 1988 and 1993. The first was the 1988 report, *The Geography of Governance,* commissioned by the Federation of PEI Municipalities and the Department of Community Affairs to review the structure of local and regional government in the province. This report recommended a reduction in the number of municipalities throughout the province. The second was the 1990 report of the Royal Commission on the Land, which recommended the amalgamation of each of the two largest urban centres with all of their smaller neighbouring municipalities, and the consolidation of most of the sparsely populated rural communities into large counties. The third was the 1991 document titled the *Municipal Study Report* commissioned by the Department of Community and Cultural Affairs, which noted the problems caused by the multiplicity of municipalities in the Charlottetown and Summerside regions and recommended their amalgamation with those cities. The fourth was the 1993 report of the Commission on Municipal Reform (Charlottetown and Summerside areas) produced in conjunction with the provincial government's *White Paper on Municipal Reform*. Ultimately, however, the only recommendations for structural reforms implemented were those calling for the amalgamation of municipalities in the Charlottetown and Summerside regions (Tindal and Tindal, 2004: 136).

Municipal structural reforms were far less encompassing in the four western provinces and in the three northern territories (Garcea, 2002a). The notable structural reform in these regions of the country involved two of the three northern territories and occurred in 1999 largely as a result of the hiving off of the eastern portion of the former Northwest Territories to create Nunavut Territory. This division reduced the number of municipal and quasi-municipal units in the NWT from 61 to 33. The restructuring that did take place in the western provinces was minimal and limited in scope and included the voluntary consolidation of a small number of municipalities such as those in Alberta's Fort McMurray and Cold Lake regions, British Columbia's Abbotsford region, and Manitoba municipalities in the Gimli region, and the voluntary dissolution of a limited number of very small municipalities. Some new municipalities were incorporated, as happened in Alberta with the Banff and Jasper townsites and the incorporation of many Alberta improvement districts as municipal districts. There was little de-amalgamation across the West, the case of note being de-amalgamation of Headingly, a suburban community that was hived off from Winnipeg (O'Brien, 1993: 32–3).

All of the western and northern jurisdictions devoted some attention to the question of structural reform either for all or parts of their respective municipal systems. Even in cases where restructuring was not at the forefront of the reform agenda or reform initiatives, it always loomed to some degree in the reform discussions (Tindal and Tindal, 2004: 86–105). There were three notable examples of structural reform being seriously considered but not acted on. In Saskatchewan the provincial government established a task force to examine the municipal system, which in its interim and final reports proposed a substantial restructuring of the entire municipal system (Saskatchewan, 2000). That proposal was abandoned due to strong opposition from many municipal officials and ratepayers. In Alberta and Manitoba the provincial governments appointed committees to investigate the merits of structural reforms in the Edmonton and Winnipeg city-regions. Whereas the Alberta committee recommended a weak form of regional government for the Edmonton region and made every effort to avoid depicting it as anything more than a loose form of inter-municipal co-operation (Alberta, 2000a, 2000b), the Manitoba committee concluded that inter-municipal collaboration was the only practical choice for the Winnipeg region (Manitoba, 1999). Both committees proffered the 'new regionalism' perspective that advocates various modes of inter-municipal and inter-authority co-ordination within various types of regions (Artibise, 1998; Sancton, 2001). In both of those cases regionalization was not achieved despite the fact that many of the key municipal stakeholders were supportive of the basic tenets of 'new regionalism'. The stumbling block to structural reform in both the Edmonton and Winnipeg city-regions was disagreement among the principal municipal government stakeholders on the precise configuration of a new regional governance framework, even if it left the current municipalities intact.

Although the structural reforms in the four western provinces and the three northern territories did not entail any major consolidation or reconfiguration of the individual municipal units, structural reforms were of some importance in some of those jurisdictions. This included the reclassification of municipalities and the configuration of some types of special-purpose bodies. In Manitoba, for example, the principal reform emanating from the new Municipal Government Act, 1996 was a revision of a five-category classification scheme to a simpler urban-rural dichotomy. Villages were dissolved and local urban districts were established in their place. A reclassification of municipalities was also undertaken in Alberta with the decision not to create any new summer villages, the elimination of the counties as a formal category, and the creation of a new category dubbed 'specialized municipalities'. A reclassification initiative also occurred in Yukon in 1998 pursuant to the new Municipal Act, which streamlined the classification of municipalities into two general types of incorporated entities (i.e., cities and incorporated municipalities) and unincorporated rural municipal entities comparable to what traditionally have been referred to as improvement districts in other jurisdictions.

Changes to the systems of special-purpose authorities occurred across the western provinces and the northern territories in varying measures (Saskatchewan, 2000: 211–42). Alberta implemented several such reforms, including the elimination of its improvement district system, the near-total elimination of its regional planning commissions, and the revamping of the system of regional services commissions. In Saskatchewan, the provincial government created a new system of regional economic development authorities during the early 1990s in place of the ones established during the 1980s. In Manitoba and British Columbia the provincial governments established some special-purpose bodies to deal with regional matters in their respective metropolitan urban centres. In Manitoba the only product of two extensive reviews (Manitoba, 1999, 2001) related to governance in the Winnipeg city-region was the creation of the Regional Planning Advisory Committee. This body is mandated to advise the province on regional planning policies and regional governance issues (Tindal and Tindal, 2004: 104–5). Recommendations on the need to consolidate and improve the regionalization of regional special-purpose authorities in the remainder of the province did not result in any reforms. In British Columbia, the provincial government created the Greater Vancouver Transit Authority (now Translink), a special-purpose agency closely allied with the Greater Vancouver Regional District. Reforms involving special-purpose authorities in the North included the permissive statutes in Yukon and the Northwest Territories that sanction the establishment of common administration or planning structures with First Nation governments. These arrangements are likely to become increasingly important in the future as both municipal and First Nation governments find it necessary to establish and institutionalize frameworks that allow for effective working relationships between them.

Overview of the Functional Reform Initiatives

Functional reforms were seriously contemplated in all provinces and territories during the recent period of reform, but in the end substantial reforms were only undertaken in a few provinces (Hobson and St-Hilaire, 1997; Tindal and Tindal, 2004: 182–95). In some jurisdictions specially appointed task forces and committees examined the need for and nature of functional reforms; in other jurisdictions limited attention was devoted to functional reform either by the provincial/territorial government on its own or in periodic discussions with representatives of municipal governments. At issue in discussions and negotiations related to functional reforms were the precise roles and responsibilities of each level of government. Two issues were particularly prominent: (1) whether such functions would be performed exclusively by one level of government versus another level of government, or by two or more levels of government; and (2) whether certain functions would be performed by smaller local municipalities or smaller local special-purpose authorities as opposed to larger regional municipalities and larger regional special-purpose bodies.

The principal focus of functional reforms—contemplated or implemented—generally involved property assessment, road planning and development, land-use planning, development and maintenance of infrastructure, services to property, and economic development. Some of the notable tendencies in the realignment of these responsibilities were as follows. The administration of property assessment tended to shift from either the municipal or provincial governments to special-purpose bodies with varying degrees of representation of both levels of government. Such assessment agencies provide province-wide assessment with varying degrees of involvement by the provincial and municipal governments. The development and maintenance of roads tended to move from the provincial government to the municipal governments. Land-use planning, infrastructure development and maintenance, and services to property were often shifted from local municipal governments and the provincial government to regional municipalities and regional authorities. Economic development and regional planning were most often shifted from municipal and provincial agencies to special regional authorities.

The most significant functional reform initiatives during this reform era were undertaken in Nova Scotia, Ontario, Quebec, and Alberta. Nova Scotia's initial effort at functional reform involved a service exchange in which municipalities assumed responsibility for policing and suburban roads (and bridges) and the province for municipal child welfare costs, nursing homes, homes for the aged, probate court and registry of deeds, and home care and boards of health. As part of the bargain provincial grants for public transit, planning, building inspection, recreation, and emergency funding were eliminated. This exchange arrangement proved not fully satisfactory almost from the onset and wide-ranging consultations commenced in 1999 in an effort to establish a more satisfactory and complete arrangement. Placed on the table for consideration were governance, revenue structure, general services, economic development, protective services, transportation, environment, land management, and recreation. These discussions have been protracted and complex, and are continuing (Vojnovic, 1999; Tindal and Tindal, 2004: 184–6).

Ontario's major functional realignments entailed a general shift of functions from the province to the municipalities (Graham and Phillips, 1998a; Sancton, 2000c: 147–9; Tindal and Tindal, 2004: 186–9). Ontario's service realignment activities included moving the property assessment administration to an autonomous municipally funded entity and transferring responsibility from the provincial government to the municipal governments for social housing, the operation of airports and most ferries, many roads, land ambulance, and water and sewer services. Although the scope of the Ontario reforms is clearly more encompassing than that in Nova Scotia, both reform initiatives suffered something of the same fate. Both initiatives were slowed by their complexities and by the unavailability of provincial funds required to complete the reforms. The larger scope of the Ontario reform owes principally to the province's ceding approximately 50 per cent of the local property tax collected by school authorities to municipalities. As in Nova Scotia, Ontario realignment (or service exchange) remains incomplete and a matter of continuing discussion as part of the unfinished reform agenda.

Alberta's major functional reform initiative was the transferal of responsibility for education from the education committees of county councils to the reorganized school districts. This reform was essential to facilitate the consolidation of the education sector in that province. Alberta also overhauled the land-use and regional planning regime, formally shifting significantly greater responsibility to the municipal level—this was especially the case for smaller authorities that relied heavily on provincial or regional planning administrations to provide expert municipal planning services. The maintenance of secondary highways was briefly transferred to rural municipalities but returned to the province after heavy lobbying. Although Alberta municipalities have always been responsible for completing municipal property assessments, the province withdrew the expert services of its Municipal Assessment Services Division concomitant with reforming the assessment system. Recently, the province adopted a policy by which Regional Health Authorities would assume land ambulance responsibilities, thereby relieving municipalities of an expensive and controversial service requirement. The new ambulance policy resulted from discussions within a Minister of Municipal Affairs' council that negotiates roles, responsibilities, and resources with municipal stakeholders.

In Quebec, functional reforms resulted in changes in the roles and responsibilities between provincial and municipal governments and among various municipal governments and local authorities (Tindal and Tindal, 2004: 183). In an effort to improve policing in municipalities with populations equal to or greater than 50,000, the province mandated that municipalities either contract for policing through the Quebec provincial police or provide policing through MRC-wide intermunicipal policing administrations. The province also required rural MRCs and new cities created through mergers in the major metropolitan regions to assume some responsibility for social housing. Some functional reforms also involved changes in the alignment of responsibilities between municipal governments and municipal authorities. In the Montreal metro area the Communauté métropolitaine de Montréal (CMM) inherited planning and management functions on a metro scale and shares several functions (water and waste management, air quality, transportation, urban and regional planning, economic development, social housing) with the region's MRCs. MRC functions were expanded to include property valuation, management of waterways, and rural parks (in the case of rural MRCs).

Functional reforms were substantially less significant in other jurisdictions. The only notable functional reforms in British Columbia involved the creation of the Greater Vancouver Transportation Authority (now TransLink), which involved shifting important region-wide transportation responsibilities from a provincially appointed authority to one directed by municipal politicians. Saskatchewan's functional reforms were limited to efforts by the provincial government to reduce or curtail its role in providing selected regulatory activity and advisory services. The province abandoned the mandatory certification of municipal administrators, leaving that to the provincial associations, and transferred responsibility for building inspections in rural and small urban communities to municipal governments. In the Northwest Territories the territorial government laid the foundations for new regional authorities to perform certain functions that traditionally have been performed by the territorial or municipal governments.

Despite a desire on the part of provincial, territorial, and municipal governments to achieve various types of functional reforms, ultimately the nature and scope of the reforms that were implemented in various provinces and territories ranged from modest to insignificant in the grand schemes of things. Differences among the various provinces both in the functional reforms that they considered and in those that they implemented were more the product of differences in the political dynamics than differences in the extant alignment of functions. Several provinces and territories, including some examined above, considered but did not implement functional reforms. For example, in New Brunswick, Frank McKenna's Liberal government contemplated functional reform in a 1992 White Paper but nothing came of this or of proposals to download road maintenance to municipalities.

Finally, contrary to conventional thinking, the downloading and uploading had less to do with shifts in which order of government would actually perform various governance, management, and service delivery functions than with their responsibility for financing their respective traditional functions. Generally, any considerations of functional reform were closely and in some instances inextricably linked to considerations of financial reform. That linkage between functions and finances had a dual effect on functional reforms; it both facilitated and served to resist such reforms. The proverbial financial 'bottom line' generally became the top consideration whenever issues of functional realignment were discussed.

Overview of Financial Reform Initiatives

As was the case with structural and functional reforms, provincial and territorial jurisdictions approached financial reforms with different levels of political imagination and resolve (Graham et al., 1998: 202–25; Siegel, 2002; Slack, 2002; Kitchen,

2003; Tindal and Tindal, 2004: 221–56). Moreover, the precise nature and scope of financial reforms considered and implemented varied among jurisdictions. Despite such differences, there was one important commonality—radical reforms of traditional revenue sources and financial responsibilities were neither contemplated nor implemented in any jurisdiction. Thus, the traditional fiscal frameworks for municipal governments remained relatively unchanged. What did change substantially was the amount of municipal revenue garnered from provincial and territorial transfers. The decline was significant in many jurisdictions and, correspondingly, the percentage increase of own-source revenues increased (Treff and Perry, 1998). Whether these changes can be properly labelled reform is a matter for debate, but reductions of transfer payments certainly have changed the relationship between provincial/territorial and municipal governments. The nature and scope of financial reforms can be usefully addressed with attention to the following: reforms of assessment and taxation matters; transfers and cost-sharing programs; and regulations over municipal loans, borrowing, debt, and deficits (Hobson and St-Hilaire, 1997).

Several provinces either reformed their property assessment valuation and administration regimes or at least reviewed them (Tindal and Tindal, 2004: 236–9). The notable system revisions were in Ontario, Saskatchewan, and Alberta, where provincial authorities moved to or sought to improve 'full market value' assessments. Current full market value assessments replaced the dated 'fair market value' assessments in Alberta and Saskatchewan and thereby provided what is generally thought to be a more equitable regime that reflects the true value of old and new properties. The 'fair market value' assessments were neither fully understood by the public nor easily administered. Reassessments sometimes languished for years, largely due to the technical requirements of valuation. These delays in timely reassessments created inequities within municipal jurisdictions but were especially confounding in efforts to define accurate equalized assessments for municipalities across a whole province. Establishing a fair equalized assessment was of special importance to provinces such as Alberta that collected province-wide revenues from local property taxes through a uniform mill rate. Variances in the accuracy of assessed values of similar properties of similar value located in different municipalities made real inequities possible. A related challenge was to establish market value mass assessments that were timely. Ontario's reforms of the late 1990s to its full market value system established two decades earlier were introduced to improve the regularity and frequency of reassessments and to establish a relatively recent standard year from which the assessments would be based (Sancton, 2000c: 150–2). In Ontario and Saskatchewan the reforms to the property assessment regimes were accompanied by the creation of specialized assessment authorities roughly modelled on the long-standing and successful British Columbia Assessment Authority. Moreover, in Alberta and Saskatchewan the assessment appeals machinery was altered to make it more accessible and streamlined.

Although tax reform was studied in a number of provinces and new municipal taxes have been proposed, on balance, the number of new taxes introduced has been limited. Tax-sharing of the provincial component of at-the-pump fuel taxes has been proposed in British Columbia and Nova Scotia and implemented in Alberta. British Columbia has proposed a variety of new municipal taxes in league with its Community Charter legislation, including a resort tax, local entertainment tax, parking stall tax, and hotel room tax. However, although the Community Charter legislation has been enacted, the tax reforms remain on the drawing board. Alberta's Special Tax was introduced to raise revenue to pay for a long list of services including waterworks, sewer, dust treatment, paving, repair and maintenance of roads, ambulance, fire protection, and recreation. Different from the province's local improvement tax that targets capital improvements, this tax permits levies for continuing maintenance and support under specific conditions. The Special Tax also can be levied to pay incentives for health professionals to reside and practise in the municipality. In an apparent effort to diversify sources of municipal revenues, Quebec added development user fees to finance various municipal expenditures that can be allocated to new real estate projects. Saskatchewan introduced the new tool of a minimum tax that municipalities can use to ensure that all properties, including those with a very small market value, pay a fair share of tax to cover the cost of municipal services.

Saskatchewan and Quebec, among others, also made changes to calculations of grants in lieu of taxes. In Quebec's case the revisions to the grants-in-lieu formula were part of an initiative to rectify distortions created by the province's earlier efforts to battle its deficits and debt. Other provinces also were involved in give-and-take financial adjustments. Alberta ceded tax recovery responsibilities to its municipalities and let them keep the funds raised through tax recovery. In the bargain the province sought to protect municipalities against inheriting cleanup costs that had accompanied municipal requisition of properties for tax arrears.

Several provinces altered taxation legislation to permit variable rates within defined zones of a larger municipality. Such innovations were necessary in some provinces—for example, Nova Scotia—that created expansive municipalities that administer urban, suburban, and rural areas. Among other provinces that wrote similar innovations into legislation are Quebec, Saskatchewan, and Alberta. Municipalities in some provinces were also permitted to distinguish between classes of property within their authority and to apply distinctions by class within the aforementioned tax zones—although this was by no means a novel provision in Canadian municipal legislation. Manitoba introduced the American innovation of tax increment financing in its new Winnipeg Charter Act. This scheme establishes a revenue shelter that receives revenues from zone or district growth to pay for infrastructure needs and development expenditures in the zone.

Provinces have traditionally tapped into the local property tax, either directly through their own requisitions or indirectly by permitting other local authorities to requisition from this base. During the turn-of-the-millennium period there were changes to established property tax-sharing practices. Ontario, for example, sought to provide municipalities with greater property tax room by dramatically reducing its use of revenues from this source. Ontario's realignment efforts were tied to ceding approximately half the school requisition of the property tax to municipalities. This manoeuvre provided—or at least appeared to provide—

Ontario municipalities with greater fiscal flexibility. Alberta assumed administration of property taxes requisitioned through municipalities for school purposes in an effort to promote equity in school funding. Although this move caused great consternation among municipalities, the province steadily dropped its levies until a recent fiscal crunch. Quebec completely ceded the property tax to municipalities in the 1980s. However, in 1997 the province moved back into the property tax domain by exacting a provincial deficit levy from municipalities to help alleviate the provincial burden. This levy was eliminated through an agreement between the province and municipalities concluded in 2000 that saw the province introduce a comprehensive package of grants, changes to the tax structure, and other reforms. There was a quid pro quo to all of this, since in exchange for the retiring of the levy municipalities ceded to the province taxes on telecommunications, natural gas, and electricity. Recently, Saskatchewan's provincial levies on health and social assistance have been reduced and a hospital levy on municipalities has been eliminated. As well, in 2003 the provincial government established a task force to review and make recommendations on changes to the system by which municipal governments and school authorities share the property tax base (Saskatchewan, 2004). Pursuant to the recommendations of that task force, the current provincial government remains committed to reduce the pressure felt by municipalities on the property tax, by limiting the level of dependency of education authorities on that tax subject to its fiscal capacity to do so in the future as part of what are being labelled 'new directions for provincial-municipal partnerships' (Saskatchewan, 2004b). Finally, some provinces have changed or revised their policies on tax exemption. Alberta municipalities now have somewhat greater say in such exemptions, and in Saskatchewan such policies have clarified precisely what types of properties are eligible for tax exemptions in both urban and rural areas.

Municipal associations have long called for tax-sharing arrangements with the provincial and territorial governments that would have municipalities acquire access to provincial revenue sources or acquire a defined share of revenue from a specified tax. All the same, during this most recent period there have been no major incursions by municipalities into provincial tax areas. Fuel taxes have been one area in which municipalities have been especially energetic in pressing their case, but little headway has been made. Indeed, while Alberta granted Edmonton and Calgary a share of the provincial fuel tax take, it unexpectedly announced cancellation of the arrangement, but then reversed itself in the face of ferocious lobbying by the mayors of these two cities. Revenue-sharing among municipalities has been implemented in some provinces. Quebec's initiative in the CMM is of special note and may be a unique and significant development. Alberta's provisions for voluntary revenue-sharing are a fairly recent reform in that province but the legislation is not unique since there are precedents in the British Columbia regional district system.

One near-universal trend in municipal finance during this period has been a substantial reduction in the level of financial resources transferred to municipalities through general or targeted grants (Tindal and Tindal, 2004: 225–7). Ontario's reduction of transfers has been 'engineered' in significant respects through its realignment campaign wherein municipalities have seen wholesale reduction in provincial transfers in exchange for new tax room in the property tax. To make good on the 'revenue-neutral' promises of the realignment initiative, Ontario created a new Community Reinvestment Fund that is essentially an unconditional grant program. Nova Scotia also implemented a revenue-neutral scheme of functional reform but that reform does not appear to have increased the tax room available to municipalities within the property tax, and the province continues to take approximately 20 per cent of property taxes. Moreover, municipalities in Nova Scotia have apparently gained slightly by way of transfers in recent years. Elsewhere there has been erosion of general operating or assistance grants, and this has not been engineered within any type of service exchange arrangement. Newfoundland's elaborate general grants scheme was reformed in 1991. The centrepiece of that reform was the Municipal Operating Grant that provided a fiscal foundation for small authority operation. Over the ensuing decade the amount of that grant declined by roughly half. In Saskatchewan municipalities experienced a similar reduction in revenue-sharing and other types of provincial grants during this reform period, with only a slight upward adjustment in the last few years. Alberta phased out its Municipal Assistance Grant (MAG) program—a general unconditional program—in 1998 and replaced it with a more modest semi-unconditional grant program with loosely defined expenditure envelopes for various services such as a police assistance grant and a public transit grant.

As with the general operating and assistance grants, and for essentially the same reasons, the provincial and territorial governments have reduced both the number and types of cost-shared programs and the level of provincial funding for them. Insofar as they have continued to participate in cost-shared programs, the general tendency among provincial and territorial governments has been to move towards more targeted conditional grants for programs and projects that they deem to be essential for communities. A substantial amount of these financial resources have been targeted for infrastructure and environmental programs and projects, especially those with the potential to maximize economic and social development as well as public health and safety. Newfoundland's 1991 restructuring of its municipal finance arrangements included revenue incentives for municipalities to collect more taxes and also provided road grants and water and sewer subsidies. Every province and territory has similar grants. One reason that targeted grants for infrastructure and environmental projects were increased during this period was the substantial amount of federal government funding for such projects made available on a cost-shared basis with provincial, territorial, and municipal governments (Andrew et al., 2002).

Another major trend in the provinces was the shifting of some financial responsibilities between the provincial and municipal governments (Tindal and Tindal, 2004: 182–95). In Ontario, for example, pursuant to 'disentanglement' there were shifts in funding arrangements with municipalities picking up full costs for policing, libraries, and public transit and larger proportions for public health and, effectively, the farm tax rebate; at the same time, the province increased its financial contributions for social assistance (Graham and Phillips, 1998a). In Newfoundland, financial responsibility for programs and services was shifted from the provincial to the municipal level in the areas of assessment, auditing, and planning. The province also established and funded an independent property assessment authority. Such shifts in financial responsibilities between the two levels of government occurred in most, if not all, jurisdictions. One of the most hotly debated issues during the recent reform period was whether the net effect of such transfers was revenue-neutral or entailed downloading or uploading.

Reforms to municipal financial management were also implemented in recent years. At least two provinces reformed the regulations relating to debt and deficits, borrowing, and the making of loans and investments. Under the new 1996 Municipal Act, Manitoba municipalities were permitted to make loans and investments. These innovations reflected the new orientation towards market-oriented municipal governance that suffuses the Manitoba legislation. The object of expanding authority for making loans was to encourage public enterprise and to encourage achieving returns on available municipal funds. Manitoba municipalities were also permitted under the 1996 legislation to form investment pools and, generally, to broaden the scope of where they can invest funds. Similar schemes were introduced in Alberta through the 1994 Municipal Government Act. While Manitoba municipalities remained tied to provincial approvals when creating an operating deficit and borrowing over a set debt limit, they were generally freed through the 1996 legislation to manage their financial affairs. Alberta accorded its municipalities similar free rein through its new legislation and also introduced a regime of debt limits to replace specific borrowing approval that had been administered by its defunct Local Authorities Board.

In summary, provincial governments appear, collectively, to have touched on many facets of financial reform, but none seems to have been truly comprehensive or radical. Proposed and actual reforms were generally intended to give municipalities greater certainty and control over their finances. Ontario appears to have been the boldest financial reformer through its ceding a large provincial share of the property tax while commensurately reducing its funding across a wide range of functional areas. Efforts by Alberta and Saskatchewan to adjust their property assessment regimes are best viewed as initiatives to catch up with the rest of the country. Changes made by Manitoba and Alberta to municipal debt regulation, loaning, and investments can also be viewed as efforts to provide municipalities with greater local control over their financial affairs. Provincial governments granted municipalities few new streams of own-source revenue. Alberta's Special Tax moves beyond standard development user fees of the type that Quebec adopted during this period. Manitoba's new TIF scheme is novel but its utility within the Canadian context is certainly not clear at this time. While British Columbia and other provinces appear to be looking at the establishment of a variety of new taxes, these have not been approved in legislation. With a few exceptions, provinces did not move to share revenue sources; instead, they not only cut back on general operating grants but also reduced program and project cost-sharing arrangements. Admittedly, grants-in-lieu-of-taxes regimes were revised in recent years to the benefit of municipalities in some provinces, but judging from history there is no guarantee such financial arrangements are immutable. Some provinces reformed debt administration and provided greater flexibility to municipalities in investment and loan matters, but in truth these innovations effectively permitted municipalities to work and take risks with their own money. The master strategy of the period is clear: financial reforms have been designed to provide municipalities with greater opportunity to work with their own taxes and revenues. This strategy did little to appease municipalities. The result is that financial concerns dominate at present and the clamour from municipalities for substantive financial reform is still loud (Boothe, 2003).

Overview of Jurisdictional Reform Initiatives

Numerous jurisdictional reform initiatives of varying magnitude and importance were undertaken over the past 15 years. Such initiatives had been on the municipal reform agendas for at least two decades (L'Heureux, 1985). The general trend was towards the enactment of permissive legislation that granted municipal governments greater authority and autonomy to conduct their affairs (Canaran, 1996; Gagnon and Lidstone, 1998; Garcea, 2002b; Lidstone, 2003; Tindal and Tindal, 2004: 197–206). This was coupled with the enhancement of democratic mechanisms to facilitate greater accountability by municipal governments to the local citizenry.

A few provincial governments declared in legislation that municipal government is an 'order of government' that is relatively autonomous within the scope of provincial legislation. British Columbia's Local Government Statutes Amendment Act, 1998 recognized municipalities as an 'independent, responsible and accountable order of government'. The Community Charter legislation expands the scope of that provision a bit further by including language that may resonate before the courts. Nova Scotia's Municipal Act of 1999 similarly recognizes municipalities as a 'responsible order of government' and the same is roughly true for the Cities Act in Saskatchewan, enacted in 2002 and in force since 2003, which declares municipalities as a 'responsible and accountable level of government within their jurisdiction' (Saskatchewan, 2002: 12). Although these declarations introduce new principles, municipalities have not openly celebrated them—largely because they are qualified by other statements in the legislation that render municipalities clearly subordinate to the provincial governments. A notable example of this is found in the Saskatchewan legislation, which declares that municipalities 'being created and empowered by the Province of Saskatchewan' are therefore 'subject to provincial laws and to certain limits and restrictions in the provincial interest as set out in this and other Acts' (Saskatchewan, 2002: 12). That such clauses appear is hardly surprising since the Canadian Constitution empowers the provinces to establish and define the nature of municipal systems within their boundaries. Nonetheless, while declaring municipal government as an order of government may be without true constitutional meaning, the political meaning seems to be one of acknowledging the fundamental importance of municipal governments. Most provincial and territorial governments provided municipalities with greater autonomy, often through more generally defined authority. They did this through innovations that are unique to this reform period—and that represent significant departures from how authority was previously granted. Alberta's Municipal Government Act, 1994 was the harbinger. This legislation defined the purposes of a municipality in legislation, substituted traditional corporate powers with 'natural person' powers, and borrowed the concept of 'spheres of jurisdiction' from federalist theory for the purpose of defining areas in which municipalities would have general freedom to make local laws. The Alberta legislation also provided municipalities with general bylaw-making powers and new powers of prohibition. The bylaw-making powers extended to all spheres of municipal juris-diction and more generally to those functions that were consistent with municipal purposes so long as these did not run afoul of provincial legislation, the Constitution, or common-law jurisprudence. Interestingly, despite all these inno-vative provisions, Alberta's legislation did not explicitly identify municipalities as an order of government. Moreover, Alberta did not provide its municipalities with much in the way of new powers. Innovations under the Alberta approach were designed to make demonstrable general grants of authority and eliminate many of the picayune specifications of corporate powers, bylaw-making powers, municipal service provision, and the like. In the wake of all this, municipalities remained corralled within specific areas of jurisdiction in which they had previously governed even if 'natural person' powers and 'spheres of jurisdiction' gave them considerably more flexibility in how they could conduct their business and relate to other governing entities.

Several provinces have adopted significant elements of the Alberta legislation with or without modification. Ontario was the first province to borrow innovative provisions from the Alberta legislation including the 'natural person' powers, 'spheres of jurisdiction', and general bylaw-making powers (Ontario, 2001). Saskatchewan also borrowed heavily from the Alberta legislation in formulating the Cities Act. In Manitoba the new City of Winnipeg Charter Act also borrows heavily from the Alberta legislation by incorporating the principles of 'natural person' powers and 'spheres of jurisdiction', something Manitoba was loath to do for other municipalities based on the recommendations of its provincially appointed municipal review committee. In British Columbia the Community Charter contains elements that aim to offer better protection to municipalities from court challenges to certain clauses of the Alberta model that its legislative reformers deemed vulnerable. Thus, service powers are distinguished from general bylaw-making powers.

Deliberations in the northern territories on jurisdictional reforms were influ-enced by Alberta's legislation, but Yukon was the only territory to adopt 'natural person' powers. None of the Maritime provinces has adopted 'natural person' powers, preferring instead to expand municipal corporate powers. Nova Scotia's rejection of 'natural person' powers did not stop the province from defining the purposes of a municipality in legislation and legitimating general bylaw-making powers within expanded areas of authority. Through these devices the province moved to expand in some measure the autonomy and local law-making authority of municipalities within its system. The rejection of 'natural person' powers was based on concerns either that they were too unbounded or that their implications for municipal government are uncertain. Similar concerns influenced the provisions on jurisdictional authority contained in Manitoba and Saskatchewan municipal legislation for rural and smaller urban municipalities because the provincial governments were not convinced that many of the small municipalities have either the inclination or the capacity to operate with such powers. In Saskatchewan it remains to be seen what effect such concerns will have on recent initiatives to produce new legislation for rural and small urban municipalities (Saskatchewan, 2004c). Negotiations revolve largely around whether such legislation should embody many of the same principles contained in the new legislation for cities.

During the recent period we have studied here, provincial governments also expanded municipal authority in specific areas, with the particulars often keyed on deficiencies or problems in extant legislation. For example, in jurisdictions such as Manitoba and Nova Scotia, where 'natural person' powers have not been adopted, specific provisions relating to such matters as engaging in partnerships and agreements have been dealt with in new sections of municipal legislation. Similarly, the 2001 amendments to Saskatchewan's urban and rural municipal legislation include provisions regarding specific matters such as street closures, traffic control regulations, and business regulations, thus reflecting an absence of broad grants of power in its general municipal legislation.

Several provincial governments have also provided their municipalities with greater freedom to define internal and external organizational arrangements. In their municipal statutes, provincial governments have previously listed responsibilities and various duties that apply directly to municipal officials. While specifications of duties and responsibilities remain in many jurisdictions, movement towards the chief administrative officer model, a policy-administration dichotomy, and a general reduction in the number of statutory officers defined under legislation has placed local administrations more firmly under the singular authority of municipal councils. The reduction of statutorily defined municipal officials and even the flexibility inherent in defining the CAO role have resulted in municipalities having greater freedom to craft and control their administrative structures. Some provinces, including Manitoba, Alberta, and Nova Scotia, have provided municipalities with greater freedoms to organize their internal governance and management machinery. Under the new City of Winnipeg Charter Act, for example, the city has the option of increasing the number of councillors and has also gained the capacity to abolish community committees. Similarly, Alberta and Nova Scotia statutes allow rural municipalities to determine whether the head of council can be elected at large. Although by no means universally, some provincial governments—Alberta, British Columbia, Manitoba, and Quebec—have also provided municipalities with greater authority over the creation and operation of selected special municipal bodies such as economic development authorities.

At least three other notable measures were designed to increase municipal authority and autonomy during this period. First, some provinces lightened their municipal oversight and regulatory regimes. Second, some provinces—notably British Columbia and Nova Scotia—formally committed themselves to consult with municipalities or their associations on proposed changes to municipal legislation and the realignment of municipal functions. Third, at least one province—British Columbia—made a commitment to limit its authority to alter the structure of the municipal system through forced amalgamations. This is a unique provision without precedent and, at this time, no other province or territory seems to be considering following its example. Such a provision was likely an anathema for many other provinces and territories since it effectively establishes something loosely akin to American 'home rule' status for municipalities. For British Columbia such a provision was consonant with its declaration that municipalities are an order of government that should have substantial autonomy in conducting their affairs.

In an attempt to provide a check on the expanded authority and autonomy of municipal governments, some provinces and territories have strengthened and tightened those elements of provincial and territorial legislation that define the rules of local democratic and accountable governance. Provinces and territories have moved with different levels of enthusiasm to achieve new balances between greater municipal authority and autonomy on one hand and greater municipal democracy and accountability on the other. Thus, a hallmark of this period is a general movement towards both municipal empowerment and citizen empowerment. Although the movement to citizen empowerment is evident, some contributors to this volume have observed that provinces and territores have not done enough in this area. There is certainly evidence to support this contention, but it is also worth noting that reforms have been directed towards an empowered citizenry by enhancing democracy and accountability in the municipal sector. Several provinces have also sought, through a number of devices, to make municipal government more transparent. British Columbia, Alberta, Nova Scotia, and others have required in legislation that councils generally conduct their business in public. Annual reporting requirements and the particulars of these, such as those proposed in the British Columbia's Community Charter, are designed to increase transparency and accountability. Information access and protection of privacy legislation has been extended to municipalities in several provinces, or municipal legislation has been invested with such provisions. Alberta provides an example here, as does Quebec. The new City of Winnipeg Charter Act extends the authority of the provincial Ombudsman to deal with issues emanating from governance, management, and administration of the city. Quebec recently passed legislation to ensure that its newly consolidated cities operate with greater transparency in the management of public funds. Indeed, the province has passed two bills that strengthen the democratic operations of local institutions, increase the level of mandatory public consultation, and make more transparent the granting of professional services contracts. Further, Quebec has introduced referendums on urban planning. Alberta and British Columbia have introduced more generous petition and counter petition features into their legislation and retained or strengthened plebiscite provisions. In these provinces, the public can register a strong and independent voice in policy-making and decision-making through these mechanisms.

Another means by which provincial legislators have sought to impose a greater degree of accountability in the municipal sector has been through statutory and regulatory provisions related to conflict of interest and unauthorized or illegal conduct by elected and appointed officials. Such provisions consist of more exacting conflict of interest rules and the establishment of more severe penalties for unauthorized or illegal conduct. Two notable examples are the code of conduct established under Winnipeg's new charter and Alberta's municipal legislation, which places chief administrative officers under much greater scrutiny and at greater risk if they engage in unauthorized activity or fail to provide adequate corporate supervision. Another notable effort to strengthen accountability within the municipal sector has been municipal election reform in various provinces during the 1990s. Two examples are the statutory provisions that sanctioned the creation of political parties at the municipal level in British Columbia and the regulation of municipal campaign contributions in British Columbia and Nova Scotia.

To enhance accountability and responsiveness at the municipal level, some provinces have sanctioned the creation of community representative committees. Generally, this occurred as part of structural reforms. In such cases several provinces have created sub-municipal representative or administrative authorities, such as the community committees in Nova Scotia, community councils in Toronto, borough committees in Quebec's amalgamated metropolitan cities, and local urban districts in Manitoba. What is significant about these innovations in terms of jurisdictional authority is that they assist in facilitating the prospects for improved oversight and control of municipal government by ratepayers. However, as noted previously, these innovations are somewhat atypical. More such bodies may be required in large municipalities in the future to improve the degree of responsiveness by municipal representatives to their ratepayers and residents.

In summary, the major thrust of jurisdictional reforms has been to enhance the authority and autonomy of municipal governments. The precise scope and value of this autonomy and authority is a matter of debate among governmental stakeholders and academics alike. While some believe that these reforms are significant, others claim them to be minimal because, as noted above, the provisions expanding authority and autonomy are qualified by other provisions either within the legislation or within subsequent regulations. At issue is the burden of these limiting provisions and whether municipalities are truly any freer to govern. Not open to debate, however, is that municipal governments still remain in a subordinate position to provincial and territorial governments. This is even true in those provinces where municipalities either have been declared orders of government or have been granted 'natural person' powers and 'spheres of jurisdiction'.

PRODUCTS OF MUNICIPAL REFORM INITIATIVES: THE OUTCOMES

The central objective in this section is threefold: first, to provide an overview of debates regarding the effects of municipal reforms on each of the three major sets of reform objectives—governance capacity, intergovernmental relations, and municipal-community relations; second, to provide a brief assessment of the overall effect of municipal reforms; and third, to provide some general guidelines for assessing the effects of such reforms.

Some important caveats are in order, however. First, the competing arguments presented here regarding the effects of reforms are necessarily offered in a polarized and an abstracted or 'ideal' form for purposes of exposition. Nevertheless, as revealed by the analyses of reform politics in the provinces and territories contained in this book, as well comparable analyses in other publications, they are by no means wholly abstract or baseless. The second caveat is that the effects of municipal reforms implemented during the period of our study have been and remain largely unclear and unexamined. Most of the assessments that exist, including those in this book, tend to be speculative in the absence of hard data tied to results, and some are polemical.

Several factors contribute to the paucity of definitive and systematic assessments. One major factor is that some of the principal protagonists of reform contests are not strongly supportive of such assessments. After all, contests over reform initiatives are often founded on hard-held views that reflect the values and subjective interests of the contestants. Claims regarding the effects of specific reform proposals are often inflated in the heat of debate. Even in the absence of energetic debate, governments and other policy actors bring the best case forward to press their preferences. These 'best cases' are usually not substantiated by systematic and objective research. Within such circumstances and practices it is hardly surprising that the evaluation stage in the policy cycle is foreshortened or even omitted by those who have been central actors in initiating and implementing a particular policy. Of course, this is especially true when only a short period of time has passed since implementation began. For governments, in particular, prospects that systematic research will reveal flaws in policy assumptions and logic, in the design of reform programs, or in program implementation are sufficient to discourage the sponsorship of such research. Those actively opposing reform initiatives are more likely to support evaluative research, but here, too, there is often less interest in systematic and scientific approaches than in what best can be described as polemical research in which the questions are chosen to support a particular policy preference.

Another major factor contributing to the paucity of definitive and systematic assessments of reforms is the difficulty in conducting such assessments. These difficulties stem from the fact that so many variables could be responsible for any change in conditions; it is very difficult to find proper indicators and measurements of the effects of reforms. A notable example of this is the challenges encountered by those who have undertaken studies regarding the effects of the structural reforms in some of the amalgamations in metropolitan urban centres across the country (O'Brien, 1996; Vojnovic 1997, 1998, 2000b; Poel, 2000; Slack, 2000: 20). These researchers found it difficult to assess the precise extent to which such reform contributed to financial savings or improved resource and asset management practices and the quality or quantity of service delivery. Moreover, the challenges faced in assessing the effects of reforms on efficiency also remind us to be careful in setting unduly high expectations when assessing reforms. None of this is to claim that systematic analysis is impossible or undesirable. Results of the Halifax reform research, for example, offer guidance to policy-makers and academic researchers concerning pre- and post-reform service delivery (McDavid, 2003). Related research on the effects of Nova Scotia's functional reforms also stands out as significant because it reveals unintended consequences of the province's policy initiative.

Effects of Reforms on Governance Capacity
Debates on Effects on Municipal Governance Capacity
The effect of municipal reforms on the governance capacity of municipal governments is debatable. Two basic alternative arguments regarding the effect of municipal reforms on the governance capacity of municipal governments could and have been made. The first is that structural, functional, financial, and jurisdictional reforms either have had or will have a positive effect in bolstering governance capacity. In making such claims, one could point to the structural reforms in metropolitan and non-metropolitan regions as important measures that have increased the governance capacity of municipal governments in such regions (Hutton, 1996). The cases in point, at least for those who have a positive view of the effects of such consolidations, are the new super-municipalities in the metropolitan and non-metropolitan city-regions of Ontario, Quebec, and Nova Scotia. These authorities have much greater scope for formulating and implementing policies and plans over a substantially larger geographic area and a larger population than was the case prior to amalgamation. Arguably, such a change has effectively created super-municipalities with enhanced power to govern the region and, perhaps ironically, to confront more effectively the provincial governments. Similarly, in making the case that municipal governance capacity has been increased one could point to the jurisdictional reforms in various provinces and territories that have provided municipal governments with greater authority and autonomy. There is certainly evidence that, in law, municipalities across the country have been granted greater latitude in policy-making, planning and development, routine business affairs, and the management of financial and human resources. One could argue that this latitude constitutes enhanced municipal capacity to govern effectively, especially among municipal governments who are willing and able to use it strategically for their respective governance purposes.

The second argument is that at most the reforms have had either no effect or at most a very limited effect on the governance capacity of the vast majority of municipal governments. The essence of this argument is that although the structural, financial, functional, and jurisdictional features of municipal governance have been changed, the results are inconsequential, ineffectual, or outright detrimental to enhanced capacity. Those hoping to see transformational change might concede that reforms have had some salutary effects for municipal governance. Yet, on balance they would deny that the reforms significantly altered municipal governance capacity. In their view, reforms have not provided municipalities with the requisite powers or financial and human resources to govern more efficaciously. The root of disappointment is found in the failure to do the following for municipal governments: grant them either constitutional status as an 'order of government'; grant them jurisdictional authority and autonomy that would guarantee an efficacious form of 'home rule'; provide them with suitable and truly elastic revenue instruments; and provide them with clarity and balance in the alignment of their roles and responsibility. The arguments of those whose expectations are less elevated, but who still see reforms as more or less ineffectual, are also grounded in perceptions or evidence that reforms implemented are inadequate and potentially even problematic. For example, while acknowledging that jurisdictional reforms provided greater autonomy in specified spheres of jurisdiction, they also observe that the absence of any new revenue sources largely mooted the autonomy. Similarly, these critics argue that efforts to establish new municipal roles and responsibilities that also aimed at an eventual revenue neutrality in policy outcome between municipalities and the province, as was the case in Ontario, for example, either truncated the intended reform or created new dilemmas for effective governance. Somewhat differently, certain proponents of the ineffectual thesis could point to the voluntary or enabling character of many jurisdictional reform provisions, which leave municipalities to their own devices when seeking to enhance governance capacity. Those who view the preponderance of municipal governments as timid, or politically constrained by their populations to adopt energetic governance reform, lament the lack of compulsion. Finally, those who view reforms as detrimental to governance capacity argue that the new structural arrangements created less easily governable municipalities or, somewhat differently, did little to address the true sources of governance problems. They could also argue, as have many who opposed reforms, that municipal governments were well run and possessed sufficient powers to serve their populations even prior to the reforms. Reforms introduced new challenges to these happy arrangements, including greater bureaucracy, less clear lines of responsibility, and greater risk to the municipal corporation.

Effects of Reforms on Provincial/Territorial Governance Capacity
The effect of municipal reforms on the governance capacity of provincial and territorial governments is also debatable. This debate can be abstracted in two basic alternative arguments. The first argument is that the municipal reforms had a substantial effect on the overall governance capacity of provincial and territorial governments. In making such an argument one could point to cases where there has been a realignment of functions and finances and argue that these reforms have contributed substantially to reducing both the functional load and the financial responsibilities of provincial and territorial governments and that this, in turn, has contributed substantially to enhancing provincial and territorial governance capacity. In making this case one could also point to provinces and territories where reductions in financial transfers to municipalities along with any downloading of functional and financial responsibilities provided provincial and

territorial governments with additional financial resources that contributed to their ability not only to alter some of their program funding priorities but also to manage their deficits and debts.

The second argument is that the municipal reforms in themselves did not have a substantial effect on the overall governance capacity of provincial and territorial governments either to perform their governance functions or to finance them. Here, one could point to cases where there has been little or no realignment of functions between the two levels of government and therefore no prospect for enhancing governance capacity from such reform. Similarly, one could point to cases where the reduction of financial transfers or the downloading of financial responsibilities to municipal governments has been relatively minimal. Somewhat differently, but still within the same line of argument, one might also claim that reduced transfers are directly responsible for growth of the so-called infrastructure deficit, which over the long run will result in no saving at all for provincial and territorial governments. Indeed, in the future it could end up costing them more to upgrade infrastructure that has been under-serviced or neglected for a long time due to financial pressures at the municipal level. This, in fact, has been the situation in many American municipalities in the recent decades and has been happening with a greater degree of frequency in many Canadian municipalities in recent years.

Effects on Intergovernmental Relations

The effect of municipal reforms on intergovernmental relations not only between municipal governments and their respective provincial and territorial governments but also among municipal governments is also debatable. The debates revolve around whether various types of reform initiatives have produced a more positive or more negative climate in intergovernmental relations, or, alternatively, have had no significant impact.

Municipal-Provincial/Territorial Relations

In the case of the relations between the municipal governments and their respective provincial and territorial governments, the contending arguments regarding the effects of reforms are as follows. The first is that some of the reforms have had a relatively positive effect. According to this argument the various reforms, but particularly the functional and jurisdictional reforms, have eliminated or at least reduced some of the major irritants between municipal governments and their respective provincial and territorial governments. In making such an argument one could posit that although the various levels of government are still not entirely satisfied with the current arrangements, at least in some jurisdictions greater clarity and balance exist now than had been the case prior to the reforms. Both the alignment of functional roles and responsibilities and the degree of authority and autonomy that many municipal governments enjoy vis-à-vis their respective provincial and territorial governments have been enhanced. One could also claim that in some jurisdictions, but by no means all, there has been a positive dividend from the special efforts that senior-level governments have made during the reform period to consult and to negotiate with municipalities on various reform matters. Finally, one could suggest that improvements in such intergovernmental relations are particularly evident in jurisdictions in which substantial reforms have been not only adopted but, more importantly, implemented in a relatively efficacious manner.

The second and contending argument is that the reforms have not had a substantial positive effect on relations between municipal governments and their respective provincial and territorial governments. Two sets of interrelated developments are relevant here: the residual or lingering effects of the major and minor conflicts that were triggered by certain types of reforms in various jurisdictions; and the continuing frustration felt not only by municipal governments in most jurisdictions, but to some extent also by provincial and territorial governments that the reforms have not yet produced the appropriate realignment of structures, functions, finances, and jurisdictional authority. One could also point to provinces and territories where the dynamic of intergovernmental relations was adversely affected by reforms; indeed, all governments had to make a concerted effort to improve such relations in the aftermath of controversial reform initiatives.

Effects on Inter-Municipal Relations

The debate regarding the effects of reforms on the dynamics and climate of relations among municipal governments also revolves around two arguments. The first argument is that reforms have had some positive effects on such relations—the effects of two key reform initiatives point to this conclusion: (1) municipal amalgamations in some regions eliminated some of the inter-municipal conflicts that existed prior to amalgamation (Blais, 1994; Coffey, 1994b; Gertler, 1996); (2) some provisions in the statutory and funding frameworks of various municipalities that in the past had been obstacles to inter-municipal collaboration have been eliminated, and in other instances provisions have been added to facilitate such collaboration.

The second argument—that the reforms have not had a notable positive effect—rests on the clearly demonstrable persistence of long-standing conflicts and resistance to collaboration and co-ordination among neighbouring municipal governments, notwithstanding any structural, functional, financial, or jurisdictional reforms implemented in recent years. That some of these conflicts have been institutionalized and internalized, creating very different and perhaps very difficult new political relationships within the newly constituted municipalities, is a key ancillary point to this argument. From this perspective one could also argue that although amalgamations may have resulted in reduced inter-municipal conflict, they have increased inter-community conflict among the constituent parts of amalgamated municipalities based on, among other things, real or perceived differences in service and taxation levels.

Effects on Municipal-Community Relations

The effect of municipal reforms on municipal-community relations is also debatable (Cooper, 1996). At issue are both the responsiveness of municipal governments to community preferences and the level of transparency and accountability on the part of municipal governments to ratepayers (Graham et al., 1998: 93–147; Tindal and Tindal, 2004: 369–73). Here, too, there are at least two basic arguments. Some would claim that reforms had a positive effect on such relations in at least some provinces or territories, especially those in which this was a central objective of the reform initiatives. In making such an argument one could point to reforms in some jurisdictions that were designed to increase municipal government responsiveness to the preferences of ratepayers through, among other things, greater use of plebiscites and referendums. One could also point to statutory provisions mandating municipal governments to increase the level of openness to their deliberations and accessibility to their documents as a means to improve transparency and accountability.

The opposing argument is that reforms have not had a tangible effect on such matters. In many jurisdictions the legislative scope of provisions to improve municipal-community relations are not substantial, nor are these provisions applied in a significant manner on the ground. In other words, what has been done has not increased significantly the responsiveness of municipal governments to community preferences or calls from the public for greater transparency and accountability. Consequently, notwithstanding the nature or scope of various reforms, little has changed in practice in terms of municipal-community relations.

In summary, the objective to this point has been to provide an overview of the actual and potential arguments related to several debates regarding the effects of municipal reforms on the three central objectives of reform—improved governance capacity of the municipal and provincial/territorial governments; improved intergovernmental relations; and improved municipal-community relations. In what follows we offer some reflections both on the overall effects of those reforms and on their relative importance as compared to other factors that may have affected governance capacity, intergovernmental relations, and municipal-community relations.

As we have seen, equally plausible arguments exist or can be made that the reforms have or have not had some positive or negative effects on the three sets of reform objectives. Municipal reforms, like policy changes at other levels of government, tend to have a Janus-like quality in that every substantive shift in policy at once solves some problems and creates new ones. The argument that cannot be made is that any of the reforms, either individually or collectively, has had a transformational effect on any of those three sets of objectives or on governance generally, either at the local level or at the provincial/territorial level. Regardless where one stands on any of the arguments regarding the effects of reform, the reality is that the structural, functional, financial, and jurisdictional configurations of municipal governments have not been changed in a fundamental manner. The same is true of the governance capacity of municipal and provincial/territorial governments, intergovernmental relations, and municipal-community relations. This is not to suggest that reforms have not produced some interesting and important changes that have had an impact on one or more of the aforementioned matters, but, for better or worse, the changes do not amount to the transformation or reinvention of municipal governance that some governmental stakeholders proposed and others opposed. This is precisely what has been suggested in one of the leading textbooks on municipal governance in Canada regarding the effect of reforms on the relations between municipal governments and their respective provincial and territorial governments. The authors of that book assert that the basic form of such relationships is not substantially different today than it was prior to this latest round of reforms. They maintain that the fundamental nature of the 'superior-subordinate' relationship between municipal governments and their respective provincial or territorial governments is still essentially unchanged (Tindal and Tindal, 2004: 203–5, 371).

Despite where one stands on any debates profiled above or on the question of whether the overall effect of municipal reforms during the turn-of-the-millennium period was either marginal or transformational, we encourage analysts and practitioners alike to produce more assessments of these reforms. Systematic analyses of the effects of reforms should keep at least three important points in mind. First, definitive assessment of the effects of reforms is very difficult, largely due to methodological problems stemming from the multiplicity of factors, other than municipal reforms per se, that might account for any real or perceived effects. Second, any assessment of the effects of reforms will have more to do with perceptions of the principal stakeholders of such matters as opposed to purely objective data (Poel, 2000). The aphorism that 'perception is reality' has some relevance in this matter because few of the effects of reforms are easily measurable or quantifiable. Third, as we noted earlier, it has not been long since some of the reforms were implemented; therefore, it may be premature to attempt a definitive assessment of their impacts because some time may have to pass for these to be manifested. Even at that point, however, one is likely to encounter the challenges of measuring or quantifying impacts. Such challenges require analysts to exercise a modicum of modesty in evaluating the precise nature of the causal chain and the effect of any particular municipal reform initiative.

THE POLITICS OF THE MUNICIPAL REFORMS

The objective in this section is to provide an overview of the nature and determinants of two facets of the politics of municipal reforms: the configuration of key governmental and non-governmental political actors involved in the deliberations regarding municipal reform agendas and initiatives, and the patterns of political interaction among them.

Configuration of Political Actors

The key political actors involved in municipal reforms were elected and appointed officials of the provincial, territorial, and municipal governments. Indeed, a major characteristic of recent municipal reform politics has been its intergovernmental nature—between provincial/territorial politicians and officials and their municipal counterparts, and between the officials of various types of municipalities. The political dynamics between such governmental actors were a central feature of the political machinations of municipal reform.

Non-governmental actors tended to become involved in the politics of munici-pal reform largely at the invitation or instigation of the various levels of govern-ment, and generally they had ample opportunity to do so. Such invitations and instigations were often tactical, as each order of government in various jurisdic-tions encouraged non-governmental actors to support its preferred vision for and approaches to municipal reform. Community groups and individual ratepayers tended to be reactive rather than proactive in their efforts to shape the reform agendas and initiatives of provincial, territorial, and municipal governments. Moreover, ratepayers tended to react much more strongly to some facets of the reform agenda than to others. The strongest reactions were generated by struc-tural reform initiatives that entailed the amalgamation of municipalities and financial reform initiatives that ratepayers feared would likely result in tax increases or user fees. The strong reactions on such reform matters can be attrib-uted to the fact that ratepayers, individually and collectively, were able to discern that they and their communities would likely experience some negative impacts, either in the pocketbook or affectively (e.g., someone born and raised in the same locale does not want to be told that by the stroke of a legislative pen his or her community no longer exists). Generally, functional and jurisdictional reforms did not engender the same degree of interest and involvement among residents, largely because their direct impact on the citizenry, if any, is not so easily discerned. A notable exception to this general observation was evident in Ontario's debate over which order of government should be responsible for funding and delivering social services. Even in that case, however, ratepayers tended to follow and side with, rather than lead, either the provincial or municipal governments on such reform initiatives.

Participation by municipal associations in shaping reform agendas and in developing and implementing reform initiatives generally also occurred in response to initiatives by the provincial and territorial governments. The extent and character of their participation differed depending on factors such as their views of the proposals, the character of provincial or territorial engagement, and the existing character of politics between municipal governments and their respective senior governments. Provincial and territorial governments could and did radicalize municipal associations either by failing to engage them in the reform dialogue or by tendering proposals that were repugnant either to all or at least to a segment of a municipal association's membership. Divided associations often had a difficult time participating in reform discourse and a seemingly common result was for a small group of the affected members to organize their own dialogue with provincial officials. Such differences tended to occur between different types of member municipalities, as either large or small municipalities felt that they had different problems and reform agendas, which were best addressed independently from those of other types of municipalities.

Business and trade associations were not conspicuous participants in municipal reform debates. Nevertheless, business persons and their representative organiza-tions were by no means absent from reform discourse. Their preferences on reforms were communicated to governments and the public either through formal consultation channels in the form of briefs to task forces and commissions, or through informal channels created by their political connections.

One of the most surprising aspects of the politics of municipal reform is that generally it was not politically partisan in nature. Indeed, amalgamation of municipalities was, for the most part, the only major issue on which some degree of partisan posturing by the competing political parties was evident. Given the substantial opposition to amalgamation whenever it was contemplated or implemented, opposition parties tended to side with those who opposed it. In siding with them they criticized either the government's stated and unstated reasons for pursuing amalgamation or the processes of amalgamation. This was certainly true in Ontario, Quebec, the Atlantic provinces, and Saskatchewan where they echoed the views of municipal officials and ratepayers in criticizing proposed and actual amalgamation initiatives. In doing so their basic strategy was to advocate the need to provide more opportunities for public consultations, which they believed were important means to facilitate the expression of local preference in framing, implementing, and even reversing such reforms. Undoubtedly, they adopted this stance because they recognized that it would likely maximize potential electoral benefits and minimize potential electoral risks for them. In this regard, it is noteworthy that there was no clear correlation between the partisan affiliation of governments and opposition parties and their preferences or positions on any of the municipal reforms that have been analyzed in this book. To cite the most obvious examples, while the Alberta and Ontario right-wing provincial governments of Ralph Klein and Mike Harris borrowed heavily from one another in their 'revolutions', and while Ontario adopted Alberta-styled municipal legislation, the provinces adopted nearly opposite approaches on matters of structural and functional reform. Clearly, factors other than political partisanship or ideology shaped the reform agendas and initiatives of provincial and territorial governments during the period we have studied.

Patterns of Political Interaction
The municipal reform initiatives of recent years produced interesting and important patterns of political interaction, particularly among the major governmental stakeholders. Those political interactions were marked by patterns of collaboration and confrontation in the relations between municipalities and their respective provincial and territorial governments (Gibbins, 2001; Berdahl, 2002).

Patterns of Interaction in Provincial/Territorial-Municipal Relations
In the case of provincial-municipal and territorial-municipal relations, collaboration appeared easiest when governments framed broad directions and principles for municipal reform, but particularly directions and principles designed to enhance the powers and resources of municipal governments. Confrontation in such relations was frequently witnessed in negotiations regarding two sets of matters: first, specific *substantive matters* regarding the precise nature and scope of reforms to certain facets of the municipal system; and second, *procedural matters* concerning the means for developing and implementing reform initiatives.

Conflict or confrontation between municipal governments and their respective provincial and territorial governments tended to be fiercest in negotiations regarding some types of structural, functional, and financial reform initiatives. The negotiations for jurisdictional reforms tended to be protracted but generally they did not engender the same degree of passion and confrontation as those other three types of reform initiatives. In all cases, however, the nature and scope of the confrontation was closely correlated with the nature and scope of the reform initiative, and more specifically with perceptions regarding the nature and scope of its effects on municipal governments, on communities, and on individuals.

To reiterate, by far the most intense and most highly publicized confrontations between provincial and municipal governments revolved around structural reforms. Such confrontations were quite evident in several provinces in which the amalgamation of municipalities was placed at the top of the reform agenda. This included not only provinces where amalgamations were initiated and ultimately implemented by provincial governments, such as Ontario, Quebec, Nova Scotia, New Brunswick, and Prince Edward Island, but also provinces where proposals for amalgamations were advanced but ultimately never implemented because the provincial governments succumbed to political pressures not to do so, as was the case in Saskatchewan and Newfoundland. Generally, the political battles on amalgamation between the provincial and municipal governments were fought within the political arena. Rarely did the protagonists take their battles into the judicial arena. Two notable cases in which they did so were the Toronto and Montreal amalgamations—the authority of the provincial governments to effect amalgamation, or at least to do so in certain ways, was challenged. In both cases the courts confirmed that the provincial governments had the authority to restructure the municipalities and amalgamation proceeded as planned.

Patterns of Interaction in Inter-municipal Relations
Inter-municipal politics also manifested similar patterns of collaboration and confrontation along the same dimensions of the municipal reform agenda. Collaboration among municipal officials and associations tended to be most pronounced on matters related to the broad principles and general directions of the reform agenda discussed above. Municipal officials and associations tended to collaborate, or at least coalesce, around the following type of matters: the desirability of enhancing their status, their financial resources, and their authority and autonomy vis-à-vis their provincial and territorial governments; the appropriate alignment of functions and finances; and voluntary restructuring. Confrontation vis-à-vis each other was rare among municipal governments when dealing with major reforms to the municipal system.

Municipal officials and their municipal associations as a rule tried to avoid conflicts among themselves when facing the provincial and territorial governments lest their positions be significantly weakened. Nonetheless, confrontations did occur from time to time since on some major matters there were substantial and fundamental differences among members of the municipal sector. Such differences were evident in conjunction with all four pillars of reform—structural, functional, financial, and jurisdictional. In the case of structural reforms, such differences were quite evident whenever models and means of restructuring the municipal system were being considered. Whereas some municipalities tended to favour some restructuring either on a limited or on a larger scale, others were consistently opposed to any restructuring on any scale. Self-interest played an important role in their respective positions. Large central urban and metropolitan municipalities tended to favour consolidation of smaller neighbouring municipalities because they believed fragmented urban systems create impediments to effective planning, development, service delivery, and equitable financial arrangements. Certainly, this was the argument advanced by mayors of central cities such as Toronto, Montreal, Halifax, Ottawa, and Hamilton on proposals for amalgamation in their locales. Suburban mayors and many of their citizens tended to offer vigorous opposition to amalgamation for a variety of reasons. One reason was the loss of community identity and local political voice. Those in smaller communities were concerned that consolidation with other larger neighbouring municipalities would compromise the sensitivity and responsiveness of elected and appointed officials to their preferences and needs. A second set of concerns focused on potential adverse effects of reforms on taxation and services. A shared concern of many ratepayers, regardless of where they lived, was that amalgamated municipalities would result in increased municipal taxes and decreased efficiency and effectiveness in service delivery.

The central cities of metropolitan regions were not the only types of municipalities that favoured some form of amalgamation. Periodically, the very same suburban municipal governments that opposed the consolidation of their municipality into a larger regional municipality favoured amalgamation of smaller neighbouring municipalities for at least some of the same reasons cited by the large metropolitan municipalites. This phenomenon was clearly evident in the controversial debates on amalgamation in Saskatchewan during 1999–2000. Although urban municipal governments in that province by and large opposed their own amalgamation with other municipalities, they favoured the amalgamation of other urban municipalities and rural municipalities. Similarly, although the vast majority of rural municipal governments in Saskatchewan opposed the amalgamation of any rural municipalities, many of them favoured the amalgamation of smaller urban municipalities into rural municipalities.

Similar differences in the positions of municipal governments were also evident in conjunction with the merits of the models of functional, financial, and jurisdictional reforms and the means for developing and implementing them. Once again, differences were more pronounced among the different types and sizes of municipalities than among those of the same type and size. In the case of functional reforms, for example, larger municipal governments were more willing than their smaller counterparts to consider reform initiatives that required them to assume management and financial responsibility for certain types of regulatory and service functions. This included some important and costly functions such as policing, building inspections, social housing, and various types of community services. The major factor accounting for those differences was the differential financial and human resources capacity of municipal governments. Unlike their larger counterparts, smaller municipalities often did not have the requisite financial and human resources to perform such functions. Consequently, they were much more concerned than their larger counterparts about any functional shifts that could potentially add even a small financial burden. For their part, many larger municipalities recognized the elaborate linkages between the wide range of necessary services and regulatory regimes that existed in urban areas and desired responsibility and resources to effect the links. A less determinate, but significant, factor was the limited view that prevailed among a substantial number of small municipal corporations and their ratepayers concerning the proper purpose and functions of government. Just as there is a local political regime that promotes territorial expansion and tighter integration within the global economy, there is a local political regime that promotes retention of existing territorial boundaries and existing economic arrangements relatively insulated from what is happening at the global level.

Some differences among larger and smaller municipalities were also evident in the case of financial reform initiatives. Notwithstanding their shared preference for increased financial resources to help them deal with the financial pressures they faced, they differed on one important matter. Larger municipalities were more willing than the smaller ones to accept lower provincial financial transfers in exchange for a higher degree of authority and autonomy to generate their own revenues. This was particularly true in cases where the provincial and territorial transfers to larger municipalities were so small and so conditional in nature that they did more to distort their priorities than to fund them at an appropriate level. Generally, the largest metropolitan urban centres that were experiencing substantial positive economic growth were the least interested in provincial transfers. The language of the 'new economy'—and the supposed significance of large urban metropolitan centres in this economy—generally led larger municipalities to argue for statutory reforms to maximize their jurisdictional authority and autonomy in dealing with taxation and financial management matters, rather than for reforms to increase their dependence on provincial transfers, with or without conditions attached, as had been the case in previous decades (Edmonton, 2003). Of course, some of those larger municipalities tended to demand expanded powers from provincial governments, and having acquired such powers they then quickly turned their attention to new financial resources, as did the big city mayors in recent years (Winnipeg, 2004a). A notable example of this tendency is Winnipeg's pursuit of a financial 'New Deal' after having obtained its new city charter (Winnipeg, 2004b).

Differences between larger and smaller municipalities were also evident in the case of jurisdictional reform initiatives. Larger municipalities seemed much more interested in increased jurisdictional authority and autonomy than smaller municipalities. The desire of the larger municipalities for expanded authority and autonomy was perhaps most evident in the new City of Toronto, which wanted to establish a charter granting the city unique and substantially greater powers than other Ontario municipalities, and in the enactment of the Cities Act in

Saskatchewan. Although smaller municipalities were often heard in the chorus echoing the calls of the larger municipalities for more powers and autonomy, generally they were not as anxious as the much larger municipalities to see such reforms. Smaller municipalities tended to worry that too much jurisdictional authority and autonomy would create governance capacity problems for them. The behaviour of small Alberta municipalities suggests that smaller municipalities tended to be concerned when they received broader powers for fear of their exposure to increased responsibility and risk.

The foregoing differences among various types of municipalities suggest that Miles's law—'where you stand depends on where you sit'—was in full swing during the turn-of-the-millennium period of municipal reform. Both the perceptions of problems and the preferences of all actors were heavily influenced by their position within the polity. The important point to remember regarding Miles's law as it applies to the municipal sector is that neither provincial and territorial governments nor municipal governments stood and sat in one place all the time. The multiplicity of issues and the various combinations and permutations that emerged at different times led governments to stand and sit variously depending on the issue. Thus, although there were some discernible and predictable tendencies and patterns in their perceptions and behaviour, these were by no means constant. All of this was clearly evident in the dynamics surrounding municipal reforms in various jurisdictions as—notwithstanding some consistency among provincial/territorial and municipal representatives on some facets of the reform agenda—their position on other facets of that reform agenda varied, even if only slightly over time depending on their calculations regarding how a particular issue affected the public interest, but also their organizational and political interests.

THE PROCESSES OF MUNICIPAL REFORM

Some broad generalizations can now be made regarding the nature of policy-making and decision-making processes used in various jurisdictions in recent years to address various municipal reform issues. More specifically, we need to consider the modes and mechanisms used for initiating, formulating, and implementing municipal reforms (Higgins, 1986). Generalizations regarding the modes of municipal reform focus on two critical matters: the nature of interaction among governmental actors and the nature of public consultations (Saskatchewan, 2000: 163–210). Generalizations regarding the mechanisms of municipal reform focus on the major types of organizational instruments used for facilitating both intergovernmental consultations and negotiations and public consultations.

Modes of Municipal Reforms
Intergovernmental Interaction
Most, if not all, of the processes used in initiating, formulating, and implementing municipal reforms were largely intergovernmental rather than purely intragovernmental in nature. They entailed various types and degrees of interaction between representatives of provincial or territorial governments and representatives of

their respective municipal governments. Generally neither provincial and territorial governments nor municipal governments acted alone in such matters; instead, they acted either in concert with or in reaction to each other. The interactions between them involved extensive consultations and negotiations. All levels of government favoured consultation and negotiation to develop and implement reform initiatives. However, in many instances when they were unable to achieve agreement with their municipal counterparts, the provincial and territorial governments were quite prepared to terminate consultations and negotiations and implement reforms by fiat. Notable examples of reforms in which the 'fiat mode' was used to formulate and ultimately to implement municipal reforms were the structural reforms in Ontario, Quebec, Nova Scotia, PEI, and Newfoundland, functional reforms in provinces such as Ontario and Alberta, and some financial reforms such as those to the property assessment systems in Saskatchewan and Alberta and the transfer of responsibility for setting the education tax mill rate in Alberta from educational authorities to the provincial government.

The extent to which municipal governments were afforded an opportunity to choose municipal reforms, rather than having them imposed by the provincial or territorial governments, is a matter of continuing debate. This issue was most pronounced in conjunction with structural reforms in various provinces (Graham and Phillips, 1997; Graham et al., 1998: 65–91; Tindal and Tindal, 2004: 85–178). Generally, the voluntary approach was heavily favoured by municipal governments across the country, but voluntarism was rarely used to achieve any significant structural reforms. Two cases in which provisions for voluntary amalgamation were included in provincial legislation, but which have not yielded any substantial results to date, are Saskatchewan and Manitoba. The recent growth in the number of regional services commissions in Alberta provides evidence of the successful use of the voluntary approach, albeit this is a special case in which each member municipality retains its corporate existence. One of the reputed virtues of British Columbia's regional districts is their ability to frame voluntary compacts for collaborative service provision under the aegis of the district authority. These examples suggest that the voluntary approach may work better for certain types of governance entities than for others. More specifically, it may be more conducive for the creation of regional special-purpose bodies that perform a limited single function than for the creation of entities that perform multiple functions or of one-tier and two-tier regional municipalities per se.

Public Consultations

Regardless of what sort of intergovernmental interaction was involved in initiating, formulating, and implementing municipal reforms, generally they also entailed some form of public consultation. Such consultations occurred in every jurisdiction on most major reform issues. Indeed, one of the striking features of the various municipal reform initiatives across Canada is that in most cases they entailed a substantial amount of public consultation either prior to or after the formulation of reform proposals. Contemporary Canadian political culture places a high value on public consultation (Graham and Phillips, 1998a). Various levels of government were well aware of this and were therefore quite prepared to include public consultation in formulating and implementing reform. This is even true in cases where governments either witnessed or anticipated strong opposition to reform initiatives. Provincial, territorial, and municipal governments alike seemed more willing to hear their critics say they were wrong than they were to circumvent the democratic rights of electors to be consulted on key public policy matters. Thus, the only real choice that provincial and territorial governments had was in how proactive they were prepared to be in publicizing and facilitating opportunities for individuals and groups to register their views on any particular reform initiative (Graham et al., 1998: 125–47; Tindal and Tindal, 2004: 331–40).

Such consultations used similar mechanisms and means to facilitate public input. The mechanisms included special committees or task forces with a mandate to conduct such public consultations. In the case of such consultations, members of the public were invited to make their views known not only to members of these committees and task forces through written submissions or at public hearings but also to members of the government, and especially the ministers responsible for municipal affairs.

Although there were substantial similarities in the public consultation processes, some differences did exist in three key areas. First, the magnitude of the efforts and resources expended by governments, committees, and task forces on public consultations varied considerably. Whereas in some cases the time, effort, and resources were substantial, in other cases they were minimal. Usually, extensive public consultations occurred when task forces were established for that specific purpose. In the absence of such task forces, opportunities for public consultation were often more limited, even in cases where provincial or territorial governments issued policy papers or draft legislation for that purpose.

Second, the magnitude of the public involvement in such consultations varied. In some instances public involvement was massive; in other cases it was minimal. Public involvement was highest whenever municipal restructuring or taxation was at issue. This was clearly evident in provinces such as Ontario, Quebec, Nova Scotia, PEI, Newfoundland, and Saskatchewan, where restructuring and/or municipal taxation issues were prominent on the municipal reform agenda.

Third, differences were also evident in the effect that such consultations had on the decisions taken by governmental officials. In some cases the effect of such consultations on the decisions taken by governmental officials to advance, modify, or terminate an initiative or a particular proposal was substantial; in other cases it was minimal or insignificant. Notable examples of public consultations that had a significant effect on governmental decisions regarding municipal reforms were the consultations undertaken in Newfoundland and Saskatchewan related to restructuring. In both cases the opposition to restructuring, which was mobilized largely by municipal officials, led the provincial governments not to proceed with restructuring that had been recommended by provincially appointed task forces (Tindal and Tindal, 2004: 97, 139–40).

Mechanisms of Municipal Reform

Most, if not all, provinces and territories that undertook a major municipal reform initiative established at least one committee or task force. The basic purpose of these was twofold: (1) to review various facets of the municipal system and make recommendations on the need for and nature of reforms; and (2) to conduct consultations on such matters with governmental and non-governmental stakeholders and the general public. Most committees and task forces were established to assist in the formulation of reform proposals prior to undertaking any reforms. A notable exception to this occurred in Ontario, where provincially appointed restructuring commissioners were appointed to facilitate, mediate, or arbitrate the amalgamation of municipalities in some regions of the province after the provincial government had already made a decision that such amalgamation should occur. Indeed, the appointment of such commissioners was used as a means to remind municipalities that amalgamation would take place; the only choice they had was between voluntary, mediated, or mandated amalgamation (ibid., 114–15).

Generally, such committees and task forces were created by the provincial and territorial governments. Only on a few occasions were they established by municipal associations. Notable examples of the latter were three task forces established by the Saskatchewan Association of Urban Municipalities. This included the Task Force on Governance and Urban Renewal created in the mid-1990s, comprised of members of its executive and staff, which produced a report containing some general directions and principles for municipal reform (SUMA, 1995), the city mayors' caucus, which was instrumental in producing the draft legislation that became the Cities Act (Saskatchewan, 2002), and the towns and villages caucus established to frame a statutory framework for such municipalities (SUMA, 2004a, 2004b).

The preferred mechanisms for performing the aforementioned functions in the municipal reform processes were autonomous special committees and task forces with varying degrees of affiliation to various governmental stakeholders, rather than provincial and territorial legislative committees. Much less common were committees and task forces that included one or two provincial legislators among a group of members who were not elected members of the legislature. A notable example of the last arrangement was the Alberta committee that reviewed and made recommendations on that province's statutory framework. Similarly, Saskatchewan's Task Force on Inter-Community Cooperation and the Quality of Life (Saskatchewan, 1993) included among its members the provincial minister responsible for municipal affairs. One plausible explanation for the reluctance to use legislative committees to explore and initiate municipal reform is that governing and opposition parties were often reluctant to use such committees for this purpose. Instead, they tended to leave their own committees free to deal with the legislative and regulatory instruments that any reform process might produce. Another plausible explanation is that representatives of the governing and opposition parties, as well as representatives of municipalities and municipal associations, were concerned that the use of legislative committees would increase the likelihood that such processes would be subjected to partisan politics. Presumably this could compromise the ability to achieve a political consensus on a coherent municipal reform plan. Whatever the reasons, the municipal reform initiatives of recent years suggest that special committees and task forces are in vogue for public consultations involving controversial and potentially controversial issues, and legislative committees are not.

This raises some important issues regarding the extent to which legislative committees should be used for purposes of municipal reform. Among other things, it may be worthwhile to consider whether legislative committees should be used more extensively than they have during the recent reform era either to conduct reviews and make recommendations based on their own analyses, or at least both to review and to make recommendations on any reports produced by various task forces and committees that do not involve legislators.

The Future of Municipal Reform in Canada

Will any significant reforms be implemented in the future, and, if so, what will be their nature and scope? Will the nature and scope of the reform agendas of the near future be similar to or different from what we have seen in the recent past? Before addressing those questions a caveat is in order. The nature and scope of both the reform agendas and reform initiatives in the future, as in the past, will be highly contingent on the dynamic interaction of several factors: the real or perceived challenges or crises facing the various levels of government; the interests, preferences, and bargaining capacities of the various governments involved; the interests and political influence of societal interests; and the prevailing public philosophies regarding the appropriate purposes and modes of governance.

The Prospect of Future Reform

The prospect of more municipal reforms in the near future is relatively good. This is so despite the fact that at this time most provinces and territories and their municipalities seem to be taking a respite from the flurry of reform initiatives undertaken during approximately the past 15 years. Politicians, administrators, organized interests, and the concerned public all seem to be feeling the effects of 'reform fatigue'. Such fatigue is the result of the fact that several reform initiatives were quite contentious and required the principal actors to expend considerable time, energy, and political and financial resources. Even when not contentious, there are semi-elastic limits to the amount of municipal reform that can be pursued since it must compete with other matters on policy agendas of provincial and municipal governments. Thus, in part, the likelihood of municipal reforms in the near future is contingent on the overall nature and scope of the reform agendas of the various levels of government.

We can expect further reforms for at least four closely related reasons. First, in most if not all provinces and territories there is what might be termed an 'unfinished reform agenda' because some contemplated or proposed reforms were not implemented. Second, it is fair to assume that reassessment by provincial, territorial, and municipal governments to some of the structural, functional, financial, and jurisdictional reforms implemented during the past 15 years will lead to some changes, either small or significant. Third, in some jurisdictions there will be calls for the implementation of reforms comparable to those implemented either for the same types of municipalities in other jurisdictions or for other types of municipalities within the same jurisdiction. This is especially true of any reforms that municipalities believe will place them on more equal footing with other municipalities within their respective provinces and territories or within any other jurisdiction in the rest of the country. Arguments by municipal governments for comparability and parity are relatively easy to make and relatively difficult to reject. Finally, major new governmental initiatives affecting municipalities introduced by any level of government in Canada will require response.

The most significant of such governmental initiatives at this juncture is the renewed effort by the federal Liberal government in recent years to deal with infrastructure and development issues that impinge on the municipal sector. For that purpose it has been seeking to build more direct policy, program, and financial linkages with municipalities (Gibbins, 2001; Berdahl, 2002; Seidle, 2002; Plunkett, 2004). This initiative began with Prime Minister Jean Chrétien's government. However, it gained considerable momentum while Paul Martin was seeking the leadership of the Liberal Party and after he replaced Chrétien as Prime Minister. During that time he promised Canadian cities a new deal (Martin, 2003). Early initiatives have included the appointment of a Prime Minister's External Advisory Committee on Cities and Communities headed by Michael Harcourt, the former Premier of British Columbia and mayor of Vancouver. Martin also appointed John Godfrey as Parliamentary Secretary to the Prime Minister with responsibility for cities. In the new government's first Speech from the Throne an increase in federal funds for cities and communities was promised. Shortly thereafter, the 2004 federal budget made a so-called down payment on its promise by eliminating all GST payments levied on municipalities (Canada, 2004). In a speech on his government's priorities made in April 2004, Martin reiterated the government's continued commitment to share with municipalities some of the revenues from gas taxes (Martin, 2004b).

The federal election of 28 June 2004, which resulted in the return of a minority federal Liberal government, has not deterred the Liberal 'new deal' initiative. The Prime Minister's advisory committee remains active, and John Godfrey has been elevated to Minister of State for Infrastructure and Communities. Further, it seemed clear from public statements made by the minister that the government was committed to providing municipalities with a share of the federal gasoline excise tax and that this would be achieved through consultations with provincial governments and would also involve municipal representatives. Indeed, according to the minister the 'new deal' is about partnerships more than about sharing the federal treasury (Canada, 2004a).

The major question surrounding the creation of such partnerships is whether in the future, as in the past, the provincial and territorial governments will continue to guard jealously against the establishment of direct relationships between the federal and municipal governments (Gibbins, 2001; Berdahl, 2002). To a large extent, of course, their position will be shaped both by the size of the financial resources that the federal government brings to the negotiating table and by the extent to which it is willing to operate according to some of the key principles and protocols of the Calgary Declaration on federal ventures into areas of provincial jurisdiction (Canada, 1997).

The federal government's revived interest in adopting a more concerted and strategic policy role in the municipal sector has led provincial ministers responsible for municipal affairs to develop a protocol that would provide the principles for the federal–provincial–municipal relationship. The protocol was the product of a meeting held in Québec City in September 2004 in anticipation of each province and territory undertaking bilateral negotiations with the federal government on that relationship in the near future. It contained two major sets of principles, one related to federal respect for provincial and territorial jurisdiction and the other related to the nature of federal funding for municipal programs. In both instances the provincial and territorial ministers appear unanimous in having the federal government respect provincial and territorial priorities and jurisdiction (New Brunswick, 2004).

Federal-municipal intergovernmental relations are likely to expand in the future since the federal Liberal government has a strong political stake in wooing the urban voter (Andrew et al., 2002). And yet, the future of federal participation in municipal affairs may be attenuated if the Liberal minority government is replaced by a federal Conservative government. The federal election of 2004 revealed a notable difference between the Liberals and Conservatives in urban policy matters. Urban priorities were clearly less urgent for the Conservatives than for the Liberals, notwithstanding a promise by the Conservatives to provide 3 cents a litre of the federal gas tax to cities.

Beyond the impetus provided by the interests of the federal government, the emergence of a closer relationship between it and municipal governments is also the result of the desire of municipalities, particularly large ones, to establish a more direct relationship with the federal government. The reason for this is that in a growing 'glocal' context the power and resources of the national state become significant for all levels of government (Courchene, 1995). In that context it is logical and appropriate that the national and local (city-region) power poles should be attracted to one another. Further, given that over the span of the turn-of-the-millennium period of reform provinces have granted municipalities increased governing authority and autonomy but not much financial resources, it is not surprising that cash-starved and increasingly internationally oriented municipalities would look to the federal government for resources and support (Gibbins, 2001). Indeed, the most intriguing question in this evolving constellation of intergovernmental fiscal relationships is whether provinces are dealing themselves out of the picture with the largest municipalities. It would appear that it is of principal interest for the federal government to establish direct and substantial relations with municipal governments to achieve various national goals related to infrastructure and development.

The Nature of Future Reform

The engaging question raised more than two decades ago as to 'whither municipal government?' still engages us today (Plunkett and Graham, 2002). Our answer to that question is that the fundamental nature of Canadian municipal governance in the near future is likely to remain relatively unchanged from what it has been in the recent past. All indications are that the reform issues and options debated by municipal, provincial, and territorial governments during the recent reform period will continue to prevail in more or less the same form for the foreseeable future. The reform die has been cast and there is little to suggest that this can be changed substantially in the near future. The traditional core issues and options of the principal components of municipal reform (structural, functional, financial, and jurisdictional) have a relatively enduring quality that are likely to shape reform agendas and the actual reforms for some time to come in each of Canada's provinces and territories. The most that could happen is that some of those reforms could be stretched beyond their traditional parameters. The proposals emanating from the City of Toronto for a substantially empowered municipality with a radically transformed alignment of jurisdictional authority and autonomy vis-à-vis the provincial government are a notable example of such 'stretching'. These proposals fall somewhere between the American style 'home rule' and German 'city-states' such as Hamburg (Toronto, 2000a, 2000b, 2000c, 2000d, 2000e). Comparable proposals for greater authority and autonomy have been articulated by other major metropolitan cities in Canada, notably Edmonton and Winnipeg (Edmonton, 2003; Winnipeg, 2004). The prospect of such a reform being implemented for Toronto or for any other metropolitan municipality is very remote unless, of course, it could be demonstrated that such an arrangement is indisputably beneficial for the 'city interest', the 'provincial interest', and possibly even the 'national interest'. However, recent reform efforts have demonstrated to practitioners and observers alike that very little about municipal reforms and the effects of the same are indisputable. Indeed, they have also demonstrated that the length and intensity of the resulting debates are directly related to the nature and scope of the reforms being contemplated.

There is one aspect of the evolving context that demands watching—the growing prospect of municipal governance, and especially major urban and metropolitan governance, occurring within a deliberately crafted and vital multi-level governance arrangements. The federal government's recent attenton to a 'new deal' for for municipalities and communities with the emphasis on tri-level (federal, provincial, and municipal) collaboration suggests that a new reform discourse may be rising. If this comes to pass, it very well may be that a new, different reform period is in the offing.

In summary, it is highly unlikely that we will see any radical departures in the nature and scope of municipal reform agendas or municipal reforms in the near future. In the more distant future, such departures may be possible if a vision of a radically different system of municipal governance in Canada is well developed and articulated. At this juncture, however, such a vision is at the preliminary stages of development and articulation in the proposals being advanced by the City of

Toronto, and, perhaps, within the nascent multi-level governance discourse and 'new deal' ideal.

THE RESEARCH AGENDA ON MUNICIPAL REFORMS

Although this book makes a contribution to understanding the nature and scope of municipal reforms in recent years in Canada's provinces and territories, much still remains to be studied of this multi-faceted and multi-layered phenomenon. To comprehend fully the developing municipal system much more extensive research and analyses are required. In effect, each contributor here has tried to do in one chapter what ideally would require at least a book-length treatment. Much more extensive research on such reforms, in the form of case and comparative studies, is required. Thus, fleshing out what is covered in this book constitutes an important and invaluable research agenda in its own right. Moreover, as explained below, some important reform initiatives were somewhat beyond the scope of this book, and these should constitute an important component of a future research agenda.

Focus on Agendas and Initiatives, Not Just Reforms

In thinking about a research agenda on municipal reforms it is useful to focus on reform agendas and initiatives, rather than just on reforms per se. That includes not only the reform agendas of both the provincial and municipal governments, but also any public or systemic agendas that entail visions or proposals for reform beyond those espoused by the provincial and municipal governments. Moreover, attention should be devoted to the reform agendas of the past as well as those of the future. In analyzing reform initiatives, attention should be devoted not only to those that resulted in reforms but also to those that did not. In examining such reform initiatives, we need to try to discern patterns of what is or is not likely to be implemented, as well as examine what accounts for the implementation of some reforms but not others. At a broader level, attention should also be devoted to the determinants and dynamics of municipal reforms.

As part of the analysis of municipal reform agendas special attention should be given to the purposes, processes, and products of various advisory bodies established to review the need for and make recommendations on the nature of municipal reforms. Such research may shed light on why such advisory bodies are established, their precise mandates, their composition, the nature of their consultation processes, the thrust of their reform proposals, and their effect on the nature and scope of the reform agendas, on the reform initiatives that were launched, and on the reforms that were actually implemented.

Finally, and more broadly, future study should explore factors that promote reform initiatives and shape reform agendas. Among critical factors to consider are the effect of national, continental, and international economic and political forces, the role of public philosophies and specific ideas such as 'new regionalism', 'city-state', and 'subsidiarity', and the role of inter-jurisdictional emulation. This is true notwithstanding the considerable references to at least some of these matters within commentaries on reform politics and initiatives, including some contained in this volume. Coupled with this is a requirement for additional efforts to build theory and to apply various theories to municipal reform analysis. A common critique of scholarship devoted to the municipal sector is that it is almost universally atheoretical or, alternatively, that it hides its theoretical assumptions. There is much to support the critique. However, that the critique is telling should not preclude a new scholarship that moves beyond the current standard.

Focus on Effects or Outcomes of Municipal Reforms

Another important focus of a research agenda is the effects or outcomes of the municipal reforms that have been undertaken or will be undertaken in various jurisdictions. Little evaluative research of this sort has been done either prior to or after municipal reform initiatives in the various provinces and territories. Notable exceptions are a couple of evaluations of amalgamations in Ontario and Nova Scotia, which have been reported in this book. Given that so much of municipal reform policy appears to have been pursued in the absence of detailed empirical research findings, a strong case can made for conducting systematic research into policy outcomes.

Although such research is highly desirable, researchers would face two major challenges. The first is establishing causal linkages between any reforms and any particular direct or indirect effects or outcomes. The second challenge is defining the proper indicators and finding the relevant data by which the effects or outcomes of reforms can be measured. These are challenges faced by analysts and advocates of municipal reforms who undertake either *post facto* or *ex ante* impact or outcome analyses. In short, establishing the effects or outcomes of reforms that have been either implemented or not implemented is a challenging task and one that is always likely to be contested, depending on the preferences and the real or prospective stakes of various stakeholders. If we are to take the research challenge seriously, the work should ideally proceed in a scientific fashion. That is, the research needs to build in increments from a sound agenda that identifies the truly important issues and proceed in some systematic form. Obviously, the challenge is a large one and certainly one in which major research funding agencies and all levels of government must be prepared to participate and contribute.

The research agenda should also include research on reforms that were beyond the scope of this book. This includes what might be termed reforms to the organizational, decision-making, and management frameworks of individual municipal governments that have been undertaken in the wake of the 'new public management movement' that has swept across the country during the last 15 years (Siegel, 1993; Borins, 1995; Barnett, 1996). In analyzing such reforms, the general analytical framework proffered in this book, which directs attention to the purposes, pillars, products, processes, and politics of reforms, should prove useful. Consideration of the existing and emerging relationship between municipal and federal levels of government is another area for future research. It will be of particular interest to ascertain whether federal-provincial relations are altered by increased federal-municipal interaction, and whether the federal-municipal agenda becomes another contested matter between the federal, provincial, and territorial governments (Canada, 2002, 2004; Andrew et al., 2002).

To reiterate, much remains to be studied beyond what has been covered in this book. The task is monumental but worthy insofar as it could contribute not only to an improved understanding of municipal reforms and municipal governance, but could undoubtedly contribute to improved municipal governance. Moreover, both the study and practice of municipal governance are of crucial importance for good governance at the local level and for good governance at all levels. The reason for this is that while it may be an unfounded exaggeration to suggest that municipal government is the most important level of government, there is no denying that it has been and remains an important one within the Canadian political system.

REFERENCES

Alberta. 2000a. Capital Region Governance Review. *Supplemental Reports and Appendices.*

———. 2000b. Capital Region Governance Review. *Setting the Stage for Strong Regions: Choices for the Future.*

Andrew, Caroline. 1995. 'Provincial-Municipal Relations; or Hyper-Fractionalized Quasi-Subordination Revisited', in James Lightbody, ed., *Canadian Metropolitics: Governing Our Cities.* Mississauga, Ont.: Copp Clark, 137–60.

———. 1997. 'Globalization and Local Action', in Thomas (1997: 139–49).

———, Katherine A.H. Graham, and Susan Phillips. 2002. *Urban Affairs: Back on the Policy Agenda. A Reflection on Contemporary Urban Policy Issues and the Federal Government's Role in Dealing with Them.* Montreal and Kingston: McGill-Queen's University Press.

Artibise, Alan F.J. 1998. *Regional Governance without Regional Government.* Background report prepared for the Regional Municipality of Ottawa-Carleton, Apr.

Barnett, Neil, and Robert Leach. 1996. 'The New Public Management and Local Governance', in Ian Hampsher-Monk and Jeffrey Stanyer, eds, *Contemporary Political Studies, 1996.* London: Political Studies Association of the United Kingdom, 1508–38.

Berdahl, Loleen. 2002. *Structuring Federal Urban Engagement: A Principled Approach.* Calgary: Canada West Foundation.

Bish, Robert L. 2000. 'Evolutionary Alternatives for Metropolitan Areas: The Capital Region of British Columbia', *Canadian Journal of Regional Science* 23, 1 (Spring): 73–87.

———. 2001. 'Local Government Amalgamations: Discredited Nineteenth-Century Ideals Alive in the Twenty-First', *The Urban Papers.* Toronto: C.D. Howe Institute Commentary No. 150.

Blais, Pamela. 1994. 'The Competitive Advantage of City-Regions', *Policy Options* 15, 4: 15–19.

Boothe, Paul, ed. 2003. *Paying for Cities: The Search for Sustainable Municipal Revenues.* Western Studies in Economic Policy No. 9. Edmonton: Institute for Public Economics.

Borins, Sandford. 1995. 'The New Public Management Is Here to Stay', *Canadian Public Administration* 38, 1: 122–32.

Boswell, Peter G. 1996. 'Provincial-Municipal Relations', in Christopher Dunn, ed., *Provinces: Canadian Provincial Politics.* Peterborough, Ont.: Broadview Press, 253–74.

Bradford, Neil. 2004. 'Place Matters in Multi-Level Governance: Perspectives on a New Urban Policy Paradigm', *Policy Options* 30, 1: 39–44.

Canada. 1997. Canadian Intergovernmental Relations Secretariat, news release, 850–065/4.

———. 2002. *Canada's Urban Strategy—A Blueprint for Action.* Final Report of Prime Minister's Task Force on Urban Issues. At: <www.judysgro.com>.

———. 2004. *Speech from the Throne.* Mimeo, 11–12.

———, Infrastructure Canada. 2004. 'Key Address to the Canadian National Summit on Municipal Governance', Speech by the Honourable John Godfrey, Minister of State (Infrastructure and Communities), 28 July.

Canadian Federation of Municipalities. 1998. *Future Role of Municipal Government.* Mimeo.

Canaran, Hemant R. 1996. 'Local Government Legislation and Structures Are Outdated Says Vancouver Lawyer Lidstone', *Municipal World* (Aug.): 6–7.

Coffey, William J. 1994a. *The Evolution of Canada's Metropolitan Economies*. Montreal: Institute for Research on Public Policy.

———. 1994b. 'City-Regions in the New Economy: The Economic Role of Metropolitan Areas', *Policy Options* 15, 4: 5–11.

Cooper, Reid. 1996. 'Municipal Law, Delegated Legislation and Democracy', *Canadian Public Administration* 39, 3: 290–313.

Courchene, T.J. 1995. 'Glocalization: The Regional/International Interface', *Canadian Journal of Regional Science* 18, 1: 1–20.

Downey, Terence, and Robert Williams. 1998. 'Provincial Agendas, Local Responses: The "Common Sense" Restructuring of Ontario's Municipal Governments', *Canadian Public Administration* 41: 234–5.

Edmonton. 2003. *Identifying and Addressing Inequities in the City of Edmonton's Relationship with the Provincial Government*. Edmonton: Corporate Services Department.

Fischler, R., and J. Wolfe. 2000. 'Regional Restructuring in Montreal: An Historical Analysis', *Canadian Journal of Regional Science* 23, 1: 89–114.

———, John Meligrana, and Jeanne M. Wolfe, 2004. 'Canadian Experiences of Local Government Boundary Reform: A Comparison of Quebec and Ontario', in Meligrana, ed., *Redrawing Local Government Boundaries: An International Study of Politics, Procedures, and Decisions*. Vancouver: University of British Columbia Press, 75–105.

Frisken, Frances. 1994. 'Metropolitan Change and the Challenge to Public Policy', in Frisken, ed., *The Changing Canadian Metropolis*. Berkeley, Calif.: Institute of Governmental Studies Press, 1–35.

———. 1997. 'Jurisdictional and Political Constraints on Progressive Local Initiative', in Thomas (1997: 151–72).

Gagnon, Kristin, and Donald Lidstone. 1998. 'A Comparison of New and Proposed Municipal Acts of the Provinces', prepared for the 1998 annual conference of the Federation of Canadian Municipalities.

Garcea, Joseph. 2002a. 'Municipal Reform in Western Canada: plus ça change plus c'est la même chose', *Organizations & Territoires* 11, 3: 101–10.

———. 2002b. 'Modern Municipal Statutory Frameworks in Canada', *Journal of Governance: International Review* 3, 2: 1–14.

Gertler, Meric. 1996. 'City-Regions and the Global Economy: Choices Facing Toronto: Principles to Guide Toronto Policy Makers', *Policy Options* 17, 7: 12–15.

Gibbins, Roger. 2001. 'Local Governance and Federal Political Systems', *International Social Science Journal* 53, 1: 163–70.

Graham, Katherine A., and Susan D. Phillips, eds. 1998a. *Citizen Engagement: Lessons in Participation from Local Government*. Toronto: Institute of Public Administration of Canada.

——— and ———. 1998b. '"Who Does What" in Ontario: The Process of Provincial-Municipal Disentanglement', *Canadian Public Administration* 41, 2: 175–209.

——— and ———. 1999. 'Emerging Solitudes: The New Era in Provincial-Municipal Relations', in Martin W. Westmacott and Hugh P. Mellon, eds, *Public Administration and Public Policy: Governing in Challenging Times*. Scarborough, Ont.: Prentice-Hall, 73–88.

———, ———, and Allan A. Maslove. 1998. *Urban Governance in Canada: Representation, Resources, and Restructuring*. Toronto: Harcourt Brace Canada.

Higgins, Donald J.H. 1986. 'The Process of Reorganizing Local Government in Canada', *Canadian Journal of Political Science* 19, 2: 219–42.

Hobson, Paul A.R., and Frances St-Hilaire, eds. 1997. *Urban Governance and Finance: A Question of Who Does What*. Montreal: Institute for Research on Public Policy.

Hutton, Thomas. 1996. 'Structural Change and the Urban Policy Challenge: Policy Responses to Transformational Change', *Policy Options* 17, 7: 3–6.

Kernaghan, Kenneth, Brian Marson, and Sandford Borins. 2000. *The New Public Organization.* Toronto: Institute of Public Administration of Canada.

Kitchen, Harry M. 1995. 'Does Amalgamation Really Produce Cost Savings?', paper presented to Municipal Amalgamation Conference, Halifax.

———. 2003. *Municipal Revenue and Expenditure Issues in Canada.* Toronto: Canadian Tax Foundation, Tax Paper No. 107.

——— and Melville L. McMillan. 1985. 'Local Government and Canadian Federalism', in Richard Simeon, research coordinator, *Intergovernmental Relations*, vol. 63 of the research studies for the Royal Commission on the Economic Union and Development Prospects for Canada. Toronto: University of Toronto Press, 215–61.

L'Heureux, Jacques. 1985. 'Municipalities and the Divisions of Powers', in Richard Simeon, research coordinator, *Intergovernmental Relations.* Toronto: University of Toronto Press, 179–214.

Lidstone, Donald. 1998. 'Lidstone Compares New and Proposed Legislation', *Municipal World* (Aug.): 9–12.

———. 2003. 'Municipal Acts of the Provinces and Territories: A Report Card', presented to the annual conference of the Federation of Canadian Municipalities.

McDavid, James C. 2003. 'The Impacts of Amalgamation on Police Services in the Halifax Regional Municipality', *Canadian Public Administration* 45, 4 (Winter): 538–65.

McFarlane, Susan. 2001. *Building Better Cities: Regional Cooperation in Western Canada.* Calgary: Canada West Foundation.

Manitoba, Capital Region Review Panel. 1999. *Final Report of the Capital Region Review Panel.* At: <www.susdev.gov.mb.ca/capreg/capreg.html>.

———, Department of Intergovernmental Affairs. 2001. *Planning Manitoba's Capital Region: Next Steps.*

Martin, Fernand. 1996. 'Montréal devant la mondialisation: Le modèle optimal reste a construire', *Policy Options* 17, 7: 16–19.

Martin, Paul. 2003. 'Towards a New Deal for Cities', presented at the Creative Cities Conference, Winnipeg, 29 May. At: <www.paulmartintimes.ca>.

———. 2004a. 'For a Competitive, Compassionate, Independent Canada', *Policy Options* 25, 2 (Feb.): 5–7.

———. 2004b. 'Martin outlines action plan for five key priorities', news release, 16 Apr. At: <www.liberal.ca/news>.

New Brunswick. 2004. Environmental and Local Government. 'Local government ministers eager to begin bilateral negotiations.' Press Release, 15 November.

O'Brien, Allan. 1993. *Municipal Consolidation in Canada and Its Alternatives.* Toronto: ICURR.

———. 1996. 'Municipal Reform in Halifax: Assessing the Amalgamation in Halifax', *Policy Options* 17, 7: 20–2.

Ontario. 2001. *New Directions: A New Municipal Act for Ontario.*

———, Minister of Municipal Affairs. 2004. 'Open Letter to Residents of the City of Kawartha Lakes', 18 Feb.

Plunkett, T.J. 2004. 'A Nation of Cities Awaits Paul Martin's "New Deal"—Federal Funds for "Creatures of the Provinces"', *Policy Options* 30, 1: 19–25.

——— and Katherine Graham. 1982. 'Whither Municipal Government?', *Canadian Public Administration* 25, 4: 603–18.

Poel, Dale. 2000. 'Amalgamation Perspectives: Citizen Responses to Municipal Consolidations', *Canadian Journal of Regional Science* 23, 1: 21–48.

Quesnel, Louise. 2000. 'Municipal Reorganization in Quebec', *Canadian Journal of Regional Science* 23, 1: 115–34.

Richmond, Dale, and David Siegel, eds. 1994. *Agencies, Boards, and Commissions in Canadian Local Government*. Toronto: Institute of Public Administration of Canada.

Sancton, Andrew. 1991. *Local Government Restructuring Since 1975*. Toronto: ICURR.

———. 1992. 'Canada as a highly urbanized nation: New implications for government', *Canadian Public Administration* 35, 2: 281–98.

———. 1994. 'Governing Canada's City Regions: The Search for a New Framework', *Policy Options* 15, 4: 12–15.

———. 1996a. 'Reducing Costs by Amalgamating Municipalities: New Brunswick, Nova Scotia and Ontario', *Canadian Public Administration* 39, 3: 267–89.

———. 1996b. 'Assessing the GTA Task Force's Proposal: A Politically More Acceptable Alternative', *Policy Options* 17, 7: 38–40.

———. 1999. 'Globalization Does Not Require Amalgamation', *Policy Options* (Nov.): 54–8.

———. 2000a. 'The Municipal Role in the Governance of Canadian Cities', in Trudi Bunting and Pierre Filion, eds, *Canadian Cities in Transition: The Twenty-First Century*, 2nd edn. Toronto: Oxford University Press, 425–42.

———. 2000b. *Merger Mania: The Assault on Local Government*. Westmount, Que.: Price-Patterson.

———. 2000c. 'Amalgamations, Service Realignment, and Property Taxes: Did the Harris Government Have a Plan for Ontario Municipalities?', *Canadian Journal of Regional Studies* 23, 1: 135–56.

———. 2000d. 'Jane Jacobs on the Organization of Municipal Government', *Journal of Urban Affairs* 22, 4: 463–71.

———. 2001. 'Canadian Cities and the New Regionalism', *Journal of Urban Affairs* 23, 5: 543–55.

———. 2002a. 'Metropolitan and Regional Governance', in Edmund P. Fowler and David Siegel, eds, *Urban Policy Issues*, 2nd edn. Toronto: Oxford University Press, 54–68.

———. 2002b. 'Municipalities, Cities, and Globalization: Implications for Canadian Federalism', in Herman Bakvis and Grace Skogstad, eds, *Canadian Federalism: Performance, Effectiveness, and Legitimacy*. Toronto: Oxford University Press, 261–77.

———. 2002c. 'Signs of Life? The Transformation of Two-tier Metropolitan Government', in Andrew et al. (2002: 179–99).

Saskatchewan. 1993. *Report of the Advisory Committee on Inter-Community Cooperation and Community Quality of Life*.

———. 1995. *Advisory Committee Report on Inter-Community Cooperation and Community Quality of Life*.

———, Task Force on Municipal Legislative Renewal. 2000. *Options 2000: A Framework for Municipal Renewal (Rural and Urban Sectors)—Final Report*.

———. 2002. The Cities Act, *Statutes of Saskatchewan, 2002*, Chapter 11.1. At: <www.city.saskatoon.sk.ca/org/clerks_office/cities_act.pdf>.

———. 2004. Commission on Financing Kindergarten to Grade 12 Education. *Final Report*.

Saskatchewan Urban Municipalities Association (SUMA). 1995. *Task Force on Urban Government Renewal, Recommendations. The ABC's of Renewal*.

———. 2004a. 'New Directions for Municipal-Provincial Partnerships', *Urban Voice* 8, 9: 1, 8.

———. 2004b. 'On the Road to a Municipal Act', *Urban Voice* 9, 2: 5.

Séguin, Rhéal. 2003. 'Quebec lays out rules for breakup of megacities', *Globe and Mail*, 29 Nov.

———. 2004a. 'Studies cite advantage of de-amalgamation: Separation from megacities in Quebec would benefit wealthy communities', *Globe and Mail*, 22 Apr., A11.

———. 2004b. 'Montreal demerger called a setback: Opponents say a return to old boundaries will further split the city linguistically', *Globe and Mail*, 22 June, A10.

Seidle, Leslie. 2002. *The Federal Role in Canada's Cities: Overview of Issues and Proposed Actions.* Canadian Policy Research Networks, Discussion Paper F/27, Nov.

Siegel, David. 1993. 'Reinventing Local Government: The Promise and the Problems', in Leslie Seidle, ed., *Rethinking Government: Reform or Reinvention?* Montreal: Institute for Research on Public Policy, 175–202.

———. 2002. 'Urban finance at the turn of the century: Be careful what you wish for', in Edmund P. Fowler and David Siegel, eds, *Urban Policy Issues: Canadian Perspectives*, 2nd edn. Toronto: Oxford University Press, 36–53.

Slack, Enid. 2000. 'A Preliminary Assessment of the New City of Toronto', *Canadian Journal of Regional Science* 23, 1: 13–30

———. 2002. *Municipal Finance and the Pattern of Urban Growth.* Montreal: C.D. Howe Institute

Smith, Patrick J. 1996. 'Metropolitan Governance: Vancouver and BC Regions: Workable Alternatives to Regional Government', *Policy Options* 17, 7: 7–11.

——— and Kennedy Stewart. 1998. *Making Accountability Work in British Columbia.* Report for the Government of British Columbia, Ministry of Municipal Affairs and Housing.

Thomas, Timothy, ed. 1997. *The Politics of the City: A Canadian Perspective.* Scarborough, Ont.: Nelson.

Tindal, C. Richard. 1996. 'Municipal Restructuring: The Myth and the Reality', *Municipal World* 107, 3 (Mar.): 3–7.

——— and Susan Nobes Tindal. 2004. *Local Government in Canada*, 6th edn. Scarborough, Ont.: Nelson Canada.

Toronto. 2000a. 'Towards a New Relationship with Ontario and Canada', press release.

———. 2000b. 'Towards a New Relationship with Ontario and Canada', Staff Report.

———. 2000c. 'The Time is Right for New Relationships with Ontario and Canada', Background Report.

———. 2000d. 'Power of Canadian Cities—The Legal Framework', Background Report.

———. 2000e. 'Comparison of Powers and Revenue Sources of Selected Cities', Background Report.

Treff, Karen, and David B. Perry. 1998. *Finances of the Nation: A Review of Expenditures and Revenues of the Federal, Provincial, and Local Governments of Canada.* Toronto: Canadian Tax Foundation.

Vojnovic, Igor. 1997. *Municipal Consolidations in the 1990s: An Analysis of Five Canadian Municipalities.* Toronto: ICCUR Press.

———. 1998. 'Municipal Consolidation in the 1990s: An Analysis of British Columbia, Nova Scotia and New Brunswick', *Canadian Public Administration* 41: 239–83.

———. 1999. 'The Fiscal Distribution of the Provincial-Municipal Service Exchange in Nova Scotia', *Canadian Public Administration* 42: 512–41.

———. 2000a. 'The Transitional Impacts of Municipal Consolidations', *Journal of Urban Affairs* 22: 285–317.

———. 2000b. 'Municipal Consolidation, Regional Planning, and Fiscal Accountability', *Canadian Journal of Regional Science* 23, 1: 49–72.

——— and Dale Poel. 2000. 'Provincial and Municipal Restructuring in Canada: Assessing Expectations and Outcomes', *Canadian Journal of Regional Science* 23, 1: 1–6.

Williams, Robert J., and Terrence J. Downey. 1999. 'Reforming Rural Ontario', *Canadian Public Administration* 42, 2: 160–92.

Winnipeg. 2004a. 'Canada's mayors unite for a "New Deal" from Ottawa and the provinces', news release, 23 Jan.

———. 2004b. 'City Council Passes New Deal', news release, 21 Apr.

Index